Adventure Guide to™
Virginia

Leonard M. Adkins

HUNTER

HUNTER PUBLISHING, INC,
130 Campus Drive, Edison, NJ 08818
732-225-1900; 800-255-0343; Fax 732-417-1744
hunterpub@emi.net

1220 Nicholson Road, Newmarket, Ontario
Canada L3Y 7V1
800-399-6858; Fax 800-363-2665

The Boundary, Wheatley Road, Garsington
Oxford, OX44 9EJ England
01865-361122; Fax 01865-361133

ISBN 1-55650-816-6

Cover photo: Natural Stone Bridge, Leo de Wys
Back cover photo: Maury River, by author
Photos on pages 51, 52, 177, 180, 205, 246, 252, 324, 374,
386 and 387 courtesy of Virginia Tourist Corporation
All other photos © Leonard M. Adkins
Maps by Kim André, © 1998 Hunter Publishing, Inc.

1   2   3   4

Acknowledgments

This book would never have become a reality without the kind and able assistance of the following folks:

Rebbecca Caudill, Phyllis Deel, Sheila F. Kuczko, and staff, Virginia Coalfield Regional Tourism Development Authority; Andy Dawson, Shenandoah Valley Travel Association; Sloane Hunter, Bedrock Inn; Ron Caldwell, Cumberland Gap Outfitters; Julia Gillespie, Doe Run Lodge; Mark Glickman, Wintergreen Resort; Julie Grimes & Pamela Jewel, Virginia Tourism Corporation; R. D. Bray, Boxwood Inn; Carol Harding, Northern Neck Tourism Council; Jim Shiner, John W. Flannagan Dam & Reservoir; Ron Kuhlman, Virginia Beach Department of Convention & Visitor Development; Manfred Locher, Bryce Resort; Madison County Tourist Office; Karen Michuad, Shenandoah National Park; Mr. & Mrs. Dale Benedict, Monte Vista B&B; Kathryn Kreiling, Colonial Inn; Woody Lipps, US Forest Service; Kenneth B. Mullens, equestrian extraordinaire and all-around good guy; Yvonne Thompson, Cuz's; Gary Waugh, Department of Conservation & Recreation; Ross L. Weeks, Jr., Historic Crab Orchard Museum & Pioneer Park; Allison Webber, Massanutten; and Wytheville Area Convention & Visitors Bureau.

Thanks once again to my parents for making everything in my life possible. Dr. Stephen Lewis and Caroline Charonko, my new life was made possible by your compassion and knowledge. Laurie, my life is with you.

www.hunterpublishing.com

Hunter's full range of travel guides to all corners of the globe is featured on our exciting website. You'll find guidebooks to suit every type of traveler, no matter what their budget, lifestyle, or idea of fun. Full descriptions are given for each book, along with reviewers' comments and a cover image. Books may be purchased on-line.

About The Author

Leonard M. Adkins has been outdoor adventuring for nearly two decades now. He has walked the full length of the Appalachian Trail four times. He has traversed the Continental Divide Trail from Canada to mexico (covering several hundred miles of New Mexico on mountain bike), Canada's Great Divide Trail, and the Pyrenees High Route along the border of France and Spain. In all, he has hiked more than 16,000 miles exploring the backcountry areas of the States, Canada, Europe and the Caribbean. Jobs as an interpreter for the Virginia State Parks system, an Assistant Director for George Mason university's Outdoor Education Center, and crew member of the 46-foot *Rebel Ann II* sailing the Caribbean have helped hone his skills and increase his appreciation and knowledge of the natural world.

When not on an extended adventure, Leonard spends his time exploring what he considers to be his own big backyard – Virginia. Lecturing and writing articles and books and publishing photographs takes up whatever spare time is left.

Along with his thru-hiking wife, Laurie, and his thru-hiking dog, MacAfee of Knob, he lives in Catawba, Virginia – just one mile from the AT.

Other Books By Leonard M. Adkins

- *Seashore State Park: A Walking Guide*

- *Walking the Blue Ridge: A Guide to the Trails of the Blue Ridge Parkway*

- *50 Hikes in Northern Virginia: Walks, Hikes, and Backpacks from the Allegheny Mountains to the Chesapeake Bay*

- *The Appalachian Trail: A Visitors Companion*

- *The Caribbean: A Walking and Hiking Guide*

Contents

■ Maps

For Laurie.
All of the best of things
I ever imagined in the world,
I found in you.

> The most beautiful thing we can experience is the mysterious.... He to whom this emotion is a stranger, who can no longer pause to wonder and stand rapt in awe, is as good as dead: his eyes are closed.
>
> Albert Einstein

Introduction

I had a lot of fun doing the field research for this book. I had experienced many wonderful adventures in Virginia, but the need for current, first-hand knowledge of the state's offerings set me off on a new exploration.

From horseback riding through the Cumberland Mountains in far Southwest Virginia to watching wild ponies scamper about as I toured Assateague Island, I now had the perfect excuse to visit places and engage in activities I had always wanted to do but could never find the time for. A walk amid the cypress swamps and luxuriant folds of Spanish moss in First Landing/Seashore State Park and a canoe trip down the sparkling waters of the Shenandoah River returned me to places I had yearned to see again. In addition, since the human body demands fuel and rest, I was able to sample the sumptuous offerings of some of the world's most innovative chefs and engage in intriguing conversations with the guests and hosts of Virginia's relaxing and historically rich bed and breakfasts.

All of this served to reinforce in my mind what I already knew – that Virginia is an exceedingly beautiful state, both in spirit and geography.

History permeates the air over this land. The first permanent English settlement in the New World was established here. Many of the movers and shakers of the drive for independence from Great Britain were born and spent their lives on its soil. The state was witness to the result – the birth of a new nation – when the British surrendered at Yorktown. Virginia bore the brunt when the nation split apart, with more than 60% of the Civil War battles taking place inside its boundaries. The state was also the site of the reunification of our country when Lee surrendered to Grant at Appomattox. The Virginia of today is rooted to this past, flavoring the outlook and daily lives of its citizens.

The topography of the state, running the gamut from the high peaks of the Allegheny Mountains along the West Virginia border to the crashing surf of the Atlantic Ocean, provides some of the best terrain for outdoor adventures. In the eastern part of the Commonwealth (which the state has dubbed itself) is the coastal plain, where land meets saltwater. Here you will discover herons and egrets fishing in small swamps, brackish ponds, and slow-moving streams.

The Piedmont in the central portion of the state is characterized by gently rolling land of hardwood forests which lead to grassy meadows with open vistas. Influenced by narrow ridgelines, the Blue Ridge Mountains rise and descend on fluctuating mountain crests; waterfalls come crashing down into small valleys and coves. The mountains of the westernmost part of the state are the least populated and most rugged; here you have an excellent chance of observing the state's diverse wildlife.

My hope is that this book will instill in you a desire to visit and experience the many wonderful things that Virginia offers. Happy adventuring!

History

Virginia's human history actually began in prehistoric times, when tribes of wanderers entered North America by crossing a land bridge from Asia. Historians believe these people gradually spread across the continent, with some eventually settling – as early as 5,000 BC – on lands that would one day be Virginia.

The customs, culture, and lives of the descendants of those first inhabitants would be changed forever when colonists in the *Susan Constant, Godspeed*, and *Discovery* sailed up the James River and established the first permanent English settlement in America in 1607. Named Jamestown in honor of King James I, the colony lost so many settlers to disease, famine, and constant Indian raids that it barely survived. However, the establishment of a second settlement at Henrico in 1611, and the exportation of tobacco to England starting in 1614, brought a change of fortune and a prosperity to the colony.

In what proved to be a forerunner to elective government, the popularly elected House of Burgesses was established in 1619. The first indentured servants from Africa arrived that same year, a precursor to slavery and a problem that could be said to have plagued the state ever since.

Continuing Indian raids led Nathaniel Bacon to organize a band of followers to attack Native American villages. Branded traitors, Bacon and his men went on to battle the governor's forces. Although the rebellion ended when Bacon died and many of his men were killed, the seeds of independence from the mother country had been sown.

The following years were prosperous ones, with the tobacco plantations thriving on the labor of black slaves. This affluence, however, brought about an increasingly heavy taxation burden and served only to fan the flames of frustration over British rule. In fact, in a move calculated to stop anti-government demonstrations, Governor John Murray Duncan abolished the House of Burgesses in 1774. That same year saw the convening of the First Continental Congress; open warfare had broken out by the time the Second Continental Congress convened the following year.

Adopting the Declaration of Independence (written, for the most part, by Virginia native Thomas Jefferson) on July 4, 1776, the Congress appointed George Washington as commander of the Continental Army. Years of bitter and costly battles eventually led to real independence when British general George Cornwallis surrendered at Yorktown on October 19, 1781.

George Washington chose land in Maryland and Virginia to be the young country's federal capitol. Native sons, such as James Monroe, John Marshall, and James Madison, gravitated to the area as they helped shape the political, social, and economic future of the United States of America.

The question of slavery continued to hang over the state and the entire country. John Brown's raid on Harpers Ferry in 1859 and Abraham Lincoln's election as president in 1860 brought the tensions to a series of crisis events. In December, 1860, South Carolina seceded from the Union; six other states soon followed. In February 1861, Jefferson Davis was sworn in as President of the Confederate States of America. In April 1861, Confederate forces lay siege to, and accepted the surrender of, the Federal Garrison at Fort Sumter, South Carolina.

The Civil War had begun. When Lincoln ordered local militia to fight for the Union, Virginia seceded to join the cause of the Confederacy.

More than half of the battles of the four-year Civil War were fought on Virginia soil, and the ghosts of those struggles still haunt the state. The sites of battles, both large (such as Manassas or Fredericksburg) and small (Hanging Rock near Roanoke) are spread throughout the state. It is almost impossible to travel through the state without stumbling upon a battlefield, monument, or structure from those dark days.

When the war ended, Virginia lay in waste. Thousands of its young men were dead, one-third of its land had become the new state of West Virginia, its farms were in ruin, the slaves that once worked them gone, and the state's currency was worthless. To survive, eastern plantation owners turned their large land holdings into sharecropping ventures, while western farmers started raising a variety of crops and livestock.

Eventually, new railroads delivered coal from the southwestern part of the state for exportation from ports in Hampton Roads, bringing much-needed funds to both areas.

The state's economy has continued to diversify and is no longer dependent on agriculture. World Wars I and II brought an influx of armed forces personnel and their families to the state's many military installations, and the Hampton Roads area experienced a boom from the expansion of the Norfolk Naval Base and the accompanying increase in shipbuilding.

The tendrils of Washington, DC continue to creep into the state; the federal government is now the single largest employer in the Commonwealth.

Geography

Geologists and geographers have divided Virginia into five physiographic regions, each with its own surface features and vegetative communities.

■ The Coastal Plain

Taking in the Eastern Shore and Tidewater Virginia, the Coastal Plain has a maximum elevation of 300 feet above sea level. Its bedrock slopes east and continues into the Atlantic, forming the continental shelf. As the Tidewater's four great rivers – the Potomac, Rappahannock, York, and James – flow east, they split the land into three peninsulas (called "necks"). Along the Atlantic coast and the shores of the Chesapeake are tidal marshes, beaches, swamps, and vegetation that is able to withstand the rigors of wind and saltwater. Inland are mixed forests of hardwoods and evergreens, notably loblolly pine.

■ The Piedmont

Encompassing Northern and Central Virginia, the Piedmont meets the Coastal Plain at the fall line, where eastern-flowing waters cross the geological dividing line between the two provinces. The fall line has determined the location of some of Virginia's larger cities. Fredericksburg, Richmond, and Petersburg were all established as transshipment centers because, upstream from them, their rivers became unnavigable for large ships bringing in cargo from the Chesapeake Bay. Characterized by a gently rolling topography that has few steep slopes, the Piedmont is over 150 miles wide near the North Carolina border, narrowing down to about 30 miles wide at the Maryland border.

■ The Blue Ridge

Also narrow at the north – sometimes no more than two miles wide – the Blue Ridge spreads out to more than 70 miles wide south of Roanoke. Shenandoah National Park, the Blue Ridge Parkway, and a portion of Southwest Virginia are within its domain. Here the mountains thrust up from the Piedmont, eventually rising to over 5,000 feet on Mount Rogers near the North Carolina border. Rivers in the northern portion of the province flow east to the Atlantic. Those in the southern portion course in the opposite direction, eventually to reach the Gulf of Mexico.

■ The Valley & Ridge

The Valley and Ridge begins at the western base of the Blue Ridge. Including the Shenandoah Valley Region and a portion of Southwest Virginia, the province is characterized by a series of parallel ridges and valleys that become progressively higher and more irregular as they rise up to the west. Its northern portion has rivers flowing to the Atlantic Ocean and the southern segment drains to the Gulf of Mexico.

■ The Cumberland Plateau

Along the Kentucky border in the state's extreme southwest is the Cumberland Plateau (also referred to as the Appalachian Province). This is where Daniel Boone made use of the Cumberland Gap as a gateway to lands lying west, and the Russell Fork River roars through one of the largest canyons east of the Mississippi River.

Climate/When To Go

Virginia can have a wide range of temperatures and conditions. Winters can be surprisingly cold or relatively mild, while summers can range from hot and humid to temperate. Spring and autumn are usually the most pleasant times of the year to be outdoors, as days warm up to a comfortable level and nights cool down for easy sleeping.

Of course, with a terrain that includes mountains over 5,000 feet as well as a coastline, conditions will vary. Snow is common in the mountains, moderate in Northern and Central Virginia, and infrequent in the Tidewater and on the Eastern Shore. When heat and humidity have taken the joy out of outdoor activities in the eastern portion of the state, the mountains will beckon with temperatures that can be more than 10° lower. The average year-round temperature along the coast is 60°, while in the mountains it is about 54°.

To a large extent, the activities you wish to pursue will determine when to visit. Most people think of the dead of winter as the time to come for skiing, but in certain years the season can extend from November into April. Canoeists and kayakers will find that snow melt and seasonal rains make the mountain rivers most challenging in the spring. By mid-summer, when many of those streams have dropped to a barely floatable level, it is time to head further east for some flatwater paddling on lakes and tidal rivers. Fall is considered by many to be the perfect season; temperatures are cooler, the autumn foliage is in full color, and crowds are fewer.

Birds singing early in the morning, flowers opening wide to soak in the noontime sun, and owls hooting in the evening make it worthwhile to visit the same place at different times of the day. Also, a spot visited in late spring will be a different experience when you return in the fall. Be willing to visit an area more than once and do not limit your outings in Virginia to just one or two seasons. Adventuring here is a year-round activity.

How To Use This Book

Heading from east to west, this book has divided Virginia into six regions – The Eastern Shore, Tidewater Virginia, Northern Virginia, Central Virginia, the Shenandoah Valley Region, and Southwest Virginia. Because they are so important for outdoor adventuring, Shenandoah National Park and the Blue Ridge Parkway have their own, separate chapters.

Each chapter begins with a short *Introduction* to the region, giving an overview of the general history and lay of the land, the sites to visit, and the adventures available.

Next are the *Information Sources*, which provide addresses and phone numbers of regional, city, and county tourist offices.

Getting Around provides transportation details. Included is information on the region's airports, railroad and bus services, and car rental agencies. Free state road maps may be obtained from most tourist offices or from the Department of Transportation, 1401 East Broad St., Richmond, VA 23219, ☎ 804-786-2838.

📖 When driving off the beaten path the *Virginia Atlas & Gazeteer* (DeLorme Mapping Co., PO Box 298, Freeport, ME 04032) is an invaluable resource. It's available at most bookstores.

The *Touring* section will take you on a driving excursion through the region, discussing the outstanding historical, cultural, scenic, or adventure attractions in each city or area along the way.

Separate sections provide in-depth details concerning the specific *adventures* in each region, with information for those who want to take off on their own or for others seeking a planned and guided tour.

Adventures On Foot

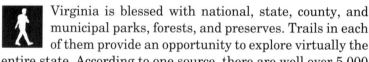

Virginia is blessed with national, state, county, and municipal parks, forests, and preserves. Trails in each of them provide an opportunity to explore virtually the entire state. According to one source, there are well over 5,000 miles of footpaths in the Commonwealth!

The longest trail is the over 500-mile stretch of the 2,100-mile Georgia-to-Maine **Appalachian Trail** (AT). Maintained by volunteer efforts, the AT enters the state at Damascus in Southwest Virginia, courses into the Allegheny and Blue Ridge mountains of the Jefferson and George Washington National Forests, passes through most of Shenandoah National Park, and leaves the state as it crosses the Shenandoah River at Harpers Ferry, West Virginia. Guidebooks, maps, and other information about the AT may be obtained from the **Appalachian Trail Conference**, PO Box 807, Harpers Ferry, WV 25425, ☎ 304-535-6331. Because Virginia contains such a large portion of the trail, the conference has split the state into four guidebooks – *Southwest Virginia, Central Virginia, Shenandoah National Park*, and *Maryland & Northern Virginia*.

You do not have to be a long-distance hiker to reap the rewards of hiking in Virginia. More than 500 miles of well-maintained and marked pathways, some as short as a tenth of a mile, radiate through Shenandoah National Park and take off from the Blue Ridge Parkway.

In addition, more than 1,700,000 acres of the George Washington and Jefferson National Forests are scored by dirt roads and over 1,900 miles of pathways – beckoning both day hikers and overnight backpackers.

Although they are usually easy to follow, trails in the national forests are generally not as well maintained or marked as those in the national or state parks. If you plan to hike any of the forest service trails, I suggest you purchase the inexpensive forest maps (about $3 to $4 each). They not only give you a broad overview of the area but they show all of the trails and can open up a whole new world of hiking options. One map takes in the entire George Washington National Forest and two cover the Jefferson. Maps and further information can be obtained from the **George Washington and Jefferson National Forests**, *5162 Valleypointe Parkway, Roanoke, VA 24019, 540-265-6054.*

Spread throughout the state are other federal lands and state, county, and municipal parks and preserves with their own systems of pathways.

As you use this book for hiking options, be sure to look over the sections on mountain biking. With few exceptions, foot travel is also permitted on most of the pathways that are open to bicycles.

Hiking Safety

Whether you are on a multi-week trek or just out for an afternoon stroll in a state park, there are certain precautions you should take:

- Always let someone know where you are hiking.

- Always carry fresh water. Water sources found in the backcountry should be treated before consumption.

- Even on warm summer days, you should have a jacket, first aid kit, extra food, and a flashlight.

- You do not have to be in the best physical shape to enjoy a walk, but do take into account the difficulty of terrain, the weather report, and your conditioning. Allow enough time to complete your outing before dark.

Camping Etiquette

To protect the resources as much as possible, you should practice no-trace hiking and camping techniques. A quick overview of this approach, as presented by the Appalachian Trail Conference:

- Stay on the footpath; short cuts erode the land.

- Use a small backpacking stove. Fires leave charred spots and destroy nutrients in the topsoil.

- Carry out everything you carried in.

- Ditching around your tent and scraping away twigs and leaves causes erosion by permitting topsoil to wash away.

- Take only pictures, leave only footprints.

- Use the privy if the campsite has one. Otherwise, dig a "cathole" of eight inches in depth and at least 200 feet from any water sources or campsites.

- Do not wash yourself, dishes, or clothing in or near water sources.

📖 For further information, **Backwoods Ethics** by Laura and Guy Waterman is an excellent resource, not only providing details on the "how" of no-trace, but also the "why."

Adventures On Wheels

 Seeing Virginia on a bicycle is one of the best ways to discover its offerings. This section is split into *Mountain Biking* and *Road Biking* subsections.

Mountain Biking

In recent years, mountain biking has gained a wide following in Virginia. The state has responded by establishing new routes for fat-tire enthusiasts. In the pages that follow, I give information on places to ride, the length and difficulty of the trip, and the scenic attractions along the way.

Mountain Biking Etiquette

Mountain biking is generally supported in Virginia, but continued access to the trails and routes is dependent upon you and your treatment of the land and fellow outdoorsfolk. Now accepted worldwide, the International Mountain Biking Association has developed a set of guidelines that make for good relations and safe riding:

■ Ride on open trails only. Respect trail and road closures and private property (it is your responsibility to know, even if signs are not posted). Obtain permits or authorization if required. Federal and state wilderness areas are off-limits to cycling and some parks and forests (both national and state) may have certain trails closed to bicycles. Leave gates as you found them, or as marked.

■ Leave no trace. Do not ride on soil after a rain. Never ride off the trail, skid your tires, or litter. Pack out everything you bring in.

- Control your bicycle. Inattention for even a second can cause disaster for you and others. Excessive speed frightens and may injure people, gives mountain biking a bad name, and can result in trail closures.

- Always yield. Make your approach known well in advance. A friendly greeting is considerate and often appreciated. Show respect when passing, slowing to a walking speed or even stopping, especially in the presence of a horse. Anticipate that other trail users may be around corners or blind spots.

- Never spook animals. Give them extra room and time to adjust to you; move slowly or dismount. Running livestock and disturbing wild animals are serious offenses.

- Plan ahead. Know your equipment, your ability, and the area in which you are riding, and prepare accordingly. Be self-sufficient at all times, keep your bike in good condition, and carry a repair kit and supplies for changing weather conditions. Keep trails open by setting an example of responsible cycling.

- Always wear a helmet.

Road Biking

Road biking in Virginia is the best way to travel large distances in a single day, yet go slowly enough to experience the sounds, smells, and beauty of the countryside.

The state is blessed with portions of three of the nation's long-distance bicycle routes. About 500 miles of the TransAmerica Bicycle Route runs from the Kentucky/Virginia border near Breaks Interstate Park to Yorktown. Close to 150 miles of the Maine to Virginia Bicycle Route follow roadways from Washington, DC to Richmond, and 130 miles of the Virginia to Florida Bicycle Route head south from Richmond to the Virginia/North Carolina border at Suffolk.

You are permitted, with a few exceptions, to ride a bicycle on any roadway in Virginia, so the possibilities for exploration and

Introduction

exercise are virtually limitless. The outings described in the road biking section are among the most often used and well-liked rides. They offer a variety of trips suitable for varying abilities and desires. Also included is information on outfitters selling, renting, or repairing bicycles and/or offering guided trips.

Road Biking Etiquette

The laws regulating bicycling on Virginia's public highways define the rights and duties of bicyclists:

- Bicyclists must obey all traffic signs, signals, lights, and markings, and must ride with the flow of traffic on the right side of the highway.

- Ride single-file on highways; you may ride two abreast only on paths or parts of highways designated exclusively for bicycles.

- Bicycles are not permitted on Interstates or most other controlled-access highways.

- Every bicycle ridden between sunset and sunrise must have a white light on its front which is visible at least 500 feet to the front. The rear must have a red reflector visible 300 feet to the rear or a red light visible 500 feet to the rear.

- Bikes ridden on highways must have brakes which will skid the wheels on dry, level, clean pavement.

Additional information concerning bicycle riding opportunities in the state may be obtained by contacting **State Bicycle Coordinator, Virginia Department of Transportation**, 1401 East Broad St., Richmond, VA 23219. ☎ 804-786-2964.

Adventures On Horseback

In Virginia, you can take off solo on designated trails in the backcountry of a national forest, arrange for an easy one-hour ride on gentle terrain, or join a multi-day guided trip, stopping each night at a comfortable inn or bed and breakfast.

This section provides you with the particulars of where you may ride, what to expect in the way of scenery when you get there, and which outfitters will take you where.

Whether you plan to go on your own or with an outfitter, the US Forest Service and the Virginia Horse Council offer a number of tips to make your ride enjoyable, safe, and environmentally friendly.

Horseback Riding Etiquette

■ Let someone know where you will be riding and camping.

■ Stay on the trail; cutting switchbacks causes erosion and damages vegetation. Keep stock from skirting shallow puddles, small rocks, and bushes.

■ Even on short breaks, tie your animal off the trail. Use tree-saver straps (do not tie horses directly to the trees).

■ Pack out everything you carried in.

■ Obtain permission before crossing private property.

■ Make sure your horse is properly shod and that all equipment and tack is in good repair.

■ Wear comfortable clothing and anticipate changes in the weather.

■ Carry a first aid kit for you and the horses.

■ Do not rush ahead, but adjust your speed to the most poorly conditioned horse or least experienced rider.

Adventures On Water

 Virginia's waters are as diverse as her terrain. This section will take you down mountain streams that will challenge the best paddlers and it will guide you on easy flatwater trips across placid lakes. While the state does not draw the large number of whitewater enthusiasts that neighboring West Virginia does, it does offer an exhilarating ride through the urban landscape of Richmond and has one of the most dangerous and challenging trips in America near the Kentucky border. I supply information on raft operators that will take you on these trips.

Also included in this section is information on dinner and sightseeing cruises suitable for the whole family, canoe and kayak rental outfitters, folks will teach you how to sail on the Chesapeake, and certified scuba diving instructors who will take you out into the Atlantic Ocean.

All adventures on and in the water can be dangerous. It is always best to learn from a competent instructor (of which a number are pointed out in this book) and always be aware of your skill level when setting out on a new trip.

Canoeing & Kayaking Safety

These are precautions you should observe while canoeing and kayaking:

- Let someone know where you will be paddling.
- Always use a personal flotation device.
- Never attempt to run a low water bridge or dam.
- Learn to read and recognize the signs of a river and never run a river in flood stage.

When a river has rapids, I have included its difficulty rating, which should help you decide if you have the skills needed to safely negotiate the stream. Do remember that the ratings apply to the river during normal conditions.

Whitewater Classification Chart	
Class I	Easy, with small waves and riffles. There are few obstructions and self-rescue is easy.
Class II	There are more easy rapids and a number of low ledges. Although there are more obstructions, figuring a way around them is easy.
Class III	For those with intermediate skills. Waves, long rapids, and obstructions require the ability to maneuver quickly. Open canoes could be swamped.
Class IV	Advanced. You will need good boat-handling abilities and may still end up in unavoidable waves, eddies, and cross-currents. You should scout a Class IV (and above) stream if it is your first time running it.
Class V	Experts only. There will be long, continuous, and obstructed rapids on an extremely complex course. Rescue spots, if any, are few and far between. Every skill of paddling will be needed.
Class VI	Extreme. Errors can result in loss of life.

Adventures On Snow

Although it can start earlier and end later, Virginia's ski season typically runs from late November to mid-March. Nighttime lows in the teens and 20s, and daytime highs in the 30s and 40s make ideal temperatures for skiing and snowboarding.

Virginia's four downhill ski resorts are located in the Shenandoah Valley Region. All have snowmaking systems and offer challenging terrain, with more than 1,000 feet of vertical drop and runs of over a mile. Each offers rental equipment and classes for beginners, as well as ski/lodging package deals.

Call ☎ 800-THE-SNOW for a free Virginia Ski Packet, which includes color brochures and discount coupons.

There are no resorts in the state dedicated exclusively to cross-country skiing, but the hiking trails and golf courses of Bryce, The Homestead, and Wintergreen can easily be used. Relevant sections of the Shenandoah Valley Region, Shenandoah National Park and Blue Ridge Parkway chapters do point out several areas that are popular with remote cross-country skiers.

Adventures In The Air

 Seeing Virginia from the air can be even more exhilarating than exploring it on the ground. Bi-planes, helicopters, hang-gliders, parasails, and hot-air balloons are ready to take you up and away.

Where To Stay

 Although it was not always possible to find one in each and every town, the establishments that have an interest in outdoor adventures (those that provide bikes and canoes or arrange outings) are given preference in this book. Included is a range of accommodations, from budget motels to expensive resorts. Because I believe that good accommodations offer more than just a place to sleep, I have also included a number of bed and breakfasts, where you will be able to interact with other guests or find out about local sites from the hosts.

Rates were current as this book went to press; all rates for B&Bs include a full breakfast. Where seasonal price scales are used, the highest rate is given. The $ codes indicate what it will cost for two people in one room for one night.

Accommodations Prices

$	below $50
$$	$51 to $80
$$$	$81 to $110
$$$$	$111 to $150
$$$$$	above $150

Businesses come and go, ownerships and rates change. It is always a good idea to contact a place in advance to obtain the most current information.

Camping

Information on public, commercial, and backcountry campsites is included in this section.

 As a general rule, those with the most amenities will be the most expensive.

With just a few exceptions, backcountry camping is free and permitted anywhere on the state's 1,700,000 acres of national forest land. Some campgrounds are open only part of the year, so call ahead.

Where To Eat

 One of the joys of traveling is discovering a new restaurant where the food, service, or ambiance is special, be it a low-cost hearty breakfast, a sumptuously flavorful dish, or an elegant atmosphere. With a couple of exceptions, I have refrained from making any unfavorable remarks; if an establishment did not meet my expectations, it was not included. The $ codes indicate what an evening meal will cost, minus any drinks, appetizers, or desserts.

Restaurant Prices

Budget [$]	less than $10
Moderate [$$]	$10 to $20
Expensive [$$$]	$20 to $30
Extra-expensive [$$$$]	above $30

Key to Abbreviations

US – identifies a federal highway (i.e., US 60).

VA – identifies a state highway (i.e., VA 31) or a county highway (i.e., VA 624).

FDR – identifies a highway on Forest Service lands, which are usually unpaved (i.e., FDR 59).

FS – Official forest service maps mark trails with the forest service inventory numbers and – to help make it easy for you to identify them on the maps – I have included them in brackets (i.e., FS 621).

Introduction

The Eastern Shore

Close to 70 miles long, 10 miles at its widest, and bounded by water on three sides, Virginia's Eastern Shore is on the southern end of the Delmarva Peninsula (parts of which belong to Delaware, Maryland, and Virginia). It is a land where time has stood still – or at least slowed down considerably.

In search of flounder, crabs, clams, oysters, and other delicacies of the deep, watermen still rise before dawn and venture onto the Chesapeake Bay or the Atlantic Ocean. Moving about in small craft often manned by just one or two people, they employ many of the same techniques that their fathers and grandfathers used decades ago.

There are no huge malls or strips of fast food restaurants. Small seafood processing plants in many of the unpretentious fishing villages are the only industry. In this age of giant multiplex cinemas, one-screen theaters survive here. The flat fields surrounding the towns are blessed with a long growing season and fertile soil, which produces a rich harvest of corn, beans, tomatoes, peppers, and other vegetables.

Once connected to the mainland only by ferry service, the peninsula's isolation came to an end with the completion of the Chesapeake Bay Bridge-Tunnel in 1964. Although the rising amounts of traffic and tourism have caused subtle changes in Eastern Shore lifestyles, the outside influences have also helped bring about an increased awareness of the need to preserve the natural world.

The Eastern Shore is situated along the Atlantic Coast Flyway. Migrating shorebirds, waterfowl, raptors, and songbirds, including sandpipers, plovers, dowitchers, knots, whimprels, ducks, geese, herons, egrets, swans, pelicans, falcons, osprey, and many more, make use of the isolated barrier islands, marshlands, and fields as major resting areas. Thousands of water fowl, such as snow geese, black ducks, mallards, and pintails, winter here. Since the completion of the bridge-tunnel, the Eastern Shore National Wildlife Refuge, Fisherman Island National Wildlife Refuge, and Kiptopeke State Park have been established for the protection of habitat crucial to the migrant and resident birds and endangered wildlife species.

The barrier islands that insulate the mainland from the ravages of the Atlantic Ocean are, without a doubt, the Eastern Shore's most outstanding and important natural feature, both to human beings and to wildlife. Nearly all of the islands are now under the protection of federal and state governments or contained within The Nature Conservancy's Virginia Coast Reserve. Established in 1943 and now a major tourist destination, Chincoteague National Wildlife Refuge safeguards Virginia's portion of Assateague Island. (Maryland's section is overseen by its state parks department and the National Park Service.)

Information Sources

Chincoteague Chamber of Commerce, PO Box 258, Chincoteague, VA 23336, ☎ 757-336-6161

Chincoteague National Wildlife Refuge, PO Box 62, Chincoteague, VA 23336, ☎ 757-336-6122

Eastern Shore Tourism Commission, PO Box 460, Melfa, VA 23410, ☎ 757-787-2460

Cape Charles-Northampton County Chamber of Commerce, PO Box 87, Cape Charles, VA 23310, ☎ 757-331-2304

New Church Welcome Center-Virginia Division of Tourism, PO Box 215, New Church, VA 23415, ☎ 757-824-5000

■ ■ ■

Getting Around

The major air connection to the Eastern Shore is via the **Norfolk International Airport** (☎ 757-857-3351), less than an hour's drive from the peninsula's southern tip and served by most of America's major airlines. More than three million passengers pass through the airport's gates every year.

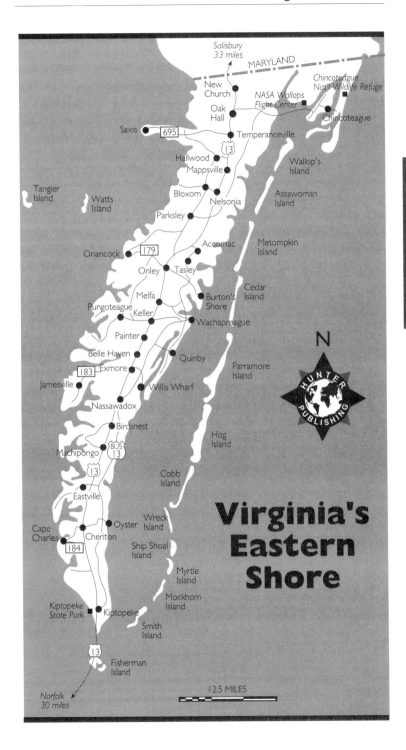

Salisbury
33 miles

MARYLAND

New
Church

Oak
Hall

NASA Wallops
Flight Center

Chincoteague
Nat'l Wildlife Refuge

Chincoteague

Saxis 695

Temperanceville

13

Hallwood

Mappsville

Wallop's
Island

Tangier
Island

Watts
Island

Bloxom

Nelsonia

Assawoman
Island

Parksley

Accomac

Metompkin
Island

Onancock 179

Onley Tasley

Melfa

Cedar
Island

Pungoteague

Keller

Burton's
Shore

Wachapreague

Painter

Belle Haven

Quinby

Parramore
Island

Jamesville

183 Exmore

Willis Wharf

Nassawadox

Birdsnest

Hog
Island

Machipongo BUS 13

13

Cobb
Island

Eastville

Cape
Charles

Oyster

Cheriton

Wreck
Island

Ship Shoal
Island

184

Myrtle
Island

Mockhorn
Island

N

**Virginia's
Eastern
Shore**

HUNTER
PUBLISHING

Kiptopeke
State Park

Kiptopeke

Smith
Island

13

Fisherman
Island

Norfolk
30 miles

12.5 MILES

Amtrak (9304 Warwick Blvd., Newport News, VA 23607, ☎ 800-872-7245) has daily train service into Newport News from Richmond and Washington, DC. For passenger convenience from Newport News, the railroad runs a shuttle van/bus into Norfolk and Virginia Beach.

Providing excellent service, **Carolina Trailways** (PO Box 28088, Raleigh, NC 27611, ☎ 919-833-3601) makes daily scheduled stops in Oak Hall, Onley, Exmore, and Cheriton. Flag stops are possible in Temperanceville, Accomac, Melfa, Nassawadox, Eastville, and the Chesapeake Bay Bridge-Tunnel.

Automobile rentals from national chains such as **Avis, Hertz, Budget**, and **Enterprise** are available at the Norfolk airport and numerous locations in the Norfolk/Virginia Beach metropolitan area. On the Eastern Shore you can rent a vehicle at the **Accomack County Airport** (29009 Terminal Drive, Melfa, VA 23418, ☎ 757-787-4600) or **Rent-A-Wreck** in Accomac (US 13N, Accomac, VA 23301, ☎ 800-787-0466).

US 13, of which the Chesapeake Bay Bridge Tunnel is a part, is the major south/north route on the Eastern Shore. Our tour branches off this four-lane highway to take in the attractions of the peninsula from the Eastern Shore National Wildlife Refuge in the south to Assateague Island in the north.

Touring

The tour begins by crossing the 17.6-mile **Chesapeake Bay Bridge-Tunnel** (PO Box 111, Cape Charles, VA 23310, ☎ 757-331-2960) from Virginia Beach to Cape Charles. Completed in 1964 at a cost of $200,000,000 and several lives, the structure is such marvel that it was awarded the status of an "Outstanding Engineering Achievement" by the American Society of Civil Engineers. You are given a ticket for a free refreshment when you pay the toll, so use it as an excuse to stop on the bridge's first island. Next to the restaurant/gift shop, a 625-foot fishing pier enables you to watch ocean-going cargo ships slowly gliding above the tunnels you'll be passing through.

Driving on, cross over Fisherman Island, a national wildlife refuge you can visit only by organized tour. Once you are across the bridge and on land once more, be sure to stop at the **Eastern Shore of Virginia National Wildlife Refuge** (5003 Hallett Circle, Cape Charles, VA 23310, ☎ 757-331-2760). Occupying land that was once a military installation, the refuge was established in 1984 for migratory and endangered species management, and for wildlife-oriented recreation. Each fall, migrating birds gather in large groups, waiting for favorable weather conditions to permit an easy crossing of the Chesapeake Bay. The visitors center is one of the best I've ever seen. You will not only come away from here with an appreciation of the wildlife, but also with a thorough understanding of how the ocean and the barrier islands affect the everyday aspects of the Eastern Shore.

Just north of the refuge, **Kiptopeke State Park** (3450 Kiptopeke Drive, Cape Charles, VA 23310, ☎ 757-331-2267) is also a stopover for migrating birds. Since 1977, members of the Virginia Society of Ornithology and the Hawk Migration Society have observed over 200,000 birds of prey at Kiptopeke. The park's 375 acres contain a hawk observatory, a hiking trail, boat ramp, campground, picnic area, and one of only two public beaches along the Chesapeake Bay on Virginia's portion of the Eastern Shore.

■ Cape Charles

The other public beach, this one in Cape Charles, is the setting for some spectacular sunsets over the bay. The small town is your first chance to become really acquainted with the lives of those who live on the Eastern Shore. This city has the largest population in the county, yet it has only 1,400 residents. A walking tour brochure available from the **Cape Charles Museum and Welcome Center** (PO Box 11, Cape Charles, VA 23310, ☎ 757-331-1008) takes you through the historic district of town, with large Victorian homes on almost every street. Cape Charles was a busy railroad hub near the beginning of the 20th century, but about all that is left from those days is one of the last remaining rail barges in the country headquartered here.

■ Eastville

The oldest continuous court records in the nation (1632) are preserved in the Eastville Clerk's Office, dating from 1830. Eastville was established in 1715 and the village's past is also preserved in its many other old structures, such as the 1731 Court House (with a museum of Indian and Colonial artifacts), the 1743 **Debtor's Prison**, and the **Eastville Inn**, dating from 1780.

If you happen to be on the Eastern Shore in early spring or mid-fall, take a tour of the **oyster house** in the small village of Willis Wharf, where you'll be amazed at the speed with which local workers can shuck oysters.

Continuing north, you'll be in Accomack County where the **Painter Gallery** (33412 Lankford Highway US 13, Painter, VA 23420, ☎ 757-442-9537) hosts a diverse array of fine arts exhibits and programs. Nearby **Wachapreague**, which bills itself as the Little City by the Sea, is where dozens of charter fishing trips, barrier island tours, and bird-watching excursions to the Virginia Coast Reserve originate.

■ Onancock

Much of the history of the Eastern Shore is discovered on a walking tour of Onancock. The Federal-style **Kerr Place** (69 Market St., Onancock, VA 23417, ☎ 757-787-8012) was built for wealthy merchant John Shepherd Kerr in 1799. Furnished in period antiques and now owned by the Eastern Shore Virginia Historical Society, the mansion is open Tuesday through Saturday, March through December. Other places of interest are the monuments to Confederate General Edmund R. Bagwell and World War I and II veterans, and the **Cokesbury United Methodist Church**, founded in 1784. **Hopkins and Brothers Store** (2 Market St., Onancock, VA 23417, ☎ 757-787-8220), one of the oldest general stores on the east coast, is listed on the US and Virginia Historic Landmark Registers. Tickets for the **Tangier Island cruises** (see page 91) are sold through the same window that passengers used more than a century ago to purchase steamboat tickets.

■ Accomac

Walking tours of Accomac take in the **Debtor's Prison** (☎ 757-787-2462), built in 1784 as the jailer's residence and furnished as it would have appeared around 1815. A perfect example of the "big house, little house, colonnade, and kitchen" style of construction is the **Seymour House** on Route 13. Using a method popular throughout the Eastern Shore, the first unit of the home was constructed in 1672. Later sections were added bit by bit, resulting in a house of various segments, sizes, and roof heights. Seven Gables, the oldest residence in the original 10-acre town site, and nearby Ailworth House, were also built in sections. There are, in fact, so many historic homes to see that one tourist brochure proclaims that Accomac has "more restored Colonial architecture than anywhere in Virginia except Colonial Williamsburg."

■ Parksley

Railroad buffs will want to take in the **Eastern Shore Railway Museum** (☎ 757-655-6271) on the site of the original depot. A 1927 observation car and a 1939 lounge car sit outside the museum, which has thousands of pieces of memorabilia from the old New York, Philadelphia, and Norfolk Railroad.

As you turn east on VA 175 toward Chincoteague, the high-tech mission and modern gadgetry of NASA's **Wallops Island Flight Facility** and **Goddard Space Flight Center** seem out of place on the sleepy Eastern Shore. Outside the visitors center are full-scale aircraft and rockets, while inside the history of flight is showcased – beginning with ancient Chinese and Greek stories and continuing up to the latest excursions into space. The balloons, rockets, and other aircraft that have been launched from its beachside pads have been some of the most important scientific flights for NASA. Although launches still occur frequently, they are not publicized.

The Eastern Shore

■ Chincoteague & Assateague Islands

Chincoteague and Assateague were both sleepy barrier islands at the northern end of Virginia's Eastern Shore until Marguerite Henry wrote her popular *Misty of Chincoteague* series beginning in 1947. Each year, Chincoteague Island draws 1½ million visitors in search of the simple island lifestyle and the ponies of Henry's books.

Amid all of the motels, restaurants, and souvenir shops, seek out the **Oyster and Maritime Museum** (7125 Maddox Blvd., Chincoteague, VA 23336, ☎ 757-336-6117). Maritime implements, shells, tools, historical artifacts, and live marine exhibits furnish a perspective on the area's seafood industry and way of life. A block away, exhibits at the **Refuge Waterfowl Museum** (7059 Maddox Blvd., Chincoteague, VA 23336, ☎ 757-336-5800) focus on the history and artistic side of waterfowl decoy carving, with a wealth of information on the wide variety of birds living in or passing through the area.

Ponies of Assateague Island.

The biggest event of the year takes place on the last continuous Wednesday and Thursday of July when the Virginia herd of ponies swims the channel from Assateague to Memorial Park on Chincoteague. Actually owned by the Chincoteague Volunteer Fire Department, some of the foals are sold at auction, with proceeds aiding fire fighting efforts. Legend has long held that the ponies are descendants of mustangs that swam ashore after a Spanish ship wrecked off the coast in the 16th century. Most likely their ancestors were placed on the island by mainland owners wanting to avoid taxation and the expense of fencing.

With a 37-mile beach, Assateague Island stretches across the border into Maryland. All of the island is public land as either the Assateague Island National Seashore administered by the **National Park Service** (Route 611, 7206 National Seashore Lane, Berlin, MD 21811, ☎ 410-641-3030), Maryland's **Assateague State Park** (7303 Stephen Decatur Highway, Berlin, MD 21811, ☎ 410-641-2120), or **Chincoteague National Wildlife Refuge** (PO Box 62, Chincoteague, VA 23336, ☎ 757-336-6122) under the jurisdiction of the Fish and Wildlife Service.

The refuge was established on the Virginia side in 1943 to protect wildlife and their habitat. Special emphasis has been placed on protecting threatened and endangered species, such as the Delmarva Peninsula fox squirrel and the piping plover. A network of roadways and hiking and biking trails lead to various points in the refuge, providing a chance to study the wildlife and vegetation of the barrier island. At the Chincoteague Refuge Visitors Center you can obtain maps, books, brochures, and other interpretive information about the refuge and its environs.

The Eastern Shore

Adventures

■ On Foot

Eastern Shore National Wildlife Refuge

 Making use of cinder-covered pathways and old roads, a half-mile interpretive trail in the refuge on Delmarva Peninsula's southern tip loops through a maritime forest of holly, loblolly pine, and locust trees draped by thick vines. Going past an old graveyard, the pathway has several segments. One ascends steps to the top of a World War II bunker for an expansive view of marshes, islands, bays, inlets, and the Atlantic Ocean. Another observation point looks inland.

With relatively mild temperatures, the national wildlife refuge is a great place to explore any time of year. Hawks, falcons, and songbirds are common from late August to November. During winter days, American woodcocks fly from fields to woods, and northern harriers and American kestrels search for prey. As temperatures warm into spring, glossy ibis, cattle egrets, and willets munch on delicacies found in shallow waters and grassy areas. At about this time, osprey arrive to begin seasonal nesting on platforms installed by refuge personnel. Use the lightly traveled, paved service roads that wind through the public lands to seek out other refuge residents, such as white-tailed deer, gray squirrels, cotton-tailed rabbits, opossums, raccoons, river otters, and red foxes.

Kiptopeke State Park

The 1½-mile **Baywoods Trail** in the park loops through open fields and an upland hardwood forest inhabited by deer, foxes, and other wildlife. Passing over secondary dunes, the pathway swings by an observation deck where you just might catch sight of a hawk or two. Although rare for the area, more than 100 red-headed woodpeckers have been spotted in a single day on park land.

A grand walking opportunity is the nearly mile-long **beach** adjacent to the park's campground. Although open to swimmers during the season, the beach is rarely crowded and makes for a wonderfully serene place to beachcomb. The Chesapeake Bay is teeming with aquatic life and a walk will usually yield an abundance of shells – oysters, blue mussels, scallops, jackknife clams. Darting from their holes near the dunes are ghost crabs, while large horseshoe crabs will sometimes wash ashore, only to crawl quickly back to water. The sky can be a great source of walking entertainment. Sometimes a brilliant blue, sometimes crowded with white, puffy cottonballs or darkened by sinister-looking storm clouds, it makes a colorful backdrop.

Indiantown Park

Often overlooked is the **nature trail** in the 52-acre Indiantown Park (7399 Indiantown Drive, Eastville, VA 23347, ☎ 757-678-0468) near Eastville. About 1½ miles, the pathway loops by a Native American burial ground in a hardwood/evergreen forest.

Chincoteague National Wildlife Refuge

Assateague Island offers the most hikes on the Eastern Shore. One of the most popular is in the **Chincoteague National Wildlife Refuge**. The paved **Woodland Trail** is also open to bicycles. The 1.6-mile loop begins off Beach Road, passes through barrier island woodlands, and goes by an observation deck overlooking a marsh where the wild ponies and Nippon sika deer graze. Although tourists are excited to see them, the non-native deer have become a detriment to the island's environment since they were introduced several decades ago. Eating saplings, they prevent young trees from growing up to replace the older, dying trees. As bits of the forest steadily disappear, the already endangered Delmarva Peninsula fox squirrel loses more and more of the habitat it needs in order to survive. A decline in the population of the native white-tailed deer has also been linked to the introduction of the sika deer.

Across Beach Road from the visitors center, the short (half-mile round-trip) **Lighthouse Trail** leads to the 124-foot **Assateague Lighthouse**, still used by the US Coast Guard to aid ship navigation.

The longest route in the refuge is the 7½-mile (one way) **Wash Flats Service Road**. From the visitors center, the gated road skirts marshes, dunes, wetlands, and man-made freshwater ponds. Along the way you are almost guaranteed to see a number of wild ponies, herons, and egrets.

Paved 3.2-mile **Wildlife Loop** is probably the most popular with hikers and bikers (it's open to motor vehicles after 3 pm each day). From the Chincoteague Refuge Visitors Center, the route encircles **Snow Goose Pool**, where geese, ducks, swans, and other waterfowl are often seen. Branching off from it is 1.1-mile **Swan Cove Trail**, which crosses over to the beach and the park service visitors center at Tom's Cove.

The National Park Service assists the Fish and Wildlife Service in providing services and managing recreational use in the Tom's Cove area. Although the loop it has developed for the **Tom's Cove Nature Trail** is less than a half-mile long, you'll want to spend a good bit of time here. A brochure (available at the trailhead) is keyed to numbered stops along the route explaining the natural history of the area as it passes through interdune, salt marsh, and shrub thicket habitats.

A rewarding overnight journey is to hike the beach from Tom's Cove in Virginia to the island's northern tip in Maryland. The beach stretches unbroken by high rise condominiums, restaurants, or motels for more than 30 miles. Imagine walking all day long with the warm sun above, the golden sands beneath your feet, and the clear blue water beside you – perhaps not seeing another person the whole time.

Isolation brings responsibility your way. No potable water is available, so carry plenty. Also, there is little shade; take coverups to protect you from the sun. Plan on a long day, as the first authorized campsite (across the Maryland border) is more than 13 miles from the Tom's Cove Visitors Center, where the required parking and backcountry use permits may be obtained.

■ On Wheels

Road Biking

 A lack of large tracts of public land precludes any real mountain biking, but the Eastern Shore's flat terrain can't be beat for road touring by bicycle. Other than main highway US 13, traffic is relatively light – and all roads either lead to small fishing villages with bed and breakfasts that cater to cyclists or out to wonderfully isolated dead-ends overlooking the Chesapeake Bay or the Atlantic coastline.

A ride that takes in the full length of Virginia's Eastern Shore begins by heading north from the **Eastern Shore National Wildlife Refuge**. **VA 600** is followed all of the way through rural Northampton County. Optional side-trips could include **VA 639** to the unspoiled fishing village of **Oyster**, or **VA 631** to **Indiantown Park** for a walk along its nature trail. Continue northward on VA 600, coming into Accomack County and bearing right onto **VA 182** to pass a number of commercial seafood houses and then turn left onto **VA 605** in tiny Quinby. Continuing on through Wachapreague, you'll pass by the **Locustville Academy**, the only surviving 1800s school building of higher education on the Eastern Shore. There is no way to avoid riding **Business US 13** as you pass through Accomac, but bear right as soon as you see the sign for **VA 679**. You can follow this lightly traveled route through such sleepy spots as Modest Town, Assawoman, Atlantic, Horntown, and Silva to the journey's end at the Maryland border.

An 11-mile round-trip ride to one of the least populated areas on the Eastern Shore follows **VA 634** from **Eastville** all the way to its end on **Savage Neck**, beside Cherrystone Inlet.

A 32-mile circuit that takes in fishing villages on both the bayside and the oceanside begins by heading south from **Onancock** on **VA 718/178** to **Pungoteague**. Turn east on **VA 180**, passing through Keller and crossing US 13 to come into **Wachapreague** for lunch at the dockside restaurant. You'll need to backtrack a bit to head north on **VA 605**, passing through tiny Chancetown and Locustville. Once in Accomac, bear left on

Business US 13, cross US 13 once more, and merge onto **VA 178** for the return to Onancock.

A longer, 90-mile circuit ride also originates in **Onancock**, taking **VA 718/178** to the south and following it through Pungoteague to Belle Haven and Exmore. You'll have to continue to the south on four-lane **US 13** for a short distance before turning onto lightly traveled **VA 618**. In Shadyside you'll once again make use of US 13, this time to ride into Eastville, where a left turn onto **VA 631** brings you to another left onto **VA 600**. Stay on this roadway until it ends and you can make a left onto **VA 605**. At the crossroads of Dougherty, head west on **VA 648**, cross US 13, and merge left onto **VA 657**. Another 1.4 miles of riding and you'll make a left onto **VA 658** to return to Onancock.

You can use the Tall Pines Harbor Waterfront Campground in Sanford as a base for a 12-mile round-trip exploration of the isolated marshes of the **Saxis Wildlife Management Area**. Follow **VA 695** west from the campground and soon bear left onto **VA 788** to its end, luxuriating in the quiet solitude of Messango Creek. Returning to **VA 695**, turn left to Saxis, where fishermen are so dedicated that you will see them going about their chores even on Sunday mornings. Continuing on, you'll come to the public boat ramp and the end of VA 695, where you can gaze out across the expanse of the Chesapeake Bay. Retrace VA 695 back to the campground, enjoying the sights and sounds of hundreds of Canada geese flying around the marshes.

Using the Stillmeadow B&B in Franktown as a base, an easy nine-mile circuit follows **VA 618, VA 620, VA 600**, and **VA 609**.

A 16-mile designated bicycle route leads from Maddox Blvd. in the town of **Chincoteague to the Chincoteague National Wildlife Refuge**, follows the Wildlife Loop, and continues on to Toms Cove Visitors Center along Beach Road. Also open to bicycle use in the refuge are the **Woodland Trail** and the **Swan Cove Trail**.

Outfitters

Bicycle rentals are available from **Piney Island Country Store** (7085 Maddox Blvd., Chincoteague, VA 23336, ☎ 757-336-6212).

■ On Horseback

Horseback riding is permitted in the **Tom's Cove** area of Chincoteague National Wildlife Refuge (☎ 757-336-6122) during certain times of the year. You should contact the refuge office before bringing your horse, as the time of year the areas are open to horses can change from year to year.

■ On Water

Virginia Coast Reserve & Mockhorn Island

Thanks to a partnership between public and private concerns, almost all of Virginia's Eastern Shore barrier islands are now protected and will remain much as they were when European settlers arrived in the early 1600s. The Nature Conservancy's Virginia Coast Reserve (PO Box 158 Brownsville, Nassawadox, VA 23143, ☎ 757-442-3049) includes 13 islands and 45,000 acres, ranging from Smith Island north to Metompkin Island. In addition, the state administers the more than 7,000-acre Mockhorn Island Wildlife Management Area (5806 Mooretown Road, Williamsburg, VA 23118, ☎ 757-253-4180).

These isolated, uninhabited islands, with their miles of inlets, acres of marshes, and mazes of tidal creeks and shallow bays, are a wilderness paddler's dream come true. You could easily canoe or kayak here for days on end without covering the same bit of water. This is a place where it is sometimes hard to tell whether you are on water or land, as the two mingle in shallow tidal flats. You are sure to see dozens of shorebirds and waterfowl and may run into a dolphin or a whale out in the ocean – but you probably will not encounter another human.

This place is only for those who feel comfortable with isolation and possess the skills necessary to navigate among myriad islands that are not much more than indistinct low shapes on the horizon. Take a compass, good maps or charts and plenty of drinking water. Be prepared for strong winds, sudden storms, and choppy water. You are permitted on the islands only during daylight hours. Camping is prohibited.

There are a number of **public ramps** that make it easy to slip your boat into the water. Among them are the ones at the end of VA 639 east of Cheriton; off VA 603 near Exmore; at Upshur Bay in Quinby; the public dock in Wachapreague; and along VA 680 next to Gargathy Bay.

Contact The Nature Conservancy (☎ 757-422-3049) if you are hesitant about paddling on your own. The organization sponsors naturalist-guided canoe/kayak/walking tours of the barrier islands on an irregular basis.

Chincoteague & Assateague Islands

Further north, **Chincoteague Bay, Assateague Channel, Chincoteague Channel**, and **Assateague Bay** are all popular paddling spots. In addition to large numbers of birds and waterfowl, you'll have the chance of spotting wild ponies, Nippon sika deer, white-tailed deer, red foxes, and maybe even an endangered Delmarva Peninsula fox squirrel. Except for four designated canoe campsites administered by the park service along Maryland's section of Assateague Island, camping is not permitted on any of the lands bordering these waters.

On the bayside, **public ramps** in Kiptopeke State Park, Cape Charles, Wardtown, and Onancock give you access to the entire Chesapeake Bay. You can head north or south from any of these, exploring the shore or paddle up one of the many creeks emptying into the bay. As part of its interpretive program, the state park conducts family-oriented, guided canoe trips through the salt marshes of the Eastern Shore.

Saxis Wildlife Management Area

By using the ramp at the end of VA 695 in the small fishing village of Saxis you could spend days exploring this area (5806 Mooretown Road, VA 23118, ☎ 757-253-4180). Its 5,570 acres are more marshland than solid ground and are riddled with scores of small creeks and passageways, with wide Messango Creek splitting the area in two. Like the barrier islands on the Atlantic side of the Eastern Shore, this is wilderness in its truest form. You'll find no houses or development of any kind and, other than an occasional fisherman, you probably will not encounter any signs of human life. This just may be the quietest and best paddling you will find on all of the Chesapeake Bay.

Eastern Shore Outfitters

Tidewater Expeditions (7729 Eastside Drive, Chincoteague, VA 23336, ☎ 757-336-6811) rents canoes and kayaks by the hour or day – and conducts hour-long guided trips and one-day sea kayak clinics.

If you want to let a motor do the work, contact **R & R Boat Rental** at the Harbor Light Motel and Marina (4183 Main St., Chincoteague, VA 23336, ☎ 757-336-5465), **Snug Harbor Cottages** (PO Box 498 Eastside Drive, Chincoteague, VA 23336, ☎ 757-336-6176), or **Capt. Bob's** (2477 Main St., Chincoteague, VA 23336, ☎ 757-336-6654).

In addition to taking the schooner *Delight* out on afternoon and sunset pleasure sails, Captains Greg and Laura Lohse run the **Low Sea Company** (Cape Charles, VA 23310, ☎ 757-331-4361), which conducts sailing classes, seminars, and coastal piloting and celestial navigation courses.

■ Ecotours

The interpretive and background information supplied by **Chincoteague National Wildlife Refuge Tours** (PO Box 252, Chincoteague, VA 23336, ☎ 757-336-6155) is about the most comprehensive you'll find. More than an hour long, the narrated bus tours wind through a part of the refuge few people see. Among other things, you will learn how freshwater ponds are manipulated to provide wildlife habitat, about the overwintering habits of snow geese and tundra swans, and of the harmful habits of the imported sika deer. The evening tour provides the best chance to see wildlife.

Captain Mike Handroth, a local fisherman of more than 20 years, pilots the *Chincoteague View* (PO Box 35, Chincoteague, VA 23336, ☎ 757-331-6861) on very reasonably priced one- and two-hour cruises to the ocean side of Assateague Island in hopes of seeing dolphins, sea turtles, and the famed wild ponies.

Providing a sort of one-stop-shopping, **Assateague Adventures** in The Mariner Motel (6273 Maddox Blvd., Chincoteague, VA 23336, ☎ 800-221-7490) has package programs that include accommodations, meals, and lectures, in conjunction with ecology, archaeology, natural history, wildlife photography, birding, boating, and bicycling tours.

In association with The Nature Conservancy, **Eastern Shore Escapes** (PO Box 395, Belle Haven, VA 23306, 888-VA SHORE) has weekend bed and breakfast package deals featuring birding, biking, or kayaking adventures. Participants are accompanied by naturalists who interpret the ecology, history, and culture of the areas being explored. This is not your typical tourist tour, but a first-class operation that will give you a very thorough understanding of the Eastern Shore.

Held in early October, the annual **Eastern Shore Birding Festival** celebrates the peak of the fall bird migration. Workshops, field trips, exhibits, canoe excursions, and nature hikes help participants experience the phenomenon of thousands of birds congregating in preparation for the annual flight to the tropics. Events take place at various sites throughout the Eastern Shore; Kiptopeke State Park and Sunset Beach Inn are the primary centers of activity. **The Eastern Shore Chamber of Commerce** (PO Box 460, Melfa, VA 23410, ☎ 757-787-2460) will provide you with a brochure and dates for registration.

In the same vein and with similar activities, the Chincoteague National Wildlife Refuge (PO Box 62, Chincoteague, VA 23336, ☎ 757-336-6122) celebrates its feathered transients with the **International Migratory Bird Week**, held every year in May.

Where To Stay

Northampton County

 Headquarters for the Eastern Shore Birding Festival held each October – and just a few minute's drive to the Eastern Shore of Virginia National Wildlife Refuge and Kiptopeke State Park – **Sunset Beach Inn** [$] (Route 13, Cape Charles, VA 23340, ☎ 800-899-4SUN) has its own restaurant, pool, boat ramp, and private beach on the bay.

Bicycles are available for guests of the **Sunset Inn B&B** [$$ to $$$] (108 Bay Ave., Cape Charles, VA 22310, ☎ 757-331-2424) to ride the mile-long Cape Charles boardwalk. Rockers on the front porch overlooking the water allow you to watch the sunset.

Just around the corner, the 1861 **Sea Gate B&B** [$$ to $$$] (9 Tazewell Ave., Cape Charles, VA 23310, ☎ 757-331-2206) also has bikes for guest use. Casual afternoon teas can help relax you for evening activities.

Upping the bicycle ante, **Wilson-Lee House B&B** [$$$] (403 Tazewell Ave., Cape Charles, VA 23310-3217, ☎ 757-331-1954), constructed in 1906, has a bicycle built for two.

Just south of Cape Charles, **Nottingham Ridge B&B** [$$ to $$$] (28184 Nottingham Ridge Lane, Cape Charles, VA 23310, ☎ 757-331-1010) has 100 acres of woodlands and dunes that lead to a private beach. Wine and cheese complement the sunsets.

The **Anchor Motel** [$$] (7120 Lankford Highway US 13, Nassawadox, VA 23413, ☎ 757-442-6363) and **Best Western** [$$] (2543 Lankford Highway US 13, Exmore, VA 23350, ☎ 757-442-7378) are centrally located within a 30-minute drive of nearly everything on Virginia's Eastern Shore.

Close to Nature Conservancy property is the **Stillmeadow B&B** [$$] (7423 Bayside Road, Franktown, VA 23354, ☎ 800-772-8397). Hosts Carroll and Irene Walker put an emphasis on outdoor activities. Besides providing bicycles for guest use, they can arrange excursions to the Barrier Islands, or help you rent a boat or arrange a fishing trip.

In a rare departure for many B&Bs, children and pets are actually welcome to enjoy the homey atmosphere of **Ballard House Family Style B&B** [$$] (12527 Ballard Drive, Willis Wharf, VA 23486, ☎ 757-442-2206). The kids are encouraged to use the attic playroom, walk the nature trail, play the piano, or dip their hands into the cookie jar. You have your choice of a low fat, vegetarian, Southern, or international-style breakfast.

Accomack County

Overlooking Occohannock Creek and the Chesapeake Bay, **Bayview B&B** [$$] (35350 Copes Drive, Belle Haven, VA 23306, ☎ 800-442-6966) sits on 140 acres of woods, farmland, and creekshore to hike along. After using the bicycles, you can relax in the pool or browse the library.

You can experience almost everything the Eastern Shore has to offer without ever venturing far from the grounds of the **Evergreen Inn B&B** [$$ to $$$] (PO Box 102, Pungoteague, VA 23422, ☎ 757-442-3375). Guests have use of a canoe, a paddleboat, or a bike. In addition, there are 25 acres to explore, including a private beach and a crabbing dock.

Sitting upon a marsh that leads to the Atlantic Ocean, **Wachapreague Hotel and Marina** [$] (17 Atlantic Ave., Wachapreague, VA 23480, ☎ 757-787-2105) has small boats for rent and arranges charter fishing trips. Pets are welcome.

True to its name, **The Spinning Wheel B&B** [$$] (31 North St., Onancock, VA 23417, ☎ 757-787-7311) has several spinning wheels amid its antique furnishings. The hosts of this restored 1890s folk Victorian home supply guests with bicycles and information on local rides.

The **Lighthouse Motel** [$$] (4218 Main St., Chincoteague, VA 23336, ☎ 757-336-5091), the **Beach Road Motel** [$$] (6151 Maddox Blvd., Chincoteague, VA 23336, ☎ 757-336-6551), and the **Sea Shell Motel** [$$] (3720 Willow St., Chincoteague, VA 23336, ☎ 757-336-6589) each have a small pool, clean rooms, and some of the lowest rates on the island of Chincoteague.

Within walking distance of the wildlife refuge and only a 10-minute drive from the seashore, **Refuge Motor Inn** [$$$]

(7058 Maddox Blvd., Chincoteague, VA 23336, ☎ 757-336-5511) offers saunas, whirlpools, and bicycles for rent. The management can also make arrangements for narrated boat cruises focusing upon the natural world around Chincoteague Channel.

Overlooking Chincoteague Channel with its own marina is **Waterside Motor Inn** [$$$ to $$$$] (3761 Main St., Chincoteague, VA 23336, ☎ 757-336-3434).

In the center of Chincoteague, air-conditioned **Island Manor House B&B** [$$ to $$$] (4160 Main St., Chincoteague, VA 23336, ☎ 800-852-1505) serves a full breakfast and afternoon tea. Make use of the bicycles, then unwind in a relaxing garden room.

Miss Molly's Inn B&B [$$ to $$$] (4141 Main St., Chincoteague, VA 23336, ☎ 800-221-5620) is an obligatory listing, as Marguerite Henry stayed here while writing *Misty of Chincoteague*. Breakfast and traditional English tea, complete with scones, are served in the gazebo.

Outdoor enthusiasts can obtain a wealth of information from Dennis Holland, the owner of **The Main Street House B&B** [$$ to $$$] (4356 Main St., Chincoteague, VA 23336, ☎ 800-491-2017). He is a former wildlife refuge manager.

Free use of bicycles and beach chairs, a hearty breakfast, and afternoon tea are the draw at **The Watson House B&B** [$$ to $$$] (4240 Main St., Chincoteague, VA 23336, ☎ 757-336-1564), a Victorian home furnished with antiques.

Chincoteague Island Vacation Cottages (6282 Maddox Blvd., Chincoteague, VA 23336, ☎ 800-457-6643) is the agent for a number of private homes on the island that are rented out by the week, miniweek, or weekend. You can greatly reduce your cost of staying in the area if you get several family members or friends to share a cottage with you.

■ Camping

You can make reservations to stay in the campground at **Kiptopeke State Park** by calling ☎ 800-933-PARK. The sites, which are within a minute's walk of the park's beach, offer drinking water, electric and sewer hookups, picnic tables, fire rings, showers, and restrooms.

A destination unto itself, 300-acre **Cherrystone Campground** (PO Box 545, Cheriton, VA 23316, ☎ 757-331-3063) has waterfront property on the Chesapeake Bay, swimming pools, crabbing piers, camping cabins, and a nature trail.

Sunsets are superb seen from the waterside tentsites in the 81-acre, family-run **Tall Pines Harbor Waterfront Campground** (VA 695, Sanford, VA 23426, ☎ 757-824-0777) on the Pocomoke Sound. Water, sewer, and electric hookups, dump stations, showers, and laundromat are available. This is a quiet, rarely crowded campground in a lovely out-of-the-way spot.

Maddox Family Camground (PO Box 82, Chincoteague, VA 23336, ☎ 757-336-3111) – with hot showers, dump station, grocery store, and laundromat – is the campground closest to Chincoteague National Wildlife Refuge.

One of the largest camping facilities in the Chincoteague area, **Tom's Cove Campground** (Chincoteague Island, VA 23336, ☎ 757-336-6498) occupies the waterfront overlooking Assateague Island. In addition to the usual campground amenities, there is a boat ramp and marina.

Also on the waterfront in Chincoteague is **Inlet View Campground** (2272 Main St., Chincoteague, VA 23336, ☎ 757-336-5126).

Six ponds on the waterfront property of **Pine Grove Campground** (5283 Deep Hole Road, Chincoteague, VA 23336, ☎ 757-336-5200) serve as a sanctuary for more than 40 species of waterfowl.

Campers Ranch (4423 Chicken City Road, Chincoteague, VA 23336, ☎ 757-336-6371) has a limited supply of equipment geared mostly toward car campers.

Where To Eat

 The dining experiences on the Eastern Shore can't help but be centered around seafood. Enjoy it, as you'll never find the local delicacies – especially crabs, clams, oysters, and flounder – to be any fresher than they are here.

Northampton County

The first spot for tourists to eat as they pour off the Bay Bridge-Tunnel is **Sting Ray's Cape Center Restaurant** [$ to $$] (Route 13, Cape Charles, VA 23310, ☎ 757-331-2505). This is a gas station/convenience store/restaurant serving breakfast, lunch, and dinner, with a surprisingly good menu. Who would have expected succulent crab, flounder, or lamb entrées, with an extensive wine list? Desserts are delicious and milkshakes are made the old-fashioned way.

The Trawler Restaurant [$$$] (Route 13, Exmore, VA 23350, ☎ 757-442-2092) serves seafood (the she-crab soup is delicious), homemade chowders, and sweet potato biscuits. If you are looking for a bit of cultural diversion, the restaurant becomes a dinner theater about four times a year.

The Italian owner puts his mark on the lasagne, calzones, eggplant dishes, pizzas, and strombolis served in the **Little Italy Restaurant and Pizza** [$ to $$] (10237 Rogers Drive, Nassawadox, VA 23413, ☎ 757-442-7831). Try the homemade tiramisu.

Accomack County

Inside a building designed to look like an old lifesaving station, **Island House** [$$$] (15 Atlantic Ave., Wachapreague, VA 23480, ☎ 757-787-2105) specializes in fresh seafood and Black Angus beef.

The Argentine owner of **Armando's** [$$] (10 North St., Onancock, VA 23417, ☎ 757-787-8044) watches over an innovative menu of seafood, veal, and pasta. Save room for equally creative and luscious desserts.

You can't get much fresher than **Flounder's** [$$] (Lankford Highway US 13, Tasley, VA 23491, ☎ 757-787-2233). The owner's husband is a local waterman who supplies the restaurant with his daily catch of oysters.

Several miles west of Chincoteague, **Wright's Seafood Restaurant** [$$$] (PO Box 130, Atlantic, VA 23303, ☎ 757-824-4012) features all-you-can-eat barbecue ribs, fried chicken, and steamed crabs and shrimp. Separate meal entrées include other fresh seafood, such as flounder.

Diners enjoying traditional seafood meals at **Etta's Family Restaurant** [$ to $$] (7452 East Side Drive, Chincoteague, VA 23336, ☎ 757-336-5644) can watch boats gliding by on Assateague Sound.

Fresh-baked breads accompany the meals of crab, shrimp, clams, beef, and chicken at the **Landmark Crab House** [$$ to $$$] (6162 Landmark Plaza, Chincoteague, VA 23336, ☎ 757-336-5552). Next door, the **Shucking House Café** [$ to $$] (Landmark Plaza, Chincoteague, VA 23336, ☎ 757-366-5145) serves breakfast and lunch at its pierside location.

The only all-you-can-eat crab and shrimp restaurant on Chincoteague Island, **Steamers** [$$] (6251 Maddox Blvd., Chincoteague, VA 23336, ☎ 757-336-6904) also has a carry-out menu.

With an Italian influence, the scents of fresh grilled fish, seafood, steaks, veal, and pasta waft out of the screened dining porch at **AJ's on the Creek** [$$] (6585 Maddox Blvd., Chincoteague, VA 23336, ☎ 757-336-5888). A fine wine list is available.

For a bit of indulgence, **Mullers Old Fashioned Ice Cream Parlour** [$] (4034 Main St., Chincoteague, VA 23336, ☎ 757-336-5894) can satisfy your sweet tooth with soda fountain treats such as sundaes, splits, malts, and Belgian waffles topped with ice cream, fresh fruit, and homemade whipped cream.

Reservations are recommended for **The Garden and Sea Inn** [$$ to $$$] (4188 Nelson Road, New Church, VA 23415, ☎ 757-824-0672). Inside an intimate dining room, the menu changes seasonally, based upon the availability of fresh seafood and regional ingredients.

Tidewater Virginia

Water rules here. Look out of any window and you are likely to see it. Virginia's Tidewater area is bounded on the east by the brackish water of the Chesapeake Bay – the world's largest estuary – and by the salt water of the Atlantic Ocean. Its land has been deeply cut and divided into three long peninsulas (or necks, as they are called locally) by four large rivers – the Potomac, Rappahannock, York, and the James. With more than 20 miles of sand and surf, Virginia Beach is the state's only ocean-front resort strip. And even the distinction between water and land is blurred at Tidewater's southernmost point along the North Carolina border. At one time, the Great Dismal Swamp spread its influence over more than 2,000 square miles. For hundreds of years men have tried to drain it, but the swamp still holds sway over 750 square miles and provides some of the best wilderness explorations in the entire state.

All of this water has influenced the daily life of the Tidewater region. As on the Eastern Shore, fisherfolk set out each day in hopes of harvesting blue crabs, oysters, and other bounties of the bay. One of the joys of traveling here is the opportunity to dine upon the fruits of their labor and to wander around the small waterside villages that have changed little through the years. Supported by some of the largest and most modern ship-building facilities in the world and America's largest naval base, the cities around the mouth of the Chesapeake Bay – known collectively as the Hampton Roads area – have grown into Virginia's most populated metropolis. Some of the Commonwealth's best natural history museums, among them the Virginia Marine Science Museum and the Virginia Living Museum, are located here. Also noteworthy are the Chrysler Museum of Art, and Nauticus, The National Maritime Center.

The first permanent English settlement in the New World, Jamestown, was established upon a bit of land along the northern shore of the James River. The area also includes Yorktown – where the last important conflict of the Revolutionary War was fought – and the restored 18th-century town of Colonial Williamsburg. The vast acreage of wetlands along the rivers, bay, and ocean – such as Back Bay National Wildlife, Ragged Island Wildlife Management Area, York River State Park, and Caledon Natural Area – are home to numerous birds and are major - resting areas on the Great Atlantic Flyway. Hiking trails and canoeable waters enable you to observe a wide array of migratory waterfowl, including ducks, swans, and geese.

Almost all of the area's national, state, county, and municipal parks and preserves are situated along a body of water, providing public access and sponsoring interpretive programs that explore the natural and human histories of the areas.

Information Sources

Hampton Visitors Center, 710 Settlers Landing Road, Hampton, VA 23669, ☎ 800-800-2202.

Newport News Tourism Development Office, 2400 Washington Ave., Newport News, VA 23607, ☎ 800-333-7787.

Isle of Wight Visitors Center, 130 Main St., Smithfield, VA 23430, ☎ 800-365-9339.

Norfolk Convention & Visitors Bureau, 232 East Main St., Norfolk, VA 23510, ☎ 800-368-3097.

Northern Neck Travel & Tourism Council, PO Box 326, Wicomico Church, VA 22579, ☎ 800-453-6167.

Portsmouth Convention & Visitors Bureau, 505 Crawford St., Suite 2, Portsmouth, VA 23704, ☎ 800-PORTS-VA.

Potomac Gateway Welcome Center, 3540 James Madison Parkway, King George, VA 22485, ☎ 540-663-3205.

City of Virginia Beach Visitor Information Center, 2100 Parks Ave., Virginia Beach, VA 23451, ☎ 800-446-8036.

Williamsburg Area Convention & Visitors Bureau, 201 Penniman Road, Williamsburg, VA 23187, ☎ 800-368-6511.

■ ■ ■

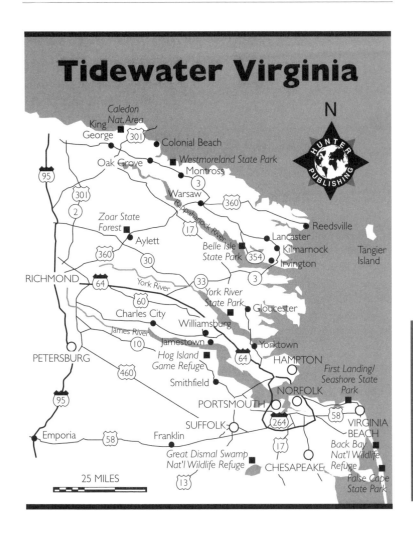

Getting Around

A couple of airports make it easy to fly into Tidewater Virginia. Just 15 miles from the Virginia Beach oceanfront, **Norfolk International Airport** (☎ 757-857-3200) is served by more than a dozen major national and regional airlines. Close to 200 flights can give you direct connections with such cities as Atlanta, Baltimore, Boston, Charlotte, Chicago, Dallas, New

York, and more. Close to the Historical Triangle, the **Newport News/Williamsburg International Airport** (☎ 757-877-0221) also has connections to major US cities via several national airlines.

Amtrak (☎ 800-872-7245) makes stops in Williamsburg and Newport News. From the Newport News station, the railroad runs a shuttle van/bus into Norfolk and Virginia Beach.

Greyhound (☎ 800-231-2222) will deliver you or pick you up in Virginia Beach, Norfolk, Hampton, Newport News (at Fort Eustis), Williamsburg, Suffolk, and Franklin. Flag stops are made

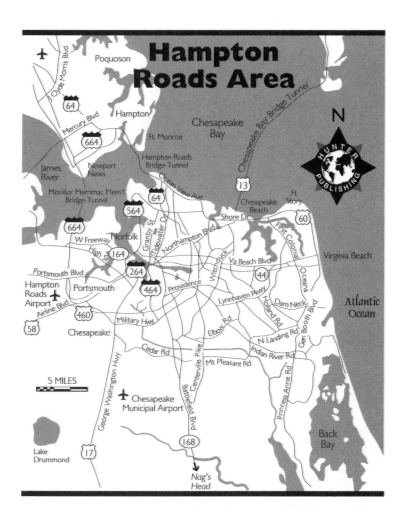

in the small Southhampton County and Sussex County towns of Courtland, Sebrell, and Homeville. Sadly, there is no bus service to the Northern Neck region.

In the larger cities of Norfolk, Virginia Beach, Chesapeake, Portsmouth, Newport News, Hampton, and Williamsburg, you will be able to **rent a car** from the major chains: Alamo, Avis, Budget, Enterprise, Hertz, National, Rent-A-Wreck, and Thrifty. Look to Enterprise and Rent-A-Wreck while in the Northern Neck region.

Touring

■ Norfolk

The tour of Tidewater Virginia begins in Norfolk, home port to more than 150 ships. This is the world's largest naval installation, so you would be remiss to overlook the **Norfolk Naval Base** (9079 Hampton Blvd., Norfolk, VA 23505, ☎ 757-444-7955). On weekend afternoons visitors are permitted to tour certain ships and there are bus tours throughout the week with naval personnel providing commentary on the base's sites and activities.

A much quieter tour would be to walk the 12 miles of pathways winding into the more than 150 acres of azaleas, camellias, rhododendrons, roses, dogwoods, hollies, and lily ponds in the **Norfolk Botanical Gardens** (6700 Azalea Garden Road, Norfolk, VA 23518, ☎ 757-441-5830). Special spots include the Fragrance, Italian Renaissance, Japanese, Colonial, and Perennial Gardens. Boat and trackless train tours are also available.

A number of tour companies provide **boat cruises** around Norfolk. Originating beside the city's revitalized Waterside Festival Marketplace, some are sightseeing tours, while others offer lunch, brunch, dinner, and moonlight cruises. (See *On Water,* below, for details on specific cruises.)

One of Norfolk's newest attractions is adjacent to the Waterside complex. **Nauticus, The National Maritime Center** (One Waterside Drive, Norfolk, VA 23510, ☎ 757-664-1000) is a $52 million, 120,000-square-foot, high-tech museum and science center with the glitz of an amusement park. Three levels of interactive exhibits include marine biology, environmental science, naval artwork, ship designing, and much, much more. You could spend a full day here and not even come close to experiencing everything. There is a wide-screen theater showing the underwater adventure film, *The Living Sea* (nominated as the Best Documentary of 1996), another with a naval battle simulation, and yet another presenting a video on the trends of the shipbuilding industry.

Norfolk

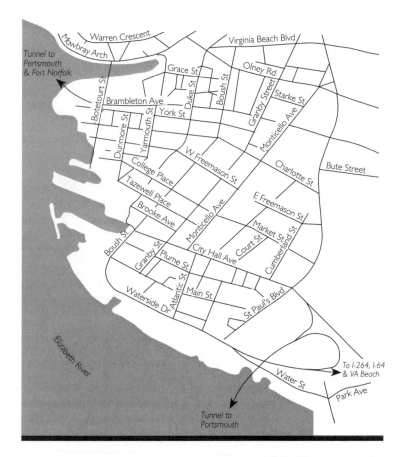

A bit more traditional in scope, the **Chrysler Museum of Art** (245 West Olney Road, Norfolk, VA 23510, ☎ 757-664-6200) was recognized by the *Wall Street Journal* as one of the nation's top 20 art museums. Inside you will find a permanent collection of more than 30,000 works of art, ranging from those of ancient Egypt to European masters and an 8,000-piece glass collection featuring more than 200 Tiffany works.

The Moses Myers House (331 Bank St., Norfolk, VA 25310, ☎ 757-664-6296) is the only historic house in the United States to provide an overview of the traditions and lives of early Jewish immigrants. The 18th-century house is furnished with belongings from five generations of the Myers family.

Virginia Beach, one of America's great Atlantic Ocean beaches.

■ Virginia Beach

From Norfolk, the tour follows US 58 east to Virginia Beach. With close to 30 miles of surf and sand, the city claims to be the world's longest beach resort. Although that may be somewhat of a nebulous distinction, there is no doubt that it is Virginia's only

Atlantic Ocean beachfront and that saltwater worshippers flock here by the thousands. A three-mile concrete boardwalk from 1st St. to 39th St. defines the main resort area and is, by far, the best spot for people-watching. Not as crowded, but still patrolled by lifeguards, are the Camp Pendleton, Croatan, Sandbridge, and Fort Story beaches.

Along the waterfront, the **Old Coast Guard Station** (24th St. & Oceanfront, Virginia Beach, VA 23451, ☎ 757-422-1587) is the state's only lifesaving/coast guard station that is open to the public. The museum showcases the early days with visual exhibits of over 600 shipwrecks and rescues along the city's shoreline.

High-rises line the shore.

The Association for Research and Enlightenment (67th St. and Atlantic Ave., Virginia Beach, VA 23451, ☎ 757-428-3588) studies Edgar Cayce's work in holistic medicine and parapsychology. There are free tours, exhibits, and lectures on dreams, life after death, holistic health, and even an ESP testing machine.

Where the Chesapeake Bay meets the Atlantic Ocean, **First Landing Cross** marks the area where, in 1607, America's first English settlers touched shore. In the same area is the **Old Cape Henry Lighthouse** (Fort Story, Virginia Beach, VA 23451, ☎ 757-422-9421). Erected in 1791, it is the oldest government-built lighthouse in the United States.

The **Virginia Marine Science Museum** (717 General Booth Blvd., Virginia Beach, VA 23451, ☎ 757-425-3474) is a major attraction. When I was employed at the nearby state park, I spent as much of my free time as possible here. I was fascinated by the sights, sounds, and knowledge I was gleaning from the museum. I always seemed to find and learn something new from the 150 interactive exhibits, the nature trail winding through a life-filled salt marsh, and the aquariums populated by sharks, sea turtles, sting rays, octopi, eels, seals, otters, and other marine life from Virginia's waters. The adjoining six-story IMAX 3D Theater, with films such as *Into the Deep,* adds to appeal of this do-not-miss place.

The 32,000 square feet of the **Contemporary Art Center of Virginia** (2200 Parks Ave., Virginia Beach, VA 23451, ☎ 757-425-0000) are dedicated to 20th-century art in painting, photography, sculpture, and other visual media. Recent themes have included ethnic works, land usage issues, and an exploration of food as an artistic medium.

If someone described a place of tannin-stained swamps surrounded by cypress trees festooned with Spanish moss, you might be inclined to think of the Okefenokee Swamp in Georgia. Yet, miles of trails wind through such an environment to ascend small sand dunes under a forest of sweetgum and loblolly trees in **First Landing/Seashore State Park** (2500 Shore Drive, Virginia Beach, VA 23451, ☎ 757-481-2131). The 2,900-acre oasis of green amid high-rises and shopping centers is a great place to escape the hyperactivity of the resort area beach. Then again, with its own mile-long band of sand on the bay, campsites, and rental cabins, you may never need to venture out of the park.

Situated on a thin strip of land south of town, **Back Bay National Wildlife Refuge** (PO Box 6286, Virginia Beach, VA 23456, ☎ 757-721-2412) contains a coastline typical of barrier is-

Tidewater Virginia

lands found along the Atlantic coast. As a haven for waterfowl – geese, swans, and ducks – the refuge provides habitat for otters, muskrats, mink, and deer. Although they are damaging to the environment, non-native pigs, nutria, and horses also roam free. A system of dikes and boardwalks are open to walkers and cyclists to explore the 4,608 acres.

Until recently you could reach **False Cape State Park** (4001 Sandpiper Road, Virginia Beach, VA 23546, ☎ 757-426-7128) only by walking or biking more than five miles through the wildlife refuge or taking a boat through the waters of Back Bay. Now a tram runs from Little Island City Park, through the refuge, and into the state park. With an unspoiled shoreline of rolling dunes topped by sea oats, salt marshes, and a bit of a forest of oak and loblolly pines, this is one of the last undisturbed coastal environs left in the East. Primitive campsites and trails enable you to discover the wonders of this place.

 No potable water is available – so be sure to bring plenty with you.

■ Chesapeake

The tour takes its leave of Virginia Beach by heading west on Pungo Ferry Road from the western shore area of Back Bay. Make a left onto Blackwater Road and follow it for several miles to a right onto Indian Creek Road. This, in turn, will lead you to **Northwest River Park** (1733 Indian Creek Road, Chesapeake, VA 23322, ☎ 757-421-3145). Even though it has a playground, picnic shelters, miniature golf course, canoes for rent, and a campground (all of which are bunched together close to the park entrance), it is more like a nature preserve than a regional park. Save for a few hiking trails and a network of old canals, most of its 763 acres have been left unspoiled, with cypress trees growing in the swamplands and backwaters of Indian Creek and Northwest River. At less than $15 a site, the park is a low-cost, quiet place to camp and explore the natural world, yet it's just a short drive from the resort amenities of Virginia Beach.

Driving a few miles farther to the west, you will run into the **Great Dismal Swamp National Wildlife Refuge** (PO Box 349, Suffolk, VA 23439, ☎ 757-986-3705). Far from "dismal," the area is a wondrous place of rich natural charm with cypress knees rising out of tannin-darkened waters and a forest of pine, cedar, blackgum, sweetgum, and oak growing upon and around the soft peat bogs. In the center of the refuge is one of only two natural lakes in all of Virginia, 3,100-acre **Lake Drummond**. (The other is Mountain Lake in Southwest Virginia.) Unlike most swamps that form a basin – catching the waters that flow into them – Great Dismal Swamp is a perched bog, with Lake Drummond occupying the higher ground and water flowing out of it into streams and manmade canals.

George Washington was so taken by the place – proclaiming it a "glorious paradise" – that he helped form the Dismal Swamp Land Company, which purchased 40,000 acres of swampland. More entrepreneurial than naturalist in makeup, the company proceeded to drain and log portions of the swamp. Logging operations continued until 1976; in fact, every acre of the swamp has been logged at least once. This has changed its ecology, but has also opened it up to hikers and bikers, who are permitted to use the 140 miles of roadways. A commercial canoe company offers day trips into the swamp and canoeists and kayakers can paddle the miles of canals. The main refuge entrance is south of Suffolk on VA 642/White Marsh Road. (A new visitors center recently opened three miles south of the North Carolina border on US 17.) This is one of the most under-visited areas in Virginia by people looking for solitude, natural beauty, and outdoor adventure; I strongly urge you to spend some time here.

■ Portsmouth

Drive north from the swamp to the **Portside Visitor Information Center** (6 Crawford St., Portsmouth, VA 23704, ☎ 757-393-5111) to obtain the **Old Towne Portsmouth** walking tour brochure. Using it as a guide, you can saunter through – as the brochure says – "the largest concentration of restored 18th-century homes between Alexandria and Charleston." Within the original 65 acres of land that made up this Colonial town in

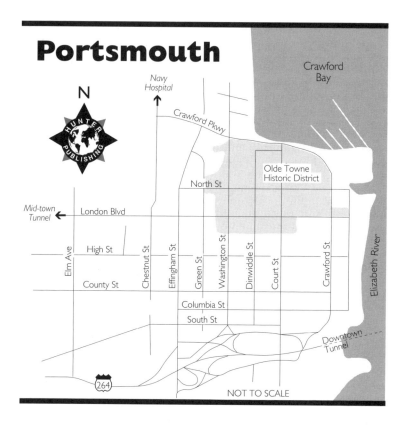

Portsmouth

Crawford Bay

Navy Hospital

N

Crawford Pkwy

Olde Towne Historic District

North St

Mid-town Tunnel

London Blvd

Elm Ave

High St

Chestnut St

Effingham St

Green St

Washington St

Dinwiddie St

Court St

Crawford St

County St

Columbia St

South St

Downtown Tunnel

Elizabeth River

264

NOT TO SCALE

1752 are worthy examples of Colonial, Federal, and antebellum houses. All are private homes closed to the public – except **Hill House** (221 North St., Portsmouth, VA 23740, ☎ 757-393-0241). Headquarters of the Portsmouth Historical Society, the four-story English basement home is now a museum containing furnishings collected by generations of the Hill family.

At one time, ships with lights attached to the tops of their tall masts were anchored for long periods in strategic places off the coast to serve as warning beacons to other ships. The **Lightship Museum** (London Slip, Portsmouth, VA 23704, ☎ 757-393-8741) served such duty for nearly 50 years. Permanently moored at the city's waterfront, this ship has been restored as a floating museum and monument to those earlier days.

Nearby, the **Naval Shipyard Museum** (2 High St., Portsmouth, VA 23704, ☎ 757-393-8591) chronicles the history of the shipyard, the Portsmouth area, and the local military forces. Included are scale models of vessels that figured into the seafaring ways of Portsmouth and surrounding cities, such as the Confederate ironclad *CSS Virginia* – known as the *Merrimac* to "unknowledgeable Yankees."

■ Smithfield Region

Traveling northwest on US 17 and VA 10, the tour leaves the large population centers behind to enter the bucolic countryside of Isle of Wight County and the town of Smithfield – producer of the world-famous, salt-flavored hams. Smithfield hams come from hogs fed peanuts from the local fields, with the meat slowly cured over hickory fires. So much meat is processed here that it was not the private slaughterhouses but the Virginia Department of Transportation that erected the road signs directing the tractor trailers loaded with livestock to the packing plants.

The production of hams has been such an important part of county life since the first salt pork curing business was established in 1779, that a portion of the **Isle of Wight Museum** (103 Main St., Smithfield, VA 23430, ☎ 757-357-7459) is devoted to its history. Other exhibits contain Native American and Civil War artifacts. Admission is free.

Settled in 1752, primarily by British merchants and ship captains, Smithfield has over 60 historic buildings that predate the Revolutionary War and a number of elaborate Victorian homes dating from the 1870s. A walking tour brochure available from the town's visitors center next to the courthouse can help bring alive the bygone days of steamboats and peanut farming.

East of town, one of the last large undisturbed brackish marshes left along the James River is protected by the **Ragged Island Wildlife Management Area** (c/o Virginia Wildlife Management Areas, PO Box 11104, Richmond, VA 23188, ☎ 804-367-1000). Marshes also make up a large portion of **Hog Island Wildlife Management Area** (RFD, Surry, VA 23883, ☎ 757-357-5224), west of Smithfield along the Isle of

Tidewater Virginia

Wight/Surry County line. Both have short hiking trails and are great places to watch thousands of shorebirds and waterfowl such as egrets, herons, geese, and ducks descend onto the marshlands during the fall migration.

Serving as your introduction to Colonial Virginia, **Chippokes Plantation State Park** (695 Chippokes Road, Surry, VA 23883, ☎ 757-294-3728) claims to be one of the oldest working farms in the country. West of Hog Island and across the James River from Jamestown, Captain William Powell received a land grant for 550 acres along Chippokes Creek in 1619, and that land is still in cultivation today. The displays and artifacts within the **Farm and Forestry Museum** portray the evolution of farm life and its agricultural implements. The stately **Chippokes Mansion** was built in 1854, and was stuccoed and painted white so that it could serve as a landmark for boats plying the James River. In addition to all of this history, Chippokes has a swimming pool, picnic area, and short hiking and biking trails.

■ Charles City County

Follow VA 10 west from the park, make a right onto VA 31, and you'll come to the **Scotland-Jamestown Ferry** (☎ 804-294-3354), one of the few automobile and passenger ferries still operating in Virginia. Although this is a utilitarian boat, the ride across the wide expanse of the James River can be a scenic and enjoyable one as you watch waterfowl and other birds wing their way above the river.

Once on the northern shore, you will be in the vicinity of Jamestown and Williamsburg, but the tour heads west on VA 614 and Scenic Byway VA 5 to parallel the James River. This is plantation country and you have the opportunity to visit some of the oldest homes in America, each surrounded by beautifully maintained acreage.

Sherwood Forest Plantation (14501 John Tyler Highway, Charles City, VA 23030, ☎ 804-829-5377) was the Georgian clapboard home of President John Tyler.

James River Plantations

Richmond • Exit 22A • 64 • 106 • 60 • 64 • 155 • 64 • 60 • 95 • 295 • Shirley • Edgewood • Indian Fields • Piney Grove • Belle Air • Exit 242 • Berkley • Tavern • 623 • Westover • Evelynton • 619 • Williamsburg • 95 • Hopewell • North Bend • Sherwood Forest • 5 • 199 • Petersburg • 10 • James River • NOT TO SCALE

N

NOT TO SCALE

The Georgian Revival-style house on the **Evelynton Plantation** (6701 John Tyler Highway, Charles City, VA 23030, ☎ 800-473-5075) was built in the 1930s using brick from the original home which had been burned during the Civil War. The founder of the plantation, Edmond Ruffin, is said to have fired the first shot of the war.

Signer of the Declaration of Independence Benjamin Harrison, and his son, the future President William Henry Harrison, were born on **Berkeley Plantation** (12602 Harrison Landing Road, Charles City, VA 23030, ☎ 804-829-6018). Birthplace of Robert E. Lee's mother, Anne Carter Lee, **Shirley Plantation** (501 Shirley Plantation Road, Charles City, VA 23030, ☎ 800-232-1613) is still owned and occupied by 10th- and 11th-generation Hills and Carters.

 TIP *To save money, buy a "Combination Ticket" if you plan to visit all four of the above plantations.*

Tidewater Virginia

■ Northern Neck Region

West of the plantations you will pick up a bit of Richmond traffic as you drive north on I-295, but will leave it behind by heading east along US 360.

Turn left onto VA 600 at Aylett and enter **Zoar State Forest** (PO Box 246, Aylett, VA 23009, ☎ 804-769-2655). Take a break from driving to walk along the Mattaponi River via the one-mile trail through a forest of large, old-growth trees.

Once you've driven all of the way through the state forest, bear right onto VA 628 so that you can soon go north on VA 625. Skirting the boundary of Fort A. P. Hill, head to the northwest on US 17, make a right onto US 301 and follow road signs to the **Caledon Natural Area** (11617 Caledon Road, King George, VA 22485, ☎ 540-663-3205). Donated to the state in 1974 by Ann Hopewell Smoot in memory of her late husband, the area is the summer home to one of the largest concentrations of bald eagles on the East Coast. Designated a National Natural Landmark, much of the area's 2,579 acres are zoned and closed off to the general public so as not to disturb the eagles. Check at the visitors center for the times and dates of special tours. Do not let the existence of these zones deter you from visiting here, as over four miles of trails – open to everyone – wind through a mature old-growth forest.

Driving east along VA 3 will give you the opportunity to make a number of interesting side-trips.

Just after crossing into Westmoreland County, make a right onto VA 634 and another right onto VA 637 to come to the **Westmoreland Berry Farm & Orchard** (Route 637 Box 1121, Oak Grove, VA 22443, ☎ 900-997-BERRY). Originally patented in 1641, the plantation has broad views of the fields sloping down to the Rappahannock. You can wander through the fields picking strawberries, blackberries, blueberries, or raspberries.

However, the best part of visiting the farm is the chance to do some walking on land above the river. In 1995, a land donation by the Vorhees family (present owners of the berry farm) to The Nature Conservancy created the **Vorhees Nature Preserve**. After checking in at the farm market, you can hike along several

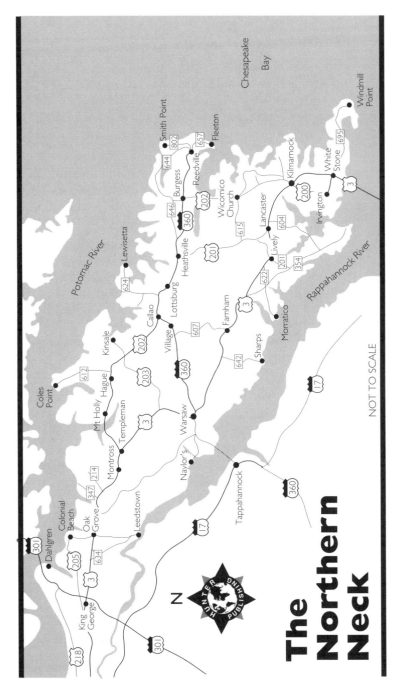

Tidewater Virginia

The Northern Neck

miles of woodland trails with observation points overlooking the river and marshes.

After your hike, continue driving on VA 637, make a left onto VA 638, and stop at **Ingleside Plantation Vineyards & Winery** (PO Box 1038, Oak Grove, VA 22443, ☎ 804-224-8687) to sample some of the best Virginia wines. With its first grapes planted in 1960, the vineyard's climate and sandy loam soil are similar to those of France's Bordeaux region.

Back on VA 3, look for a sign directing you to the **George Washington Birthplace National Monument** (Rural Route 1 Box 717, Washington's Birthplace, VA 22443, ☎ 804-224-1732). Born on February 22, 1732, Washington spent the first three years of his life here before his family moved to Mount Vernon. Walking a small network of trails will help you gain insight into the life of America's first president and the era in which he lived. The **Memorial House**, built in the 1930s, is typical of the 18th-century plantation homes of the area. Also built in the 1930s, the **Kitchen House** stands on the site of the original kitchen. The park service manages some of the 500 acres of the monument as a demonstration and working farm, using the agricultural techniques of the 1700s.

Just a few miles further east, the Commonwealth of Virginia developed **Westmoreland State Park** (Route 1, Box 600, Montross, VA 22520, ☎ 804-493-8821) in 1933, making it one of Virginia's original state parks. In addition to hiking the trails, swimming in an Olympic-size pool, staying in the campground or a rental cabin, or renting a boat to paddle the Potomac River, you could search the riverfront below Horsehead Cliffs for the fossilized remains of crocodiles, stingrays, porpoises, turtles, whales, sharks, and other marine life that lived in the Miocene Sea some 15 million years ago.

Almost within shouting distance of the park is **Stratford Hall Plantation** (Stratford, VA 22558, ☎ 804-493-8038), the birthplace of Robert E. Lee. Like Washington's birthplace, Stratford Hall was once part of an enormous tract patented by Nathaniel Pope in the 1650s. In 1716, Colonel Thomas Lee purchased about 4,000 acres and built what became the home to several generations of one of Virginia's premier families. Privately owned, the 1,500-plus acres that remain are operated as a plantation much in the way it would have been worked during Robert's lifetime. Livestock graze open meadows, and fields are cultivated by traditional methods. More than three miles of scenic nature trails offer a varied landscape and a quiet trek through the woods.

Continuing east on VA 3, the **Westmoreland County Museum** (PO Box 247, Montross, VA 22520, ☎ 804-493-8440) in Montross has special exhibits and Colonial artifacts highlighting the history of the county.

In Warsaw, the **Richmond County Museum** (PO Box 884, Warsaw, VA 22572, ☎ 804-333-3607) has a permanent collection of domestic and agricultural memorabilia depicting the county's rural lifestyle since its earliest days. If you feel the need to stretch your legs, there is a one-mile interpretive nature trail winding through the forest and along creeks on the campus of the Rappahannock Community College.

It is finally time to leave VA 3 and follow US 360 to the shores of the Chesapeake Bay and into historic **Reedville**. The menhaden fishing industry was so strong at the beginning of the 20th century that this now-sleepy village was reportedly the richest town per capita in the United States. The wealth of the times is reflected in the Victorian mansions lining Main St. Representing a waterman's home from those earlier days, the **Reedville Fisherman's Museum** (Box 360, Reedville, VA 22539, ☎ 804-453-6529) houses artifacts and material covering the history of the menhaden industry.

You can board a boat in Reedville that will take you across the waters of the Chesapeake Bay to tiny, isolated, and most interesting **Tangier Island**. (See *Cultural Tour*, below, for details.)

Since you are as far as you can go to the east, backtrack a few miles and turn south on VA 20, merging onto VA 3 near Kilmarnock. Follow road signs to **Historic Christ Church** (PO Box 24, Irvington, VA 22480, ☎ 840-438-6855). The church has changed little since it was built by Robert "King" Carter in the early 1700s. Remaining are the triple-decker pulpit with a dome-topped sounding board and the wainscoted box pews. The church is still used but, because heating and electrical lighting systems were never installed, services are held only during the

Tidewater Virginia

summer months. Artifacts and displays help clarify the history of the church.

West of Kilmarnock, **Belle Isle State Park** (Route 3 Box 550, Lancaster, VA 22503, ☎ 804-462-5030) is one of the newest parks in Virginia. Its 773 acres were purchased with funds from the Parks and Recreational Facilities Bond, which the citizens of the state voted for in 1992. Providing access to the Rappahannock River as well as Deep and Mulberry creeks, the park has a diversity of wildlife. Canoeing these waters, you just may see a blue crab, wild turkey, deer, fox, raccoon, opossum, osprey, or even a bald eagle. Facilities in the park are still under development, but it is open year-round and has a couple of trails which you can use to explore this land once inhabited by the Powhatan Indians.

South of Kilmarnock in Irvington, **The Tides Inn** (Box 480, King Carter Drive, Irvington, VA 22480, ☎ 800-843-3746) is consistently rated by readers of *Condé Nast Traveler* magazine as one of the top resorts in the world. AAA must agree, as it has given the resort a four diamond rating. Surrounded by the waters of Carter's Creek, the resort has 45 holes of golf, beach activities, tennis courts, and much, much more. If you do not have the funds to stay here (a little over $200 a night), at least stop by for a meal in the award-winning restaurant and take a stroll around the grounds.

■ The Historical Triangle

After driving across the Rappahannock River, continue south on US 17. You will soon cross over the York River and come into the area known as the Historical Triangle, made up of Yorktown, Williamsburg, and Jamestown.

It can be somewhat confusing as to who operates what in this area. Basically, the US National Park Service has the administrative responsibility for the Colonial National Historical Park, which includes the Yorktown National Battlefield, Jamestown Island, and the 23-mile Colonial Parkway that links the two via Williamsburg. The private Colonial Williamsburg Foundation owns and operates all of the facilities and interpretive programs in Williamsburg. In addition, the state of Virginia even has a

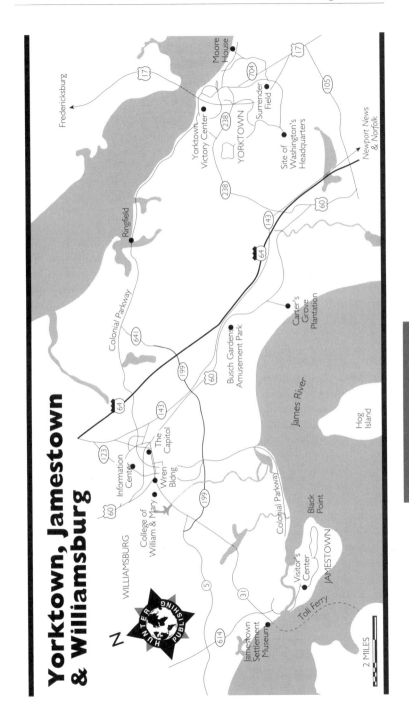

Yorktown, Jamestown & Williamsburg

Tidewater Virginia

couple of museums with living history demonstrations. Stop at the **Yorktown & Yorktown Battlefield Colonial National Historical Park Visitors Center** (PO Box 210, Yorktown, VA 23690, ☎ 757-898-3400) to pick up some information. Many places have separate admission fees and you could end up spending a lot of money here.

 To save a few dollars be sure to inquire about combination tickets permitting you access to several different sites.

Founded in 1691, **Yorktown** became a busy tobacco port during the early 1800s. However, its place in the history books was assured in October 1781, when Britain's Lord Cornwallis surrendered to George Washington, ending the American Revolutionary War. You can walk through the Moore House where the terms of the surrender were negotiated and wander through Surrender Field, where British troops laid down their arms.

Another place of interest in town is the park service's visitors center, which includes Washington's canvas field tents and exhibits portraying the events that took place here. The story of the revolution unfolds inside the **York Victory Center** (PO Box 1976, Yorktown, VA 23690, ☎ 757-253-4838) with galleries, a timeline walkway, films, and more than 500 original Revolutionary War artifacts. Outside is a recreated Continental Army camp and 18th-century farm, with costumed interpreters cooking, gardening, and demonstrating military techniques of the day.

From Yorktown, you can enjoy views of the York River as you drive west along the Colonial Parkway to arrive at the **Colonial Williamsburg Information Center** (PO Box 1776, Williamsburg, VA 23187, ☎ 800-447-8679) for brochures and tickets. There is so much to see here that you could easily spend days wandering through the town, which began as an outgrowth of Jamestown in 1633. A mile long and almost a half-mile wide, the 173-acre outdoor living history museum has more than 500 public buildings, private homes, stores, and taverns. Interpreters dressed in period clothing practice historic trades and crafts, and tend gardens.

TIP *Although I must admit to being somewhat of a skinflint when it comes to admission charges, I would urge you to pay the $30 or so to experience Williamsburg. I've never been anywhere else that does a better job of interpreting the early history of our country.*

From Williamsburg, drive the Colonial Parkway to **Jamestown**, the site of the first permanent English settlement in the New World. Arriving in May, 1607 aboard the *Susan Constant, Godspeed,* and *Discovery*, a band of 104 men and boys set about establishing the colony. Ill-equipped for the task at hand, they were, in large part, held together by the determination of Captain John Smith. Yet, the London Company, which had sponsored the venture, continued to send more settlers. During the winter of 1609-10 – known as the "starving time" – the colony of 500 was reduced to just 60.

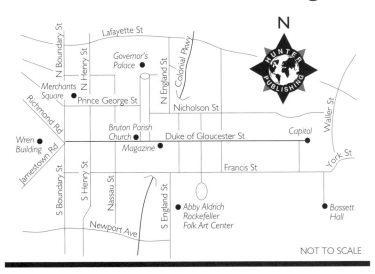

NOT TO SCALE

Tidewater Virginia

Life remained a struggle for many years; a generation later personal bickering brought about an open revolt, with Nathaniel Bacon and his followers burning the town. Partially rebuilt, it never again became an active community. The only thing that remains from those days is the **1639 Old Church Tower**, which is now attached to the Memorial Church, built in 1907. In cooperation with the park service, archaeologists have exposed foundations and restored streets and property ditches. To fully appreciate all that is here, you should take part in a guided interpretive tour of the island or pick up a walking tour brochure in the visitors center.

With its own admission fee, the adjacent **Jamestown Settlement** (PO Box 1607, Williamsburg, VA 23187, ☎ 757-253-4838) is a living history museum that recreates colonial life. Included are replicas of James Fort and a Powhatan Indian village.

■ Newport News

Newport News Park.

When you have had your fill of Colonial history, go south to **Newport News Park** (13564 Jefferson Ave., Newport News, VA 23603, ☎ 757-886-1533). This is one of the country's largest city-owned parks and it has many miles of walking routes through dense forests, well removed from automobiles and the resulting din of traffic noise – all the more amazing when you realize it sits in one of Virginia's most heavily populated areas.

In order to meet the diverse recreational needs of so many people, the park provides bicycle and boat rentals, an archery range, 36 holes of golf and a driving range, picnic shelters, an arboretum, an interpretive center, playgrounds, concessions, and

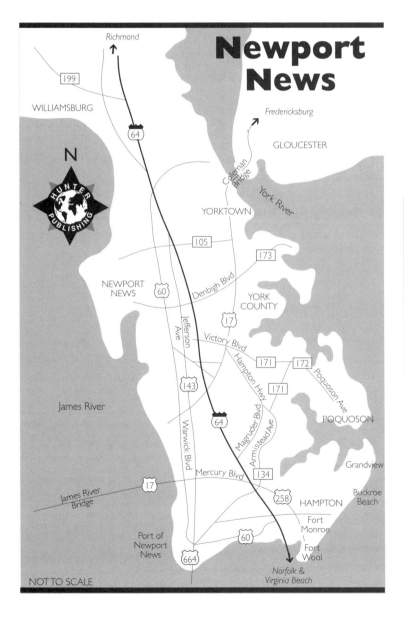

Tidewater Virginia

a campground with close to 200 sites. Yet, all of these facilities are concentrated in just a few hundred acres. Some 40 miles of pathways and fire roads can lead you to dark stands of loblolly pine, past overgrown reminders of wars past, and into lushly green and quiet swamplands. Walkers and bicyclists have the opportunity of seeing more than 70 different types of spring flowers, over 100 summer and fall blossoms, 60 species of trees, and so much wildlife that it takes an eight-page pamphlet just to list all of the native species.

You will also find some nice walking and hiking trails on the 550 acres of the **Mariner's Museum** (100 Museum Drive, Newport News, VA 23606, ☎ 757-596-2222). Narrated by James Earl Jones, the award-winning film, *Mariner*, begins your tour of America's only international maritime museum dedicated to preserving the heritage of the sea. There are collections of miniature ship models, works of scrimshaw, antique boats, maps, a working steam engine, and scheduled appearances of costumed interpreters.

Admission is free to the adjacent **Peninsula Fine Arts Center** (101 Museum Drive, Newport News, VA 23606, ☎ 757-596-8175), which has changing exhibits of contemporary art from national traveling exhibits and from regional artists.

At the **Virginia Living Museum** (524 J. Clyde Morris Blvd., Newport News, VA 23607, ☎ 757-595-1900) a boardwalk winds through seven acres of forest, meadow, and marshland, letting visitors observe a number of animals, such as raccoons, beavers, otters, deer, foxes, bobcats, skunks, and bald eagles, in their natural habitat. An aquarium and touch tank lets you get close to creatures of the deep. Expect to spend a substantial amount of time here as there is also a planetarium, a botanical garden, indoor and outdoor aviaries, fossils and prehistoric exhibits, and a not-to-be-missed 60-foot scale model of the James River.

If you want to get even closer to the water, the two-hour **Newport News Harbor Cruise** (917 Jefferson St., Newport News, VA 23607, ☎ 757-1533) will take you across the James River and through most of the waters of the Hampton Roads area to glide past the Newport News Shipyard, the Norfolk Naval Base, and the site of the Civil War battle between the ironclads, the *Monitor* and the *CSS Virginia*. For those who are more interested in the natural world, the same company offers an eight-hour trip down the Intracoastal Waterway toward North Carolina.

■ Hampton

In downtown Hampton, the neighboring city to Newport News, the **Virginia Air and Space Center/Hampton Roads History Center** (600 Settlers Landing Road, Hampton, VA 23669, ☎ 800-296-0800) is the official visitors center for the **NASA Langley Research Center**. Interactive exhibits will let you simulate visiting Mars, launching a rocket, or working as an astronaut in space. Ten air and space craft, including the Apollo

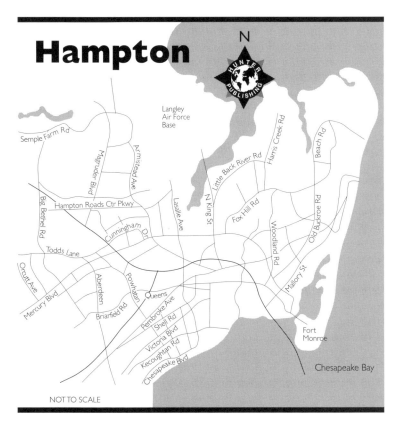

12 command module, are suspended from the ceiling. A large-screen IMAX theater shows a series of rotating films.

Inside the **Hampton University Museum** (Hampton University, Hampton, VA 23668, ☎ 757-727-5308) is a collection of more than 2,700 artifacts and objects of art representing a myriad of ethnic cultures from Native American to African. Also on display are Oceanic artifacts and works by Harlem Renaissance artists.

Your driving tour of Tidewater Virginia comes to an end as you use the I-64 bridge to leave Hampton and return to the starting point, Norfolk.

Adventures

■ On Foot

Norfolk/Virginia Beach/ Chesapeake/Portsmouth

FIRST LANDING/SEASHORE STATE PARK: This may be the best opportunity on all of the East Coast to explore myriad ecological zones with very little effort. Five thousand years of geological, biological, and botanical evolution on a piece of land hemmed in by three major bodies of water have crowded much into these 2,900 acres. Turtles bask in the sun, snakes skim across the water, woodpeckers laugh, and the calls of owls echo through the forest. It is possible to leave a quiet beach, walk over a hickory-covered dune into a fiddler crab-infested salt marsh, go through a lowland forest of sweetgum and red maple, and end up at a freshwater swamp – all in a short 20-minute walk.

The park's showpiece, the 1½-mile-circuit **Bald Cypress Trail,** is the most popular in the park – and with good reason. Elevated boardwalks cross over tannin-darkened swamps, while Spanish moss hangs in luxuriant folds from stately bald cypress and black gum trees. Branching off the Bald Cypress Trail, the 2½-

mile-circuit **Osmanthus Trail** has boardwalks bringing hikers into intimate contact with the swamp and lagoon environment. The four-mile one-way **Long Creek Trail** is one of the most varied in the park. Along its route it is possible to be in heavy forest one moment and in an open salt marsh the next. The trail crosses 50-foot dunes, passes by White Hill Lake – home to a number of nesting osprey – and goes out to the isolated, narrow beaches on Broad Bay. The low-cost *Seashore State Park: A Walking Guide and Naturalist's Primer*, available in the visitors center, provides detailed mile point-by-mile point descriptions of these and the park's other 10 miles of pathways.

BACK BAY NATIONAL WILDLIFE REFUGE: This 4,608-acre refuge was established in 1938 to provide habitat for migrating and wintering waterfowl, particularly greater snow geese. Habitat management, such as water level manipulation, has created a system of roadways and dikes, some of which can be used for hiking and biking. In addition, there are a few short, designated walking paths. From the visitors center, the .8-mile round-trip **Bay Trail** winds through wax myrtle and live oak to an observation platform overlooking the inland bay waters. Also departing from the visitors center, the half-mile round-trip **Seaside Trail** is a sandy pathway heading east to the beach and the Atlantic Ocean. The **East Dike** and the **West Dike** parallel each other down the more-than-four-mile length of the refuge, providing access to False Cape State Park. Cross-dikes between freshwater lakes connect with the two main dikes.

In order to protect migrating species, all of the pathways and dike systems are closed to visitors during the winter. However, you are still permitted to walk the four miles of oceanside beach.

FALSE CAPE STATE PARK: Until recently you could only reach False Cape State Park by walking or biking over five miles through the wildlife refuge or taking a boat through the waters of Back Bay. Now a tram runs from Little Island City Park, through the refuge, and into the park. This is a great place to spend several days and is the only place in all of the Hampton Roads area where you are permitted to do any overnight, backcountry camping on public lands. You do not need a permit for day hikes, but overnighters must obtain one from Seashore State Park in Virginia Beach (☎ 757-481-2131) before coming to this park. There is no potable water, so be sure to bring plenty with you.

The 2.4-mile one-way **Barbour Hill Nature Trail** has numbered stops keyed to a booklet available at the park's entrance station. You will learn of the important role loblolly trees play, what migrating dunes are, come to understand the complex makeup of the thicket habitat, and gain valuable information about Back Bay and its bird, mammal, amphibian, and reptile inhabitants. The main park road (which receives only park personnel traffic) stretches for four miles to the environmental education center (open only to organized groups). Here it meets up with the three-mile one-way **Dudley Island Trail**, which will lead you into the most isolated part of the park and eventually out to the Atlantic Ocean at the Virginia/North Carolina border. Numerous short pathways branch off the Dudley Island Trail and the main park road, heading either to the ocean or to the waters of Back Bay. The quiet, the solitude, and the uncommon environment make False Cape State Park a wonderful spot; make it a point to visit here – you will not be disappointed.

NORTHWEST RIVER PARK: All of the trails in this Chesapeake park are interconnecting loops, making it possible for you to take short strolls or longer treks through the quiet swamplands and mixed hardwood forest. The longest pathway, the **Indian Creek Trail**, provides access – in one way or another – to all of the park's other trails. Be on the lookout for mink, otter, raccoon, and nutria. Elevated boardwalks, observation decks, benches, footbridges, and well-signed intersections will help you get to know this environment.

GREAT DISMAL SWAMP NATIONAL WILDLIFE REFUGE: Except for a couple of marked routes, you should not expect to find such niceties when hiking in the Great Dismal Swamp National Wildlife Refuge, the largest expanse of public wildlands in Tidewater Virginia. Two centuries of logging and draining have left a network of more than 140 miles of old roadways, making it possible to explore every corner of the refuge. Be aware, though, that these gated roads are not marked or signed in any way and the flat terrain makes it hard to get your bearings. If you are not used to hiking in such situations, go with someone who is familiar with the area, or at least learn to use a map and compass. However, if you are prepared, hiking along these roads is some of the most extraordinarily isolated trekking in the state. The entire time you are in the refuge you may not see another person. You might, however, spot a bobcat or a black bear!

At the refuge's entrance on VA 642 east of Suffolk is the not-to-be-missed showpiece trail, the signed **Dismal Town Boardwalk Trail**. The mile-long trail winds through a representative portion of the swamp on an elevated boardwalk, with observation decks and benches permitting restful contemplation of the surroundings. Also signed and departing from VA 642, the **Washington Ditch Trail** heads arrow-straight for 4½ miles to the heart of the swamp, Lake Drummond. Be aware that the refuge is for day use only.

Smithfield Region

CHIPPOKES PLANTATION STATE PARK: The focus here is on the agrarian way of life of days gone by, so it is only natural that its main pathway, the one-mile one-way **Lower Chippokes Creek Trail** begins at the plantation mansion and meanders through farmland and forest before dropping down to the creek. Actually, the best walking in the park is beside the James River on two miles of fossil beach that was once the bottom of the sea.

Be sure to check on the tides at the visitors center if you do not want to get your feet wet!

Northern Neck Region

At one time, the Northern Neck Region was sorely lacking in public lands for rambling and roaming. Acquisitions by the state in the last several decades have changed the situation for the better – so much so that day hikers now have a wide choice of places and environments to visit.

CALEDON NATURAL AREA: The land for Caledon Natural Area was donated to the state in 1974 by Ann Hopewell Smoot in memory of her late husband, and has since become the summer home to one of the largest concentrations of bald eagles on the East Coast. Much of the area's 2,579 acres are zoned and closed off to the general public so as not to disturb the eagles, but interpreters do lead guided tours through these zones, so you should check at the visitors center for times and dates.

The natural area does have a system of five interconnecting loop trails that are open to the public year-round. The .7-mile **Laurel Glen Trail** leads into a climax forest and along a creek lined with lush vegetation. Numbered signposts along the .9-mile **Fern Hollow Trail** are keyed to a brochure available from the visitors center. Amazingly, decades after the blight, you can still find the remains of American chestnut trees along the 1.1-mile **Poplar Grove Trail**. You will find a stone survey marker dating from the 1700s on the 1.1-mile **Benchmark Trail**. With more ups and downs than you would expect of a trail in the Tidewater, the 1.1-mile **Cedar Ridge Trail** descends into ravines and climbs over ridges as it passes through an old-growth forest. You are likely to come upon hawks, pileated woodpeckers, deer, and rabbits. Caledon is for day use only; pets are prohibited on the trails.

WESTMORELAND STATE PARK: One of the six original state parks opened to the public in 1933, Westmoreland has a prime vantage point overlooking the Potomac River. Six short trails interconnect for a total of six miles. The .6-mile one-way **Big Meadow Trail** begins by skirting the top of Horsehead Cliff for a great view. Upstream, sometimes hidden by haze, are the buildings of Colonial Beach, while across the six-mile-wide river is southern Maryland. The route then drops you to a beach on the Potomac River, which at this point is brackish because you are only 30 miles from the Chesapeake Bay. Because of the salinity, creatures normally associated with bays or oceans are able to survive here. You may find a blue crab or horseshoe crab washed up on the sand. The trail returns to the woods and comes to an observation platform overlooking Yellow Swamp. Here you will meet up with the **Turkey Neck Trail**, which connects with the park's other pathways.

RAPPAHANNOCK RIVER NATIONAL WILDLIFE REFUGE: Along Cat Point Creek west of Warsaw off VA 634, several miles of trails past marshes, old farm roads, and through woodlands will allow you to have some great birding and wildlife observing in this refuge.

BELLE ISLE STATE PARK: Bounded by water on three sides, the 773 acres of Belle Isle State Park were purchased with funds from the Parks and Recreational Facilities Bond, which the citizens of the state voted for in 1992. Still in the development stage, the park has only recently opened year-round. Several short trails of not much more than a mile follow old roads through fields, marshes, and wetlands to the banks of the Rappahannock River. Managed by the personnel of Belle Isle State Park are three new natural area preserves acquired by the state in the mid-1990s:

- **Bush Mill Stream Natural Area Preserve:** Near Heathsville, this preserve's freshwater meets salt water in marshes and mud flats between steep-sided slopes covered in forest. A 1½-mile trail heads through the woods and down to the water where observation decks overlook a heron feeding area.

- **Hughlett Point Natural Area Preserve:** Off VA 605 north of Kilmarnock, this preserve contains excellent examples of tidal and non-tidal wetlands, dunes, undeveloped beaches, and upland forest. About two miles of old farm road and pathways (some on boardwalks to get you across wet areas) lead out to the beach and observation decks with wide bay views. From this vantage point, the Chesapeake Bay looks much as it did at the time of Captain John Smith's explorations in the early 17th century.

- **Bethel Beach Natural Area Preserve:** South of the Rappahannock River and east of Topping, short pathways course through the Bethel Beach Natural Area Preserve's constantly changing sandy beach, low dune, and salt marsh habitats. Over 90 species of birds have been seen on the preserve, which also protects the globally rare northeastern beach tiger beetle. You can reach the preserve by taking VA 611 south of Matthews, turning right on VA 643, and then left onto VA 609.

Tidewater Virginia

BEAVERDAM PARK: At the end of VA 616, a 3½-mile nature trail loops through 635-acre Beaverdam Park (Gloucester County Parks and Recreation, PO Box 157, Gloucester, VA 23601, ☎ 804-693-2107). A brochure available from the park office is keyed to more than 50 sites along the route, which offers pleasing views of the park's small lake.

Historical Triangle

YORK RIVER STATE PARK: Just off I-64 about 10 miles west of Williamsburg, this is an engaging mix of tidal marshes, river shorelines, and coastal and upland forests. More than 15 miles of interconnecting pathways, some open to bikes and some to horses, reach into almost every corner and ecological zone of the large, 2,505-acre park.

The 1.6-mile loop **Taskansis Creek Trail** is an interpretive trail with numbered stops keyed to a booklet available from the visitors center. As you wind through a woodland with mountain laurel and galax, then into a tidal marsh, you will be learning about Christmas ferns, the continuous tidal fluctuation in the marsh, forest succession, animal tracks, and more.

The 1.6-mile round-trip **Pamunkey Trail** branches off the 1.3-mile **Backbone Trail** to descend to an observation deck overlooking a marsh and the York River. Following the one-mile **Majestic Oak Trail** will bring you onto a boardwalk and into intimate contact with the tidal marsh.

Newport News/Hampton

NEWPORT NEWS PARK: This one of America's largest city-owned parks, with over 30 miles of designated hiking trails going past breastworks remaining from Civil War days, through forests of oak, hickory, holly, dogwood, and loblolly pine, and into a swamp filled with the thick vegetation of arrow arum.

The land is so level here that you could walk all day long and never break a sweat.

Because the park is so large and has so many interconnecting trails and old roadways, you should stop at the interpretive center to obtain a map and have an orientation conversation with park personnel.

■ On Wheels

Mountain Biking

Norfolk/Virginia Beach/ Chesapeake/Portsmouth

FIRST LANDING/SEASHORE STATE PARK: The only route in the park open to bicycles is the six-mile one-way **Cape Henry Trail,** which passes by just about every type of environment the park has to offer – swamp, dunes, pine-hardwood forest, salt marsh, beach, and lake. The northernmost mile is paved and begins off Kendall St. in the Cape Henry Shores housing development. (Beginning there, instead of the visitors center where most folks do, will save you paying the park's parking fee.) The middle portion of the trail is actually an old roadway of hard-packed dirt and gravel – suitable for those who are riding skinny-tire bikes. After traversing 64th St., the Cape Henry Trail crosses a boardwalk over a swampy area, becomes quite sandy, and emerges out of a marsh next to a bathing beach on Broad Bay.

BACK BAY NATIONAL WILDLIFE REFUGE/ FALSE CAPE STATE PARK: This may just be the flattest area in the state on which to ride for miles and miles. It is the only part of Tidewater Virginia where you can combine backcountry camping with your riding. In all, there are nearly 30 miles of trails, dikes, old roadways, and beach open to mountain bikers.

From the refuge visitor contact station you may ride past freshwater impounds on either the **East Dike** or the **West Dike** for more than four miles to the state park. Once in the

Tidewater Virginia

park, you can follow the **Main Trail** for almost four more miles to the site of the old Wash Woods Cemetery. Along the way are opportunities to branch out onto a number of side trails leading either to the bay or the ocean. For a change of pace, there are 10 miles of Atlantic Ocean beach on which you could make the return ride during low tide – when the sand closest to the ocean is hard-packed. No matter how long your ride is, be sure to bring plenty of water with you, as there is no potable water in either the refuge or the state park.

Obtain the required permit from Seashore State Park in Virginia Beach (☎ 757-481-2131) before beginning your ride if you want to camp at one of False Cape's backcountry sites.

LONE STAR LAKES PARK: Administered by the City of Suffolk, 1,172-acre Lone Star Lakes Park (Department of Parks & Recreation, PO Box 1858, Suffolk, VA 23439, ☎ 757-255-4308) is centered around nine freshwater lakes that were once marl pits. (Marl is loose or crumbling earth that contains deposits of calcium carbonate and is used as a fertilizer.) A day-use area, the park has four short hiking trails totaling about 1½ miles, but no designated bike trails. However, bicycles are permitted on the system of miles of unpaved backcountry roads, making for some flat, easy riding through a forest of beech, locust, cedar, sweetgum, and sycamore.

GREAT DISMAL SWAMP NATIONAL WILDLIFE REFUGE: Two centuries of logging and draining have left a network of more than 140 miles of old roadways, making it possible to explore every corner of the Great Dismal Swamp National Wildlife Refuge.

These gated roads are not marked or signed in any way and the flat terrain makes it hard to get your bearings. If you are not used to biking in such situations, you should take someone with you who is familiar with the area, or at least be proficient in using a map and compass.

You may not see another person the entire time you are in the refuge. To get a feel for the swamp, first-time biking visitors should use the marked and maintained, 4½-mile one-way **Washington Ditch Trail**, which heads arrow-straight to the heart of the swamp, Lake Drummond.

Smithfield Region

CHIPPOKES STATE PARK: Bicyclists are permitted on two miles of almost-level trail in Chippokes State Park. Lined by bald cypress, the 1.3-mile one-way **College Run Trail** connects the plantation mansion to the beach area. The half-mile **James River Trail** is a roadway leading down to the river.

Historical Triangle

WALLER MILL PARK: Amazingly challenging for a mountain bike trail in the Tidewater area, the four-mile **Dogwood Trail** in Waller Mill Park (Department of Parks & Recreation, 202 Quarterpath Road, Williamsburg, VA 23185, ☎ 757-220-6178) owes much of its existence to the efforts of a local mountain biking association. The singletrack route traverses a rolling terrain and rises over small ridges, running beside the Waller Mill Reservoir and into a forest of gum, hazelnut, maple, and loblolly pine.

 Be alert, as you might scare up a wild turkey or deer when making a turn.

The park is reached by taking I-64 Exit 243 north of Williamsburg and heading west on Rochambeau Drive. In a little over a mile, make a left onto VA 645 and follow it to the park's entrance.

YORK RIVER STATE PARK: The terrain is not quite as rigorous as that in Waller Mill, but the mountain bike trails can provide a nice afternoon's outing. A physical fitness trail with designated exercise stops, the dirt road 1.3-mile-loop **Woodstock Pond Trail** encircles the pond. It connects with the 2.6-mile round-trip **Backbone Trail**, the park's main route through forest and open meadows. Expect some soft sandy spots and some ups and downs as the 2.8-mile round-trip **Riverview Trail** drops about 50 feet to the cliffs and banks overlooking the York River. On a hillside above two small streams – and with a few rapid drops – the 1.2-mile round-trip **White Tail Trail** dead-ends in the forest in the southeastern corner of the park. A concessionaire rents bicycles.

Newport News/Hampton

NEWPORT NEWS PARK: In cooperation with a group of local fat tire enthusiasts, the **Harwood Mills Mountain Bike Trail** was established in the southeast corner of Newport News Park. The beginning of the trail may be reached by taking I-64 Exit 258, driving north on US 17 for close to four miles, and turning left onto VA 620 to the designated parking area. About 5.4 miles in total length, the trail is unique in that it has three distinct sections built and signed for novice, advanced, and expert riders. The terrain is not really that difficult on any of the sections, but the twists, turns, and obstacles placed in the way will put your bike handling skills to the test. Traffic is routed in one direction, so be sure to pay attention to the signs.

Newport News Park Bikeway.

With a parking area on Richneck Road off VA 105 (Fort Eustis Blvd.) the park's **Richneck Road Trail** has 5.3 miles of novice-level, gravel and natural surface roadway on which to ride.

Beginning at the campsite office in the main section of the park, a designated **Bikeway** makes a loop for 5.3 miles on dirt and gravel roads that are so hard-packed that skinny tire bikes should also be able to negotiate it. The terrain is almost level; throughout the entire course you will have a total elevation gain of not much more than 100 feet. About halfway into the ride, where honeysuckle and poison ivy vines drape over the trees, you have the option of taking a short side route into the **Colonial National Historical Park** – and thus gain access to some paved road riding on the **Colonial Parkway**.

Bikes are available for rent in the park.

Road Biking

TransAmerica Bicycle Route

The final (or beginning, depending on which way you are going) 62 miles of the 4,100-mile TransAmerica Bicycle Route are located within Tidewater Virginia. Marked by "Bike-76" signs along the highways, the route enters the region at the town of Glendale, just east of Richmond. Heading to the south on VA 156, it turns to the east, following Scenic Byway VA 5 through Charles City County and going by the numerous plantations along the James River. Crossing the Chickahominy River and coming into Jamestown, the route picks up the Colonial Parkway, passes through Williamsburg, and comes to its eastern terminus beside the Victory Monument in Yorktown.

Norfolk/Virginia Beach/ Chesapeake/Portsmouth

The city of Virginia Beach has more than 60 miles of designated and marked bicycle routes winding into nearly every corner of the city. Unfortunately, many of those miles are on highly congested roadways. A much more pleasant outing would be to ride the first four miles of the hard-packed dirt **Cape Henry Trail** through First Landing/Seashore State Park, then connect with the three-mile paved boardwalk along the beach from 39th St. to 1st St. at Rudee Inlet.

Smithfield Region

Using **Chippokes State Park** as a base and crossing one swamp stream after another, an easy day's loop ride begins by leaving the park's visitors center and heading south along VA 634. Coming to VA 633, follow it to the right for just a short distance before making a left to continue along VA 634 and cross Chippokes Creek. Head east on VA 10 for less than two miles to make a right onto VA 617. (At this point you could make a short side-trip to tour **Bacon's Castle**, a restoration of an English-style garden discovered on the grounds of a 17th-century house.) Riding through flat and rolling swampish-type land, turn right on VA 626, crossing over the streams of Mill Swamp and Golden Hill Swamp. Make a right onto VA 634, another right on VA 10, and then a quick left back onto VA 634 to return to the park.

Historical Triangle

In an area swarming with tourists, a 12½-mile one-way ride can get you from York River State Park to Williamsburg without too much car traffic. The ride begins at the visitors center in the state park by following VA 696 to the south to make a left turn onto VA 606, then a right turn onto VA 646 soon thereafter. Continuing to the south on a service road next to I-64, the ride intersects VA 132 and then follows VA 132Y to the Williamsburg Information Center.

There are a couple of other scenic rides that originate from the Williamsburg Information Center (which can provide you with maps):

The 16-mile **Carter's Grove Plantation Loop** follows VA 132Y to VA 132 from the information center before heading south along Henry St. and then east on Newport Ave. Leaving Williamsburg, the itinerary follows South England St. to enter the scenic Carter's Grove Country Road.

The traffic is light along this roadway, but be prepared for some quick turns, climbs, and spots of loose gravel.

Unfortunately, the final portion of the ride is along heavily traveled US 60 to return to the starting point.

Getting into more open country, and also departing from the Williamsburg Information Center, the 23-mile **Jamestown Loop** takes VA 132Y to VA 132, and turns west along a bikeway on Business US 60. Turning to the southwest on VA 615 and to the west on VA 612, you will be on gently undulating terrain as you cross over Long Hill Swamp and head south on VA 614. You have the option of taking a five-mile side-trip onto Jamestown Island before hopping on the Colonial Parkway to return to the starting point.

Connecting Jamestown to Williamsburg and Yorktown, the 23-mile **Colonial Parkway** is closed to commercial traffic, which makes for a pleasant ride along flat-to-gently rolling terrain. Interpretive markers, pullouts, and picnic areas provide resting spots overlooking the waters of the James and York rivers.

Outfitters

Headquartered in Williamsburg, **Bike Virginia** (Box 203, Williamsburg, VA 23187, ☎ 757-229-0507) puts together fully supported bicycle vacations focusing on various aspects of the entire state. The tours come complete with camping/motels, food, and entertainment.

Bikesmith of Williamsburg (515 York St., Williamsburg, VA 23187, ☎ 757-229-9858) can help if your bike needs repair. They also sell bikes.

Tidewater Virginia

■ On Water

Norfolk/Virginia Beach/ Chesapeake/Portsmouth

 Unique to all of Virginia, the **Virginia Beach Scenic Waterway System** provides almost boundless paddling within the city limits of Virginia Beach. Beginning in the north with the beach and tidal marshes at Lynnhaven Inlet, the main trail, the **Lynnhaven River – West Neck Creek – North Landing River Trail**, follows the Lynnhaven River through a suburban landscape to enter a major drainage canal. Leaving the houses behind, it moves into its most scenic stretch in narrow, cedar- and cypress-lined West Neck Creek, where you might see deer, otters, raccoons, turtles, herons, and ospreys. Coming into the wider waters of the North Landing River, you have your choice of continuing south into North Carolina or turning to the west along the Intracoastal Waterway. In addition to the launch sites along this main route, the municipal government has provided a number of others on many other streams and bays throughout the city. A map of the system and launch sites can be obtained at the Virginia Beach Visitors Center.

Canoes are available for rent in Chesapeake's **Northwest River Park**, enabling you to paddle by cypress trees and knees growing in the swamplands and slow-moving, dark waters of Indian and Smith creeks and the Northwest River. Only those who rent a boat are permitted to use the park's ramp. However, everyone may use the hand-carry launch sites on either Smith Creek Road or Indian Creek Road.

Part of the Intracoastal Waterway, the 22-mile **Dismal Swamp Canal** connects the Elizabeth River in Virginia to the Pasquotank River in North Carolina. The oldest continuously operated canal in the United States, it no longer sees commercial traffic, but does get quite a bit of use by pleasure craft during the spring, summer, and fall.

About three miles north of the North Carolina border, a large parking area and boat ramp on US 17 provides access to the canal for those of you with your own canoe or kayak. While the canal is worth a paddle, the better trip would be to head south for half a mile. You'll then make a turn to the right for three miles of paddling upstream on the 50-foot-wide Feeder Ditch, heading into the heart of the Great Dismal Swamp. Portage around the water control structure and you are on 3,100-acre **Lake Drummond**. There is a very good possibility that you may be the only person on the three-mile-wide lake. Things are quiet here, with just the cry of a pileated woodpecker or the nearly silent slithering of a snake to break the stillness. The lake has no real defined boundary as its water just seems to continue into the surrounding forest. I cannot urge you enough to visit this lake; no other place in Virginia has such a primeval feel, of days long ago when our ancestors first walked the earth.

 Be aware that the Great Dismal Swamp National Wildlife Refuge is a day-use area and that you must be out by sunset.

If you do not want to go on your own, Randy Gore of **Tidewater Adventures** (110 West Randall Ave., Norfolk, VA 23503, ☎ 757-480-1999) is a self-described "National Outdoor Leadership School Graduate, American Canoe Association Certified Kayak Instructor, and all around fun guy," who provides guided kayak ecotours of the Great Dismal Swamp, Broad Bay, and Back Bay. He also offers beginning and intermediate kayak classes and rolling clinics.

You can satisfy a need for speed in the ocean by renting waverunners and jet boats from **Oceanfront Water Sports** (31st St. & Oceanfront, Virginia Beach, VA 23451, ☎ 757-491-1117).

Cruising along the inland waters of Virginia Beach, the 80-foot yacht *Discovery* (600 Laskin Road, Virginia Beach, VA 23451, ☎ 757-422-2900) offers lunch, dinner, and sightseeing tours. You can rent a ski boat, jet boat, or pontoon boat from **SeaVenture** (☎ 757-422-0079) at the same address.

Built in the 1980s to resemble a tall ship of the 1800s, the many sails of the 135-foot *American Rover* (PO Box 3125, Norfolk, VA 23514, ☎ 757-627-SAIL) can be a beautiful sight as it leaves the Waterside Festival Marketplace for two- and three-hour trips through Hampton Roads harbor.

Tidewater Virginia

The *Carrie B* (Waterside Festival Park, Norfolk, VA 23503, ☎ 757-393-4735), a replica of an 1800s Mississippi riverboat, also cruises the harbor for 1½-hour and 2½-hour trips.

The *Spirit of Norfolk* (110 West Plume St., Suite 116, Norfolk, VA 23503, ☎ 757-625-1463) looks more like a ship you would see cruising the Caribbean. With room for 450 passengers, it provides buffet lunch and dinner sightseeing trips on the Elizabeth River from the marketplace to the naval base.

Concentrating on the lower Chesapeake Bay, **SPAR Charters** (8172 Shore Drive, Norfolk, VA 23518, ☎ 757-588-2022) can set you up with captained or bareboat (meaning you sail the boat yourself) multi-day sailing cruises. If you have always admired those who are able to handle a sailboat themselves, SPAR Charters also has classes on how to trim a sail or tack to port.

Just off the coast of Virginia Beach, the Atlantic Ocean is littered with dozens of shipwrecks that the **Lynnhaven Dive Center** (☎ 757-481-7949) can take you to, on either the *Cindy Loo* or the *Miss Lindsey*.

If you don't know the first thing about diving, the PADI instructors at the **Mid-Atlantic Dive Center** (☎ 757-420-6179) have courses that can quickly get you breathing safely underwater.

Smithfield

Smithfield Paddlers (South Church St., Smithfield, VA 23431 ☎ 757-357-5843) in the Pagan River Shoppes next door to Smithfield Station can get you outfitted and pointed in the right direction to enjoy some of Tidewater Virginia's easiest canoeing through the marshlands of Cypress Creek or the open waters of the Pagan River. They also rent bikes to landlubbers.

Northern Neck Region

Canoes are available for rent by the hour or day in **Westmoreland State Park**, permitting you to paddle the wide expanse of the Potomac River. The water is so calm and slow-moving here that a concessionaire even rents pedal boats.

Guided canoe trips through the slow waters and marshes of the Rappahannock River and Mulberry and Deep creeks are offered on a scheduled basis by the staff and volunteers of **Belle Isle State Park**. These are fascinating tours that bring to life the eight different types of wetlands in and around the park.

If you have always wanted to experience a sea kayak's unique versatility to explore rivers, marshes, and oceans, **River Rats** (PO Box 247, Ophelia, VA 22530, ☎ 804-453-3064), on the Little Wicomico River, has classes designed to make you proficient enough to take off on your own. In addition, they will put together guided tours or rent you a kayak if you demonstrate the required ability to handle one.

The **Mattaponi River Company** (Route 1, Box 25, Aylett, VA 23009, ☎ 800-769-3545) not only rents canoes by the day, but leads guided, nature-oriented trips on the Mattaponi and Pamunkey rivers. Trips last anywhere from three hours to all day.

Historical Triangle

Known for its rare and delicate estuarian environment, where freshwater and saltwater meet, **York River State Park** is the site of regularly scheduled, naturalist-led canoe trips on Taskinas Creek and the surrounding marshes – which have been designated a Chesapeake Bay National Estuarian Research Reserve. Canoes, life jackets, and paddles are rented by the hour if you wish to do some exploring on your own.

■ In The Air

Norfolk/Virginia Beach/Chesapeake/Portsmouth

Certainly not cheap, but a thrill nonetheless, **Adventure Parasail** (200 Winston Salem Ave., Virginia Beach, VA 23451, ☎ 757-422-UFLY) has no age limit and can accommodate up to three people at a time – while providing a different perspective on the ocean and the beach.

Tidewater Virginia

They taught George Bush how to do it, and they can teach you, too. How to jump out of an airplane and survive, that is. Anyone under 230 pounds and over 18 years of age can static line or tandem jump with **Skydive Suffolk** (200 Airport Road, Suffolk, VA 23434, ☎ 757-539-3531).

The same regulations apply for the tandem jumps at **Chesapeake Skydive Adventures** (1771 West Road, Chesapeake, VA 25320, ☎ 757-471-7245).

■ Ecotours

Each year, fin whales, bottlenose dolphins, humpback whales, and other marine animals migrate to the waters off the Virginia Beach coastline. The **Virginia Marine Science Museum** sponsors two-hour boat trips to see these wonderful creatures. Each excursion is an education program guided by knowledgeable museum interpreters. Times and dates can change from year to year, but generally the whale-watching trips are conducted from December to March, while the dolphin-watching trips go to sea from June to September/October. During the summer, the museum also sponsors "Ocean Collection Trips," on which museum interpreters collect a sampling of marine life – such as seahorses, jellyfish,

Secluded Tangier Island.

crabs, and stingrays – to display in temporary aquariums on board.

Outdoor Experience, Inc. (PO Box 5755, Virginia Beach, VA 23455, ☎ 757-464-5794) rents kayaks and conducts guided kayak nature tours through the waters and swamps in and around the Hampton Roads area. Overnight guided camping trips are also arranged.

Recently the **Colonial Inn** [$$$ to $$$$] (2809 Atlantic Ave., Virginia Beach, VA 23451, ☎ 800-448-2786) has begun putting together package deals for those interested in naturalist-led whale- and/or dolphin-watching trips, bird-watching explorations, scuba diving, kayak tours of the ocean and remote waterways, day hiking journeys, and more.

Tangier Island

Set in the heart of the Chesapeake Bay, tiny Tangier Island is a world unto itself. With its highest point only four feet above sea level, the island is about five miles long and only 1½ miles at its widest; more than half of its acreage is marshland. Sighted by Captain John Smith and settled by Cornish fishermen in the 1600s, the island's inhabitants still speak with the Elizabethan accents and idioms of their ancestors. Most still make their living from the waters of the bay, heading out early in the morning from the island's many marshy channels.

Visitors from the Tidewater area are usually day-trippers that arrive by way of a 1½-hour narrated boat ride aboard the *Chesapeake Breeze* (Tangier & Chesapeake Cruises, Inc., Route 1 Box 1332, Reedville, VA 22539, ☎ 804-453-2628). The boat sails daily – May to October – from its dock in Reedville. Reservations are necessary. Most visitors stay on the island only for the couple of hours that the boat is docked, during which time they have a meal and take a quick minibus tour.

But the best way to really appreciate the uniqueness of this place is to spend the night. After the other tourists have gone, you will get a chance to have unhurried conversations with the residents and take a stroll along the mile-long beach. As the day comes to an end, you can

Tidewater Virginia

watch thousands of fiddler crabs make mass a migration across the narrow roadways or just enjoy the sunset spreading a reddish glow across the marshland channels and the waters of the bay.

You have a choice of three bed & breakfasts if you plan to stay for the night. **Shirley's Bay View Inn B&B** [$$] (PO Box 183, Tangier, VA 23440, ☎ 757-891-2396) is one of the oldest homes on Tangier. The slow pace of the island is visible from its front and side porches. **The Sunset Inn** [$$] (16550 West Ridge Road, Tangier, VA 23440, ☎ 757-891-2535) has motel-like rooms with private baths and serves a continental breakfast. **Hilda Crockett's Chesapeake House** [$$] (PO Box 194, Tangier, VA 23440, ☎ 757-891-2331), which has been welcoming guests since 1940, is beginning to show its age. In its favor, the nightly rate includes a family-style seafood dinner and a breakfast.

In what is a long standing tradition, most people who come to Tangier Island, especially day-trippers, head to **Hilda Crockett's Chesapeake House** for a family-style lunch of crab cakes, clam fitters, and vegetables. However, in all honesty, my wife and I found that the closed curtains on the windows, unadorned gray walls, and long folding tables were more akin to an institutional hall than to a pleasurable dining experience.

If you pass up the Chesapeake House, head to either **The Islander Seafood Restaurant** (☎ 757-891-2249) or **Fisherman's Corner** (☎ 757-891-2571) for tasty crab cakes, other seafoods, and sandwiches.

With no more than five miles of narrow paved roads and alleyways, automobiles are almost non-existent and most folks get around by walking, biking, or riding golf carts. You can join them by renting a golf cart for the hour, half-day, or day from **RB's Rentals** (☎ 757-891-2240), located beside the boat dock. They can also set you up with a canoe or kayak and direct you to the best paddling spots inside the island's marshes or along the shoreline.

Where To Stay

Norfolk

 Closest accommodations to the airport are in the uniquely designed **Norfolk Airport Hilton** [$$$ to $$$$] (1500 North Military Highway, Norfolk, VA 23502, ☎ 757-466-8000). The **Quality Inn-Lake Wright** [$$$] (6280 Northampton Blvd., Norfolk, VA 23502, ☎ 757-461-6251), with more than 400 rooms, is accessed from the same I-64 Exit as the airport.

A bit farther away, but in the same vicinity – and with lower rates – is the **Colonial Inn-Airport** [$$ to $$$] (6360 Newton Road, Norfolk, VA 23502, ☎ 757-461-1081).

Some of the lowest rates in town are found at the **Tides Inn** [$$] (7950 Shore Drive, Norfolk, VA 23518, ☎ 757-587-8781). It is close to the Little Creek Naval Base and only about a 15-minute drive from the resort strip in Virginia Beach.

The Holiday Sands [$$ to $$$] (1330 East Ocean View Ave., Norfolk, VA 23503, ☎ 800-525-5156) has its own beach on the Chesapeake Bay.

The only hotel overlooking the city's harbor is the deluxe **Omni Waterside Hotel** [$$$$] (777 Waterside Drive, Norfolk, VA 23510, ☎ 800-THE-OMNI). The large marble entranceway and lobby has such comfortable furnishings and seating that you may never want to go to your room.

Located within the Ghent Historic District, the **Page House Inn** [$$$ to $$$$] (323 Fairfax Ave., Norfolk, VA 23507, ☎ 800-695-1487) calls its complimentary morning meal a continental+ breakfast. The Georgian Revival home has whirlpool baths and a "European soaking tub," which is a bit shorter but five inches deeper than a standard tub. If you really want to pamper yourself, ask to stay in the Bath Suite, which has an unbelievably large sunken tub.

Virginia Beach

As with beach areas around the world, the breadth of accommodations here runs the gamut from low-cost rooms several blocks from the beach to high-rise, super deluxe suites overlooking the ocean. Unless noted, all of the motels listed below have swimming pools.

At the **Belvedere Motel** [$$$] (36th St., Virginia Beach, VA 23458, ☎ 800-425-0612), all of the rooms have private balconies overlooking the beach. The motel provides complimentary bicycles for its guests.

Smaller and a bit more cozy than most of the other oceanfront motels, the **Idlewhyle** [$$$] (2705 Altlantic Avenue, Virginia Beach, VA 23451, ☎ 800-348-7263) also has bicycles for free guest use.

At the northern end of the boardwalk, the **Thunderbird Motor Lodge** [$$ to $$$$] (35th & Oceanfront, Virginia Beach, VA 23451, ☎ 800-633-6669) permits you to have small pets in its oceanfront rooms. Bicycles are available for rent.

For an extra few dollars a day, your pet will also be permitted to stay at the **Ocean Holiday Hotel** [$$$ to $$$$] (2417 Atlantic Ave., Virginia Beach, VA 23451, ☎ 800-345-7263).

To enjoy the beach in grand style, check into **The Cavalier** [$$$ to $$$$] (42nd St. & Oceanfront, Virginia Beach, VA 23451, ☎ 800-980-5555). For about the same as it would cost to stay in a Marriot or Ramada, this landmark resort can provide a beach vacation with all the elegance of yesteryear. Experiences such as this are harder and harder to come by unless you spend a minor fortune. Although the beachfront portion that opened in 1987 is nice enough, for the full experience try to get a room in the original 1927 structure.

The following four places are only one block from the beach, but should save you some money.

Look to **The Balboa** [$ to $$$] (29th St. & Pacific Ave., Virginia Beach, VA 23451, ☎ 800-771-8266) for some of the lowest rates in town.

Free bike use and fairly low rates are draws at the **Blue Marlin Motel** [$$ to $$$] (2411 Pacific Ave., Virginia Beach, VA 23451, ☎ 800-643-3230).

Even if you want a hot tub in your room or a two-room suite, staying at **Murphy's Emerald Isle** [$$ to $$$] (1005 Pacific Ave., Virginia Beach, VA 23451, ☎ 800-237-9717) will save money compared to most oceanfront motels.

Angie's Guest Cottage [$ to $$] (302 24th St., Virginia Beach, VA 23451, ☎ 757-428-4690) is the local American Youth Hostel. The beach house has a European atmosphere and provides a free continental breakfast.

The **Church Point Manor House B&B** [$$$$ to $$$$$] (4001 Church Point Road, Virginia Beach, VA 23455, ☎ 757-460-2657) is away from the resort area. It has a private dock on the Lynn-haven River and a canoe available for guest use (access to miles and miles of paddling on the city's excellent Scenic Waterway System is offered).

If your time in Virginia Beach is going to be a week or more, you will probably save quite a lot by renting a cottage through **Atkinson Realty** (54th & Atlantic Ave., Virginia Beach, VA 23451, ☎ 800-766-0409).

The **Colonial Inn** [$$$ to $$$$] (2809 Atlantic Ave., Virginia Beach, VA 23451, ☎ 800-448-2786), with its own swimming pool and rooms overlooking the beach, is as nice as any oceanfront spot. Yet, in the past few years, Sales Manager Kathryn Kreiling has also helped establish it as the premier place to stay in town if you are looking to do some outdoor adventuring. The motel has package deals for those interested in whale- and/or dolphin-watching boat trips, bird-watching explorations, scuba diving, kayak tours of remote waterways, day hiking journeys, and more.

Chesapeake/Portsmouth

Some of the lowest rates in the area are offered at the **Hampton Inn** [$$] (701A Woodlake Drive, Chesapeake, VA 23320, ☎ 800-HAMPTON).

All of the rooms are large, well furnished suites, yet rates at the **Comfort Suites** [$$ to $$$] (1550 Crossways Blvd., Chesapeake, VA 23320, ☎ 800-428-0562) are no more than those at the nearby **Holiday Inn** [$$ to $$$] (725 Woodlake Drive, Chesapeake, VA 23320, ☎ 800-HOLIDAY).

You will have your choice of views at the **Holiday Inn Waterfront** [$$$] (8 Crawford Parkway, Portsmouth, VA 23704, ☎ 800-HOLIDAY) in Portsmouth. Some rooms overlook the sailboats docked at the adjoining marina, while others let you observe the busy water traffic making its way along the Elizabeth River.

The Olde Towne Inn B&B [$$$ to $$$$] (420 Middle St., Portsmouth, VA 23704, ☎ 800-353-0278) is nestled in the city's historic district and has a gas fireplace in the central parlor.

Smithfield Region

The prime spot to stay is **Smithfield Station** [$$ to $$$$$] (415 South Church St., Smithfield, VA 23430). Uniquely modeled after a Victorian Coast Guard Station, it has rooms overlooking beautiful views and sunsets on the marshes and open water of the Pagan River. The 61-slip marina makes it easy for those passing by in a yacht to stop in and enjoy a meal in the superb seafood restaurant. An adjacent facility rents canoes to explore the waterways and bicycles to ride through the town's historic district.

The restored 1807 **Four Square Plantation B&B** [$$] (13357 Four Square Road, Smithfield, VA 23430, ☎ 757-365-0749) sits on four acres.

About four miles southeast of Smithfield in Benns Church, the **Econo Lodge** [$$] (20080 Brewers Neck Blvd., Benns Church, VA 23314, ☎ 757-357-9057) provides basic, low-cost motel rooms.

Charles City County

In keeping with the antique atmosphere of the county, the best places to stay are in restored plantation homes.

The 1819 **North Bend Plantation B&B** [$$$$] (1220 Weya-noke Road, Charles City, VA 23030, ☎ 800-841-1479) provides bicycles for exploring the area and a swimming pool in which to cool off.

The nature trail, flower garden, and swimming pool of the Piney Grove at **Southall's Plantation B&B** [$$$$ to $$$$$] (916920 Southall's Plantation Lane, Charles City, VA 23030, ☎ 704-829-2480) are designed to keep you active and relaxed while on the grounds of the 1800s plantation.

Northern Neck Region

In Essex County, the plantation home of the **Linden House B&B** [$$ to $$$$] (PO Box 23, Champlain, VA 22438, ☎ 800-622-1202) dates from 1735 and offers four rooms and two suites, some with fireplaces. The 204 acres of gently rolling pasture al-low plenty of elbow room.

In Colonial Beach, the **Days Inn** [$$ to $$$] (30 Colonial Ave., Colonial Beach, VA 22443, ☎ 804-224-0404) has a swimming pool as well as a beach on the Potomac River.

One mile northwest of Montross, the **Porterville B&B** [$$] (Route 3 Box 1002, King's Highway, Montross, VA 22520, ☎ 804-493-9394) makes a great base from which to explore nearby Westmoreland State Park, George Washington Birth-place, and Stratford Hall.

Nearby, and with wonderful views overlooking the Potomac River, is the **Mount Holly House B&B** [$$ to $$$] (PO Box 130, Mount Holly, VA 22524, ☎ 804-472-3336). It was built in 1876 to serve the needs of travelers and merchants along the steamboat routes. The waterfront location lends itself to swim-ming, canoeing, and crabbing from the private beach.

On Munday Point – a two-mile spit of land – guests of the **Cats Cove Cottage** [$$] (PO Box 621, Callao, VA 22435, ☎ 804-529-5056) can explore the creek in provided rowboats and canoes or use the available bicycles to ride to the end of the Point and gaze out across the Potomac River to the Maryland shore.

To the west in Warsaw, the rates can't be beat at the **Green-wood B&B** [$] (Route 2, Box 50, Warsaw, VA 22572, ☎ 804-

Tidewater Virginia

333-4353). The Georgian-style home has 12 large rooms, each with central heat and individual air-conditioning.

A traditional fisherman's village with boat cruise connections to Tangier Island, Reedville has an almost embarrassing number of bed & breakfasts. Three that seem to draw guests back time and again are listed below:

On the waterfront, the **Bailey-Cockrell House B&B** [$$] (Main St., Reedville, VA 22539, ☎ 804-453-5900) provides its guests with bikes and paddleboats as well as some of the lowest rates in town.

In addition to a private beach, bikes are also available for guest use at **Cedar Grove B&B** [$$ to $$] (Route 1 Box 2535, Reedville, VA 22539, ☎ 804-453-3915).

The 1895 **Victorian Morris House** [$$ to $$$$] (PO Box 163, Reedville, VA 22539, ☎ 804-453-7016) also offers bikes, and has water views from every room.

South of Kilmarnock in Irvington, **The Tides Inn** [$$$$$+] (Box 480, King Carter Drive, Irvington, VA 22480, ☎ 800-843-3746) is consistently rated by readers of *Condé Nast Traveler* magazine as one of the world's top resorts. AAA has given it a four diamond rating. Surrounded by the waters of Carter's Creek, it has 45 holes of golf, beach activities, tennis, and more.

Just across the creek on its own 175-acre peninsula, **The Tides Lodge** [$$$$ to $$$$$] (Box 4, Irvington, VA 22480, ☎ 800-438-6000) is owned by the same corporation. A bit smaller in size than The Tides Inn, the lodge has its own resort-style amenities.

Historical Triangle

The Yorktown Motor Lodge [$ to $$] (8829 George Washington Highway, Yorktown, VA 23692, ☎ 757-898-5451) provides clean, basic, low cost rooms.

On the York River waterfront, the **Duke of York Motor Inn** [$$] (508 Water St., Yorktown, VA 23690, ☎ 804-898-3232) has some rooms with balconies overlooking Coleman Point.

The Marl Inn [$$$ to $$$$] (220 Church St., Yorktown, VA 23690, ☎ 800-799-6207) serves a continental breakfast and provides free use of bicycles.

Williamsburg is one of the top tourist destinations in the state, attracting more people – and therefore having an abundance of accommodation choices – than the entire Virginia Beach/Norfolk metropolitan area. If you are calling ahead to make reservations for a trip to Williamsburg, be sure to ask the motel if it has any promotional packages. They could save you quite a few dollars in admission fees.

For some of the lowest rates in Williamsburg, check into the **Bassett Motel** [$] (800 York St., Williamsburg, VA 23185, ☎ 757-229-5175). All 18 rooms on this small property are well maintained.

Other low-rate motels in the area include the **Colonial Motel** [$$] (1452 Richmond Road, Williamsburg, VA 23185, ☎ 757-229-3621), the **Governor Spotswood Motel** [$$] (1508 Richmond Road, Williamsburg, VA 23185, ☎ 757-229-6444), and the **Motel Rochambeau** [$ to $$] (929 Capitol Landing, Williamsburg, VA 23185, ☎ 757-229-2851).

The chain motels are well represented in Williamsburg. **Best Western Colonial Capitol Inn** [$$ to $$$] (111 Penniman Road, Williamsburg, VA 23187, ☎ 800-446-9228) has a pool and permits small pets. The **Ramada Inn-Historic District** [$$$ to $$$$] (351 York St., Williamsburg, VA 23185, ☎ 800-962-4743) has an indoor heated pool with Jacuzzi and offers package plans. An indoor heated pool, sauna, and whirlpool at the **Hampton Inn Historic Area** [$$$ to $$$$] (505 York St., Williamsburg, VA 23185, ☎ 757-229-6444) may help you relax after a day of sightseeing.

If cost is no object and you want to experience elegance, refinement, hospitality, and a bit of history, check into the **Williamsburg Inn** [$$$$ to $$$$$+] (PO Box 1776, Williamsburg, VA 23187, ☎ 800-447-8679). Situated on 400 acres, the luxury inn has 45 holes of golf, meticulously maintained gardens and lawns, swimming pools (one is spring-fed), whirlpool, spa, sauna, and more.

Tidewater Virginia

The Williamsburg Inn is owned by the Colonial Williamsburg Foundation, so be sure to check on the available special package deals, which can end up saving you a lot of money.

If you just can't get enough history, consider a stay at the **Newport House B&B** [$$$$] (710 South Henry St., Williamsburg, VA 23185, ☎ 757-229-1775); the host is an author of history studies and a retired museum director.

Only three blocks from the historic district, the **Colonial Capital B&B Inn** [$$$ to $$$$$] (501 Richmond Road, Williamsburg, VA 23185, ☎ 800-776-0570) provides its guests with bicycles. Across from William and Mary College, the **Candlewick B&B** [$$$ to $$$$] (800 Jamestown Road, Williamsburg, VA 23185, ☎ 800-418-4949) also has bikes for guest use.

The two guest rooms in the **Alice Pearson House B&B** [$$ to $$$] (616 Richmond Road, Williamsburg, VA 23185, ☎ 800-370-9428) are furnished in fine antiques, oriental rugs, and unique linens. Fireplaces add a touch of warmth during the winter months.

There is a nature trail at the **War Hill Inn B&B** [$$$ to $$$$] (4560 Long Hill Road, Williamsburg, VA 23188, ☎ 800-743-0248), which sits on 32 acres about two miles from Williamsburg.

Newport News/Hampton

Newport News has a number of reasonably priced motels within a few minute's drive of the airport. With some of the lowest rates, the **Econo Lodge-Oyster Point** [$ to $$] (11845 Jefferson Ave., Newport News, VA 23606, ☎ 757-599-3237) and the **Budget Lodge** [$ to $$] (930 J. Clyde Morris Blvd., Newport News, VA 23601, ☎ 757-599-5647) provide clean, basic rooms. The **Host Inn** [$ to $$] (985 J. Clyde Morris Blvd., Newport News, VA 23601, ☎ 888-599-3303) has an outdoor pool.

The **Ramada Inn and Conference Center** [$$ to $$$$] (950 J. Clyde Morris Blvd., Newport News, VA 23601, ☎ 800-841-1112) has some reasonable rates for the quality of its facilities.

Rates are also reasonable for the 16 rooms at **The Inn at Kiln Creek** [$$] (1003 Brick Kiln Blvd., Newport News, VA 23602, ☎ 757-874-2600), especially as you have all of the amenities of a golf course resort.

Within walking distance of Newport News Park, the **Days Inn** [$$] (14747 Warwick Blvd., Newport News, VA 23601, ☎ 757-874-0201) and the **Mulberry Inn** [$$] (16890 Warwick Blvd., Newport News, VA 23603, ☎ 757-887-3000) both have swimming pools and provide airport transportation.

In Hampton, the **Red Roof Inn** [$ to $$] (1925 Coliseum Drive, Hampton, VA 23666, ☎ 757-838-1870) has about the lowest rates in town and permits small pets.

Within walking distance of the Hampton Coliseum, the **Fairfield Inn** [$ to $$] (1905 Coliseum Drive, Hampton, VA 23666, ☎ 800-228-2800) has a few rooms overlooking the swimming pool.

The restored, turn-of-the-century **Victoria House B&B** [$$ to $$$$] (4501 Victoria Blvd., Hampton, VA 23669, ☎ 757-722-2658) is located inside the city's designated historic district.

■ Camping

Virginia Beach/Chesapeake/Suffolk

The two campgrounds closest to the main beach area are almost resort spots in and of themselves. In addition to the usual campground amenities, **Holiday Trav-L-Park** (1075 General Booth Blvd., Virginia Beach, VA 23451, ☎ 800-548-0223) has miniature golf, a playground, four swimming pools, outdoor game facilities, hayrides, live entertainment, and bingo. Guests have free beach parking.

Just a couple of blocks away, the **Virginia Beach KOA Resort Kampground** (1240 General Booth Blvd., Virginia Beach, VA 23451, ☎ 800-KOA-4150) also has swimming pools and miniature golf. It offers a free trolley to the beach.

Tidewater Virginia

By time you pay the fee to camp in the KOA, you could add just a few more dollars and stay in one of the air-conditioned Kamping Kabins.

With its own beach on the Chesapeake Bay, **First Landing/Seashore State Park** has sites nestled between sand dunes and under the shade of live oak trees. There are no water or electric hookups here, but there is a dump station and restrooms with warm showers. This is a popular place and, even though there are more than 200 sites in the park, you should make your reservations as early as possible by calling ☎ 800-933-PARK.

About the quietest and cheapest sites in the beach area are in **North Shore Campground** (3257 Colechester Road, Virginia Beach, VA 23456, ☎ 757-426-7911) near Sandbridge Beach.

The quietest of all would be the 12 primitive backcountry sites in **False Cape State Park**. Some are near the ocean, some tucked behind dunes, and others under tall loblolly pines. Permits must be obtained at Seashore State Park in Virginia Beach (☎ 757-481-2131.) This is a great place to be if you truly want to escape the crowds, but remember you must walk or bike (backpacks or camping equipment are not permitted on the tram) more than five miles through Back Bay National Wildlife Refuge and through a part of the park to reach the sites.

 False Cape has no potable water, so carry in more than you think you will need. I love this place; but my suggestion is to go in the spring or fall to escape the sometimes oppressive heat and an even more oppressive bug population.

Operated by the city of Chesapeake – but still within reasonable driving distance of the ocean – **Northwest River Park** has shaded sites on 733 acres. Besides providing hiking trails, a lake to canoe upon, and a miniature golf course, there are electric hookups, a camp store, and dump station.

Privately owned **Chesapeake Campground** (693 South George Washington Highway, Chesapeake, VA 23323, ☎ 757-485-0149) has two pools, a tennis court, and rental bikes.

The farthest from the beach, but also the lowest in cost by far, are the sites in 64-acre **Portsmouth Park Campground** (4700 Sleepy Hole Road, Suffolk, VA 23435, ☎ 757-538-4102). There is a laundromat, dump station, and an 18-hole golf course.

Smithfield Region

About 15 miles west of Smithfield, visitors are welcome at the **White Tail Family Nudist Resort** (39033 White Tail Drive, Ivor, VA 23866, ☎ 757-859-6123). Facilities include a pool, spa, clubhouse, and RV and tent sites.

Northern Neck Region

You can make reservations for one of the more than 100 sites in **Westmoreland State Park** by calling ☎ 800-933-PARK. RVs seem to favor the larger sites in Campground A, while tenters tend to enjoy the smaller, but more wooded sites of Campground B. There are no hookups in Campground C. The park also has 25 housekeeping cabins available for rent – some by the night, others by the week.

Once you arrive at the **Cole's Point Campground** (PO Box 77, Coles Point, VA 22442, ☎ 804-472-3955) on the Potomac River you may never leave. All of the sites have water, electric, and sewer or pump out service. There are laundry facilities and camping supplies, a gift store, a restaurant, and boats and canoes for rent. If you get tired of the swimming pool, five miles of hiking and biking trails wind through the property, with bikes available for rent.

The hiking trails at **Heritage Park Resort** (2570 Newland Road, Warsaw, VA 22572, ☎ 804-333-4038) overlook Menokin Bay and the Rappahannock River. Boats and canoes are available for rent, and resort personnel lead half-day guided canoe trips through the wetlands of Cat Point Creek.

Tidewater Virginia

The **Chesapeake Bay/Smith Island KOA** (Route 1 Box 1910, Reedville, VA 22539, ☎ 804-453-3430) is where you will find the dock for the Smith Island, Maryland scenic cruise boats, and for boats taking campground guests on narrated trips of the Potomac River. Pets are permitted in the campground, which has waterfront sites, a swimming pool, and boat and bicycle rentals.

With large waterfront sites on the Rappahannock River, the **Bethpage Camp Resort** (PO Box 178, Urbana, VA 23175, ☎ 804-758-4349) has just about everything you would need for a family vacation: boat ramp, marina, playground, recreation room, outside sporting facilities, tennis court, swimming pool, and beach.

In Deltaville, **Bush Park Camping Resort** (PO Box 589, Deltaville, VA 23043, ☎ 804-776-6750) also has some sites close to the Rappahannock River. Amenities here include a pool, boat ramp, phone hookups, and dump station. Pets are not permitted.

Historical Triangle

The **Williamsburg KOA Resort** (5210 Newman Road, Williamsburg, VA 23188, ☎ 757-565-2907) rents bicycles and provides free transportation to the area's attractions.

With well over 435 sites crammed onto 34 acres, I'm not sure if the **Holiday Trav-L-Park Fair Oaks Family Campground** (901 Lightfoot Road, Williamsburg, VA 23188, ☎ 757-565-2101) really qualifies as a campground as much as it deserves to be called a small town. However, if you make a certain level of purchases at the nearby Williamsburg Pottery, your night's stay is free.

A bit more spread out are the 600 sites on 200-acre **Jamestown Beach Campsites** (PO Box CB, Williamsburg, VA 23187, ☎ 757-229-7609), which sits on the shores of the James River – adjacent to Jamestown Island. Feeling energetic? Take part in the free dances with live music on the beach.

A little more laid back and along the lines of a traditional campground, **Kin Kaid Campground** (559 East Rochambeau

Drive, Williamsburg, VA 23188, ☎ 757-565-2010) only has 50 sites on 88 acres. Pets are permitted.

Newport News/Hampton

In a wooded setting adjacent to Lee Hall Reservoir, the 180-site campground in **Newport News Park** has picnic tables, grills, laundromat, phones, camp store, dump station, playground, and water and electrical hookups. With most of the park's 8,000 acres left in a natural state, this is one of the nicest car camping spots in Tidewater Virginia.

Although it has much less acreage than Newport News Park, the Hampton City-operated **Gosnold's Hope Park** (Little Back River Road, Hampton, VA 23669, ☎ 757-850-5116) still makes for a pleasant and quiet camping experience.

Where To Eat

With water playing such an important role in the everyday life of the Tidewater area, it is no surprise that seafood figures prominently on the menus of the local restaurants, even those with ethnic backgrounds. My advice is to stay away from things deep-fried and be adventurous in trying new dishes. Be ready to enjoy some of the freshest seafood in the East!

Norfolk

A local favorite – with views of the Chesapeake Bay – **Ship's Cabin Seafood Restaurant** [$$ to $$$] (4110 East Ocean View Ave., Norfolk, VA 23518, ☎ 757-362-4659) has a changing menu to take advantage of the freshest seasonal ingredients. Always on the menu are crab soup, crab cakes, seafood kabobs, and oysters sautéed with wine, butter, and shallots.

Overlooking Little Creek Harbor, the **Blue Crab Bar & Grill** [$$] (4521 Pretty Lake Ave., Norfolk, VA 23518, ☎ 757-362-8000) has a creative seafood menu with a bit of a Cajun and Caribbean accent.

The bistro-style **Bienville Grill** [$$] (723 West 21st St., Norfolk, VA 23517, ☎ 757-625-5427) will also transport you to Cajun country with gumbos, étouffées, pan-fried catfish, and dishes featuring crawfish, oysters, andouille sausage, and tasso ham.

The buffet at the **India Restaurant** [$ to $$] (5760 Northampton Blvd., Norfolk, VA 23502, ☎ 757-460-2100) lets you sample just about everything on the menu – beef, lamb, and seafood, curried and tandoori dishes, as well as a good selection of vegetarian fare.

If you wake up with a sweet tooth for breakfast, the **French Bakery & Delicatessen** [$] (4108 Granby St., Norfolk, VA 23504, ☎ 757-625-4936) will satisfy it with donuts, French pastries and eclairs.

Virginia Beach

It seems that every ocean resort area in America now has the obligatory all-you-can-eat seafood buffets and Virginia Beach is no exception. Among the many to be found along the main drag are at **Seafood Harbor** [$ to $$] (32nd St. & Atlantic Ave., Virginia Beach, VA 23451, ☎ 757-428-6220), **Capt. John's Crab House** [$ to $$] (33rd St. & Atlantic Ave., Virginia Beach, VA 23451, ☎ 757-425-6263), and **Emilio's** [$ to $$] (35th St. & Atlantic Ave., Virginia Beach, VA 23451, ☎ 757-491-2675).

If it's just crabs you are looking for, **The Happy Crab** [$ to $$] (550 Laskin Road, Virginia Beach, VA 23451, ☎ 757-437-9200) has a buffet of blue crabs, softshell crabs, crab legs, crab soup, crab Newberg, crab cakes, and more. It will even provide a free Taxi-Crab to and from the restaurant.

It's not on the oceanfront, but for a bit more refined dining experience head to **Alexander's on the Bay** [$$ to $$$] (4536 Ocean View Ave., Virginia Beach, VA 23451, ☎ 757-464-4999). The chefs are creative here, with dishes such as tuna Norfolk (sautéed tuna topped with backfin crab meat, artichoke hearts, and hollandaise sauce) and seafood Madagascar (lobster, shrimp, and scallops cooked in peppercorn sauce).

How can you go wrong when the locals have voted the **Duck-In & Gazebo** [$ to $$] (3324 Shore Drive, Virginia Beach, VA 23451, ☎ 757-481-0201) as the top overall seafood restaurant with the best steamed shrimp, best view, best crab cakes, best sunset, best lunch, and best outdoor dining?

Waffles and Company [$] (18th St., & Pacific Ave., Virginia Beach, VA 23451, ☎ 757-491-0363) will help you get your day started.

Italian dining is best at **Aldo's Ristorante** [$$ to $$$] (1860 Laskin Road, Virginia Beach, VA 23454, ☎ 757-491-1111), especially the wood-burning brick oven-baked pizzas.

The brick oven in **Anatola Turkish Cuisine** [$$] (2158 North Great Neck Road, Virginia Beach, VA 23451, ☎ 757-496-9777) is used to bake delicious pita bread to accompany sautés and kebobs of chicken, lamb, beef, or shrimp. Lots of vegetarian dishes, also. Belly dancing on Friday and Saturday nights!

Unfortunately, the best Mexican restaurant in all of Virginia Beach (and Virginia!), Lista's, closed several years ago. Not quite Mexican, but with more of a Southwest Tex/Mex menu, the **Coyote Café & Cantina** [$] (972A Laskin Road, Virginia Beach, VA 23451, ☎ 757-425-8705) helps to fill the void with its spicy wild boar tamales, duck confit wontons, and wild mushroom and scallops pasta.

Chesapeake

Reservations are recommended for **The Locks Pointe** [$$ to $$$] (136 Battlefield Blvd. North, Chesapeake, VA 23320, ☎ 757-547-9618). You can watch boaters glide along the Intracoastal Waterway as you enjoy inventive fresh seafood dishes cooked with spices, sauces, and cheeses. Save room for equally interesting desserts.

Also on the Intracoastal Waterway, **Cara's** [$$] (123 Battlefield Blvd. North, Chesapeake, VA 23320, ☎ 757-548-0006) serves up sesame seed chicken with Cumberland sauce, steak Chesapeake, and salads large enough to be a meal. Here you need to save room for the peanut butter pie.

Tidewater Virginia

Traditional Mexican cuisine, plus several vegetarian offerings, lure diners into the **Three Amigos** [$ to $$] (200 Battlefield Blvd. North, Chesapeake, VA 23320, ☎ 757-548-4105).

Portsmouth

Café Europa [$ to $$$] (319 High St., Portsmouth, VA 23704, ☎ 757-399-6652) is romantic, with lace curtains and antique chandeliers, recognized for faultless service, and known for unsurpassed French and Italian cuisine This small hideaway is located in Olde Towne. Veal, such as veal romanola and veal martini, is the specialty of the house.

American home cooking is the order of the day at **Mom's Best Deli** [$] (340 Broad St., Portsmouth, VA 23704, ☎ 757-399-1199). The menu includes chicken and dumplings, corned beef and cabbage, and homemade desserts. Be sure to try one of the meringue pies.

The **Scale O'De Whale** [$$ to $$$] (3515 Shipwright St., Portsmouth, VA 23704, ☎ 757-483-2772) is actually a ship permanently moored in a marina. After eating the Neptune Feast, consisting of lobster, stuffed shrimp, and filet mignon, you might want to wait a while before asking for an order of the bread pudding mixed with lemon custard.

Smithfield

East of town you will find a number of fast food and Italian and Chinese restaurants near the intersection where Business VA 10 splits off from VA 10. For the best spots, you should continue into town.

Overlooking the wetlands and waters of the Pagan River, the **Smithfield Station Restaurant** [$ to $$$] (415 South Church St., Smithfield, VA 23430, ☎ 757-357-1752) features the famous Smithfield ham at breakfast, lunch, and dinner. Not to be overlooked are the wonderfully prepared fresh seafood dishes.

Much along the same lines are the ham and seafood meals served to the general public at the **Smithfield Inn B&B** [$$ to $$$] (112 Main St., Smithfield, VA 23430, ☎ 757-357-1752).

Charles City County

You can admire the landscape while enjoying your meal of Southern American cuisine on the porch of the restored farmhouse at the **Indian Fields Tavern** [$$ to $$$] (9220 John Tyler Highway, Charles City, VA 23030, ☎ 804-829-5004). Sunday brunch always draws a crowd.

Going along with its setting, **The Coach House Tavern** [$$ to $$$] (12602 Harrison Landing Road, Charles City, VA 23030, ☎ 804-829-6003), within the Berkeley Plantation, is open for refreshments and traditional Colonial dining. Reservations are required for dinner.

Northern Neck Region

With a screened porch overlooking the Potomac River in Colonial Beach, the **Dockside Restaurant** [$ to $$] (PO Box 400, Colonial Beach, VA 22443, ☎ 804-224-8726) features fresh, steamed, or boiled seafood, steaks, and a raw bar.

About a half-mile west of Colonial Beach, the weekend seafood buffet at **Wilkerson's Seafood Restaurant** [$ to $$] (Route 2 Box 11, Colonial Beach, VA 22443, ☎ 804-224-7117) draws both locals and travelers.

It is almost obligatory to tour Robert E. Lee's birthplace while traveling in the Northern Neck, so you might as well partake of the food and drink in the **Stratford Hall Dining Room** [$$] (Stratford, VA 22558, ☎ 804-493-8119) before you leave.

On the way to Reedville, **Bambery's on the Green** [$ to $$] (PO Box 209, Callao, VA 22435, ☎ 804-529-5200) in Callao provides upscale dining in a casual atmosphere overlooking the Valley Green Golf Course.

The family-style dining at **Rosie Lee's Restaurant & Lounge** [$ to $$] (PO Box 206, Burgess, VA 22432, ☎ 804-453-6211) is popular for breakfast, lunch, and dinner.

Located in the restored 1880s Reedville Market, **Elijah's** [$$ to $$$] (Main St., Reedville, VA 22539, ☎ 804-453-3621) has fresh seafood, soups, and salads. The local crabs are served as crab cakes, steamed crabs, soft crabs, crab imperial, and more.

You can come by land or water and eat in or take out the steamed crabs, crab cakes, and seafood salads at **Cockrell's Creek Seafood Deli** (Fleeton Road., Reedville, VA 22539, ☎ 804-453-6326).

Somewhat of an economic hub in the Northern Neck, **Kilmarnock** has a number of good restaurants worth checking out:

Stay at **Lee's Restaurant** [$ to $$] (Main St., Kilmarnock, VA 22482, ☎ 804-435-1255) long enough and you are almost sure to meet the entire population of town. The family-style cooking and congenial mom-and-pop atmosphere may just make you decide to take up residence.

Chesapeake Café [$$ to $$$] (Route 3 North, Kilmarnock, VA 22482, ☎ 804-435-3250) serves local crab and seafood in addition to prime rib and daily regional specialties. The Angler's Cove Lounge has lighter fare and spirits.

From the decor and the high quality of its food, you would never know that the building now occupied by **The Northside Grill** [$ to $$$] (555 Main St., Kilmarnock, VA 22482, ☎ 804-435-3100) was once a Dairy Queen. Owner Mike Robertson has turned the place into such a good restaurant that people drive miles for meals of seafood, steaks, salads, and burgers. The chef's daily specials are always innovative and delicious.

Patrons of the **Crab Shack Restaurant** [$ to $$] (PO Box 816, Kilmarnock, VA 22482, ☎ 804-435-2700) can watch the sun set over Indian Creek and the Chesapeake Bay while dining on fresh seafood, beef, and chicken.

South of Kilmarnock in Whitestone, **Willaby's** [$ to $$] (PO Box 1122, White Stone, VA 22578, ☎ 804-435-0044) satisfies lunch appetites with gourmet burgers, special sauces, and desserts.

The elegant restaurant at **The Tides Inn** [$$$] (PO Box 480, Irvington, VA 22480, ☎ 804-438-5000) has a different menu every night with regional favorites and gourmet fare. Wear a jacket or be denied dinner!

River's Inn [$ to $$$] (8109 Yacht Haven Drive, Gloucester Point, VA 23062, ☎ 804-642-9942) offers blue crabs, oysters, clams, shrimp, grilled fish, and duck. Dining on the outdoor

Crab Deck is a bit more casual and features steamed blue crabs, oysters, sandwiches, and micro-brewed beers.

Historical Triangle

Fresh seafood with a Greek accent is not the only reason to dine at **Nick's Seafood Pavilion** [$ to $$$] (Water St., Yorktown, VA 23690, ☎ 757-887-5269). Be prepared for a decor of pink tablecloths, chandeliers, a tile floor, statues surrounded by green plants, and a wait staff dressed in bolero vests and hats.

Within **Colonial Williamsburg** are a number of restored 18th-century taverns serving traditional menus in an historical decor. One of the largest, with 11 dining rooms, is **Shields Tavern** [$$ to $$$] (Duke of Gloucester St., Williamsburg, VA 23187, ☎ 757-220-7677). It features spit-roasted beef and fowl, Virginia ham, and an appetizer sampler with a variety of tidbits from the 18th century.

Also with 11 dining rooms is the **King's Arms Tavern** [$$ to $$$] (Duke of Gloucester St., Williamsburg, VA 23187, ☎ 757-229-1000). It has balladeers to serenade those who are dining on Smithfield ham with grape sauce, oyster-stuffed filet mignon, and an old Virginia favorite, peanut soup.

Brunswick stew is popular at **Chowning's Tavern** [$$ to $$$] (Duke of Gloucester St., Williamsburg, VA 23187, ☎ 757-229-2141), where the drinks at happy hour are not the typical beer and wine, but grog and juleps.

George Washington was a frequent diner at **Christina Campbell's Tavern** [$$ to $$$] (120 East Waller St., Williamsburg, VA 23185, ☎ 757-229-1000). Be sure to try the Chesapeake Bay jambalaya with scallops and country ham.

Despite the name, America's first president never ate at the **George Washington Inn Smorgasbord** [$$] (500 Merrimac Trail, Williamsburg, VA 23185, ☎ 757-220-1410). Steamed, baked, fried, broiled, boiled, grilled – just about any meat, vegetable, or dessert you can think of can be found on the buffet table.

You don't have to leave the historic district to find some fast food. **A Good Place to Eat** [$ to $$] (410 Duke of Gloucester St.,

Williamsburg, VA 23187, ☎ 757-229-1000) serves muffins and pancakes for breakfast, and burgers, sandwiches, fries, and milkshakes for lunch and dinner.

Departing from the historic theme and heavy foods of the Williamsburg restaurants, the **Trellis Café, Restaurant & Grill** [$$ to $$$] (403 Duke of Gloucester St., Williamsburg, VA 23187, ☎ 757-229-8610) changes its menu seasonally to take advantage of the freshest seafood and produce. Even the ice cream is made on the premises.

Low cost and generous portions of Cantonese, Mandarin, Szechuan, and Hunan dishes at **The Dynasty** [$ to $$] (1621 Richmond Road, Williamsburg, VA 23185, ☎ 757-220-8888) are enough to lure customers away from other establishments.

Newport News/Hampton

Herman's Harbor House [$ to $$$] (663 Deep Creek Road, Newport News, VA 2302, ☎ 757-930-1000) specializes in seafood and, most notably, crab cakes. The decor is nautical. You may have to search a bit for the restaurant as it is located in a residential area. Call ahead for directions.

The steak and lobster kew is a favorite choice from the Chinese-American menu at **Port Arthur** [$ to $$] (11137 Warwick Blvd., Newport News, VA 23606, ☎ 757-599-6474).

The **Kappo Nara Seafood and Sushi Restaurant** [$$] (550 Oyster Point Road, Newport News, VA 23602, ☎ 757-249-5395) is known for its authentic sushi and Japanese cuisine. To meet all tastes, there are also some seafood and steak meals prepared American-style.

Decidedly not American are the rouladen and schnitzel served in **Das Waldcafe** [$ to $$] (12529 Warwick Blvd., Newport News, VA 23606, ☎ 757-599-6035). Hazelnut cake for dessert!

Lots of windows at **Fisherman's Wharf** [$$ to $$$] (14 Ivy Home Road, Hampton, VA 23669, ☎ 757-723-3113) in Hampton provide expansive views of the busy Hampton Roads harbor. The menu is heavily tilted toward seafood, with baked shrimp stuffed with crab meat being a popular selection.

Fairly low prices and large portions of chicken, seafood, and other offerings make dining at **Sammy & Nicks Family Restaurant** [$ to $$] (2718 Mercury Blvd., Hampton, VA 23666, ☎ 757-838-9100) a wise economic decision.

Just a few doors down (with branches in Virginia Beach and Williamsburg), **Captain George's Seafood Restaurant** [$$ to $$$] (2710 West Mercury Blvd., Hampton, VA 23666, ☎ 757-826-1435) claims to have the largest all-you-can-eat buffet, with over 70 items.

Fire and Ice [$ to $$$] (2040 Coliseum Dr., Hampton, VA 23666, ☎ 757-826-6698) has a diverse menu not often found at a restaurant located within a shopping center. The onion-crusted salmon is a pleasant surprise.

Tidewater Virginia

Northern Virginia

From its cities and suburbs crowded with employees of the federal government to the sparsely populated foothills of the Blue Ridge Mountains, Northern Virginia is the state's most diverse region. Super-modern shopping malls and six-lane highways full of traffic exist alongside the preserved buildings and cobblestone streets of the Colonial era. The surrounding countryside is known as Horse and Hunt Country, where fox hunts and steeple chases on large landholdings still take place. The effects of the federal government's influence and money fade as you travel further south and west, where rural farms and smaller cities and towns become the norm.

Surprisingly, there is ample opportunity in this heavily populated area to do some great outdoor adventuring. Federal, state, regional, and county parks – such as Mason Neck State Park, Great Falls Park, the Washington and Old Dominion Trail, and Burke Lake Park – have preserved parcels of open space where you can hike, bike, and horseback ride. Just a few miles north of the nation's capitol, the Potomac River presents canoeists and kayakers with the opportunity for easy flatwater paddling and some of the most exhilarating whitewater in the state.

To the south and west of the metropolitan Washington, DC area, Lake Anna attracts sailing enthusiasts, and the adjoining state park has miles of hiking trails on which to discover the area's rich natural and human history. Scenic Byway VA 231 runs along the edge of Shenandoah National Park, providing almost continuous views of the mountains and connecting with smaller country lanes perfect for afternoon drives or quiet, daylong bike rides. On the eastern rampart of the Blue Ridge Mountains, Sky Meadows State Park has one of the most spectacular vistas in all of Virginia, taking in a vast sweep of the rolling Piedmont landscape.

Much of America's historical drama has been played out in Northern Virginia. Alexandria was a flourishing port town long before the streets of Washington, DC were laid out; a walking tour of the Old Town portion of the city passes more than 400 buildings remaining from those days. George Washington, Thomas Jefferson, John Adams, and other personalities from America's earliest days walked these same streets and called the city home.

North of Alexandria is Arlington County, the second smallest county in the country – much of it owned by the federal government. On the confiscated estate of Robert E. Lee is Arlington National Cemetery, with the Tomb of the Unknowns, the eternal flame of John F. Kennedy's grave, and Iwo Jima – the US Marine Corps War Memorial.

Like the rest of the state, Northern Virginia was the scene of intense fighting during the Civil War. Just a few miles west of Arlington, the Manassas National Battlefield Park preserves the site of two of those battles. The First Battle of Manassas is considered by historians to be the first major battle of the war, while the Second Battle of Manassas opened the way for the Southern forces to drive into Northern territory. To the south, the Fredericksburg and Spotsylvania National Military Park preserves the sites of four major battles that were fought in and near Fredericksburg.

Information Sources

Alexandria Convention & Visitors Assoc., 221 King St., Alexandria, VA 22314, ☎ 703-838-4200.

Arlington Convention & Visitors Service, 735 S 18th St., Arlington, VA 22201, ☎ 800-677-6267.

Fairfax County Convention & Visitors Bureau, 8300 Boone Blvd., Suite 450, Tysons Corner/Vienna 22182, ☎ 703-790-3329.

Fairfax Visitors Center, 10209 Main St., Fairfax, VA 22030, ☎ 800-545-7950.

Fredericksburg Visitors Center, 706 Caroline St., Fredericksburg, VA 22410, ☎ 800-678-4748.

Loudon Tourism Council, 108-D South St., Southeast, Leesburg, VA 20175, ☎ 800-752-6118.

Prince William County/Manassas Conference & Visitors Bureau, 14420 Bristow Road, Manassas, VA 20112, ☎ 800-432-1792.

Spotsylvania County Department of Tourism & Visitors Center, 4704 Southpoint Parkway, Fredericksburg, VA 22407, ☎ 800-654-4118.

Foothills Travel Association of Virginia, 183A Keith St., Warrenton, VA 20188, ☎ 540-347-4414.

■ ■ ■

Northern Virginia

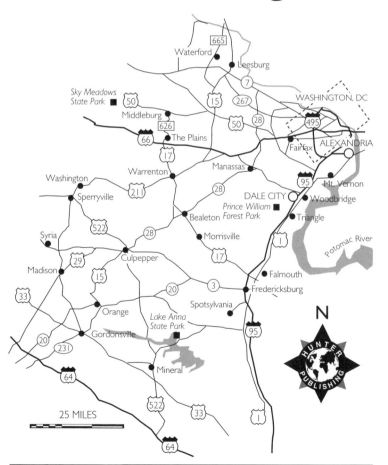

Getting Around

If you fly into Northern Virginia, it will be into one of two of the busiest airports in the country. **Dulles International Airport** (☎ 703-572-2700), about a 30-minute drive from Washington, DC, is served by just about every major carrier and has connections to cities both domestic and foreign. Along the Potomac River in Alexandria, Ronald Reagan **Washington National Airport** (☎ 703-417-8372, or 800-833-0415) has scheduled service with at least 10 national airlines.

Heading southwest from Washington, DC, **Amtrak** (☎ 800-231-872-7245) makes stops in Alexandria, Manassas, and Culpepper. A different route south from the city has stops in Alexandria, Woodbridge, Quantico, and Fredericksburg.

Taking **Greyhound** (☎ 800-231-2222) gives you a bit more flexibility, with stops in Washington, DC, Arlington, Culpepper, Fairfax, Fredericksburg, Gordonsville, Middleburg, Orange, Springfield, Triangle, Upperville, Warrenton, and Woodbridge. Flag stops are made in Centreville and Gainsville. Fredericksburg and Springfield are also served by **Carolina Trailways** (☎ 919-833-0627).

Touring

■ Arlington County Area

GREAT FALLS PARK: The tour begins by leaving Dulles Airport, heading north on VA 28, and then east on VA 7. In just a few miles, turn onto VA 193 and finally onto VA 738 to arrive at Great Falls Park (PO Box 66, Great Falls, VA 22066, ☎ 703-285-2966), one of the most scenic outdoor recreation spots in the vicinity of the capital. The park sits on the fall line, the point where the Piedmont meets the Coastal Plain. The Potomac River – having gathered strength and force from its humble beginnings in the mountains of West Virginia – rushes and roars over the rough, jagged rocks of narrow Mather Gorge. This display of power can be breathtaking and beautiful. In recent years the falls have become a favorite of expert, almost-daredevil, paddlers. The park is also popular because of its picnic areas, scenic overlooks of the river, and network of close to 15 miles of hiking, biking, and horseback riding trails.

Arlington & Fairfax Counties

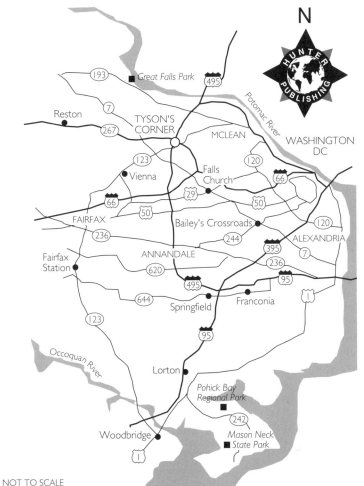

NOT TO SCALE

GEORGE WASHINGTON MEMORIAL PARKWAY: Continue east from the park on VA 193, turn north on I-495, and follow signs directing you onto the George Washington Memorial Parkway (c/o Turkey Run Park, McLean, VA 22101, ☎ 703-285-2606). A limited-access highway, the scenic parkway parallels the Potomac River. It travels through heavy forests, by pristine marshlands, and alongside landscaped areas. The blossoms of azalea, mountain laurel, day lilies, crab apple, pear, redbud, and dogwood trees make it especially charming in the spring and early summer. Stretching for 23 miles from I-495 to Mount Vernon, the parkway provides access to numerous parks, recreation areas, and historical sites – such as Fort Hunt, Theodore Roosevelt Island, Jones Point Lighthouse, Lady Bird Johnson and Turkey Run parks, and Dyke Marsh.

ARLINGTON NATIONAL CEMETERY: Drive around a bend in the Potomac, exit the parkway, and follow signs to the Arlington National Cemetery (Arlington, VA 22211, ☎ 703-692-0931). Although there is no charge to walk or drive through, the best way to grasp the significance of this huge burial ground – where more than 200,000 men and women are interred – is to take the guided tourmobiles that leave from the visitors center. You are permitted to get off/on at any of the main sites, such as the Tomb of the Unknowns and the gravesites of John F. Kennedy, Robert F. Kennedy, Jacqueline Kennedy Onnassis, and William Howard Taft. It is also possible to take a self-guided tour of Arlington House, the residence of Robert E. Lee and his family for 30 years.

THE NEWSEUM: If you feel up to facing the horrendous traffic of downtown streets, admission to the Newseum is also free (1101 Wilson Blvd., Arlington, VA 22209, ☎ 703-284-3722). It opened in mid-1997. The only interactive museum of news, it gives visitors a behind-the-scenes look at how and why news is made. You can experience what it is like to be a reporter, radio announcer, or news anchor. Artifacts and memorabilia enable you to relive great moments in history.

■ Alexandria & Vicinity

ALEXANDRIA: From the Newseum, make your way back to the George Washington Memorial Parkway (sometimes referred to in this area as the Mount Vernon Memorial Parkway) and follow it south.

OLD TOWN: In the mid-1700s, surveyor John West, Jr., and his teenage assistant George Washington, "laid of in streets and 84 half-acre lots" the town of Alexandria. The small city became a boom town after the Revolutionary War due to burgeoning tobacco farms, its access to international shipping, and its proximity to Washington, DC – the seat of the new federal government. George Washington and the prominent Lee family of Virginia took up residence here, and many reminders of those glory days can still be found. A walking tour brochure from the visitors center in **Ramsay House** (221 King St., Alexandria, VA 22314, ☎ 314-838-4200), the oldest structure in town, can direct you to the best sites.

If you are not a resident of Alexandria, be sure to ask for the pass which gives you 24 hours of free parking.

George Washington and Robert E. Lee were pewholders at the red brick Georgian-style **Christ Church** (118 North Washington St., Alexandria, VA 22314, ☎ 703-549-1450). Although it has been altered since it was first used in 1773, much of the church has been restored to its original appearance.

The **Old Presbyterian Meeting House** (321 South Fairfax St., Alexandria, VA 22314, ☎ 703-549-6670) was the site of Washington's funeral. The original structure was burned after being hit by lightning in 1835, but its replacement was built around the old walls in much the same style as its predecessor.

Also restored to its late 18th-century appearance, the **Stabler-Leadbeater Apothecary Museum** (105 South Fairfax St., Alexandria, VA 22314, ☎ 703-836-3713) counted both Washington and Lee among its regular customers. In fact, among its many hand-blown medicinal bottles, pill rollers, and mortars and pestles, is a record of an order from Mount Vernon for a bottle of castor oil.

Northern Virginia

Gadsby's Tavern (134 North Royal St., Alexandria, VA 22314, ☎ 703-838-4242) was a center of social and political life in the beginning days of our country, attracting such notable figures as Washington, Jefferson, and Adams. Guided tours take you through its rooms, which have been restored to their 18th-century appearance. If you're hungry, three of the rooms have been converted into Colonial-style **Gadsby's Tavern Restaurant**.

Built in the late 1830s as a lecture and concert hall, the **Lyceum** (201 South Washington St., Alexandria, VA 22314, ☎ 703-838-4994) also served as a hospital during the Civil War and as a private residence. Today it is a museum concentrating on the city's history.

Interpreting the role of African-Americans in that history is the focus of the **Alexandria Black History Resource Center** (638 North Alfred St., Alexandria, VA 2314, ☎ 703-838-4356). The permanent collection of letters, photographs, documents, and other artifacts is complemented by rotating exhibits.

MOUNT VERNON: About 10 miles south of downtown, via the George Washington Memorial Parkway, is George Washington's Potomac River plantation: Mount Vernon (Mount Vernon, VA 22121, ☎ 703-780-2000). There is no official guided tour, but any questions you may have can be answered by assistants found throughout the mansion home. The plantation has been accurately restored to its appearance during the last year of Washington's life. Any visit here should also include a stroll over the 500 acres of grounds, with 12 outbuildings, gardens, and George and Martha Washington's graves.

Travel to the southwest from Mount Vernon on VA 635, then south along US 1 for several miles to VA 242, where you make a turn to the east. This leads to the sites described below:

POHICK BAY REGIONAL PARK: In addition to a campground, one of the largest swimming pools on the east coast, a picnic area, golf course, and boat ramp, the park (6501 Pohick Bay Drive, Lorton, VA 22079, ☎ 703-339-6104) has several short hiking trails (totaling about four miles) that twist and turn through stands of holly and laurel and pass by small lily-covered inlets.

GUNSTON HALL: Gunston Hall (Lorton, VA 22079, ☎ 703-550-9220) is reached by continuing on VA 242 for a short distance past the regional park. A two-mile trail shows off the natural beauty of George Mason's homestead. Mason was the author of the 1776 Declaration of Rights of Virginia, which stated, "All men are by nature equally free and independent and have certain inherent rights."

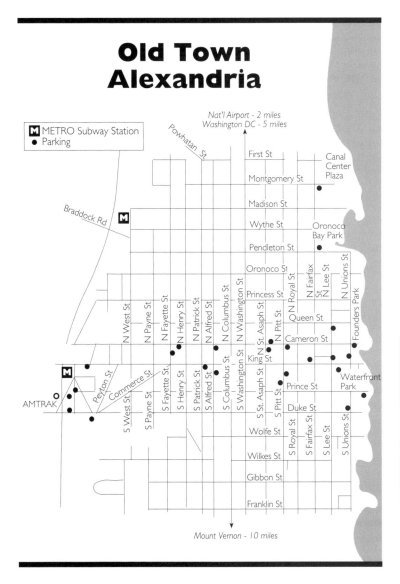

Old Town Alexandria

METRO Subway Station
● Parking

Nat'l Airport - 2 miles
Washington DC - 5 miles

Powhatan St

First St
Montgomery St
Madison St
Wythe St
Pendleton St
Oronoco St
Princess St
Queen St
Cameron St
King St
Prince St
Duke St
Wolfe St
Wilkes St
Gibbon St
Franklin St

Canal Center Plaza

Oronoco Bay Park

Braddock Rd

N West St
N Payne St
N Fayette St
N Henry St
N Patrick St
N Alfred St
N Columbus St
N Washington St
N St. Asaph St
N Pitt St
N Royal St
N Fairfax St
N Lee St
N Unions St
Founders Park

AMTRAK

Peyton St
Commerce St
S West St
S Payne St
S Fayette St
S Henry St
S Patrick St
S Alfred St
S Columbus St
S Washington St
S St. Asaph St
S Pitt St
S Royal St
S Fairfax St
S Lee St
S Unions St

Waterfront Park

Mount Vernon - 10 miles

Northern Virginia

MASON NECK NATIONAL WILDLIFE REFUGE: Beyond Gunston Hall the roadway becomes VA 600, which you follow until you can make a right onto VA 5783. This road cuts through the Mason Neck National Wildlife Refuge (14416 Jefferson Davis Hwy, Suite 20, Woodbridge, VA 22191, ☎ 703-690-1297), which was established in 1969 as the country's first national sanctuary for the endangered bald eagle. A brochure available at the start of the three-mile **Wood Marsh Trail** provides information on places such as Eagle Point, which overlooks the 250-acre Great Marsh. It is estimated that at least 30 pairs of eagles nest here in winter and spring to mate and raise young.

MASON NECK STATE PARK: Continuing to drive through the refuge, come to 1,804-acre Mason Neck State Park (7301 High Point Road, Lorton, VA 22079, ☎ 703-550-0960), overlooking Belmont Bay. Eagles are often spotted in this day-use area, which has a canoe launching site, picnic area, and a small, wonderfully designed network of hiking trails.

POTOMAC MILLS OUTLET MALL: After a visit to the state park, retrace your steps, return to VA 1, and head south, crossing the Occoquan River and passing by the Potomac Mills Outlet Mall (☎ 800-VA-MILLS) in Dale City, which features outlet prices in more than 220 stores. This mall has now become the number one tourist attraction in the state – a sad comment on the priorities of our society.

PRINCE WILLIAM NATIONAL FOREST PARK: For a much more natural way to spend your day, continue south to the Prince William National Forest Park (PO Box 209, Triangle, VA 22172, ☎ 703-221-7181). The quiet beauty of this component of the national park system is made all the more remarkable by the fact that it is less than an hour's drive from downtown Washington, DC. This close proximity to large numbers of people attracts many visitors, yet I have always found the trails to be wonderfully underused. In addition to nearly 35 miles of hiking trails, the park provides picnic areas, group-camping cabins, interpretive programs, two campgrounds, and a backcountry camping area reachable only by foot. Sitting on the fall line – the place where the Piedmont drops onto the coastal plain – the park's lush forest is home to a great number of creatures and evidence of beaver can be seen along most streamside trails.

Fredericksburg

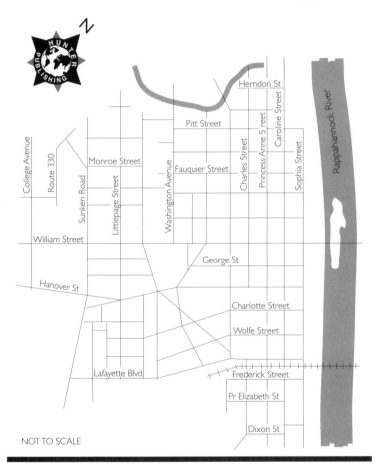

Herndon St
Pitt Street
Monroe Street
Fauquier Street
William Street
George St
Hanover St
Charlotte Street
Wolfe Street
Lafayette Blvd
Frederick Street
Pr Elizabeth St
Dixon St

College Avenue
Route 330
Sunken Road
Littlepage Street
Washington Avenue
Charles Street
Princess Anne Street
Caroline Street
Sophia Street
Rappahannock River

NOT TO SCALE

■ Fredericksburg

The tour continues by driving south on US 1 to Fredericksburg which, like Alexandria, was a favorite haunt of such luminaries as Washington, Jefferson, and James Monroe. A walking tour of the downtown historic district (brochures available from the visitors center) is the best way to discover the oldest part of town and its 350 original buildings from the 1700s and 1800s.

MARY WASHINGTON HOUSE: In 1772, George Washington bought his 62-year-old mother the Mary Washington House (1200 Charles St., Fredericksburg, VA 22407, ☎ 540-373-1569) so that she would be comfortable and "free from care." Mary Ball Washington lived here until her death in 1789. Guided, 30-minute tours are given by interpreters in period clothing.

KENMORE: Married to George Washington's first cousin, and later to his only sister, Betty, Fielding Lewis was one of the wealthiest planters in Fredericksburg. He completed construction of Kenmore in 1775 (1201 Washington St., Fredericksburg, VA 22401, ☎ 540-373-3381). Lewis' plantation originally contained 1,300 acres planted in tobacco, flax, and grains. Today only four acres of lawn remain, but the magnificent home has been restored to its Colonial elegance; all of the woodwork, paneling, and elaborate plasterwork are original. Tours through the house, furnished with authentic Lewis family pieces, conclude in the kitchen, where spiced tea and gingerbread from a recipe of Mary Washington's are served.

JAMES MONROE MUSEUM & MEMORIAL LIBRARY: America's fifth president lived for three years in the home that now houses the James Monroe Museum and Memorial Library (908 Charles St., Fredericksburg, VA 22401, ☎ 540-654-1043). One of the country's largest collections of Monroe memorabilia includes the formal clothing he wore as US ambassador to the court of Napoleon, furniture he purchased while in Paris, and the gun and canteen he carried into battle during the Revolutionary War.

FREDERICKSBURG AREA MUSEUM & CULTURAL CENTER: Much of the town's history is conveyed in the exhibits at the Fredericksburg Area Museum and Cultural Center (907 Princess Anne St., Fredericksburg, VA 22404, ☎ 540-371-3037), which is housed in the 1816 Town Hall. The second floor focuses on Native American history.

FERRY FARM: Just one mile east of Fredericksburg on VA 3 is Ferry Farm (PO Box 5933, Falmouth, VA 22403, ☎ 540-373-3381), where George Washington lived from age six to 20. Admission is free to this site at which, according to legend,

Washington chopped down the cherry tree and threw the coin across the Rappahannock River.

CIVIL WAR BATTLEFIELDS: Four major Civil War battles were fought at **Fredericksburg** and nearby **Chancellorsville, The Wilderness**, and **Spotsylvania Court House**. Today the National Park Service preserves some of the lands on which those conflicts occurred. The four sites are a short drive apart, each one offering a variety of history lessons and outdoor hiking opportunities. The **Fredericksburg Battlefield Visitors Center** (1013 Lafayette Blvd., Fredericksburg, VA 22401, ☎ 540-373-6122) can supply you with maps and information about each site.

C.F. PHELPS WILDLIFE MANAGEMENT AREA: If you want to do some true backcountry camping while in the area, head northwest from Fredericksburg on US 17. Just after Morrisville, go west on VA 634, make a left on VA 637, and another left on VA 651 to enter the C.F. Phelps Wildlife Management Area (1320 Belman Road, Fredericksburg, VA 22401, ☎ 540-899-4169). Like other such areas in the Commonwealth, it is maintained in a primitive state and used primarily for hunting and fishing. Yet, a network of about 15 miles of gated roads and unmarked trails twist through the 4,500 acres, providing access to some positively isolated camping spots.

▪ Lake Anna

The tour now leaves the traffic congestion of Fredericksburg and I-95 by heading southwest on VA 208. After making twists and turns through Spotsylvania and the tiny settlement of Brokenburg, look for road signs to **Lake Anna State Park** (6800 Lawyers Road, Spotsylvania, VA 22553, ☎ 540-854-5503). The signs will direct you to make a right onto VA 601 and then a left to the park's entrance on VA 7000.

In the flat-to-rolling lands of the Piedmont, Lake Anna was created to supply cooling for Virginia Power Company's North Anna Nuclear Power Station – about three miles from the state park. With eight miles of shoreline, the park opened to the public in 1983 and offers picnic areas, a boat ramp, excellent nature and history exhibits in the visitors center, swimming in the lake, interpretive programs, and network of trails allowing you to roam its 2,000 acres.

A sandy beach at Lake Anna State Park.

■ Orange

From the state park, drive through rural countryside, taking VA 601 and VA 612 to the west, and coming into Orange. This small town is the seat of what was once the largest county in the state. Before the Revolutionary War, its boundaries extended into unexplored lands, as far west as the Mississippi River and north to the Great Lakes.

MONTPELIER: About four miles south of town on VA 20 is Montpelier (☎ 540-672-2728), the home of Orange's most famous resident and fourth president of the United States, James Madison. After Madison's death, the estate changed hands many times before being purchased by William du Pont, Sr. in 1901. The du Ponts made numerous changes to the main house and the grounds. Today a research and restoration effort is under way, but you are permitted to wander through the 55-room house and the estate's 2,700 acres. Self-guided tours take in an arboretum, formal garden, nature trails, and a steeplechase course still in use.

JAMES MADISON MUSEUM: In town, this museum (129 Caroline St., Orange, VA 22960, ☎ 540-572-1776) contains Madison artifacts such as presidential correspondence, personal library books, and clothes and fashions of his wife, Dolly.

■ Madison County & Vicinity

The topography begins to change as you head west from Orange on VA 230 and then to the north on Scenic Byway VA 231. Madison County is an exceptionally beautiful piece of rural real estate, sitting – as a tourist brochure proclaims – on the sunrise side of the Blue Ridge Mountains.

MADISON: Although it has all of the modern amenities, downtown Madison, the county seat, is the quintessential small town of an America most of us assume no longer exists. Everyone seems to know everybody else, and the local drug store still operates a soda fountain. The visitors center, located in the 1790 Madison Arcade, can provide a walking tour map to help you better appreciate the town.

The **Kemper Residence** is the post-war home of Confederate Major General James Lawson Kemper, wounded at Gettysburg and later elected governor of Virginia. Used as a hospital during the Civil War, the sanctuary of the 1834 **Piedmont Episcopal Church** was refurbished with walnut paneling donated by Mrs. Herbert Hoover. The 1830 **Madison County Court House** has arcades with the same proportions as those found on the campus of the University of Virginia.

PRINCE MICHEL DE VIRGINIA: Less than 10 miles north of town on US 29 is Prince Michel de Virginia (HCR 4 Box 77, Leon, VA 22725, ☎ 800-869-8242), a leading winery in the state and one of the best places to take a tour and learn how a vineyard operates. In a museum are antique winemaking equipment from France, rare old wine bottles, and a video presentation relating the history of viticulture. A self-guided

Northern Virginia

tour leads along a visitors' gallery, with visual displays on grape growing and wine making. Of course, you are also invited to sample the vineyard's products before departing.

BEALTON: The tour continues north of the winery on US 29, swings around Culpepper, merges onto VA 28, and turns south on US 17 to Bealton. From May to October, an airstrip in this small town in the heart of Northern Virginia is the site of the **Flying Circus Airshow** (Routes 17 & 644, Bealton, VA 22712, ☎ 540-439-8661). Each Sunday afternoon there are demonstrations of barnstorming acrobatic flying, wing walking, hot-air balloons, and open cockpit planes. You can also take rides in the biplanes.

■ Leesburg & Vicinity

Old farm cabin at Sky Meadows.

SKY MEADOWS STATE PARK: From Bealton, take US 17 north through Warrenton to head west on I-64, and then northwest along US 17. In Sky Meadows State Park (11012 Edwards Lane, Delaplane, VA 22025, ☎ 540-592-3556), large, rich green fields dapple vast areas of the hillside as the topography sweeps upward from the rolling Piedmont to meet the eastern slopes of the Blue Ridge Mountains. Once a working farm, the park has a picnic area, visitors center in historic Bleak House, hiking trails, a bridle path, and a hike-in primitive backcountry campsite. One of the hiking trails has what I consider to be among the best grandstand views in all of Virginia. From a perch on the mountains, the rolling and flatter lands of the Piedmont stretch out before you. Cattle graze in the meadow directly below, rectangular fields of nearby farms alternate with strips of woodlands, vultures soar on rising thermals, and, on clear days, the high-rise buildings of the Dulles-Fairfax area can be seen poking above the horizon.

MANASSAS NATIONAL BATTLEFIELD PARK: After your visit to the state park, retrace the same route to I-64 and drive east to VA 234 and the Manassas National Battlefield Park (6511 Sudley Road, Manassas, VA 22110, ☎ 703-361-1339), the site of two intense, bloody, and significant battles of the Civil War. In one of the first major conflicts of the war in July, 1861, Union troops were driven back to Washington by forces under the command of General Thomas J. Jackson. One year later, in August, 1862, General Robert E. Lee, now in command of the Confederates and aided by the steadfast forces of General Stonewall Jackson, employed brilliant military tactics to force General John Pope's Union army to withdraw and, once again, retreat to Washington.

A one-mile walking tour will take you to sites on Henry Hill, where the first battle climaxed on July 21, 1861. The Second Battle of Manassas is best seen by completing the 12-mile driving tour where wayside exhibits contribute to your understanding of the events. Be sure to stop at the visitors center to obtain detailed information; there are additional walking trails and other places of interest throughout the National Battlefield Park's 5,000 acres.

HORSE COUNTRY: Continuing to the northwest from the battlefield on VA 234, the tour now enters the heart of Virginia's "horse and hunt country." Less than a hour's drive from Washington, DC, some of the most expensive real estate in the Commonwealth is bordered by miles of white-painted wooden fences and the open meadows and fields of thoroughbred horse farms. Steeple chasing, fox hunting, and horse races are a part of life here.

Northern Virginia

OATLANDS PLANTATION: Turning north on US 15, pass by Oatlands Plantation (20850 Oatlands Plantation Lane, Leesburg, VA 20175, ☎ 703-777-3174), which has its own equestrian center for horse races and shows. Once part of a 5,000-acre plantation, the mansion – made of materials obtained from the estate – was built in 1803 by George Carter. Tours include the interior of the house, furnished with American, English, and French antiques. The surrounding 260 acres are said to have one of the finest boxwood gardens in America, dating back 200 years.

LOUDON MUSEUM: Continue driving north on VA 15 to Leesburg and the Loudon Museum (16 Loudon St., Leesburg, VA 20178, ☎ 703-777-7427), which records the history of Loudon County. Included are Native American artifacts, items from the Civil War, and the audiovisual presentation, *A Special Look at Loudon*. You can pick up a brochure here describing a walking tour of Leesburg. Among the 50 attractions grouped around the courthouse square are Queen Ann-style townhouses and George Washington's headquarters.

MORVAN PARK: One mile north of Leesburg, Morvan Park (PO Box 6228, Leesburg, VA 20178, ☎ 703-777-2414) typifies the lifestyle and atmosphere of this corner of Northern Virginia. The estate was once the home of Thomas Swan, a governor of Maryland, and later the home of Virginia Governor Westmoreland Davis. The 1,500-acre park includes a 28-room mansion, boxwood gardens, the Windmill Carriage Museum, the Morvan Park International Equestrian Institute, and the Museum of Hounds and Hunting – with artifacts and video presentations on the history of fox hunting.

WATERFORD: About four miles northwest of Leesburg on VA 662 is a place that exemplifies a much simpler lifestyle than that of the plantation. Waterford was first settled by Quakers and Germans in the 1730s. It is now one of only three villages designated National Landmarks. A stroll through the restored town will show how each generation built upon what was already there.

To wrap up your explorations of Northern Virginia, head east on VA 7 and then south on VA 28, returning to Dulles International Airport.

Adventures

■ On Foot

Arlington County Area

Stretching north along the Potomac River are a series of parks, natural areas, and monuments that help preserve the river's natural area, and provide marvelous places to take a walk.

THEODORE ROOSEVELT ISLAND PARK: Heading north on the George Washington Memorial Parkway, road signs will direct you to this park (c/o Turkey Run Park, McLean, VA 22101, ☎ 703-285-2600). Sitting in the middle of the Potomac River within sight of the DC skyline, the 88-acre park has about two miles of pathways. The most enjoyable path wanders into a rare tidal freshwater marsh on the southern end of the island.

From Roosevelt Park, the **Potomac Heritage Trail** heads north for close to 10 miles, winding between the river and the parkway, and passing through woodlands, floodplains, creekside environments, and high bluffs overlooking the river. Part of a planned long-distance trail that may one day stretch from Washington, DC to western Maryland, the pathway provides a hiking alternative to driving along the parkway. It also connects with pathways in other parks along the river: the 1½-mile **Windy Run Trail** leads to a 45-foot waterfall in Windy Run Park; the 1.1-mile **Donaldson Run Trail** in Zachary Taylor Park follows a creek valley to the Potomac River; and the **Gulf Branch Trail** leads down to the river in Glebe Road Park.

The northern end of the Potomac Heritage Trail is in **Turkey Run Park** (McLean, VA 22101, ☎ 703-285-2600), located on high bluffs overlooking the river. Several short trails – all much less than a mile – wander through the park and down to the river.

GREAT FALLS PARK: Further north, and administered under the auspices of the George Washington Memorial Parkway,

Great Falls Park is a centerpiece of outdoor recreation along the south bank of the Potomac River. A network of about 15 miles of trails traverse swampy areas, parallel the river, and enter forests crowded with sycamores, oaks, and beeches. Springtime brings a profusion of flowers, such as phlox, wild ginger, trillium, and Virginia bluebells. Inhabiting the 800-acre park are fox, beaver, muskrat, deer, rabbit, skunk, opossum, raccoons, and a variety of birds.

All of the park's trails interconnect in some way, so you can make your outing about as long or as short as you wish. Among the more scenic routes, the **Swamp Trail** winds into a low area where interpretive signs have detailed information on plants and wildlife. The park's most strenuous route is the **Great Falls Trail**, which provides an intimate contact with Mather Gorge by dropping down to the water's edge. Passing by remains of earlier days – such as an old iron forge and a gristmill, and the gates and dams of the old canal system – the **Patowmack Canal Trail** begins next to Wing Dam. The moderately strenuous **River Trail** begins at the visitors center, climbs over rocks, leads to overlooks of waterfalls and Falls Island, and connects with pathways in adjacent Riverbend Park.

RIVERBEND PARK: Extending along two miles of the Potomac River floodplain, Riverbend Park (8814 Jeffery Road, Great Falls, VA 22066, ☎ 703-759-3211) is operated by the Fairfax County Park Authority. An interpretive route (brochures available in the nature center), the **Pawpaw Passage Trail** makes a loop into the woods.

The Pawpaw

The pawpaw's four- to five-inch fruit, which resembles a short, fat banana, starts out green, but ripens to a purple-brown. Its meat, with the consistency of an over-ripe banana, was a food source for rural families and is still considered something of a delicacy by many people.

Connecting with the Pawpaw Passage Trail, the **Potomac Heritage Trail** (not the same as the trail of the same name in Turkey Run Park) lies along the floodplain, passing under

A pawpaw along the trail.

beech, sycamore, birch, and poplar trees before connecting with the River Trail in Great Falls Park.

Alexandria & Vicinity

Heading south from Theodore Roosevelt Park (see above) the **Mount Vernon Trail** (c/o Turkey Run Park, McLean, VA 22101, ☎ 703-285-2600) is a hiking and biking trail that parallels the George Washington Memorial Parkway for close to 18 miles before coming to an end at Mount Vernon. Along the way, it provides access to numerous sites and other hiking trails along the Potomac River:

- **The Lyndon Baines Johnson Memorial Grove** and **Lady Byrd Johnson Park**, with a grove of white pines, dogwoods, azaleas, and rhododendron.

- **Olde Town Alexandria**, with its assortment of historic structures.

- The half-mile round-trip **Jones Point Trail**, leading to the **Jones Point Lighthouse**.

- The 3½-mile trail through **Dyke Marsh**, where more than 250 species of birds have been observed.

ACCOTINK BAY WILDLIFE REFUGE: Southwest of Mount Vernon, US 1 cuts through the middle of the US Army's Fort Belvoir, providing access to the Accotink Bay Wildlife Refuge (Environmental & Natural Resource Division, 9430 Jackson Loop Building 1441, Fort Belvoir, VA 22060, ☎ 703-806-4007).

Located on the grounds of the military base, the refuge has a network of pathways (about six miles in total length) winding into its 1,300 acres; maps and brochures at the trailhead on Pohick Road can help you get oriented. Well maintained and signed, the pathways – with boardwalks, benches, and footbridges – run beside Accotink Bay and Creek, and will take you through wetlands, marshes, and forests of sweetgum, beech, and river birch. Over 200 birds, such as egrets, ducks, herons, and bald eagles, have been seen here, while the work of beavers is evident.

MASON NECK STATE PARK: Even though it is far north of the mouth of the Chesapeake Bay, Mason Neck State Park's shoreline is still subject to the ebb and flow of the Atlantic Ocean's tides. This means the area's marshlands provide the right habitat for saltwater creatures such as an occasional blue crab, and attract a wide variety of birds and waterfowl. Despite its proximity to large population centers, hikes in the park present the opportunity to see, or at least observe signs of, a diverse array of wildlife. It is a perfect spot to delight in the sprinting leaps of a white-tailed deer, the cry of an osprey, the gobble of a wild turkey, or the bark of a red fox calling out for its young. The one-mile loop **Bayview Trail** is an interpretive pathway running beside the bay, with boardwalks over marshlands. The one-mile **Kanes Creek Trail** has a short side trail leading to a blind overlooking the creek – a local late-fall-to-early spring roosting spot for bald eagles.

PRINCE WILLIAM NATIONAL FOREST PARK: You could easily spend several days wandering along the 35 miles of interconnecting trails in Prince William National Forest Park. Of those trails, one of the most scenic routes is probably the **North Valley Trail**, which gives access to Quantico Falls as the pathway courses through an isolated valley created by the North Branch of Quantico Creek. It is hard to believe you are only about 20 miles from downtown Washington as you walk through the wide and quiet valley beside the South Branch of Quantico Creek on the **South Valley Trail**. Like the beaver who live here and the deer who use it to quench summer thirsts, you might want to cool your feet or take a quick wade.

LOCUST SHADE REGIONAL PARK: A short drive from the national forest park, this 778-acre park (4701 Locust Shade Drive, Triangle, VA 22712, ☎ 703-221-8579) has the 2.2-mile **Locust Shade Trail**, which loops through a tranquil woodland, making use of footbridges to cross over a number of small streams. The 1½-mile **South Trail** is also a loop that follows the crest of a ridgeline into the same kind of environment. The park entrance is off US 1 near Triangle.

Fredericksburg

FREDERICKSBURG & SPOTSYLVANIA NATIONAL MILITARY PARK: All four sites of the Fredericksburg & Spotsylvania National Military Park have trails that are both historic and worthwhile because of the natural beauty of the sites.

 Be sure to stop at the visitors center at 1013 Lafayette Blvd. in Fredericksburg to obtain maps and directions to the individual sites.

The five-mile one-way **Lee Drive Trail**, a popular jogging trail for the citizens of Fredericksburg, is just a few minute's drive from the Fredericksburg visitors center and has historic markers identifying the events and sites of the battle that took place here in December 1862.

Stonewall Jackson was fatally wounded by his own men a few miles west of Fredericksburg during the battle of Chancellorsville (April 27-May 6, 1863). The 3½-mile **Chancellorsville History Trail** and the one-mile **Hazel Grove Trail** lead hikers past important points of the battle.

In May 1864, the Wilderness Battlefield was the site of the first conflict between the forces of Union lieutenant Ulysses S. Grant and those of Confederate General Robert E. Lee. The two-mile **Jordan Flank Attack Trail** loops through the site.

A number of trails, including **Bloody Angle, Laurel Hill**, and **McCoull/Harrison**, twist through what is now peaceful woodlands and bucolic meadows at Spotsylvania. The battle was so intense from May 8 to May 21, 1864, that the Union and Confederate armies sustained a combined estimated loss of more than 25,000 men.

Outdoor Adventures (4721 Plank Road, Fredericksburg, VA 22407, ☎ 540-786-3334) sells all of the equipment you would ever need to go walking, hiking, camping, or canoeing.

Lake Anna

LAKE ANNA STATE PARK: A network of interconnecting trails in this park allows you to roam its 2,000 acres to discover natural secrets and beauties, along with reminders of the human activity that has taken place here. The .3-mile **Old Pond Trail** is an interpretive loop with numbered stops keyed to a brochure available in the visitors center. Running along the shore of the lake, the 1½-mile **Railroad Ford Trail** makes use of an old railroad grade on which trains during World War I carried iron ore destined to be made into bullets and shell casings. There has been talk of restoring the old plantation home that is reached by following the 1.7-mile **Glenora Trail**. Other trails in the park loop through woods and fields close to the lake, lead to a cove where the work of beavers is evident and heron troll the shallow water, and swing by a chimney marking the site of an old homestead.

Leesburg & Vicinity

SKY MEADOWS STATE PARK: The contrast of open meadows and deep forests, coupled with an elevation difference of 1,840 feet as a high point and 640 feet as a low one, ensures that wildflower lovers are in for a treat at Sky Meadows State Park (see page 130 for dircctions.). A system of trails wanders through the fields, into the woods, and along streams, touching upon most of the highlights. Entering a mature oak forest, the one-mile loop **Snowden Interpretive Trail** provides information about animals of the park and their relationship to their surroundings. Less than a mile one-way, the **Piedmont Overlook Trail** ascends to one of the best views in all of Virginia's state parks. Each less than two miles, the **South Ridge**, **North Ridge**, and **Gap Run Trails** individually ascend the mountainside to converge and connect with the park's 3½-mile section of the **Appalachian Trail** (AT).

G.R. THOMPSON WILDLIFE MANAGEMENT AREA: You could either hike south along the AT for a couple of miles or drive south on US 17 and VA 688 from the state park to the G.R. Thompson Wildlife Management Area (PO Box 349, Sperryville, VA 22740, ☎ 703-825-3653). About seven miles of the AT run along the crest of the Blue Ridge Mountains here, connecting with a system of more than 20 miles of trails wandering through the area's 4,160 acres. Except for the **Ted Lake Trail** (accessed from a parking area on VA 688), most of the pathways are not named or marked. However, armed with a good map (obtained from the above address), you should definitely visit this underused area, especially in the spring when – literally – tens of thousands of trillium are in bloom!

Headquartered in The Plains, **Mountain Memory Walks** (PO Box 281, The Plains, VA 20198, ☎ 800-872-0344) puts together a wide variety of group walking and hiking vacations. The trips range from easy day walks to weekend journeys or week-long hikes into the mountains. Bed and breakfasts or country inns provide the overnight accommodations.

■ On Wheels

Mountain Biking

Arlington County Area

West of Arlington in Annandale is an easy 4½-mile gravel bike path that connects **Wakefield Park** with **Lake Accotink Park** (c/o Fairfax County Park Authority, 3701 Pender Drive, Fairfax, VA 22030, ☎ 703-246-5700). A loop around the lake is also open to bikes, adding to the riding opportunities here. Wakefield Park is reached by taking I-66 Exit 5 and heading west for no more than .3 mile on VA 620 to the park entrance. For Lake Accotink you should head east from I-66 Exit 5 for about a half-mile on VA 620 to make a right onto Hemming Ave., which leads you to the park.

Alexandria & Vicinity

PRINCE WILLIAM NATIONAL FOREST PARK: About 16 miles of gated gravel roads are open to mountain bikes in Prince William National Forest Park. Although there are no real circuit rides available (most of the roads are just one-way dead-ends of no more than two miles), they all do lead off from the park's main paved road, which is also open to bicycles. You could ride all day long – on a terrain that can be demanding at times – by first riding one gated road, returning to the main road, and then riding out another gated route, and so on.

BURKE LAKE PARK: Another popular riding route is in Burke Lake Park (7315 Ox Road, Fairfax Station, VA 22039, ☎ 703-323-6600), which is operated by the Fairfax County Park Authority. The five-mile **Burke Lake Trail** encircles the 218-acre lake, winding up and over small hillocks as you pass from one little cove to another.

 Warning. You will need to be alert for a couple of things: Pedestrians also make use of Burke Lake Trail and the resident beavers sometimes drop a small tree across the route.

GREAT FALLS PARK: Because of its proximity to the great populations of the Washington area, Great Falls Park may just be the most popular off-road riding spot in Northern Virginia. Almost six miles of interconnecting trails are designated for mountain bike use. The **Ridge Trail** runs from the park entrance road to make a fairly quick descent to the **Difficult Run Trail**. That pathway descends along the banks of Difficult Run Creek to wonderful views of the Potomac River, Great Falls, Mather Gorge, and Sherwin Island. The **Old Carriage Road** pretty much runs from one end of the park to the other, connecting with the above two trails.

Road Biking

Interstate Bicycle Route 1

This route generally follows the Virginia to Maine Bicycle Route. Marked by "Bike-1" signs along the highways, it enters Northern Virginia at Arlington and goes through Old Town Alexandria before swinging west to Manassas. From there it turns to the south, running into Fredericksburg and Caroline County, and entering Central Virginia in Hanover County.

Arlington County Area

WASHINGTON & OLD DOMINION TRAIL: Possibly the best ride in all of Northern Virginia is along the Washington & Old Dominion Trail (c/o Northern Virginia Regional Park Authority, 5400 Ox Road, Fairfax Station, VA 22309, ☎ 703-352-5900). The paved trail stretches from the urban atmosphere of Alexandria 45 miles to the quiet countryside in Purcellville. (A shorter pathway with a natural surface for hikers and horseback riders begins in Vienna and runs alongside the paved route for about 30 miles.) Following the railbed of the Washington & Old Dominion Railroad, which operated from 1859 to 1968, the trail was one of the country's first successful rail-to-trail conversions. Often used as a commuter route for cyclists, the trail can be quite congested along its eastern end as it passes shopping centers, condos, and suburban homes. However, as you continue west, the numbers of riders diminish and the scenery turns to farmland, forests, and open meadows.

A brochure describing the trail is available from the regional park authority. Also available (at a fairly low cost) is the detailed *Washington & Old Dominion Trail Guide*, which includes milepoint information, street and road accesses, and a listing of restaurants and bike shops along the way. The eastern trailhead is next to I-395, close to the Arlington County/Alexandria border; the western trailhead is close to Main St. in Purcellville.

DESIGNATED TRAILS: In addition to the W&OD Trail, Arlington County has miles and miles of on- and off-road routes open to cyclists that are detailed on a map available from the

Arlington County Bicycle Coordinator, 2100 Clarendon Blvd., Suite 717, Arlington, VA 22201, ☎ 703-358-3699.

A perfect example of the possible rides available on these routes is a 17-mile circuit journey which begins at the parking area for Roosevelt Island on the George Washington Memorial Parkway. Head to the west along the **Custis Bikeway** (beside I-66) and then south along the W&OD Trail. Coming to the **Wayne F. Anderson Bikeway** you will make a turn east to finally head north along the **Mount Vernon Trail** and return to the starting point. (See page 135 above for details on the Mount Vernon Trail.)

POTOMAC OVERLOOK TOUR: In the northern section of Arlington County, the easy 6½-mile-loop **Potomac Overlook Tour** follows Marcey Road out of the Potomac Overlook Regional Park to head north along Military Road. Going south, turn onto North Old Glebe Road, North Glebe Road, and George Mason Drive. Making use of a marked off-road bicycle route, you'll come to Yorktown Blvd., which you follow east, before turning onto another off-road route. This one will take you back to Military Road, which returns you to the beginning point of the ride.

> 📖 Additional commuting and touring routes in the Washington metro area (which includes the eastern portion of Northern Virginia) are identified on the map, *Bicycle Routes in the Washington Area*. It can be purchased from the Metropolitan Washington Council of Governments (777 North Capitol St. Northeast, Suite 300, Washington, DC, 20002, ☎ 202-962-3200). Even more information and routes can be found in the *Greater Washington Area Bicycle Atlas* from the Washington Area Bicyclist Association (818 Connecticut Ave. Southwest #300, Washington, DC, 20006, ☎ 202-872-9830).

Spokes, Etc. (1545 North Quaker Lane, Alexandria, VA 22314, ☎ 703-820-2200) has bicycles for sale and should be able to help if you have any problems with the one you already own.

Fredericksburg

OLD TOWN: The Fredericksburg Old Town area can be toured on three-, five- and 20-mile routes and information can be obtained from the Fredericksburg Visitors Center. Additional riding routes will be found in guides available from the **Fredericksburg Cyclists** (PO Box 7844, Fredericksburg, VA 22404).

Outfitters

Old Towne Bicycles (1907 Plank Road, Fredericksburg, VA 22401, ☎ 540-371-6383) and **Bike Works** (104 William Street, Fredericksburg, VA 22405, ☎ 540-373-8900) can direct you to other local riding places and can take care of any bike sale and repair.

Lake Anna

A circuit ride of more than 30 miles begins by using the small town of **Mineral** as a base. From town, head east along VA 618 to cross Freshwater Creek and make a left onto VA 700. You will follow this road to its end at the **North Anna Nuclear Power-plant,** overlooking Lake Anna. In addition to providing facts about the powerplant, the information center has hands-on and electronic displays concerning nuclear power generation.

From the powerplant, retrace the ride along VA 700 to make a right onto VA 652. You will have to put up with a bit of traffic as you make a left and ride along VA 208. Soon after that roadway merges with US 522, leave it by bearing right onto VA 623. Several miles later, intersect and turn left onto VA 22/208, which returns you to the starting point.

Madison County Area

A very pretty morning's ride can take you from breakfast at a B&B to lunch at a mountain inn – if you don't mind a few stiff ups and downs. Having spent the night and enjoyed a leisurely breakfast at **Dulaney Hollow B&B** (see page 155), head north on Scenic Byway VA 231. In just a few miles, make a left onto VA

643, paralleling Popham Run and riding in the shadow of Old Rag Mountain. You will have to negotiate several hills and twists and turns before bearing left onto VA 600. Make a right onto VA 670 to reach the **Graves Mountain Lodge** (see page 154) where, if you have made reservations, you can join other guests in a very filling family-style lunch.

Outfitters

Based in Culpepper County, **Bike Adventures** (17295 South Cambridge way, Jeffersonton, VA 22724, ☎ 540-937-4908) arranges one-day bike tours for both serious and casual cyclists.

Leesburg & Vicinity

South of Leesburg is a moderately easy circuit ride of about 20 miles that begins in **Middleburg**. Head south on VA 626, making a stop to tour and sample the products at the **Piedmont Winery**. After you have rested a bit and let the wine run its course through your system, continue south into the small settlement of **The Plains** on VA 626. Heading west, follow VA 55 for several miles to make a right onto VA 709 at **Brookes Corner**. In five to six miles look for the right turn onto VA 715. Less than a mile later, bear left onto VA 705, which will take you to a left onto VA 626 and the return to Middleburg. If you did not have a meal at **The Rail Stop** in The Plains, head to the bakery in Middleburg (just to the left of the supermarket) for a tasty lunch.

Outfitters

In Leesburg, **Bicycle Outfitters** (19 Catoctin Circle Northeast, Leesburg, VA 20178, ☎ 703-777-6126) should not only be able to tell you about some other favorite local spots to ride, but can also take care of any needed repairs (or be happy to sell you a new bicycle).

■ On Horseback

Arlington County Area

 See the **Washington & Old Dominion Trail** (page 141 above) for information on one of the longest (approximately 30 miles) rides in all of Northern Virginia.

You could spend the better part of a day riding and enjoying the environs around the Potomac River by combining the network of trails that are open to horses in **Riverbend Park** with those in **Great Falls Park**. Some paths will bring you to overlooks of the river, while others take you into a forest away from the crowds.

Alexandria & Vicinity

Although it can get crowded on the weekends during summer, **Pohick Bay Regional Park** has four miles of designated bridle trails winding through a forest of hardwood and pine that can get you away from the hustle and bustle. A few spots will give you views onto the bay, where you have a good chance of spotting ducks, geese, and maybe even a bald eagle. Muskrat slides are also in evidence.

The **Bull Run-Occoquan Trail**, open to both horseback riders and hikers, runs for more than 17 miles, linking together and passing through four parks operated by the Northern Virginia Regional Park Authority. Beginning at **Bull Run Regional Park**, the route makes it possible to ride a full day to the trail's end in **Fountainhead Park**, remaining on public land all of the way. Sketch maps of the trail are available at either of the parks' visitors centers.

Madison County Area

Affiliated with Graves Mountain Lodge, **Overnight Wilderness Outfitters** (c/o Graves Mountain Lodge, Syria, VA 22743, ☎ 540-923-5071) rents horses and leads guided one-hour, half-day, full-day, and overnight rides through the meadows and into the mountains around the lodge. The rides are geared to the ability of the riders. You can also arrange to stable your own horse. Owners Tom Seay and Patricia Goodwin were the organizers and guides of the 1995 American Transcontinental Trailride from Georgia to California.

Windin Farm (PO Box 165, Wolftown, VA 22748, ☎ 540-948-6260) provides riding lessons for you and boarding and training sessions for your horse.

Leesburg & Vicinity

The **Shadow Mountain Farm** (110 East Market St., Leesburg, VA 20176, ☎ 703-771-3356) conducts guided Western trail rides over rolling farmland and wooded trails. Special events include cattle roundups.

Southwest of Leesburg, **Sky Meadows State Park** has close to five miles of designated bridle trails winding through bottomland forest and along a number of streams. There are also stalls and facilities for overnight primitive horse camping.

A bit further south in Fauquier County is one of the premier equestrian centers in the East. The **Marriott Ranch** (5305 Marriott Lane, Hume, VA 22639, ☎ 540-364-2627) sits on a 4,200-acre Texas longhorn cattle ranch. Open all year, guides take guests on rides throughout this vast acreage.

■ On Water

Arlington County Area

 Only for those with advanced paddling skills, an exciting run of about one mile can be had on **Difficult Run** near Great Falls Park. The put in is on busy VA 193 (be mindful of traffic zooming by). Be ready for Class III-IV rapids, and make sure to portage around the Class VI falls. After the falls, stay to the left channel around the island before coming to the Potomac River, where you will take out a bit downstream. See chart on page 16 for whitewater classifications.

Alexandria & Vicinity

BULL RUN-OCCOQUAN RIVER VALLEY: The Bull Run-Occoquan River Valley is a valuable conservation area, preserving marshes and forests and protecting the shoreline of Occoquan Reservoir, the source of water for a large percentage of Northern Virginia's population. Just about anyone, even rookies, will be able to paddle the winding course of the streams for well over 20 miles from the put-in at **Bull Run Regional Park** (near the city of Manassas Park) to the take-out at **Fountainhead Regional Park** (off Hampton Road northwest of the town of Occoquan).

Additional put-in/take-out spots on VA 28 and VA 612 (in **Bull Run Marina Park**) let you decide just how long the journey will be. Despite continued, rapid development in the region, the Bull Run-Occoquan trip will take you past a shoreline that is a nesting place for ducks, geese, osprey, wild turkeys, and other birds. Chipmunks, squirrels, raccoons, foxes, snakes, turtles, and a large population of deer inhabit the land. Numerous gnawed trees, especially in and near the Hemlock Overlook Regional Park, are evidence of an active beaver population.

Once you are at Fountainhead Park (which rents rowboats during the usual tourist season), you've entered the flatwater of 2,100-acre **Occoquan Reservoir**, where you could easily spend a full day exploring little coves and inlets.

POHICK BAY AREA: Launching facilities at **Pohick Bay Regional Park** and **Mason Neck State Park** give you access to the estuarian habitats along Pohick Bay, Accotink Bay, the Potomac River, and Occoquan and Belmont bays. When the wind is calm and water not choppy, a strong paddler could make an enjoyable, but long day-trip through all of these waters from the regional park to the state park. If you want to do some open water paddling, leave from Mason Neck State Park and head south through Belmont and Occoquan bays to the launch site at **Leesylvania State Park** on Powell's Creek. Be prepared for strong winds and choppy water.

If you'd like some company and want to learn a bit of natural history while paddling, join a naturalist on one of the guided ca-

Northern Virginia

noe trips on the waters around Mason Neck State Park. (You need to provide your own canoe or kayak.)

Fredericksburg

AQUIA CREEK: North of Fredericksburg, intermediate paddlers will enjoy a Class I-III run along Aquia Creek. Putting in at VA 610 west of Garrisonville, you will need to watch out for a low concrete bridge and some downed trees. However, the nine-mile run is exceptionally pretty for this part of the state, passing by rhododendrons and hemlocks growing along the stream's high banks and cliffsides. The flatwater of **Smith Lake** announces the end of the journey. You can take out at the dam on VA 659.

Outfitters

Clore Brothers Outfitters (5927 River Road, Fredericksburg, VA 22407, ☎ 540-786-7749) rents canoes, runs a shuttle service, and arranges group trips.

In addition to renting/selling equipment for canoeing, tubing, and rafting – and providing a shuttle service – the **Rappahannock Outdoor Educational Center** (3219 Fall Hill Ave., Fredericksburg, VA 22401, ☎ 540-371-5085) also offers instructional classes.

Lake Anna

All manner of watercraft enthusiasts, from sailboaters to jet skiers to powerboaters and canoeists, are drawn to the 13,000 acres of Lake Anna. Numerous commercial marinas and a ramp in Lake Anna State Park provide access to the 17-mile-long lake.

Orange County Area

RAPIDAN RIVER: For more than 20 miles, from a put-in on US 522 east of Orange to a take-out on VA 610 at **Elys Ford**, the Rapidan River, with nothing more than a few ledges and riffles, is a great outing for the entire family just learning how to paddle. Those of you with a bit more experience could continue downstream of Elys Ford, negotiating a couple of Class II rock gardens and a possible Class III rapid, before taking out at Motts Run Landing below the confluence of the Rapidan and Rappahannock rivers.

RAPPAHANNOCK RIVER: For its part, the Rappahannock River usually provides year-round running for close to 25 miles from the put-in at **Kellys Ford** (VA 620) to the take-out at **Motts Run Landing**. Passing through virtually undeveloped land for most of the way, you have the option of staying at the commercially owned Rappahannock River Campground (see page 158) about halfway into the trip.

Madison County Area

ROBINSON RIVER: Pastoral farmland, Class III ledges, and an occasional osprey are what draw intermediate paddlers to the Robinson River, whose headwaters rise in nearby Shenandoah National Park. The put-in is northwest of **Madison** on VA 649, a short distance downstream from Graves Mountain Lodge. The river is stocked with trout at least twice a year, so you might want to try your luck with rod and reel as you head toward the take-out on VA 636 (just before reaching busy US 29).

THORNTON RIVER: North of Madison, the Thornton River in Rappahannock County provides experienced paddlers with seven miles of nearly continuous Class II-III rapids. Cliff facings, large hemlock trees, and rolling farmland border the river, but you may be too busy to notice as you need to be alert for fences or downed trees across the river that may require a portage. The put-in is at **Fletchers Mill** on VA 620 (southeast of Sperryville) and the take-out is at **Rock Mills** on VA 626.

Leesburg & Vicinity

POTOMAC RIVER: One of America's most scenic waterways, the Potomac River provides close to 30 miles – from Leesburg to Great Falls Park – of delightful canoeing and kayaking for paddlers of all skill levels. Below here, the river reaches its fall line and becomes narrow, swift, and dangerous. However, if you are an expert, this stretch will give you a thrill, with narrow channels, 90° turns, and drops of 22 feet or more.

 Anyone attempting this should go with someone who has made a successful run; you are also required to register with park rangers and police before beginning the trip. Have fun, this is a great thrill, but do not take it lightly. Many have lost their lives here.

Where To Stay

Arlington County Area

 Being next door to Washington, with the Pentagon and other federal government offices nearby, means that you will be hard-pressed to find any budget-priced motels in Arlington.

As usual, you need to look to a locally owned establishment to find the best rate. The **American Hotel** [$$] (1400 Jefferson Davis Highway, Arlington, VA 22202, ☎ 800-548-6261) is the last of those to survive near Reagan National Airport. There is nothing fancy here, but the owners keep the rooms clean and tastefully decorated.

Other motels with some of the lowest rates around include **Days Inn Arlington** [$$ to $$$] (2201 Arlington Blvd., Arlington, VA 22201, ☎ 800-329-7466), **Best Western Arlington Inn and Tower** [$$ to $$$] (2480 South Glebe St., Arlington, VA 22206, ☎ 800-426-6886), and the **Washington/Arlington Cherry Blossom Travelodge** [$$ to $$$] (3030 Columbia Pike, Arlington, VA 22204, ☎ 800-578-7878).

If money is no object, **The Ritz-Carlton Pentagon City** [$$$$$+] (1250 South Hayes St., Arlington, VA 22202, ☎ 800-241-3333) will do very nicely. Adjoining the Fashion Center Mall and Pentagon City metro station, all 345 rooms have fabric wallpaper and cherrywood furniture. There is twice-daily maid service and tea served in the afternoon.

Also in the upper stratosphere for rates is the **Hyatt Regency Crystal City** [$$$$$] (2799 Jefferson Davis Highway, Arlington, VA 22202, ☎ 800-233-1234), with an exercise room, small pool, and three-story atrium.

In the mid-range of rates for Arlington are **Quality Inn-Iwo Jima** [$$$ to $$$$] (1501 Arlington Blvd., Arlington, VA 22209, ☎ 703-524-5000) and **Days Inn Crystal City** [$$$ to $$$$] (2000 Jefferson Highway, Arlington, VA 22202, ☎ 703-920-8600).

In Fairfax, a short drive from Arlington, the **Bailiwick Inn B&B** [$$$$ to $$$$$] has 13 rooms featuring antiques, fireplaces, queen-size feather beds, and Jacuzzis.

A bit further away, but certainly quieter, the **Bennet House B&B** [$$$] (9252 Bennet Drive, Manassas, VA 20110, ☎ 703-368-6121) is in the historic district of Old Town Manassas. There is only one guest room, so your afternoon tea is sure to be quite intimate.

Alexandria

Travelers on a limited budget will certainly fare better in Alexandria than Arlington. Some of the most reasonable rates in town are at the **Comfort Inn Mount Vernon** [$$] (7212 Richmond Highway, Alexandria, VA 22306, ☎ 703-765-9000), **Days Inn-Alexandria** [$$] (110 South Bragg St., Alexandria, VA 22312, ☎ 703-354-4950), **Red Roof Inn** [$$] (5975 Richmond Highway, Alexandria, VA 22303, ☎ 703-960-5200), and **Travelers Motel** [$$] (5916 Richmond Highway, Alexandria, VA 22303, ☎ 703-329-1310).

Reasonably priced, considering that it sits on seven acres at the north end of Old Town Alexandria, is the **Best Western-Old Colony** [$$$ to $$$$] (615 First St., Alexandria, VA 22314, ☎ 800-528-1234), with an exercise room, whirlpool, and sauna.

Also in Old Town, the **Morrison House** [$$$$$+] (116 South Alfred St., Alexandria, VA 22314, ☎ 800-367-0800) was built in 1985, but has the look and feel of an 18th-century federal-style brick inn. Huge mahogany armoires hide the televisions.

Northern Virginia

The **Holiday Inn Hotel & Suites** [$$$ to $$$$] (625 First St., Alexandria, VA 22314, ☎ 800-HOLIDAY) is adjacent to the George Washington Memorial Parkway in Old Town. There is a pool, exercise room, and sauna; complimentary transportation to Reagan National Airport and metro stations is provided.

Overlooking Washington, DC, the **Ramada Plaza Hotel** [$$$ to $$$$] (901 North Fairfax St., Alexandria, VA 22314, ☎ 800-272-6232) has its own tennis court, rooftop pool, and jogging trails.

Pretty much a resort unto itself, the **Radisson Plaza at Mark Center** [$$$$$+] (5000 Seminary Road, Alexandria, VA 22311, ☎ 800-333-3333) has two lighted tennis courts, four racquetball courts, health club, indoor/outdoor pool, jogging trails, and bicycles for rent.

Fredericksburg

The farther away you get from Washington, the less it costs you to stay under a roof. In Fredericksburg, you can find a number of rooms with a rate of about $50 (or less) a night.

Some of the lowest rates are offered at the **Days Inn Fredericksburg North** [$ to $$] (14 Simpson Road, Fredericksburg, VA 22406, ☎ 540-373-5340), **Econo Lodge Central** [$ to $$] (I-95 & VA 3, Fredericksburg, VA 22404, ☎ 800-424-4777), **Royal Inn Motel** [$ to $$] (5309 Jefferson Davis Highway, Fredericksburg, VA 22408, ☎ 540-891-2700), and **Heritage Inn** [$ to $$] (5308 Jefferson Davis Highway, Fredericksburg, VA 22408, ☎ 800-787-7440).

The **Holiday Inn Fredericksburg North** [$$] (564 Warrenton Road, Fredericksburg, VA 22405, ☎ 800-465-4329) has a swimming pool and laundry facilities.

The **Sheraton Inn & Conference Center** [$$$ to $$$$] (2810 Plank Road, Fredericksburg, VA 22404, ☎ 800-682-1049) provides lighted tennis courts, a swimming and wading pool, exercise room, and Colonial-style furniture in the rooms.

In the center of Old Town Fredericksburg is the 18th-century **Richard Johnston Inn** [$$$ to $$$$] (711 Caroline St., Fredericksburg, VA 22401, ☎ 540-899-7606). The nine rooms are decorated with period furniture – and the Old Town Trolley stops at the front door.

A few blocks away, a picket fence and shutters accent the curved, two-story **Fredericksburg Colonial Inn** [$$ to $$$] (1707 Princess Anne St., Fredericksburg, VA 22401, ☎ 540-371-5666). A wide staircase leads to a landing and onto the second floor. Each of the 30 rooms has a different decorating scheme.

Surrounded by pastures, woods, and fields, the 1838 Classical Revival **La Vista Plantation B&B** [$$] (4420 Guinea Station Road, Fredericksburg, VA 22408, ☎ 800-529-2823) has large trees framing the two-story front portico. You can have your choice of a two-bedroom apartment (sleeps six) or a huge formal room with a mahogany four-poster bed.

In nearby Spotsylvania, a private deck overlooks the stream and millpond, while water rushes over the millrace at the 18th-century **Roxbury Mill B&B** [$$$ to $$$$$] (6908 Roxbury Mill Road, Fredericksburg, VA 22553, ☎ 540-582-6611).

Lake Anna Area

Open year-round, the **Anna Point Inn** [$$] (13701 Lake Anna Lane, Mineral, VA 23117, ☎ 800-476-0454) has 30 efficiency units with complete kitchens. Free boat slips are provided to guests.

All 28 rooms at the **Lakewood Motel** [$ to $$] (5152 Courthouse Road, Spotsylvania, VA 22554, ☎ 540-894-5844) have two double beds, microwave, and refrigerator. The same is true of the 15 rooms in the **Lighthouse Inn** [$ to $$] (4634 Courthouse Road, Spotsylvania, VA 22554, ☎ 540-894-5249).

Orange County

The 1830 federal-style **Holladay House B&B** [$$$ to $$$$$] (155 West Main St., Orange, VA 22960, ☎ 800-358-4422) sits in the center of town. You may have breakfast in the dining room or have it brought to your room.

Northern Virginia

Also in town, the **Hidden Inn B&B** [$$$ to $$$$$] (249 Caroline St., Orange, VA 22960, ☎ 540-672-3625) is a late 1800s Victorian farmhouse. The 10 rooms are in four different buildings spread out on eight acres.

Gordonsville

South of Orange, Gordonsville (which is just a short drive from Lake Anna) has three B&Bs of note:

A restored three-story Victorian mansion, **Tivoli B&B** [$$$ to $$$$] (9171 Tivoli Drive, Gordonsville, VA 22942, ☎ 800-840-2225) sits on a hilltop overlooking a 235-acre cattle farm. The four bedrooms have private baths and fireplaces, while the ballroom has a grand piano for guests.

After roaming the grounds of the 2,000-acre farm at the **Rocklands B&B** [$$$ to $$$$$] (17439 Rocklands Drive, Gordonsville, VA 22942, ☎ 540-832-7176), you could relax in the secluded swimming pool or stroll the private gardens. Horseback riding can be arranged.

Situated on 2½ acres in town, the 1880s **Rabbit Run B&B** [$ to $$] (305 North High St., Gordonsville, VA 22942, ☎ 540-832-2892) has the most reasonable rates around and innkeepers who are eager to please.

Madison County

Five generations of the same family have been welcoming guests to the **Graves Mountain Lodge** [$$$ to $$$$$] (Route 670, Syria, VA 22743, ☎ 540-923-4231), which overlooks the eastern rampart of Shenandoah National Park. Accommodations include a choice of rustic cabins or motel-type rooms. (Although the scenery is great anywhere on the grounds, the rooms in Ridgecrest have the best views.) After a 30-minute walk on the nature trail or through the 200-acre orchard, you could relax in the pool or take a horseback ride in the surrounding mountains. The overnight rate includes breakfast, lunch, and dinner. The family style cooking (do not expect anything fat free!) has such a reputation that local folks make reservations a week in advance for a meal.

The pre-Civil War home of **Shenandoah Springs B&B** [$$$ to $$$$] (PO Box 770, Madison, VA 22727, ☎ 540-923-4300) also has views of the national park, as well as facilities on its grounds for horseback riding, fishing, swimming, canoeing, and cross-country skiing.

The cottage of **Rag Mountain Retreat** [$$$] (HCR 2 Box 196, Syria, VA 22743, ☎ 540-923-4973) sits in the shadow of Shenandoah National Park's Rag Mountain. The screened porch and wraparound deck let you enjoy all of this scenery.

About 11 miles north of Madison lies **Dulaney Hollow B&B** [$$ to $$$] (Star Route 2 Box 215, Etlan, VA 22719, ☎ 540-923-4470). Children are welcome to stay with parents in either the antique-furnished rooms or the rustic cabins. A country-gourmet breakfast complements the surrounding mountain view.

Rappahannock County & Area

On a working cattle farm in neighboring Rappahannock County, the **Caledonia Farm B&B** [$$$ to $$$$] (47 Dearing Road, Flint Hill, VA 22627, ☎ 800-BNB-1812) offers bikes, hayrides, lawn games, a hot tub, and a piano.

The 12 rooms at **The Inn at Little Washington B&B** [$$$$$++; rates start at close to $300 and climb from there] (Middle and Main Sts., Washington, VA 22747, ☎ 540-675-3800) have the only AAA five diamond-rated accommodations in the entire state. Each room is furnished with imported English antiques and lush fabrics. Fresh flowers, heated towel racks, twice-daily maid service, and afternoon tea with scones makes this a place that people return to again and again. Reservations need to be made as early as possible. The inn's restaurant has been named the country's Restaurant of the Year by the James Beard Foundation.

Leesburg & Vicinity

Look to the **Leesburg Days Inn** [$$] (721 East Market St., Leesburg, VA 22075, ☎ 703-777-6622) for some of the lowest rates in Virginia's horse country. Pets are accepted.

Northern Virginia

Other places to check into if you are watching the vacation dollars are the **Ramada Inn** [$$ to $$$] (1500 East Market St., Leesburg, VA 22075, ☎ 703-771-9200) or the **Best Western** [$$ to $$$] (726 East Market St., Leesburg, VA 22075, ☎ 703-777-9400). Both have swimming pools.

If you avoid the suites, the **Carradoc Hall Hotel** [$$ to $$$] (1500 East Market St., Leesburg, VA 22075, ☎ 800-552-6702) is in the same rate range. Although it shows a few signs of age, it is an interesting place to stay in that the hotel consists of a 1700s mansion and a connecting long structure with a white porch railing.

The exterior of the **Lansdowne Resort** [$$$$$+] (44050 Woodridge Parkway, Leesburg, VA 22075, ☎ 800-541-4801) was designed with inspiration from Frank Lloyd Wright. On the grounds of the 300-room luxury hotel are lighted tennis courts, an 18-hole golf course, and a 5,000-square-foot health club, complete with wooden lockers and trainer. Horseback rides can be arranged.

The six rooms in the 1769 Federal **Norris House Inn B&B** [$$$ to $$$$] (108 Loudon St. Southwest, Leesburg, VA 21075, ☎ 800-644-1806) are furnished with canopy, feather, and antique beds. The verandah overlooks an award-winning garden.

About 10 miles west of town in Lincoln is the **Springdale Country Inn B&B** [$$$ to $$$$] (PO Box 80, Lincoln, VA 20160, ☎ 800-388-1832). Once a boarding school – and a stop on the Underground Railroad – the B&B has reconstructed gardens and paths along a brook on the grounds, and is within three miles of the Washington & Old Dominion Trail.

The **Ashby Inn B&B** [$$$ to $$$$$] (692 Federal St., Paris, VA 22130, ☎ 540-591-3900) is a little farther south in the small village of Paris. Views from the rooms or dining patio take in the surrounding countryside. Guests have the option of dining in the adjoining restaurant. The menu changes, and choices can range from home-cured salmon gravlax to local wild mushrooms on toast or duckling with turnips.

■ Camping

Arlington County Area

West of Arlington, **Lake Fairfax Park** (1400 Lake Fairfax Drive, Reston, VA 22090, ☎ 703-471-5414) has a campground with 136 sites that are usually open from March through November. Providing recreational opportunities for local residents, the park has a swimming pool, playground, nature trails, and a lakeside beach. Small boats are available for rent to explore the 30-acre lake.

Alexandria & Vicinity

Close to Manassas, the 150 sites at **Bull Run Regional Park** (7700 Bull Run Drive, Centreville, VA 22020, ☎ 703-631-0550) are nicely shaded and fairly private. The 2,000-acre park has hiking trails, a swimming pool, showers, and a dump station.

Set on 888 acres, **Burke Lake Park** (7315 Ox Road, Fairfax Station, VA 22039, ☎ 703-323-6600) has more than 150 sites and some of the lowest rates you will find in the Washington, DC area. The park is open year-round, but camping facilities are usually closed from October to late April.

One of the few regional parks whose camping facilities are open year-round, **Pohick Bay Regional Park** (6501 Pohick Bay Drive, Lorton, VA 22079, ☎ 703-339-6104) has 150 tightly packed sites. While here you can hike the park's trail, swim in the pool, or rent a paddleboat or small sailboat.

Also open year-round, **Prince William National Forest Park** (PO Box 209, Triangle, VA 22172, ☎ 703-221-7181) gives you a number of camping options. Catering to self-contained travelers, the **Travel Trailer Village** can accommodate RVs up to 35 feet and has a dump station, snack bar, and pool. **Oak Ridge Campground**, which almost always seems under-used, sits at the far end of the park, is quiet and shady, and has flush toilets but no showers. More primitive is **Chopowamsic Creek Backcountry Area**, a hike-in-only area where you can have your choice of staying in designated sites or choosing your own

Northern Virginia

backcountry spot. No water or facilities of any kind are provided. Permits may be obtained at the park office.

Fredericksburg

The **Fredericksburg/Washington, DC South KOA** (7400 Brookside Lane, Massaponox, VA 22408, ☎ 800-KOA-1889) provides free weekday shuttles to the train station and puts together low-cost tours of Washington, DC. Facilities include a dump station, heated pool, and a playground. Paddleboats and bicycles are available for rent.

Only one mile from I-95 Exit 143A, **Aquia Pines Camp Resort** (3701 Jefferson Davis Highway, Stafford, VA 22554, ☎ 800-726-1710) also offers tour packages of Washington, DC. Additionally, it runs a shuttle bus to the Smithsonian.

West of Fredericksburg, the 47 sites of the **Rappahannock River Campground** (33017 River Mill Road, Chancellorsville, VA 22736, ☎ 540-399-1839) sit under tall shade trees. Kayaks and canoes are available for rent.

If you want to do some (free!) backcountry camping, drive northwest from Fredericksburg on US 17. Just after Morrisville, go west on VA 634, make a left on VA 637, and another left onto VA 651 to enter the **C.F. Phelps Wildlife Management Area** (1320 Belman Road, Fredericksburg, VA 22401, ☎ 540-899-4169). Like other such areas in the Commonwealth, it is maintained in a primitive state and used primarily for hunting and fishing. Primitive camping is permitted anywhere (except in a few posted spots) on the area's 4,500 acres.

Lake Anna

Rocky Branch Marina (5153 Courthouse Road, Spotsylvania, VA 22553, ☎ 540-895-5475) and **Dukes Creek Marina** (3631 Breakneck Road, Spotsylvania, VA 22533, ☎ 540-895-5065) are both located along the north shore of the lake. Each has launch sites and a convenience store.

Christopher Run Campground (7149 Zachary Taylor Highway, Mineral, VA 23117, ☎ 540-894-4744) sits on the south side of Lake Anna with a dump station, boat ramp and marina, plus a swimming beach, and camp store.

A few miles west of the lake, **Small Country Campground** (4400 Birdmill Road, Louisa, VA 23093, ☎ 540-967-2431) has a short nature trail, small lake, and a heated swimming pool.

Madison County

About two miles south of Madison on US 29, **Shenandoah Hills Campground** (Route 1 Box 7, Madison, VA 22727, ☎ 540-948-4186) has a pool, playground, dump station, camp store, and recreation room.

Leesburg & Vicinity

Being in a commercial area close to I-64, **Hillwood Camping Park** (14222 Lee Highway, Gainesville, VA 20155, ☎ 703-754-4202) is not the quietest of places, but it is almost within sight of Manassas National Battlefield. There are phone hookups, flush toilets, and a pool.

In the same vicinity, **Greenville Farm Family Campground** (14004 Shelter Lane, Haymarket, VA 20169, ☎ 703-754-7944) is on the grounds of a working farm. There are four fishing ponds, a pool, dump station, and swimming pool.

You have to hike almost a mile to reach the quiet backcountry sites at **Sky Meadows State Park**. You can choose from one of 12 designated sites (each with picnic table, tent pad, and fire ring) or stay in a shelter that was once a farm shed. A pump is at the site, but the water is not potable.

Adjacent to the state park, more than 20 miles of trails will take you to just about every corner of the 4,000-acre **G.R. Thompson Wildlife Management Area** where, except at parking areas or a few posted sites, you can set up your tent anywhere you wish.

Northern Virginia

Where To Eat

Arlington County

There is no doubt that the place to head for breakfast (served all day) is the **Metro 29 Diner** [$ to $$] (4711 Lee Highway, Arlington, VA 22207, ☎ 703-528-2464). There is also an extensive lunch and dinner menu.

The **Little Café and Bakery** [$$] (2039 Wilson Blvd., Arlington, VA 22201, ☎ 703-522-6622) features Mediterranean cuisine, with specialties from Spain. Live flamenco dancing.

A few blocks away you can enjoy live Greek entertainment and cuisine at **Aegean Taverna** [$ to $$] (2950 Clarendon Blvd., Arlington, VA 22204, ☎ 703-841-9494).

Chicken, beef, pork, and seafood prepared according to traditional Thai recipes is the specialty of the **Star of Siam** [$$] (1735 North Lynn St., Arlington, VA 22209, ☎ 703-524-1208).

Named one of the "100 Top Value Restaurants" by *Good Housekeeping*, the **Nam Viet Restaurant** [$ to $$] (1127 North Hudson St., Arlington, VA 22204, ☎ 703-522-7110) serves authentic and fresh Vietnamese cuisine.

Another low-cost Vietnamese restaurant, the **Queen Bee** [$] (3181 Wilson Blvd., Arlington, VA 22201, ☎ 703-527-3444) is so popular that you may have to wait awhile before being seated.

Sidewalk dining (weather permitting) adds to the ambiance of **Chez Froggy** [$$ to $$$] (509 South 23rd St., Arlington, VA 22202, ☎ 703-979-7676). Daily specials depend on the availability of fresh ingredients, but most people come – at least the first time – for the frogs' legs sautéed in butter and garlic.

Do not look for a fine dining atmosphere at the **Delhi Dhaba Indian Café** [$] (2424 Wilson Blvd., Arlington, VA 22201, ☎ 703-524-0008). What you will find is authentic (and low-priced) northern Indian dishes served on Styrofoam plates. Try the lamb or chicken kabob, which are cooked in tandoori ovens.

Alexandria

One of the stops you will be making on a walking tour of Old Town is **Gadsby's Tavern** [$$ to $$$] (134 North Royal St., Alexandria, VA 22314, ☎ 703-838-4242), so stay and enjoy a meal based upon tastes from the Colonial days. English trifle and Sally Lunn bread are just a couple of the offerings.

In a restored 18th-century warehouse, the **Fish Market** [$ to $$] (105 King St. at Union St., Alexandria, VA 22314, ☎ 703-836-5676) serves traditional seafood dishes, clam chowder, and crab cakes.

In the Torpedo Factory Food Pavilion, **Radio Free Italy** [$ to $$] (5 Cameron St., Alexandria, VA 22314, ☎ 703-683-0361) serves up wood-fired oven-baked pizzas along with other traditional Italian offerings.

The pub atmosphere at **Murphy's** [$ to $$] (713 King St., Alexandria, VA 22314, ☎ 703-548-1717) has made it a local favorite. Irish bands entertain evening guests dining on corned beef and cabbage, stew, and burgers.

Microbrews on tap and an innovative menu have also made **Bilbo Baggins** [$$ to $$$] (206 Queen St., Alexandria, VA 22314, ☎ 703-683-0300) popular with the locals. Look for daily specials such as grilled salmon topped with fiddlehead greens or regular menu items like chicken Queen St. and Bilbo's bread.

Also in Old Town is **Le Refuge** [$$ to $$$] (127 North Washington St., Alexandria, VA 22314, ☎ 703-548-4661), whose atmosphere is appropriate for the country-style French dishes it serves. Favorites are the bouillabaisse, veal Normande, and homemade pâtés.

You would never know from the bright decor and the quality of the French, Italian, and California cuisines that the building housing **Tempo** [$$] (4231 Duke St., Alexandria, VA 22304, ☎ 703-370-7900) was once a service station.

President Clinton and Vice President Gore have dined on the Cajun and Creole seafood at **RT's Restaurant** [$$$] (3804 Mount Vernon Ave., Alexandria, VA 22305, ☎ 703-684-6010), so why not you?

Northern Virginia

Fredericksburg

Breakfast is served all day in Old Town at the **Liberty Town Delicatessen** [$ to $$] (600 William St., Fredericksburg, VA 22401, ☎ 540-371-3344), which also provides freshly made soups, salads, and sandwiches.

A few blocks away, **Sammy T's** [$] (801 Caroline St., Fredericksburg, VA 22401, ☎ 540-371-2008) has an extensive selection of vegan and vegetarian meals, in addition to fresh soups, salads, and breads at bargain prices. Open for breakfast.

A classical guitarist serenades weekend diners savoring the Northern Italian cuisine of fresh pasta, seafood, and poultry at **Ristorante Renato** [$$ to $$$] (422 William St., Fredericksburg, VA 22401, ☎ 540-371-8228).

Head to **La Lafayette** [$$ to $$$] (623 Caroline St., Fredericksburg, VA 22401, ☎ 540-373-6895) for traditional French fare making use of fresh local ingredients.

Goolrick's [$] (901 Caroline St., Fredericksburg, VA 22401, ☎ 540-373-9878) claims to be the oldest continuously operating soda fountain in America.

It is only natural that trains are the decorative theme at the **Sophia Street Station** [$ to $$] (503 Sophia St., Fredericksburg, VA 22401, ☎ 540-371-3355), located in an old railroad depot overlooking the Rappahannock River. Offerings are from a typical American menu of burgers, sandwiches, and entrées.

Near I-95 Exit 130, **Allman's Barbecue** [$ to $$] (2000 Augustine Ave., Fredericksburg, VA 22404, ☎ 373-9881) is known for its pit-cooked pork barbecue.

South of town at I-95 Exit 118, Colonial-costumed waitresses at the **Old Mudd Tavern** [$$] (5144 Mudd Tavern Road, Thornburg, VA 22565, ☎ 540-582-5250) bring out traditional dishes of seafood, steak, and vegetables from a kitchen that also bakes its own breads.

Lake Anna Area

The **Lakewood Restaurant** [$ to $$] (5152 Courthouse Road, Spotsylvania, VA 22553, ☎ 540-895-5844) serves breakfast, lunch, and dinner and has a weekend buffet.

The **Anna Point Shoreside Café** [$ to $$] (13721 Lake Anna Lane, Mineral, VA 23117, ☎ 540-895-5353) and the **Lighthouse Carryout** [$] (4634 Courthouse Road, Spotsylvania, VA 22553, ☎ 540-895-5249) both feature fresh steamed crabs, shrimp, and burgers. They are open only seasonally.

Madison County

Madison County has a surprising array of dining choices for a rural area.

In town, **Beulah's Madison Cafeteria** [$] (Main St. at Washington St., Madison, VA 22727, ☎ 540-948-7131) serves up home cooking, both cafeteria and restaurant style.

Also in town, **Bertine's North** [$ to $$] (206 South Main St., Madison, VA 22727, ☎ 540-948-2463) features international and Caribbean cuisine with pasta, seafood, and steak cooked on hot lava rocks. The chocolate mousse pie is a good choice for dessert.

A bit lighter in fare, the **Bleak House Tea Room** [$ to $$] (Main St., Madison, VA 22727, ☎ 540-940-3645) has lunches and traditional teas.

You should head about one mile east of town on VA 230 if you want to grab a quick sandwich made on home-baked bread (or just want to try one of the pastries) at **Yoder's Country Food Market** [$] (☎ 540-948-3000).

South of town in Shelby, **The Bavarian Chef** [$$ to $$$] (Route 29, Shelby, VA 22727, ☎ 540-948-6505) has a German atmosphere and cuisine. Extensive selection of beer and wine.

North of town, reservations are required to partake of the fresh fruit, vegetables, and herbs used in the continually changing French menu that is accompanied by the establishment's own wines at **Prince Michel de Virginia** [$$$$+] (HCR 4 Box 77, Leon, VA 22725, ☎ 800-869-8242).

Northern Virginia

Leesburg & Vicinity

Green Tree [$$] (15 South King St., Leesburg, VA 22075, ☎ 701-777-7246) serves up a dish said to have been one of Thomas Jefferson's favorites (calf's liver soaked in milk). Other authentic 18th-century entrées include bread pudding and a beef dish called Robert's Delight.

More in line with the 20th-century palate are the rib-eye steaks and other grilled items at the **Potomac Grill** [$$ to %%%] (44050 Woodbridge Parkway, Leesburg, VA 20176, ☎ 703-729-4073), overlooking the open countryside and mountains of Lansdowne Resort.

Also in the resort, the **Riverside Hearth** [$$ to $$$] (44050 Woodbridge Parkway, Leesburg, VA 20176, ☎ 703-729-4073) has a health-conscious lunch and dinner buffet.

Inside a converted 1899 mill, the **Tuscarora Mill Restaurant** [$$ to $$$] (203 Harrison St., Leesburg, VA ☎ 703-771-9300) has been featured in a number of magazines for its extensive wine list and innovative menu.

With a bistro-type atmosphere, the **Lightfoot Café** [$$ to $$$] (2 West Market St., Leesburg, VA 22075, ☎ 703-771-2233) bakes its own bread to accompany a seasonally changing menu.

Drive a few miles south of town to The Plains in Fauquier County for a hearty country breakfast at **The Rail Stop** [$ to $$] (PO Box 337, The Plains, VA 20198, ☎ 703-253-5644). Also served are seafood, subs, sandwiches, and daily specials.

Fiddler's Green [$$ to $$$$] (right by the railroad tracks in The Plains, ☎ 540-253-7022), is one of the better restaurants in this area. Try their Sunday brunch.

Central Virginia

From the Falls of the James River in Richmond, west to the foothills of the Blue Ridge near Charlottesville, and south to tobacco farms along the North Carolina border, Central Virginia is the Old Dominion's heartland. There are no dramatic mountain ranges rising to meet the sky, but there is a quiet, serene beauty here, borne by a landscape of rolling meadows, hardwood and pine forests, and waterways wending their way through limestone and clay.

Vast acreages of publicly owned land such as those found in the Blue Ridge are absent, but more than a dozen parcels of state-owned property – state parks and wildlife management areas – let you explore the region on foot, bike, or horseback without treading on the rights of private landowners.

Some of the state's best boating spots are in Central Virginia. Most of the region's state parks – Fairy Stone, Bear Creek Lake, Holliday Lake, Twin Lakes, and Pocahontas – have small lakes perfect for a day of family paddling. Occoneechee State Park and Staunton River State Park sit on the shore of the state's largest inland body of water, John H. Kerr Lake. Also known as Buggs Island Lake, it has close to 50,000 acres of surface water and 800 miles of shoreline. Only 50 miles away and surrounded by the foothills of the Blue Ridge Mountains is Smith Mountain Lake, the state's second largest lake. Both have such immense areas of open water that sailboats are common. Long, meandering streams, such as the James and Appomattox rivers draw kayakers and canoeists with hundreds of miles of flatwater and occasional stretches of whitewater rapids.

Like the rest of the state, Central Virginia was the site of battles both major and minor during the Civil War. Richmond was the Capitol of the Confederacy during the war and, as such, was the North's prime military objective. Nearby Petersburg endured a 10-month siege as Union troops came ever closer to Richmond. Upon the fall of Richmond, Confederate President Jefferson Davis fled to Danville, making it essentially "The Last Capitol of the Confederacy." Brother stopped fighting brother and the

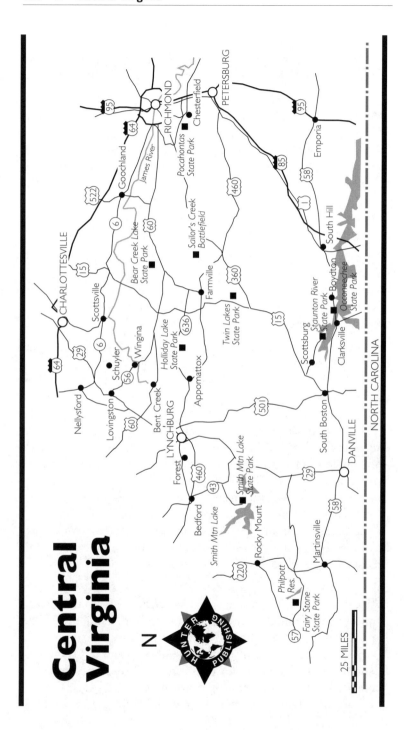

United States became one again when Confederate General Robert E. Lee surrendered to Union General Ulysses S. Grant in Appomattox.

Today the heart of Central Virginia is a tranquil, rural land of large tobacco, soybean, and corn fields bordered by cities. The capitol of the state, Richmond, has a population of well over 200,000 and maintains the Southern aristocratic sophistication of its earliest days. Danville is the tobacco and textile capital of the state, while Lynchburg, with several colleges inside its city limits, is a major seat of higher education. Once the home of Thomas Jefferson, James Monroe, and other prominent figures of America's past, Charlottesville is the site of the University of Virginia.

Information Sources

Appomattox Visitor Information Center/Chamber of Commerce, PO Box 704, Appomattox, VA 24522, ☎ 804-352-2621.

Bedford Area Chamber of Commerce & Visitors Center, 305 East Main St., Bedford, VA 24523, ☎ 540-586-9401.

Charlottesville/Albemarle County Visitors Center, PO Box 161, Charlottesville, VA 22902, ☎ 804-977-1783.

Danville Area Chamber of Commerce and Visitors Center, 635 Main St., Danville, VA 24541, ☎ 804-793-5422.

Farmville Area Chamber of Commerce, 116 North Main St., Farmville, VA 23901, ☎ 804-392-3939.

Lynchburg Chamber Visitors Center, 12th & Church Sts., Lynchburg, VA 24504, ☎ 804-847-1811.

Nelson County Division of Tourism, PO Box 636, Lovingston, VA 22949, ☎ 800-282-8223.

Petersburg Visitors Center, PO Box 2107, Petersburg, VA 23804, ☎ 800-368-3595.

Metro Richmond Convention & Visitors Bureau, 550 East Marshall St., Richmond, VA 23219, ☎ 888-RICHMOND.

Smith Mountain Lake Visitors Center, 2 Bridgewater Plaza, Moneta, VA 24121, ☎ 800-676-8203.

Pittsylvania County Chamber of Commerce, 38 North Main St., Chatham, VA 24531, ☎ 804-432-1650.

■ ■ ■

Getting Around

A choice of several airports makes it quite easy to fly into Central Virginia.

Richmond International Airport (☎ 804-226-3000) is served by a number of major national and regional airlines, with direct flights to such cities as Atlanta, Boston, Chicago, Dallas, and New York and connections to just about anywhere in the world. An inexpensive alternative is to fly into Washington, DC's **Reagan Airport** (recently renamed from National) and then have **Groome Transportation** (☎ 800-552-7911) deliver you to Richmond in a minibus for less than $30.

On the western side of Central Virginia, **Charlottesville-Albemarle Airport** (☎ 804-973-8341) is served by Comair, USAir, and United Express. Another option is to fly USAir or United Express into the **Roanoke Regional Airport** (☎ 540-362-1999) on the western side of the Blue Ridge Mountains.

On one route, **Amtrak** (☎ 800-872-7245) makes stops in Richmond and Petersburg. Stops on another route through Virginia are in Charlottesville, Lynchburg, and Danville.

Greyhound (☎ 800-231-2222) stops in Charlottesville, Lovingston, Amherst, Lynchburg, Bedford, Chatham, Danville, Appomattox, Richmond, Petersburg, and South Hill. **Carolina Trailways** (☎ 919-833-0627) makes stops in Richmond, Jetersville, Farmville, Keysville, and South Boston.

In the larger cities of Richmond, Petersburg, Lynchburg, and Charlottesville you will be able to **rent a car** from the major chains: Alamo, Avis, Budget, Enterprise, Hertz, National, Rent-A-Wreck, and Thrifty. Look to **Able Rentals** (303 West Church St., Martinsville, VA 24114, ☎ 804-632-9831) in Martinsville and **General Aviation** (Danville Regional Airport, Danville, VA 24541, ☎ 804-793-7033) in Danville for cars when in these smaller towns.

Touring

■ Richmond

The number and diversity of museums in the city can be overwhelming. You could easily use up weeks and weeks of vacation time without coming close to seeing all of the exhibits within the city limits. With something of a bias toward my personal favorites, I have picked out the six that are most deserving of your time and attention.

One of the best of its kind, the **Virginia Museum of Fine Arts** (2800 Grove Ave., Richmond, VA 23221, ☎ 804-367-0844) presents an overview of world art from ancient times to the present. The collection includes art nouveau, art deco, French paintings, contemporary American art, and an impressive assortment of art from Nepal, Tibet, and India. The museum also has the largest pubic display (outside Russia) of objets d'art created by Peter Carl Fabergé.

The **Science Museum of Virginia** (2500 West Broad St., Richmond, VA 23220, ☎ 800-659-1727) has more than 250 interactive exhibits on astronomy, chemistry, electricity, physics, crystals, aerospace, and more. Within its walls is the most lifelike motion picture experience you'll ever have. The films shown in the five-story Ethyl Universe IMAX Theater put you in the middle of the action. Scheduled presentations include *Alaska, Spirit of the Wild* and *Everest*. Pay whatever it costs – the experience is unforgettable.

If the raven's "Nevermore" still sends chills up your spine, get thee to the **Edgar Allan Poe Museum** (7th & Byrd St., Richmond, VA 23219, ☎ 804-697-8108) for the world's largest collection of Poe artifacts and memorabilia. One of the four buildings comprising the museum has a history of its own: The Old Stone House (ca 1736) is believed to be the oldest structure still standing within Richmond's original boundaries.

Make a visit to the 1812 federal-style **Valentine Museum** (1015 East Clay St., Richmond, VA 23219, ☎ 804-649-0711) to understand what Richmond life was like for Poe's contemporaries. Focusing not just on the lifestyle (wall murals, a spiral staircase, and grand furnishings) of home owner and attorney John Wickham, the museum has set out to provide a picture of all of Richmond's citizens – including that of Wickham's house slaves.

Smaller in scale, both in its physical housing and its number of exhibits, the **Black History Museum and Cultural Center of Virginia** (00 Clay St., Richmond, VA 23219, ☎ 804-780-9093), does an admirable job of preserving and presenting the history and culture of Virginia's African-Americans.

A dozen blocks away, and established more than 100 years ago, the **Museum of the Confederacy** (1201 Clay St., Richmond, VA 23219, ☎ 804-649-1861) houses the most extensive collection of Confederate memorabilia in the country. Through period clothing, weapons, art, personal effects, and historical papers, the museum documents the Southern leaders, major events, and campaigns of the War Between the States. There are also examinations of the everyday lives of the average Confederate soldier and those of both free and enslaved African-Americans.

Next door, the **White House of the Confederacy** served as the official residence of Confederate President Jefferson Davis from 1861 to 1865. Years of restoration have returned the mansion to its original Victorian lavishness. Admission to both structures costs close to $10.

Richmond's homage to the Confederacy and its leaders is exemplified by the number, size, and respect paid to the statues and sculptures on **Monument Ave**. Along this broad roadway you'll find stylized likenesses of President Jefferson Davis, Generals Robert E. Lee, Stonewall Jackson, and J.E.B. Stuart, and Commander Matthew Fontaine Maury. To insure that visitors un-

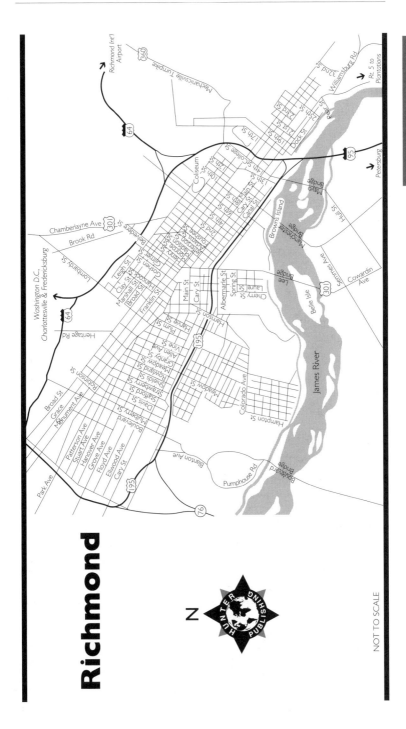

Richmond

NOT TO SCALE

derstood the importance the city placed upon the memory of Robert E. Lee, the governor of Virginia insisted the statue be at least as high as the one of George Washington in Richmond's Capitol Square. From this history of the avenue, it should be easy for you to imagine the controversy that arose when the memorial to tennis great Arthur Ashe was dedicated at the intersection of Roseneath and Monument avenues!

Confederate President Davis, along with two American Presidents (Monroe and Tyler), six Virginia governors, and two Confederate generals, J.E.B. Stuart and George Picket, are all interred in the **Hollywood Cemetery** (412 South Cherry St., Richmond, VA 23219, ☎ 804-648-8501). Maps marking the graves are for sale in the office on weekends; however, if you are truly fascinated by the history of these men and other people buried here, take part in the **Richmond Discoveries** (8620 Varina Road, 28233, ☎ 804-795-5781) guided walking tours – usually conducted on the last Sunday of each month from March through October.

As the capital of the Confederacy, Richmond was the North's prime military objective during the Civil War and experienced seven major Union assaults. The **Chimborazo Visitors Center** (3215 East Broad St., Richmond, VA 23223, ☎ 840-226-1981) is the best place to get an overview of the conflicts. Be sure to pick up the brochure describing the 60-mile automobile tour of the various sites which make up the **Richmond National Battlefield Park**. In addition to putting the battles into context for you, most of the sites, such as Cold Harbor and Fort Darling, have short walking trails to stretch your legs and increase your knowledge of history at the same time.

Stop by the **Richmond Convention and Visitors Bureau** (550 East Marshall St., Richmond, VA 23219, ☎ 888-RICHMOND) for a brochure that will direct you on a 1½-mile route taking in 10 historic sites, such as the John Marshall House, St. Paul's Episcopal Church, the James River, and the state capitol building. Be sure to go the 19th-floor **Observation Deck in City Hall** to obtain a bird's eye view of the city.

When the noise, hustle, and bustle of downtown become too much, escape for some quieter (and shadier) walking within the 80 acres of **Lewis Ginter Botanical Gardens** (1800 Lakeside

Ave., Richmond, VA 23228, ☎ 804-262-9887). Planned so that floral displays are ongoing throughout most of the year, the gardens' self-guiding tour snakes through seasonal growths of rhododendrons, azaleas, lilies, daffodils, Venus fly traps, pitcher plants, and many rare species of flowering vegetation.

Once the transportation lifeblood of the city, the James River and its environs serve as a recreational resource for Richmond's population. With five distinct sections, the **James River Park** (c/o Richmond Department of Parks and Recreation, 900 East Broad St., Richmond, VA 23219, ☎ 804-780-5695) can provide a number of spots for walkers, hikers, and bikers, as well as access to the river for fishing. The main section of the park is on the south side of the river along Riverside Drive. In another section, accessible from a parking lot on 22nd St., a staffed visitors center can supply information, a trail guide, maps, and interpretive literature and tours. A one-mile loop around the perimeter of **Belle Isle** is popular with both walkers and cyclists, while the 1.25-mile **Pleasant Creek Trail** winds through the Pony Pasture portion of the park, passing by tulip poplar, river birch, sycamore, and dozens of wildflowers in season. This is a favorite site for bird-watchers. A moderately easy whitewater canoe route also begins here. In contrast, other sections of the James River – as it passes through the urban Richmond landscape – has such challenging Class II-IV rapids that it draws skilled whitewater enthusiasts from around the country.

■ Petersburg

As the site of the last major decisive battle of the Civil War, monuments, museums, and battlefields continue to be the focus as you drive south into Petersburg via I-95.

A self-guided driving tour through the 1,500 acres of **Petersburg National Battlefield Park** (1539 Hickory Hill Road, Petersburg, VA 23803, ☎ 804-732-3531) can help put the 10-month siege of the city in perspective. At an outrageous cost in men's lives, Union General U.S. Grant began a relentless effort in mid-June 1864 to capture the city, which finally fell on April 2, 1865. (One week later the war came to an end when Lee surrendered to Grant at Appomattox Court House.) Among other sites, the Battle Trail – designated a National Recreation Trail in 1981 – swings by Meade Station (one of the Union's railroad supply spots), preserved fortifications, and Fort Friend. A side trail leads to The Crater, a 170-foot-by-60-foot depression made when the 48th Pennsylvania Infantry blew a hole in the Confed-

Petersburg

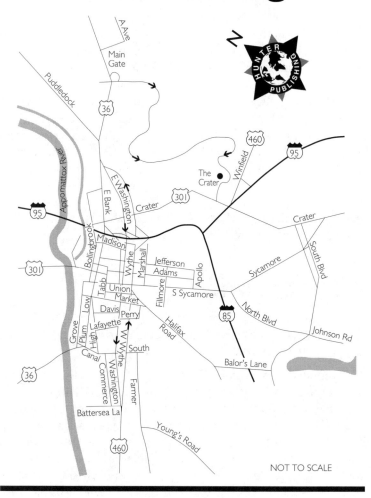

NOT TO SCALE

erate defenses with four tons of powder – after tunneling under the enemy's lines!

If you plan to spend more time touring Petersburg, your next stop should be the **Visitors Center** (15 Bank St., Petersburg, VA 23804, ☎ 800-368-3595) to pick up brochures describing walking tours of the town's historic districts, along with a Petersburg Pass. The pass will gain you admission to the **Siege Museum** (15 West Bank St., Petersburg, VA 23804, ☎ 804-733-2400) with its exhibits and films documenting the Civil War's longest siege, and the **Old Blanford Church** (319 South Crater Road, Petersburg, VA 23804, ☎ 804-733-2400), whose 15 original stained glass windows designed by Louis Comfort Tiffany were donated by individual southern states. Approximately 30,000 Confederate soldiers are buried in the adjoining cemetery. Also included in the Petersburg Pass is admission to the 1817 **Farmers Bank** (19 Bollingbrook St., Petersburg, VA 23804, ☎ 804-733-2400), the **Centre Hill Mansion** (Centre Hill Court, Petersburg, VA 23804, ☎ 804-733-2401), which showcases the creature comforts of the Southern lifestyle in the 1800s, and the **Trapezium House** (244 North Market St., Petersburg, VA 23804, ☎ 804-733-2402). The latter has no parallel sides or right angles because its owner, Charles O'Hara, believed the superstitions of his West Indian slave, who thought that such things could hide the ghosts of evil spirits.

On a lighter note, 137-acre **Appomattox Riverside Park** (River Road, Petersburg, VA 23803, ☎ 804-733-2394) has canals for fishing and canoeing and provides access to the rapids.

The **Pamplin Park Civil War Site** (6523 Duncan Road, Petersburg, VA 23803, ☎ 804-861-2408) is just off I-85 as you head southwest out of Petersburg. At the war site is a self-guided tour of the trench lines, fields, and earthworks the two sides fought over in the latter days of the war.

■ South Hill Area

Having left the heavy population concentrations of Richmond and Petersburg behind for the open land of the Piedmont, stop for a quick tour in South Hill. Side by side are the **Virginia S.**

Evans Doll Museum, with more than 500 dolls and carriages dating from 1869 to the 1980s, and a replica of the Atlantic and Danville Railroad (circa 1955) in the **South Hill Model Railroad Museum** (201 South Mecklenberg Ave., South Hill, VA 23970, ☎ 804-447-4547). During the season, tours of tobacco farms and warehouses originate from this same address.

Most visitors to South Hill are actually traveling farther southwest on US 58 to enjoy some swimming, boating, fishing, camping, and hiking at 50,000-acre **John H. Kerr Lake** (Route 1 Box 76, Boydton, VA 23917, ☎ 804-738-6143). Along with adjoining **Lake Gaston**, more than 50 miles of lake water straddle the Virginia/North Carolina border.

Facilitating an exploration of the area is **Occoneechee State Park** (Route 2 Box 3, Clarksville, VA 23927, ☎ 804-374-2210), named for the Native Americans who had lived in the area for hundreds of years. Taking general revenge against any natives they could find for Indian murders near Richmond, a group of Colonial settlers led by Nathaniel Bacon massacred most of the Occoneechees in 1676. The few survivors fled into what is now North Carolina.

Within the state park's 2,690 acres are hiking trails, a bathing beach, picnic shelters, and a campground. Two boat ramps allow access for motorboats, jet skis, water skis, and sailboats. Each year an increasing number of people are making the discovery that winds coming out of the west are ideal for sailboarding.

Also on land once associated with the Occoneechee Indians, **Staunton River State Park** (Route 2 Box 295, Scottsburg, VA 24589, ☎ 804-572-4623) occupies a peninsula of more than 1,000 acres stretching into the lake at the confluence of the Staunton and Dan rivers. Within the park is the site where – in April 1864 – a small Confederate group of old men and young boys held off an assault by 5,000 well-armed Union soldiers. In addition to the same amenities as Occoneechee State Park, Staunton River State Park has a swimming pool, housekeeping cabins, tennis courts, and designated mountain bike trails.

Staunton River State Park.

■ South Boston

West of Staunton River State Park, **South Boston Historical Museum** (801 North Main St., South Boston, VA 24592, ☎ 804-572-9200) houses the permanent collection of memorabilia relating to the area's history. Attracting much larger crowds is the .4-mile track at the NASCAR-sanctioned **South Boston Motor Speedway** (Route 360 East, PO Box 758, South Boston, VA 24592, ☎ 804-572-4947).

■ Danville

The tour continues west along US 58/360 to Danville, where there were once more than 30 water mills within the city limits. Still in operation, the Dan River Company operates the world's largest single-unit textile mill.

Rich farmland around the city has made it the country's largest market for bright-leaf tobacco and the self-proclaimed "world's best tobacco market." The method of selling piles of loose leaf tobacco by auction originated at Neal's Warehouse in the city in 1858 and today, from mid-August through November, visitors are welcome to watch the entertaining auctions in the city's six warehouses (which have a staggering combined space of more than one million square feet). If you want to understand the proceedings a bit better, **Tobacco Auction Tours** (635 Main St., Danville, VA 24541, ☎ 804-793-5422) can help interpret the auctioneer's chant.

Tobacco and textiles combined to bring copious amounts of money into the city near the turn of the 20th century. A walking tour brochure available from the **Visitors Center** (635 Main St., Danville, VA 24541, ☎ 804-793-5422) will take you through the eight blocks of **Millionaire's Row**, considered by many to be the pre-eminent collection of Edwardian and Victorian architecture in the South.

Confederate President Jefferson Davis and his cabinet fled to Danville as Lee retreated from Richmond; they heard of the General's surrender at Appomattox while staying in the Sutherlin Mansion in Danville. Today, the house is the **Danville Museum of Fine Arts and History** (975 Main St., Danville, VA 24541, ☎ 804-793-5644), which contains original and period furnishings and rotating art exhibits by regional and national artists.

Stars & Bars Dispute

The museum has been the site of an ongoing dispute over the display of the "Stars and Bars." Southern proponents insist – that to be historically correct – the flag should fly over this last capitol of the Confederacy. Opponents maintain it is nothing more than a symbol of slavery and racism.

The **Danville Science Center** (677 Craighead St., Danville, VA 24543, ☎ 804-791-5160) presents educational and entertaining science exhibits in an historic train station and is open seven days a week.

Danville

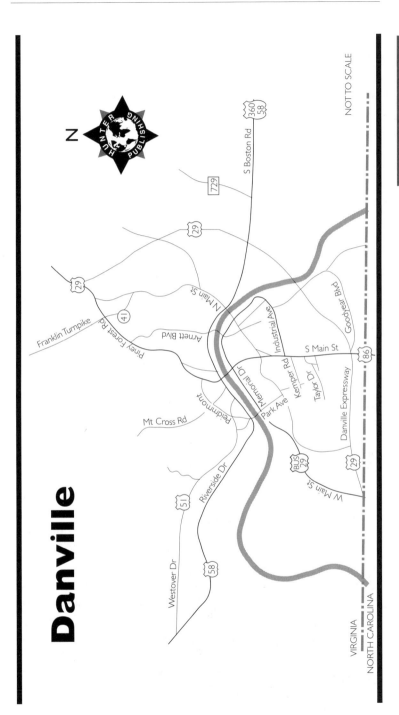

■ Martinsville

Driving west on US 58, the topography begins to change as you enter the eastern edge of the Blue Ridge Mountains at Martinsville.

Billing itself as "perhaps the world's most beautiful, comfortable race track," the **Martinsville Speedway** (PO Box 3311, Martinsville, VA 24115, ☎ 540-956-3151) hosts such stock car events as the Miller Genuine Draft 500, Hanes 500, Goody's 500, and the Winston Classic. The annual attendance at these loud, exhaust-filled events, in which vehicles go around and around the same course at high speeds for hours on end, far exceeds the number of visitors to all of the area's other attractions.

From the summits of the Blue Ridge Mountains to the beaches of the Eastern Shore, the **Virginia Museum of Natural History** (1001 Douglas Ave., Martinsville, VA 24112, ☎ 540-666-8600) does an excellent job of acquainting participants in its programs with what is truly special and important about the state – its natural heritage. Exhibits cover astronomy, oceanography, biology, and botany, with special displays focusing on exotic insects, volcanoes, Native American heritage, and dinosaurs (check out the life-sized ground sloth model and the computer-animated triceratops!).

Philpott Reservoir Area.

During the summer, outdoor recreation in the area is often centered around **Philpott Lake** (Route 6 Box 140, Bassett, VA 24055, ☎ 540-629-2703). Congress authorized construction of the lake, nestled in the rolling foothills of the Blue Ridge, in 1944 for flood control and hydroelectric power generation. Nearly 3,000 acres of surface water and over 100 miles of shoreline attract motorboaters, water skiers, sailboaters, jet skiers, canoeists, and kayakers. Close to a dozen campgrounds – some operated by the US Army Corps of Engineers, others by private concerns – reflect the lake's popularity.

Located on a western arm of Philpott Lake, **Fairy Stone State Park** (Route 2 Box 723, Stuart, VA 24171, ☎ 540-930-2424) is named for the cross-shaped staurolite stones found only in this area.

Tears of Fairies

A local legend states they are the crystallized tears of fairies who wept upon hearing the sad news of the crucifixion of Christ. Geologists say they are actually the result of intense heat and pressure produced during the formation of the Appalachian Mountains. Since you are permitted to search for and keep any of the cross-shaped stones you may happen to find on park property, it might be a bit more romantic to believe the fairy story.

Within the park's 4,570 acres are 168-acre **Fairy Stone Lake**, a bathing beach, a 51-site campground, picnic areas, cabins, rowboats, and paddleboats for rent. The lake has been known to yield walleyes and bluegills to anglers; catfish in the 20-lb. range are not uncommon.

▪ Bedford & Vicinity

Driving north from Martinsville on US 220, turn onto VA 122 in Rocky Mount to make a stop at the **Booker T. Washington National Monument** (Route 3 Box 310, Hardy, VA 24101). Although he only lived here for his first nine years, the national park service site commemorates the life of this important author and black educator who helped found Tuskegee Institute. A self-guiding tour follows the .25-mile loop **Plantation**

Trail through the historic sections of the park, passing by the original kitchen cabin (Washington's birthplace), smokehouse, tobacco barn, and blacksmith shed. Native plants and trees grow along 1½-mile-loop **Jack-O-Lantern Branch Trail**. This pathway winds through a wooded area which is very much as it was when Washington was growing up.

A few miles beyond the monument is a regional visitors center (2 Bridgewater Plaza, Moneta, VA 24121, ☎ 800-676-8203) whose staff can help you make the most of your time at **Smith Mountain Lake**. The lake was formed in the 1960s by the damming of the Roanoke River to generate electrical power for the Appalachian Power Company (now American Electric Power). A visitors center at the dam, just off VA 40 on VA 608, is full of hands-on exhibits and interesting audio-visual displays on how the lake was formed.

As with all such large artificial lakes, motorboating, water skiing, sailing, and fishing are popular activities. Yet I can't help but believe that the idea for the lake came from real estate developers as much as from the need for electric power. It is over 40 miles long, holds 20,000 acres of water, and has 500 miles of shoreline, but out of all of this, tiny **Smith Mountain Lake State Park** (Route 1 Box 41, Huddleston, VA 24104, ☎ 540-297-6066) is the only bit of land that is open to the public. Every other inch of shoreline has been turned into housing developments, private home lots, or commercial enterprises – restaurants, motels, bait and tackle shops, and more than 25 marinas. At the state park are hiking trails, paddleboat and canoe rentals, a boat ramp, and a campground. The only public swimming beach on the entire lake is here – all of 250 yards long.

Driving VA 122 north of the lake will bring you into the small city of Bedford, which lost more men in the World War II D-Day invasion than any other community in the United States. Among the first wave of soldiers to invade Nazi-controlled northern France were 35 Bedford soldiers; within the first 15 minutes 19 were killed and four more died before the end of the battle. Charles Shultz, creator of the *Peanuts* comic strip, recently donated a million dollars toward the construction of the city's planned National D-Day Memorial.

American Indian artifacts, Civil War relics, 19th-century clothing, photographs, a Benjamin Franklin printing press, and other exhibits in the **Bedford City/County Museum** (201 East Main St., Bedford, VA 24523, ☎ 540-586-4520) help paint a picture of its history.

■ Lynchburg

The tour now turns back to the east as you drive US 221 out of Bedford to **Poplar Forest** (PO Box 419, Forest, VA 24551, ☎ 804-525-1806), the home that Thomas Jefferson designed and used as his personal retreat. Restoration work on the octagonal house has begun and you can observe the methods archaeologists use to uncover bits and pieces of the plantation's history.

Home of Lynchburg College, Randolph-Macon Women's College, Virginia Seminary and College, and Jerry Falwell's Liberty College, Lynchburg serves as the cultural center of the western Piedmont.

Maier Museum of Art (2500 Rivermont Ave., Lynchburg, VA 24503, ☎ 804-947-8136), on the campus of Randolph-Macon Women's College, houses a permanent collection of such 19th- and 20th-century American artists as Thomas Hart Benton, Edward Hicks, Mary Cassatt, Winslow Homer, Childe Hassam, Jamie Wyeth, James McNeil Whistler, and Georgia O'Keefe.

The **South River Meeting House** (5810 Fort Ave., Lynchburg, VA 24502, ☎ 804-239-2548) traces the history of the early pioneer Quakers. Though they led the way in the settlement of Lynchburg during the mid-1700s, economic conditions – and their opposition to slavery – forced them to leave the area by the 1840s. The founder of the town, John Lynch, and several other early civic leaders are buried in the adjacent cemetery.

The **Lynchburg Museum** (901 Court St., Lynchburg, VA 24505, ☎ 804-847-1459) also highlights the story of the Quakers as well as other bits of city history.

Exhibits in the **Pest House Medical Museum** (4th & Taylor Sts., Lynchburg, VA 24505, ☎ 804-847-1811) give a completely different perspective on the past. Dr. John Jay Terrel had his medical office in the white frame building that has been con-

Lynchburg

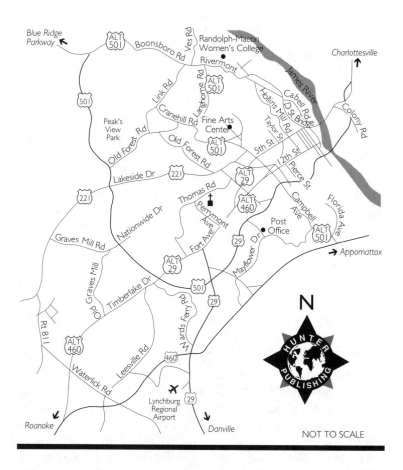

nected to a structure used as the Pest House quarantine hospital during the Civil War. A clinical thermometer, chloroform mask, hypodermic needle, operating table, and period furnishings demonstrate the standard of medicine in the latter part of the 19th century.

Saluting its ties with the James River, Lynchburg celebrates the **Bateaux Festival** each year in June. Costumed crews manning reconstructed bateaux embark upon an eight-day journey, recreating the days when the flat-bottomed boats were poled downstream to transport tobacco and other goods to Richmond.

■ Charlottesville

The tour takes its leave of Lynchburg by heading north on US 29 into Nelson County, where a short side-trip allows you to relive the halcyon days of a simpler life – as portrayed on television. Schuyler (pronounce Skyler) was the fictional setting for TV's Walton family, and **Walton's Mountain Museum** (PO Box 124, Schuyler, VA 22969, ☎ 804-831-2000) is located in the same building where series creator, Earl Hamner, Jr., attended school. You can step back in time to recreations of John-Boy's bedroom, the Walton's kitchen and living room, and Ike Godsey's store. Good Night, John-Boy; Good Night, Mary Ellen; Good Night, Jim-Bob; Good Night, Mama!

In the foothills of the Blue Ridge Mountains, Charlottesville was the home of a number of illustrious figures of American history. Thomas Jefferson founded and designed the buildings for the University of Virginia. The school's board of directors included Jefferson, James Madison, and James Monroe. Merriwether Lewis, who with William Clark explored the vast western lands of the Louisiana purchase, was born near here.

With its classical pavilions, spacious and smooth lawns, giant ancient trees, winding walls enclosing gardens, and close to 20,000 students, the **University of Virginia** (University Blvd., Charlottesville, VA 22902, ☎ 804-924-7969) helps set the cultural pace of life for the city. Tours of Jefferson's "academical village" originate in the Rotunda (inspired by Rome's Pantheon) and take in the oval chemistry room, the Rotunda bell once used to wake students for classes, the library, a room furnished as it would have been in 1826 when Edgar Allan Poe occupied it as a student, and the colonnaded Dome Room. If you wish to meander on your own, the visitors center in the Rotunda can provide you with the Academic Walk brochure, which takes in 22 points of interest on the campus.

Charlottesville was one of the first American cities to prohibit cars in a portion of its central downtown district. The result has been a thriving mall area full of restaurants, bookstores, theaters, and the **Virginia Discovery Museum** (☎ 804-977-1025), with hands-on presentations ranging from an 18th-century pioneer log cabin to an arts and crafts studio to a computer laboratory. The Fun and Games room includes bowling and giant checkers.

A few blocks off the Mall, **McGuffey Art Center** (201 2nd St. Northwest, Charlottesville, VA 22902, ☎ 804-295-7973) is where local artists and craftspeople have studio exhibits and sell their works.

On the outskirts of town is Charlottesville's "Triple Crown" of tourist attractions. Located on a mountaintop, and designed by our nation's third president, **Monticello** (PO Box 316, Charlottesville, VA 22902, ☎ 804-984-9822) is considered Thomas Jefferson's architectural masterpiece. Construction of the home began in 1769, but Jefferson continued to expand, remodel, and rebuild parts of the house for the next 40 years. Guided tours include 10 of the main floor's principal rooms where nearly all of the furniture and other items were owned by the Jefferson family. The seven-day clock Jefferson invented still works and is on display in the entrance hall. The tour also passes by the 1,000-foot-long vegetable garden and the restored orchard and vineyard. Nearby, Jefferson's gravestone is inscribed with his own words: "Here lies Thomas Jefferson, Author of the Declaration of American Independence, of the Statute of Virginia for Religious Freedom, and Father of the University of Virginia."

The home of America's fifth president, **Ash Lawn-Highland** (James Monroe Parkway, Charlottesville, VA 22902, ☎ 804-296-1492) is not quite as palatial as Monticello, but retains much of the feel of the early 1800s when James Monroe and his family lived here. Sheep, cattle, and horses are pastured in the open meadows and peacocks wander through boxwood gardens. Vegetable and herb gardens and living history demonstrations of spinning and weaving add to the atmosphere. The 535-acre estate is now owned by Monroe's alma mater, the College of William and Mary, and guided tours include the main house (with many original Monroe possessions), the overseer's cottage, smokehouse, and restored slave quarters.

Historic Downtown Charlottesville

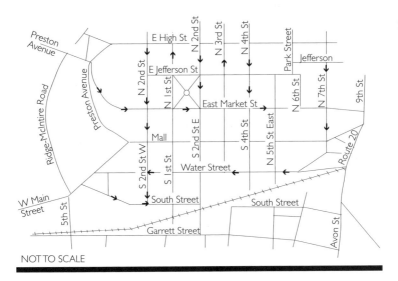

NOT TO SCALE

Almost within shouting distance of the above two estates is the **Historic Michie Tavern** (683 Thomas Jefferson Highway, Charlottesville, VA 22902, ☎ 804-977-1234). Originally built close to Monticello in 1784 to accommodate travelers with food, drink, and lodging, the tavern was moved to its present site in 1927. Featured in guided tours are the ladies' and gentlemen's parlors, a ballroom, private quarters, log kitchen, dairy, wellhouse, and smokehouse. Quite appropriately, the **Virginia Wine Museum** is located in the tavern's old wine cellar. Living history programs encourage visitors to write with a quill pen, join in a Virginia Reel, or drink a secret tankard recipe. Many visitors forgo all of this and simply enjoy a lunch of regionally renowned Southern cuisine served on pewter plates in the 200-year-old log cabin.

■ Appomattox

The tour turns south into the heart of the Piedmont and Central Virginia by following VA 20, US 60, and VA 24 to **Appomattox Court House National Historical Park** (PO Box 218, Appomattox, VA 24522, ☎ 804-352-8987), the site of Lee's surrender to Grant. A village of nearly 30 structures has been restored or reconstructed on the park's 1,700 acres to appear much as it did when the Civil War ended on April 9, 1865. Among those open to visitors are the Court House (now the park visitors center), Meeks General Store, Woodson Law Office, Clover Hill Tavern, the county jail, and the McClean House (a reconstruction of the private home in which Grant and Lee negotiated terms of the surrender). Walking the six-mile-loop **Appomattox History Trail** gives you a chance to meander by most of the major sites in the park, as well as to escape into some of its more remote and shaded spots.

Even more remote are the trails and pathways of nearby **Buckingham-Appomattox State Forest** (Route 3 Box 133, Dillwyn, VA 23936, ☎ 804-983-2175) and **Holliday Lake State Park** (Route 2 Box 622, Appomattox, VA 24522, ☎ 804-248-6308). In addition to hiking trails, picnic areas, campsites, and paddleboat, rowboat, and canoe rentals, a 115-acre lake inside the park furnishes boating, swimming, sandy beach sunbathing, and fishing opportunities.

■ Farmville

You can continue the tour by driving east from Appomattox on either four-lane US 460 or scenic Virginia Byway VA 24, VA 626, and VA 636. Either way, once you are in Farmville, pick up a tour brochure at the **Chamber of Commerce** (116 North Main St., Farmville, VA 23901, ☎ 804-392-3939) to walk through this small town of 19th-century architecture. You will encounter a city park along the Appomattox River and small locally owned shops and restaurants.

North of town, you can take a much longer and wilder walk on the 16-mile one-way **Willis River Trail** as it winds through **Cumberland State Forest** (Route 1 Box 250, Cumberland, VA

23040, ☎ 804-492-4121) and **Bear Creek Lake State Park** (Route 1 Box 253, Cumberland,VA 23040, ☎ 804-492-4410). Only 326 acres in size, the focal point of the park is its 40-acre lake. Paddleboats and rowboats can be rented by the hour or the day, while a ramp provides lake access for those with their own boats (no gasoline engines permitted). Local anglers come here in search of channel catfish, northern pike, crappie, and large-mouth bass. A 125-yard-long beach for swimmers and sunbathers, seven miles of hiking trails, a campground, and the only public archery range in Virginia's state park system round out the amenities.

Equestrians should be happy to note that south of Farmville, **Prince Edward-Gallion State Forest** (c/o Appomattox-Buckingham State Forest, Route 3 Box 133, Dillwyn, VA 23936, ☎ 804-492-4121) has many miles of gated and secondary roads open to horseback riders. Adjoining **Twin Lakes State Park** (Route 2 Box 70, Green Bay, VA 23942, ☎ 804-392-3435) has bicycles for rent to ride on designated trails and roadways. Also in the park, hiking trails encircle the two lakes, rental cabins and a campground enable you to stay overnight, rowboats and paddleboats can be rented by the hour, and a sandy beach is next to one of the lake's swimming areas. On an interesting historical note, the lakes were segregated from around 1939 to 1964, with rangers ensuring that blacks and whites were directed to their respective lakes.

East of Farmville, **Sailor's Creek Battlefield Historic State Park** (c/o Twin Lakes State Park, Route 2 Box 70, Green Bay, VA 23942, ☎ 804-392-3435) was the scene of the last major battle of the Civil War in Virginia. On April 6, 1865, Confederate General Robert E. Lee lost more than 8,000 men and a quarter of his supplies, forcing him to surrender at nearby Appomattox 72 hours later. Self-guiding pathways with stops explain the events of the day; reenactments and interpretive programs are offered at various times throughout the year.

The driving tour, which has taken in hundred of miles of the Central Virginia region, comes to an end as you return to Richmond via US 360.

Adventures

■ On Foot

Richmond & Vicinity

For a densely populated urban area, Richmond has an unusually large amount of land on which to roam. There are no areas large enough for long overnight hikes, but there is certainly ample room to stretch your legs.

JAMES RIVER PARK: In the James River Park (c/o Richmond Department of Recreation and Parks, 900 East Broad St., Richmond, VA 23219, ☎ 804-780-5695) you can combine the **Riverside Trail** with the **Geology Trail** for more than a mile of walking. In another section of the park, one-mile round-trip **Huguenot Trail** heads through a floodplain forest on its way to a favorite fishing spot.

MAYMONT PARK: A dairy farm turned into a 100-acre Victorian estate, Maymont Park (1700 Hampton St., Richmond, VA 23220, ☎ 804-358-7166) has about four miles of trails winding along magnolia-lined drives, through terraced Italian and Japanese gardens, into natural wildlife habitats and an aviary, and over hills to the James River.

HENRICUS HISTORICAL PARK: South of the city limits in Chesterfield County is a 1½-mile one-way trail in Henricus Historical Park (c/o Chesterfield County Parks and Recreation, PO Box 40, Chesterfield, VA 23832, ☎ 804-748-1623). Sir Thomas Dale established the town of Henricus in 1611, planning to build a major university. But an Indian massacre in 1622 brought the town to ruin. Running from a boat launch on the river, and with interpretive signs telling of the town's history, the trail has observation decks and viewpoints overlooking the James River.

POCAHONTAS STATE PARK: Less than 20 miles from downtown, Pocahontas State Park (10301 State Park Road, Chesterfield, VA 23838, ☎ 804-796-4255) is one of the most popular and largest state parks in the Old Dominion. The one-mile-loop **Ground Pine Path** has numbered signs keyed to an interpretive booklet available at the visitors center. Along the way you'll learn about wild grapes, loblolly trees, sensitive ferns, pawpaw trees, and running cedar. **Powhatan, Third Branch, Beaver Lake**, and **Awareness** are the names of the other trails totaling more than nine miles and giving you the chance to see an opossum, raccoon, or fox.

POWHATAN WILDLIFE MANAGEMENT AREA: Two areas west of Richmond can provide some primitive hiking experiences for those up to the challenge. Like all such areas operated by the state, their trail systems are rarely signed, marked, or well maintained. The office for the Powhatan Wildlife Management Area (Box 46, Farmville, VA 23901, ☎ 804-367-1000) is about 25 miles west of Richmond (four miles west of the town of Powhatan) on US 60. The staff there can provide you with a map of the area's approximately 13 miles of pathways and old roads. Interconnecting, they wind through 4,400 acres of piedmont forest land, providing ample opportunities for loop hikes.

AMELIA WILDLIFE MANAGEMENT AREA: The same is true of the approximately eight miles of trails and roadbeds in the 2,200-acre Amelia Wildlife Management Area (c/o Box 46, Farmville, VA 23901, ☎ 804-367-1000). It may be reached by driving west on US 360 from Richmond, making a right onto VA 609 in Amelia Court House, another right onto VA 616, and then a left into the management area on VA 652.

Outfitters

Blue Ridge Mountain Sports (1500 Midlothian Turnpike, Richmond, VA 23235, ☎ 804-965-794-2004 and 10164 West Broad St., Glen Allen, VA 23060, ☎ 804-965-0494) has all the equipment you may need to purchase for camping trips or hikes of any length.

South Hill/South Boston

JOHN H. KERR LAKE: Often overlooked as a hiking opportunity is the US Army Corps of Engineers' 7½-mile one-way **Eagle Point Trail** on the northern side of John H. Kerr Lake (also known as Buggs Island Lake). The beginning of the trail may be reached by driving west from South Boston on US 58 to Boydton for a turn onto VA 705. Follow this route for a little over four miles and bear right on VA 823 to the trailhead parking area. Isolated and not well used – but blazed – the trail winds in and out of coves created when the dam flooded the land, crossing over high points and fording several water runs. If you keep a sharp eye out, you just may discover evidence of human habitation from pre-dam days. The hike ends as the trail emerges onto a woods road to arrive at VA 705 (about three miles beyond the VA 823 turnoff).

OCCONEECHEE STATE PARK: The showpiece walking route in Occoneechee State Park is the **Plantation Trail**, wending its way by the ruins and old garden grounds of the former Occoneechee Plantation. About a mile long, the pathway is in a woodland of black locust, maple, cedar, and black walnut. Signs point out various sites and describe life as it was on the plantation in the late 1800s. Really just connector routes to various points in the park, the **Warrior's Path**, **Mossy Creek Trail**, and **Big Oak Trail** add another 1½ miles of walking treadway. The state park is reached by driving west from South Hill on US 58 and going through Boydtown and Finchley to the park's entrance on the left.

STAUNTON RIVER STATE PARK: Since most visitors to Staunton River State Park have set their sites on having fun on 50,000-acre John H. Kerr Lake, you will probably not see anyone – other than a lone fisherman or two – the whole time you are walking the **River Bank Trail**. The park is located on the site where the Dan River meets the Staunton River (known further upstream as the Roanoke River) and you will be walking along the banks of both waterways on this moderately easy 7½-mile loop. I have always enjoyed my walks here. Not only does the trail have the distinction of being one of the longest single pathways in Central Virginia, it also has wonderful views of the rivers and wildlife sightings can be frequent. Be on the lookout for ducks, geese, and herons in the water; deer, turkey, raccoon, snakes, turtles, and frogs may draw your attention back to the land.

The park's other pathways, the **Campground, Crow's Nest, Robin's Roost, Tutelo**, and **Loblolly Trail** are just short trails of no more than .6-mile, and connect the River Bank Trail to the campground, visitors center, and park roadway. The .6-mile loop **Captain Staunton's Interpretive Trail** has signs marking and describing significant natural and historical spots.

Danville

WHITE OAK MOUNTAIN WILDLIFE MANAGEMENT AREA: The White Oak Mountain Wildlife Management Area (Route 6, Box 410, Forest, VA 24551, ☎ 804-525-7522) borders the slow moving waters of the Bannister River. Like other wildlife management areas, most of the eight miles of walking opportunities here are on an interconnecting network of unsigned and unmarked pathways and dirt roadbeds. An exception is the **Hiawatha Nature Trail,** with interpretive signs winding close to the river for approximately one mile. To reach the area, drive north of Danville on US 29, make a right onto VA 640 for close to eight miles, and bear left into the management area on VA 707.

Martinsville Area

FAIRY STONE STATE PARK: For a state park in Virginia, Fairy Stone State Park has an amazing amount of land devoted to hiking trails – more than 25 miles of pathways in all. Actually more in the mountains than in the Piedmont, you can expect a great variety of terrain suitable for all levels of fitness. The moderately easy **Oak Hickory Trail** loops for 1.2 miles through a forest of rhododendron, oak, poplar, beech, and maple. The **Chipmunk Trail** and the **Little Mountain Falls Trail** are two of the more strenuous in the park, connecting with the **Deer Run Trail, Fox Path Trail**, and **Hawk's View Trail**.

You should feel comfortable about being in more isolated sections of the park before embarking upon the **Iron Mountain Trail, Whiskey Run Trail**, or **Stuart's Knob Trail**. Totaling almost four miles, the three pathways interconnect to take hikers by old iron mine sites, past azalea and redbud in bloom in the spring, and up to rocky Stuart's Knob.

PHILPOTT LAKE: The US Army Corps of Engineers has developed more than a dozen picnic, recreation, and camping areas around 10,000-acre Philpott Lake. Within a number of the areas are short trails – usually no more than a mile in length. A couple, such as the **Salthouse Branch Nature Trail** and **Smith River Trail**, have signs along the way interpreting the natural and human history of the area.

Bedford & Vicinity

SMITH MOUNTAIN LAKE STATE PARK: The 1,500-acre Smith Mountain Lake State Park is the only bit of publicly owned land on all of the lake's more than 500 miles of shoreline. Therefore, the park's trail system (about five miles total) plays an important role in acquainting visitors with the natural world around the lake. Consisting of two loops, 1.6-mile **Chestnut Ridge Trail** passes through a mixed forest of locust, sourwood, and beech trees, with running cedar covering much of the ground. Swinging by views of the lake and its inlet, the pathway passes the remains of an old tobacco barn whose logs still have mud chinking clinging to them. The tin roof and stove pipe are scatted across the ground and the drying rafters are still in evidence. The 1.3-mile-loop **Turtle Island Trail** has signs keyed to a brochure that discusses natural cycles and human use of the land. Each less than a mile, the **Beech Wood Trail, Lake View Trail**, and **Tobacco Run Trail** all bring you to viewpoints overlooking the lake.

Lynchburg

The city has developed three walking tours through its historic districts of **Diamond Hill, Garland Hill**, and **Courthouse Hill**. You can obtain a brochure from the visitors center (12th & Church Sts., Lynchburg, VA 24504, ☎ 804-847-1811).

BLACKWATER CREEK NATURAL AREA: One of the best hikes within the limits of any of Virginia's cities is the **Blackwater Creek Trail** in the Blackwater Creek Natural Area (c/o Lynchburg Parks and Recreation Department, Lynchburg, VA 24501, ☎ 804-847-1640). Crossing over a couple of swinging bridges and using a constructed boardwalk to cling to rock walls above a creek gorge, the 5½-mile trail is a hike that is just about as exciting as some you'll find in the best backcountry. Along with tramping through a forest of oak, hickory, beech, tulip, poplar, dogwood, mountain laurel, and an abundance of wildflowers, you just might happen to see a fox, a deer, or a family of wild turkeys. Branching off the main trail into two loops of one mile in total length are the **Ruskin Freer Trails**.

Appomattox & Vicinity

HOLLIDAY LAKE STATE PARK: Northeast of Appomattox via VA 24, VA 626, and VA 692, the **Lakeshore Trail** in Holliday Lake State Park makes a loop of a bit more than 4½ miles. The well-defined and moderately easy pathway rings the 150-acre lake set amid the rolling hills of the Piedmont. Crossing a number of tributaries, it provides a chance to watch beavers go about their busy work or to see great blue herons trawl the lake's shallow waters in search of a meal. Among other trees, the forest contains a mix of dogwood, white pine, red cedar, poplar, oak, and Virginia pine. You will also be walking by cattails, alders, and other moisture-loving plants along the shoreline. The other significant pathway in the park, the **Dogwood Ridge Trail**, is a short loop near the campground.

Farmville Area

TWIN LAKES STATE PARK: South of Farmville via US 460, VA 696, and VA 629, the two main pathways in Twin Lakes State Park – appropriately enough – encircle the two lakes. The shorter, one-mile loop **Goodwin Lake Trail** crosses a number of bridges, goes over the dam, and into an area inhabited by beavers. The longer four-mile loop **Otter's Path Trail** winds around Prince Edward Lake in a mixed forest of beech, maple, hickory, and white pine. Rising and falling – steeply in places – along the slopes above the lake, the trail passes through muskrat, beaver, raccoon, fox, and turkey habitat. Hawks, owls, herons, and wood ducks have been spotted around the lake. The park's other trail, the one-mile **Dogwood Hollow Nature Trail**, has numbered stops keyed to a brochure that explains the process of succession, that is, how the land has changed from the open farmland of the 1800s to the forest of today.

BEAR CREEK LAKE STATE PARK: Also within a short driving distance of Farmville is Bear Creek Lake State Park, within the confines of Cumberland State Forest. Drive north from Farmville on VA 45 to make a left onto US 60, soon turning right onto VA 629 to the park entrance. The five connecting pathways in the park have a total distance about five miles. The 1½-mile **Circumferential Trail**, as its name suggests, goes around the small lake. It is one of the park's longest pathways, and provides the best opportunity to observe ducks or watch a quail take flight. The easy 1½-mile **Lost Barr Trail** is an interpretive trail with the chance to learn a bit of natural history and lakeshore ecology.

■ On Wheels

Mountain Biking

Richmond & Vicinity

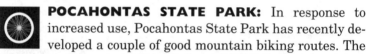

POCAHONTAS STATE PARK: In response to increased use, Pocahontas State Park has recently developed a couple of good mountain biking routes. The fairly easy, five-mile **Old Mill Bicycle Trail** begins at the visitors center and encircles 24-acre Beaver Lake. Local enthusiasts recently helped add another 10 miles, with separates routes for beginning, intermediate and expert riders. Signs direct traffic in one direction on all trails. In the meantime, don't overlook the network of more than 20 miles of old logging roads that have been signed and opened to bicycles in the acreage surrounding the main segment of the state park. The visitors center can supply you with a map to keep you from becoming disoriented; a park concessionaire rents bikes.

IRON BRIDGE PARK: Although small in size, Iron Bridge Park (c/o Chesterfield County Parks and Recreation, PO Box 40, Chesterfield, VA 23832, ☎ 804-748-1623) has more than six miles of designated mountain bike trails ranging from easy doubletrack to somewhat technical singletrack. Obstacles such as a few downed trees or stream crossings will keep you on your toes.

You may reach the park from Richmond proper by driving south on VA 10 (Broad Rock Road) toward the Chesterfield Airport. Road signs will direct you into the park, where there is a bulletin board with information and trail maps.

POOR FARM PARK: The Poor Farm Park (c/o Hanover Country Parks and Recreation, 200 Berkley St., Ashland, VA 23005, ☎ 804-798-8062) is probably the most popular mountain biking spot around Richmond. On nice weekends it is not uncommon to come upon dozens of folks enjoying the five-mile network of designated single track. The lay of the land makes it suitable for riders of all levels, from easy terrain along Stagg Creek to steep inclines and other obstacles designed to test your skills. The park can be reached by driving I-95 north of Richmond to Ashland. Follow VA 54 west to make a left onto VA 810 and enter the park.

Petersburg

PETERSBURG NATIONAL BATTLEFIELD: With names like Encampment Trail, Attack Road Trail, Jordon Point Road, and Battery Trail, more than five miles of dirt tracks connect in some way with each other and with the park's main roadway in Petersburg National Battlefield (1539 Hickory Hill Road, Petersburg, VA 23803, ☎ 804-732-3531). This opens up a whole range of possible rides that take you by some of the most important historical spots in the park. If you don't want to go off-road, blacktopped **Siege Road** is also a designated bicycle route.

Martinsville

FAIRY STONE STATE PARK: Although there are only two miles of designated, paved bicycle routes in Fairy Stone State Park, it should be enough to encourage you to exercise your calf muscles and explore the park's foothill terrain. (Route 2 Box 723, Stuart, VA 24171, ☎ 540-930-2424.)

Charlottesville

WALNUT CREEK PARK: Local riders put in well over 300 hours of labor and cooperated with the county park system to construct a five-mile loop in Walnut Creek Park. A wonderful ride through a forest of maple, dogwood, and rhododendron, the route has switchbacks negotiating steep hillsides, a picturesque lakeside portion, and ruins of farm life from days gone by. If all goes as planned, the park will soon have more miles of trails. You can drive here by taking US 29 south of Charlottesville, crossing I-64, and bearing left onto VA 708. Coming to VA 631, turn right for a half-mile to the park entrance on the left. More information about the park may be obtained from the Albemarle County Parks & Recreation Dept., 401 McIntire Road, Charlottesville, VA 22901, ☎ 804-296-5844.

Road Biking

TransAmerica Bicycle Route

More than 170 miles of the 4,100-mile TransAmerica Bicycle Route are located within Central Virginia. Marked by "Bike-76" signs along the highways, the route enters the region by dropping from the Blue Ridge Mountains at Rockfish Gap beside I-64 and US 250. Making use of lightly traveled roads for most of the way, it heads east, passing through or coming close to the communities of Greenwood, Whitehall, and Charlottesville. From there it passes by Virginia's famous landmarks of Ashlawn, Monticello, and Historic Michie Tavern. Continuing east, it passes through Palmyra, crosses I-64, and makes use of highway bridges to cross over several fingers of Lake Anna. Staying just north of Richmond, the route advances into Ashland, Mechanicsville, a portion of the Richmond National Battlefield Park, and Glendale. Here it enters the Tidewater region of the state – less than 65 miles from its eastern terminus in Yorktown.

Interstate Bicycle Route 1

Interstate Bicycle Route 1 generally follows the Virginia to Maine Bicycle Route. Marked by "Bike-1" signs along the highways, it enters Central Virginia in Hanover County and heads southwest through Chesterfield, Powhatan, Amelia, Nottoway,

Lunenburg, and Mecklenburg counties. Once across the state line, it connects with the North Carolina system of bicycle routes.

Richmond

Based west of Richmond, **Old Dominion Bicycle Tours** (3620 Huguenot Trail, Powhatan, VA 23139, ☎ 804-598-1808) puts together tours taking in just about every region of the state.

Martinsville

So scenic that it has been designated a part of the Virginia Byway road system, a one-way ride of about 35 miles rises out of Martinsville on VA 108. Crossing the Henry County/Franklin County line on VA 890, it passes through a pastoral valley surrounded by the Fork, Chestnut, and Turkeycock mountains. The ride ends at Penhook on US 40. (If you are still feeling energetic, five to six more miles of riding along VA 660 and VA 920 will lead you to Little Bull Run on the southern side of Smith Mountain Lake.)

If you run into any repair problems, **Severts Bicycle Repair Shop** (1046 Graves, Martinsville, VA 24114, ☎ 540-632-5709) should be able to help.

Charlottesville/Nelson County

Southwest of Charlottesville, neighboring Nelson County has developed three rides through its rural countryside.

South of Lovingston and Shipman, the 29-mile **Oak Ridge Loop** heads north from a designated parking lot on VA 650. Making use of VA 56, VA 639, VA 617, VA 623, VA 766, VA 624, US 29, VA 718, VA 651, VA 653, and VA 710, the ride takes in an extremely beautiful stretch along the Rockfish River and has a couple of country stores along the way to provide snacks and refreshments.

You can relive days of the past (at least as television portrayed them) and take in a bit of canoeing with an outfitter on the James River while on the 31-mile **Walton's Mountain Mu-**

seum Loop. From the museum's parking lot in Schuyler, take a counter-clockwise route by following VA 617, VA 693, VA 722, VA 602, VA 626, VA 627, VA 715, VA 719, VA 717, VA 630, VA 6, and VA 800.

Built in 1794, reconstructed in 1845, and still in continuous operation, the water-driven millstones of **Woodson's Mill** are the starting point for a loop ride of 24 miles. In a counter-clockwise direction from the mill, follow VA 778, VA 676, VA 56/151, VA 680, and VA 666. Along the way, there are shaded picnic sites providing access to wading pools in the cool water coming out of the mountains via the Tye River.

Outfitters & Information Sources

More information on all three of the above rides can be obtained by contacting the **Nelson County Division of Tourism** (PO Box 636, Lovingston, VA 22949, ☎ 800-282-8223).

Blue Wheel Bicycles (19 Elliewood Ave., Charlottesville, VA 22901, ☎ 804-977-1870) and **Blazing Saddles** (101 14th St., Charlottesville, VA 22901, ☎ 804-293-3868) can take care of your bike needs, either sales or service.

■ On Horseback

Richmond & Vicinity

DOREY PARK: With 400 acres, Dorey Park (PO Box 27302, Richmond, VA 23273, ☎ 804-672-5100) has several miles of trails open to riders. The park may be reached by taking Exit 195 off I-64 to Laburnam Ave., which is followed for three miles. Turn left onto Barbytown Road and continue for over a mile to the park entrance.

POWHATAN WILDLIFE MANAGEMENT AREA & POCAHONTAS STATE PARK: Horseback riding is permitted on the many miles of forest roads and unmaintained pathways of Powhatan Wildlife Management Area (Box 46,

Farmville, VA 23901, ☎ 804-367-1000). Equestrians are also permitted to use the forests roads and pathways of the portion of Pocahontas State Park (10301 State Park Road, Chesterfield, VA 23838, ☎ 804-796-4255) that is south of VA 655. The routes wind beside slow-moving streams and through forests of redbud, alder, sumac, beech, sweetgum, loblolly pine, and oak.

 Proof of an equine encephalitis test is required.

Charlottesville Area

On property situated along the eastern flank of the Blue Ridge Mountains in neighboring Nelson County, **Rodes Farm Inn** (Rodes Farm Drive, Nellysford, VA 22958, ☎ 804-325-8260) takes participants on trail rides, sunset rides, and – using English saddles – guided walking rides. Ponies are available for the kids.

Just west of Charlottesville there are miles of wooded trails ideal for first-time riders at **Montfair Stables** (Crozet, VA 22932, ☎ 540-823-6961). The stables also have riding lessons and half-hour, one-hour, half-day, and all-day guided trail rides, with overnight camping trips offered once a month from May through September.

Appomattox

HOLLIDAY LAKE STATE PARK: Surrounded by Buckingham-Appomattox State Forest, there are close to a dozen miles of bridle trails in Holliday Lake State Park. Your horse will have an easy time with the rolling terrain and you will enjoy a forest of cedar, poplar, Virginia and shortleaf pine, hickory, oak, alder, dogwood, and ash. The urge to sample some of the ripe huckleberries in the middle of summer may slow your progress.

■ On Water

Richmond & Vicinity

 JAMES RIVER: This may be the only spot in the country where you can have an intense whitewater raft experience while passing through an urban landscape.

Outfitters

The **Richmond Raft Company** (4400 East Main St., Richmond, VA 23231, ☎ 804-222-7238) is the lone professional outfitter licensed to take you on a guided trip down the Falls of the James and through the obstacles presented by Class II-IV rapids. Several excursions of varying lengths and difficulties are available and each trip is preceded by an orientation and safety session.

 Lone kayakers and canoeists also paddle the water of the James through Richmond, but the falls and numerous man-made obstacles make it imperative that you be accompanied by someone familiar with the river your first time out. Do not underestimate the difficulty of running the river here; many have lost their lives. Permits are required from the city when the water is running at high levels – some places become Class VI at such times.

Those looking for more of a flatwater experience should put in upstream at **Huguenot Woods**, but be sure to take out at the Williams Dam before entering the Class II rapids near Pony Pasture.

SWIFT CREEK LAKE: If you don't want to face the uncertainties of the open water of the James River, head a few miles south of town to the peaceful surface of 150-acre Swift Creek Lake in Pocahontas State Park. This close to a big city, you may be pleasantly surprised by the beauty of the surrounding scenery. Canoes and rowboats may be rented by the hour or day.

APPOMATTOX RIVER: West of Richmond, beginner paddlers can enjoy the Appomattox River from an informal put-in near Jones Lake on VA 609 to the take-out below the VA 604 bridge. The eight miles of easy water between the two spots passes through the **Amelia Wildlife Management Area**, so you might want to bring along some camping gear to enjoy a night beside the river.

Outfitters

If you are worried about your skills on the water, **Old Dominion Adventures, Inc.** (10210 Thor Lane, Mechanicsville, VA 23111, ☎ 804-559-5632) has group and private whitewater kayak and canoe instruction for beginner to intermediate levels.

West of Richmond, **West View Livery and Outfitters** (1151 West View Road, Goochland, VA 23603, ☎ 804-457-2744) rents canoes, paddles, and tubes, and will provide shuttles and orient you as to the possibilities along their portion of the James.

Adventure Challenge (8225 Oxer Road, Richmond, VA 23235, ☎ 804-276-7600) can help make you more proficient in whitewater rafting and kayaking, sea kayaking, and canoeing. They will also custom-design trips or tours for you.

Petersburg

LAKE CHESDIN: For those seeking a lazy afternoon's paddle, three trailerable put-ins give you access to Lake Chesdin, a few miles west of Petersburg.

APPOMATTOX RIVER: If you want a bit more of a challenge, make use of the wonderfully constructed canoe put-in just below the Lake Chesdin Dam for some Class I-III paddling on the Appomattox River. The first three or so miles are fairly easy, passing by old locks and allowing you to explore the placid water of an old canal system. Novices should probably bring their trip to an end at the VA 600 take-out; the next three miles into

Petersburg involve ledges and a portage (or a nasty ride) over a spiked dam before the take-out on VA 36 in Petersburg.

South Hill/South Boston

JOHN H. KERR LAKE: Virginia's largest lake attracts boating enthusiasts of all kinds. Water-skiers, sailboaters, jet-skiers, powerboaters, and even sailboarders zip along 50,000-acre John H. Kerr Lake's open waters. Canoeists and kayakers most often search out the hidden coves and inlets along its 800 miles of shoreline. Commercial marinas located around the lake rent a variety of watercraft.

Martinsville

FAIRY STONE STATE PARK: A concessionaire rents rowboats and paddleboats during the summer months so you can have a lazy day of paddling on the park's 168-acre lake. A boat ramp is available for those who have brought their own non-gasoline-powered watercraft. (Route 2 Box 723, Stuart, VA 24171, ☎ 540-930-2424.)

PHILPOTT LAKE: The hidden coves of nearby Philpott Lake enable canoeists and kayakers to slip off into quiet, isolated spots away from the scores of jet-skis, sailboats, sailboards, powerboats, and pontoon boats. A number of commercial marinas rent just about any type of craft you would want for exploring the 2,880-acre lake. (Route 6 Box 140, Bassett, VA 24055, ☎ 540-629-2703.)

Bedford

SMITH MOUNTAIN LAKE: Nearly 40 miles long, and with more than 500 miles of shoreline, Smith Mountain Lake has become a boater's vacation destination. Many folks bring their own sailboat, canoe, powerboat, kayak, jet-ski, or fishing boat to enjoy the water. If you don't have a watercraft of your own, **Captain's Quarters** (☎ 540-721-7777), **Campers Paradise** (☎ 540-297-6109), or **Saunders Parkway Marina** (☎ 540-297-4412) will rent you one. If you want to purchase one, **Webster Marine Center, Inc.** (☎ 540-297-5228) and **CB Rentals**

and Sales (☎ 800-203-7358) would like to talk to you. Information on the various regulations concerning boating on the lake can be obtained at the visitors center overlooking Smith Mountain Dam (☎ 540-985-2587).

Although families with lots of children are usually onboard, the lunch, brunch, dinner, and sightseeing cruises aboard the *Virginia Dare* (Route 1 Box 140, Moneta, VA 24121, ☎ 800-721-3273) can still be a romantic way to get to know the lake.

Located at the Virginia Dare Marina, **Smith Mountain Lake Kayak Company, Inc.** (1830 Blue Bend Road, Rocky Mount, VA 24151, ☎ 800-483-8026) provides all the equipment you need for a two-hour kayak tour of the lake. If you need lessons, morning sea kayak lessons are held Monday through Friday throughout the summer.

Smith Mountain Lake.

Lynchburg Area

TYE RIVER: North of Lynchburg in Nelson County, experienced canoeists and kayakers delight in nine miles of spectacular mountain scenery on the Tye River by putting in on VA 56 near Nash. High cliffs, interesting rock configurations, and steep slopes covered by heavy forest line the river.

 Be prepared for drops, narrow turns, and nearly continuous Class II-IV rapids for the first half of the trip; things mellow out a bit before the take out on VA 56 at Massies Mill.

JAMES RIVER: Northeast of Lynchburg there are more than 40 miles of the James River suitable for beginners and families wanting an easy float trip. Nothing harder than a Class II rapid will be encountered and you could easily portage around it. Be on the lookout for ospreys, great blue herons, ducks, hawks, wild turkeys, deer, beaver, raccoons, and more. In addition, small islands could be used as campsites for overnight trips. Boat ramps on US 60/VA 26 at Bent Creek, VA 56 in Wingina, VA 602/VA 626 near Howardsville, and VA 20/VA 6 at Scottsville let you decide just how long or short a trip you want to take.

Outfitters

James River Runners, Inc. (10082 Hatton Ferry Road, Scottsville, VA 24590, ☎ 804-286-2338) is one of the most respected outfitters in the state, renting canoes, rafts, tubes, and providing shuttles on the James.

Wingina Water Sports (717 Cabell Road, Wingina, VA 24599, ☎ 804-263-6671) and **James River Reeling & Rafting** (Main & Ferry St., Scottsville, VA 24590, ☎ 804-286-4FUN) provide basically the same services.

ROANOKE RIVER: South of Lynchburg along the Campbell County/Halifax County line, the Roanoke River (also known as the Staunton River) has numerous islands on which to camp, provides the opportunity for some fishing, and gives you a chance to see deer, turkeys, great blue herons, and ospreys. You can put in at a boat ramp on VA 761 at Long Island and take out at another boat ramp on US 501 at Brookneal – where a state fish hatchery produces walleye, striped bass, and channel catfish. Apprentice paddlers with a bit of experience (or someone to show the way) should be able to negotiate the 11 or so miles with Class I-II obstacles.

Charlottesville Area

RIVIANA RIVER: East of Charlottesville there is a moderately easy 17-mile stretch of the Riviana River which canoeists and kayakers of all skill levels can enjoy. A hand-carry put-in next to VA 729 near Shadwell gets you into the river. You paddle by farmland and low hills dotted with hemlock trees. Folks doing this trip often report seeing ospreys, turkey vultures, great blue herons, and kingfishers before taking out at the Virginia Game Commission's launch site on US 15 in Palmyra.

Be prepared half-way through the journey for a drop of about two feet along an old dam. (More advanced paddlers can continue downstream from Palmyra for another 15 miles to the James River, but should be prepared for some Class III conditions.)

Appomattox

HOLLIDAY LAKE STATE PARK: Unique to the state park system, Holliday Lake State Park has a self-guided aquatic trail marked by 10 learning stations on its 115-acre lake. Among other things, paddlers can learn about freshwater invertebrates, beaver dams, northern water snakes, and life in the lake's shallower waters. Paddleboats, rowboats, and canoes are available for rent by the hour or the day. (Route 2 Box 622, Appomattox, VA 24522, ☎ 804-248-6308.)

Farmville Area

TWIN LAKES STATE PARK: The combined surface area of both lakes in Twin Lakes State Park (Route 2 Box 70, Green Bay, VA 23942, ☎ 804-392-3435) is only 51 acres, so you are probably not going to spend days exploring here. Yet, the placid water and Piedmont scenery around the lakes can provide a nice, quiet day's worth of paddling. The same is true of the 40-

acre lake in **Bear Creek Lake State Park** (Route 1 Box 253, Cumberland, VA 23040, ☎ 804-492-4410). Rowboats, paddleboats, and canoes are available for rent by the hour in both parks.

WILLIS RIVER: Used by anglers, yet more often than not overlooked by canoeists and kayakers, the easy flowing waters of the Willis River through Cumberland State Forest will take you past some of the quietest 10 miles of scenery you are likely to find in Central Virginia. Check at the state forest office (off VA 628 in the state forst, ☎ 804-492-4121) for the most current conditions; most folks use one of the dirt forest roads for a put in spot and then take out beside VA 608 in Trenton Mill. If you want a longer journey, continue on to the James River for close to 10 more miles to a boat ramp next to VA 45 in Cartersville.

 Be vigilant for downed trees along any and all parts of the Willis River.

■ In The Air

Smith Mountain Lake/Bedford

 You are not only treated to spectacular views of the mountains during hot-air balloon rides with **Blue Ridge Balloons** (Route 2 Box 86, Wirtz, VA 24184, ☎ 800-519-6092), but also to the breathtaking expanse of the blue waters of Smith Mountain Lake nestled within the confines of the foothills.

Charlottesville

Having taken more than 15,000 passengers, **Bear Balloon Corporation** (231 Turkey Ridge Road, Charlottesville, VA 22903, ☎ 800-476-1988) flies every day at sunrise (weather permitting). Chief pilot Rick Behr flies one of the largest passenger-carrying balloons in America – over 11 stories tall and holding 24,000 cubic feet of hot air. The one-hour flights over the western Piedmont end with a champagne celebration at the Boar's Head Inn.

Hot-air balloon rides, airplane tours, and even flight instruction can be obtained through the **Blue Ridge Flight Center** (306 Bowen Loop, Charlottesville, VA 22911, ☎ 804-978-2114).

Where To Stay

Richmond

 Located close to the airport, **Airport Inn Motel** [$$] 5121 South Labumam, Richmond, VA 23231, ☎ 804-222-2828), **Econo Lodge** [$ to $$] (5408 Williamsburg Road, Sandston, VA 23150, ☎ 804-222-1020), and **Best Western Airport Inn** [$ to $$] (5700 Williamsburg Road, Sandston, VA 23150) have some of the lowest rates in and around Richmond.

In the northern part of the metro area is the no frills, but well-kept **Alpine Motel** [$ to $$] (7009 Brook Road, Richmond, VA 23227, ☎ 804-262-4798).

To be close to the downtown district, but still keep costs down, check into **Days Inn North** [$ to $$] (1600 Robin Hood Road, Richmond, VA 23220, ☎ 800-325-2525).

On the other end of the rate spectrum and in the center of town is one of Richmond's most famous landmarks, the **Jefferson Hotel** [$$$$$] (Franklin & Adams St., Richmond, VA 23220, ☎ 800-424-8014). Using a unique blend of Renaissance and other architectural styles, the hotel was built in 1895, fell onto hard times in the mid-1900s, and was restored to its magnificence in the 1980s with a $34 million renovation. Just walking into the colonnaded lobby, with its polished marble *Gone-with-the-Wind* staircase, tells you what your stay will be like here. The fireplace in the library is solid African mahogany.

The European-style **Berkeley Hotel** [$$$ to $$$$$] (1200 East Cary St., Richmond, VA 23219, ☎ 804-780-1300) caters to business travelers with quality furnishings and amenities.

Within walking distance of downtown's historical sites, the **Radisson Hotel Richmond** [$$$ to $$$$] (555 Canal St., Richmond, VA 23219, ☎ 800-333-3333) has a grand view overlooking the James River.

Also in the heart of Richmond, **West-Bocock House B&B** [$$] (1107 Grove Ave., Richmond, VA 23220, ☎ 804-358-6174) is an historic townhouse built in the latter part of the 19th century. Guest rooms have private baths, French linens, and fresh flowers.

In the Historic Church Hill District, the five rooms and two suites of the 1845 **William Catlain House B&B** [$$ to $$$] (2304 East Broad St., Richmond, VA 23223, ☎ 804-780-3746) are furnished with period antiques and have warming fireplaces.

Almost next door, the suites in **Mr. Patrick Henry's Inn** [$$$ to $$$$] (2300 East Broad St., Richmond, VA 23223, ☎ 804-644-1322) also have fireplaces, in addition to private baths and kitchenettes (which you won't have to use since the inn is also the site of a gourmet restaurant and English pub).

Once you find out about the hot tubs, fireplaces, private balconies, wine in the evening, and fresh cinnamon rolls in the morning, you may never want to check out of your waterfront room at **Uli Manor** [$$$ to $$$$$] (14042 Southshore Road, Midlothian, VA 23112, ☎ 804-739-9817) in neighboring Chesterfield County. However, you should at least take advantage of the canoeing there.

Petersburg

Less than 10 minutes from the national battlefield park, **Best Western** [$$] (405 East Washington St., Petersburg, VA 23803, ☎ 800-528-1234) permits small pets.

Clustered around I-95 Exit 45 are **Days Inn** [$$] (12208 South Crater Road, Petersburg, VA 23805, ☎ 800-325-2525), **Quality Inn** [$$] (12205 South Crater Road, Petersburg, VA 23805, ☎ 800-284-9393), and **Econo Lodge** [$ to $$] (12001 South Crater Road, Petersburg, VA 23805, ☎ 800-55ECONO). Each has a pool and exercise room.

Close to Old Town and only five minutes from I-85 and I-95, the Queen Anne Victorian **Owl and Pussycat B&B** [$$ to $$$]

(9405 High St., Petersburg, VA 23803, 888-733-0505) will let you bring your pet for a small additional charge.

Set on four acres and listed on the state and national registers of historic places, 1750 manor house **Mayfield Inn B&B** [$$ to $$$] (3348 West Washington St., Petersburg, VA 23803, ☎ 800-538-2381) has a 40-foot swimming pool and large herb garden to relax by.

South Hill/South Boston

For the lowest rates in South Hill, head for either the **Comfort Inn** [$ to $$] (918 East Atlantic St., South Hill, VA 23970, ☎ 804-447-2600) or the **Econo Lodge** [$ to $$] (623 Atlantic St., South Hill, VA 23970, ☎ 804-447-6985). Both accept pets.

Guests of the **Holiday Inn** [$$] (Box 594, South Hill, VA 23970, ☎ 800-HOLIDAY) have free privileges at the town's health club. This older, but well-maintained motel is built around a swimming pool courtyard.

Because the 1899 farmhouse is within walking distance of John H. Kerr Lake, the hosts of **Needmoor B&B** [$$] (801 Virginia Ave., Clarksville, VA 23927, ☎ 804-374-2866) have taken to arranging sailing lessons for their guests. If you don't want to skim across the water, you may make free use of the bicycles to explore nearby Occoneechee State Park or Prestwould Plantation, before a relaxing evening in the porch rockers.

West of the lake in South Boston, the **Days Inn** [$ to $$] (Route 3 Box 11, South Boston, VA 24592, ☎ 804-572-4941) and the **Super 8 Motel** [$ to $$] (1040 Bill Tuck Highway, South Boston, VA 24592, ☎ 804-572-8868) will usually have the lowest rates in the area.

Close to Staunton River State Park is the **Best Western Howard House Inn** [$$] (2001 Seymour Dr., South Boston, VA 24592, ☎ 804-572-4311).

When you stay south of town in the antebellum **Oak Grove Plantation B&B** [$$] (1245 Cluster Springs Road, Cluster Springs, VA 24535, ☎ 804-575-7137) the hosts are inviting you into the home built by their ancestors in 1820. Walking trails and small streams wind through the property's 400 acres.

Danville

A whirlpool, heated swimming pool, a free hot breakfast, and some of the lowest rates in town are available to guests of **Stratford Inn** [$$] (2500 Riverside Drive, Danville, VA 24540, ☎ 800-326-8455). Pets are accepted.

Five minutes from downtown and next to a large shopping mall, the **Howard Johnson Hotel** [$$ to $$$] 100 Tower Drive, Danville, VA 24540, ☎ 800-654-2000) is on a hilltop overlooking the highway.

Some of the rooms of the **Best Western** [$$ to $$$] (2121 Riverside Drive, Danville, VA 23541, ☎ 800-528-1234) overlook the Dan River.

About 20 miles north of Danville, a wooded country setting with formal gardens surrounds **Eldon-The Inn at Chatham B&B** [$$ to $$$$] (1037 Chalk Level Road, Chatham, VA 24531, ☎ 804-432-0935). On the premises is a gourmet restaurant staffed by a Culinary Institute of America-trained chef.

Martinsville/Collinsville

Basic, low-cost rooms are available at **Super 8** [$ to $$] (960 North Memorial Blvd., Martinsville, VA 24112, ☎ 540-666-8888) and the **Innkeeper** [$$] (Route 2 Box 565, Martinsville, VA 24113, ☎ 540-666-6835).

The **Best Western** [$ to $$] (PO Box 1183, Martinsville, VA 24114, ☎ 800-528-1234) permits pets and has an exercise room. The swimming pool is next to a quiet, wooded area.

In the mountains west of town and convenient to both Fairy Stone State Park and the Blue Ridge Parkway, **Mountain Rose B&B** [$$ to $$$] (Route 1 Box 280, Woolwine, VA 24185, ☎ 540-930-1057) has five spacious rooms with private baths, six porches, a spring-fed pool, and 100 private acres to roam.

North of Martinsville in Collinsville, the **Fairystone Motel** [$ to $$] (626 Virginia Ave., Collinsville, VA 24078, ☎ 540-647-3716) and the **Econo Lodge** [$ to $$$] (800 South Virginia Ave., Collinsville, VA 24078, ☎ 540-647-3941) consistently have the lowest rates around.

Pets are accepted at the **Dutch Inn** [$$ to $$$] (633 Virginia Ave., Collinsville, VA 24078, ☎ 540-647-3721), which offers a pool, whirlpool, sauna, and exercise room.

Smith Mountain Lake/Bedford

Campers Paradise [$$ to $$$] (Route 4 Box 50, Moneta, VA 24121, ☎ 540-297-6109) has rooms overlooking the water at Smith Mountain Lake.

The **Manor at Taylor's Store B&B** [$$$ to $$$$] (8812 Washington Highway, Smith Mountain Lake, VA 24184, ☎ 800-248-6267) is a resort unto itself. Originally built in 1820, the house has been renovated with luxurious amenities such as private porches, fireplaces, exercise room, hot tub, and billiard room. You can swim and canoe in the six spring-fed ponds within the estate's 120 acres – which are laced with hiking trails. You can even arrange to take off from the back lawn on a hot-air balloon ride.

Stone Manor B&B [$$ to $$$] (Rural Route 2 Box 268, Goodview, VA 24095, ☎ 540-297-1414) has a swimming pool and private boat docks on its 690 feet of lakefront.

If your stay at the lake is going to be an extended one, you should contact **CB Rentals & Sales** (12 Bridgewater Plaza, VA 24121, ☎ 800-203-7368) or **Royal Rental Agency** (Route 5 Box 113-A, Moneta, VA 24121, ☎ 800-296-SMLR). Both are agents for a variety of rental properties around the lake.

About 20 miles away in Bedford, the **Best Western Terrace House Inn** [$$] (921 Blue Ridge Ave., Bedford, VA 24523, ☎ 540-586-8286) provides basic, fairly low-cost accommodations.

You will pass through a covered bridge to take advantage of the pool, exercise room, horses, and walking trails at **Reba Farm Inn** [$$ to $$$] (3094 Sheep Creek Road, Bedford, VA 24523, ☎ 800-333-3574).

Central Virginia

Lynchburg

As to be expected in a city of 70,000 people with several institutions of higher learning, the choice of accommodations in Lynchburg covers the full spectrum of rates and styles.

There are no grand, restored hotels in the downtown district, but in the heart of town is the **Holiday Inn** [$$ to $$$] (601 Main St., Lynchburg, VA 24504, ☎ 800-HOLIDAY), with more than 200 rooms.

Strung along one of the main business routes are the **Best Western** [$$] (2815 Candler's Mountain Road, Lynchburg, VA 24502, ☎ 800-528-1234), and the **Lynchburg Hilton** [$$$ to $$$$] (2900 Candler's Mountain Road, Lynchburg, VA 24502, ☎ 800-445-8667).

The **Days Inn** [$$ to $$$] (3220 Candler's Mountain Road, Lynchburg, VA 24502, ☎ 800-787-DAYS) will provide you with free bowling privileges at the neighboring lanes.

The comfortable rooms are clean and well-cared for at the small, family run **Timberlake Motel** [$] (11222 Timberlake Road, Lynchburg, VA 24502, ☎ 804-525-2160).

Although it is located next to a shopping mall, some of the rooms in the **Howard Johnson Lodge** [$$ to $$$] (PO Box 10729, Lynchburg, VA 24506, ☎ 800-446-4656) have private patios looking at the Blue Ridge Mountains.

Magnificent woodwork, a huge grand hall, luxurious guest rooms, and a columned porte-cochère set apart the elegant Spanish Georgian **Lynchburg Mansion Inn B&B** [$$$ to $$$$] (405 Madison St., Lynchburg, VA 24504, ☎ 800-352-1199). It is located in the Garland Hill Historic District.

Sundried tomato quiches, garlic home fries, sourdough biscuits, and pecan coffee help you greet the morning in the **Once Upon A Time B&B** [$$] (1102 Harrison St., Lynchburg, VA 24504, ☎ 804-845-3561), the 1874 Victorian Mansion of Lynchburg's first millionaire.

North of town, children are welcome in the **Winridge B&B** [$$ to $$$] (116 Winridge Drive, Madison Heights, VA 24572, ☎ 804-384-7720), where you can stroll through the gardens or gaze onto the mountains from a hammock beneath shade trees.

In neighboring Amherst County there are many acres on which to stroll, bird- and animal-watch, or just enjoy views of the mountains at the **St. Moor House B&B** [$$] (1518 High Peak Road, Monroe, VA 22574, ☎ 804-929-8228).

Further north in Amherst County, grand vistas of the Blue Ridge Mountains enhance **Fair View B&B** [$$] (2416 Lowesville Road, Amherst, VA 24521, ☎ 804-277-8500), an Italianate-Victorian farmhouse with three guests rooms.

Charlottesville & Vicinity

If you wish to be close to the university, **Econo Lodge** [$ to $$] (400 Emmet St., Charlottesville, VA 22903, ☎ 800-424-4777), **Budget Inn** [$ to $$] (140 Emmet St., Charlottesville, VA 22903, ☎ 804-293-5141), and **Best Western-Cavalier Inn** [$$] (105 Emmet St., Charlottesville, VA 22903, ☎ 804-296-8111) can provide you with basic, lower cost rooms.

Adjacent to the university's medical center is the **Red Roof Inn** [$$] (13th & West Main St., Charlottesville, VA 22901, ☎ 800-THE-ROOF).

A bit further away are the **Holiday Inn-North** [$$] (1600 Emmet St., Charlottesville, VA 22901, ☎ 804-293-9111) and the **Quality Inn** [$$] (1600 Emmet St., Charlottesville, VA 22901, ☎ 804-971-3746).

If you are flying in, you should know that the **Double Tree Hotel** [$$$ to $$$$] (2350 Seminole Trail, Charlottesville, VA 22901, ☎ 804-973-2121) and its heated indoor and outdoor pools are close to the airport.

You can walk out of the front door of the **Omni Charlottesville** [$$$ to $$$$$] (235 West Main St., Charlottesville, VA 22901, ☎ 804-971-5500) and onto the western end of the downtown pedestrian mall.

Built by Thomas Jefferson's master craftsman, James Dinsmore, the **1817 Historic B&B** [$$$ to $$$$$] (1211 West Main St., Charlottesville, VA 2903, ☎ 800-730-7443) is also in the heart of Charlottesville, providing easy access to the pedestrian mall and the university.

Barely three miles from downtown are the 53 acres of the **Boar's Head Country Resort** [$$$$ to $$$$$] (PO Box 5307, Charlottesville, VA 22905, ☎ 800-476-1988) with its spa, fitness rooms, adjacent golf course, 20 tennis courts, and hot-air ballooning.

Just a short distance from I-64, you can wander through 40 acres of gardens or make use of the private pool, spa, tennis court, or lake at **Clifton-The Country Inn B&B** [$$$$$] (1296 Clifton Inn Dr., Charlottesville, VA 22911, ☎ 804-971-1800). Afternoon tea, in-room fireplaces, and an open policy on the cookie jar add to the relaxing atmosphere.

There are 70 serene acres on which you may roam at **The Inn at Sugar Hollow Farm B&B** [$$$ to $$$$] (PO Box 5705, Charlottesville, VA 22905, ☎ 804-823-7086). Weekend guests can enjoy family-style dinners featuring fruit and vegetables from the farm's organic gardens.

About 15 miles south of town, you can take easy walks on 50 acres of tranquil rolling fields at the **High Meadows B&B** [$$$ to $$$$$] (High Meadows Lane, Scottsville, VA 24590, ☎ 800-232-1832). The classic European auberge is known for its suites with fireplaces, tended flower gardens, complimentary Virginia wine tastings, and gourmet breakfasts.

In the same area, the **Deerfield B&B** [$$$$] (Rural Route 3 Box 573, Scottsville, VA 24590, ☎ 800-545-1744) sits on 200 acres overlooking the James River. You are sure to get personal attention here as there are only two guest rooms. In addition, the hosts can arrange a hot-air balloon ride from the front lawn.

Hot-air ballooning can also be organized through the **Palmer Country Manor B&B** [$$$ to $$$$$] (Route 2 Box 1390, Palmyra, VA 22963, ☎ 800-253-4306), about 25 miles southeast of Charlottesville. A swimming pool, five miles of hiking trails, and complimentary bicycles help you enjoy and explore the manor's 180 acres and surrounding countryside.

Appomattox

The **Budget Inn** [$ to $$] (714 West Confederate Blvd., Appomattox, VA 24522, ☎ 804-352-7451) has a pool, and accepts small pets. It's a good base from which to explore the national historic park without spending all of your vacation funds.

You can soak in the small-town atmosphere from the front porch, verandah, and deck of the in-town **Babcock House** [$$ to $$$]. The restored 1890s home has five guest rooms and welcomes children.

Farmville Area

Just about next door to each other at the junction of the US 460 bypass and US 15, the **Days Inn** [$$] (Route 15 South Box 714, Farmville, VA 23901, ☎ 800-DAYS-INN) and the **Comfort Inn** [$$] (Route 15 South Box 1740, Farmville, VA 23901, ☎ 804-392-8163) both have swimming pools. Restaurants are nearby.

North of town near Bear Creek Lake State Park, **Tranquillity Farm B&B** [$$] (Rural Route 3 Box 174, Dillwyn, VA 23936, ☎ 800-831-2492) has comfortable guest rooms, a fireplace in the sitting room, and well-tended grounds.

Southeast of Farmville, **Grey Swan Inn B&B** [$$] 615 South Main St., Blackstone, VA 23824, ☎ 800-509-3567) was built in 1902 and served as a social gathering place for prominent Virginians. The front porch looks out upon the streets of small-town America.

■ Camping

The campgrounds in the state parks of Pocahontas (near Richmond), Occoneechee (east of South Hill), Staunton River (east of South Hill and west of South Boston), Fairy Stone (west of Martinsville), Smith Mountain Lake (south of Bedford), Holliday Lake (close to Appomattox), Bear Creek Lake (north of Farmville), and Twin Lakes (south of Farmville) all have dump stations, restrooms, and showers (cold only at Smith Mountain Lake). Fairy Stone and Staunton River also have housekeeping cabins available for rent. Reservations for campsites or cabins may be arranged by calling ☎ 800-933-PARK.

Camping at Bear Creek Lake.

Richmond Area

North of Richmond, **Americamps/Best Holiday Trav-L-Park** (11322 Air Park Road, Ashland, VA 23005, ☎ 804-798-5298) caters to RV campers with a dump station, phone hook-ups, swimming pool, and recreation room.

Southwest of Richmond, the **Amelia Family Campgrounds** (9720 Military Road, Amelia, VA 23002, ☎ 804-561-3011) is a small, but well-maintained campground with a dump station, flush toilets, hot showers, and a swimming pool. A small grocery store also has a few limited camping supplies.

You can experience some (free!) primitive backcountry camping less than an hour's drive from Richmond in the **Amelia Wildlife Management Area**. Except for land adjacent to Saunders Pond and Amelia Lake, you are permitted to set up anywhere within the area's 2,200 acres. There are some great sites overlooking the Appomattox River.

Except within 100 yards of any creek or lake, backcountry camping is also permitted in **Powhatan Wildlife Management Area**, about 25 miles west of Richmond along US 60.

In the same vicinity as the wildlife management area, the 228 acres of **Cozy Acres Family Campground** (2177 Ridge Road, Powhatan, VA 23139, ☎ 804-598-2470) provides a bit more of a civilized experience, with phone hookups, flush toilets, swimming pool, groceries, and a coin laundromat. Note: By the time you pay the fee to stay here, you could add just a few more dollars and have lodging in a low-cost motel.

Petersburg

As with most of the components of this campground chain, the **South Forty KOA** (2809 Courtland Road, Petersburg, VA 23805, ☎ 804-732-8345) is fairly deluxe, with a dump station, phone and cable TV hookups, flush toilets, swimming pool, and campstore. Paddleboats and bicycles are available for rent, as are three Kamping Kabins.

South Hill/South Boston

Maintained by the US Army Corps of Engineers (Route 1 Box 76, Boydton, VA 23917) along the shores of John H. Kerr Lake are **Ivy Hill** (☎ 804-252-0903), **North Bend Park** (☎ 804-738-6662), **Rudds Creek** (☎ 804-738-6662), **Buffalo Landing** (☎ 804-374-2063), and **Longwood** (☎ 804-372-7112) campgrounds. Each has a dump station, flush toilets, drinking water, and a boat ramp. With 25 sites, Ivy Hill has the lowest rates, while the highest rates are at the 100 sites at Rudds Creek and the 55 sites in Longwood. Backcountry camping is also permitted around the lake, but you should contact the Corps of Engineers to obtain current information and regulations.

Danville Area

North of Danville, **Swan Lake Campground** (593 Keeling Drive, Keeling, VA 24566, ☎ 804-836-4880) has moderately shaded sites near the lake, with a dump station, phone hookups, swimming pool, and paddleboat and rowboat rentals. Nature and recreation programs are offered during the summer.

Also on a lake, but further north, **Elkhorn Lake Campground** (PO Box 160, Java, VA 24565, ☎ 804-432-9203) is family oriented and provides summer recreation programs and nature trails on its 580 acres. This is pretty much a self-contained resort destination with dump stations, cable-TV hookups, three swimming pools, a waterslide, and boat ramp. Boats and paddleboats are available for rent.

Except where posted, primitive backcountry camping is permitted throughout the entire 2,700 acres of the **White Oak Mountain Wildlife Management Area**.

Martinsville Area

Operated by the US Army Corps of Engineers (Route 6 Box 140, Bassett, VA 24055, ☎ 540-629-2703), **Horseshoe Point, Jamison Mill, Salthouse Branch**, and **Ryan's Branch** campgrounds are all on the northeastern shore of Philpott Lake, while **Goose Point Campground** is on the southwestern side. All of them (except no-fee Ryan's Branch) have dump stations, flush toilets, and hot showers. **Mize Point Campground** and **Deer Island Campground** offer a bit of a backcountry camping experience – as they are accessible only by boat. About two miles from the Philpott Park put-in, the sites on Deer Island have picnic tables, grills, pit toilets, and drinking water.

Bedford Area

Blue Ridge Campground and Marina (Route 2 Box 610, Wirtz, VA 24184, ☎ 540-721-FUNN) is a rustic 38-acre camp on the southern portion of Smith Mountain Lake with flush toilets, campstore, swimming beach, boat slips, and rental boats.

In the same vicinity, **Crazy Horse Campground and Marina** (Route 3 Box 392, Moneta, VA 24121, ☎ 540-721-2792) has full hookups, dump station, a swimming pool, general store, and restaurant.

Charlottesville & Vicinity

Close to Monticello, **Charlottesville KOA** (3825 Red Hill Road, Charlottesville, VA 22903, ☎ 804-296-9881) has Kamping Kabins, a large swimming pool, and a separate tenting area.

West of Charlottesville, the 47 acres of **Yogi Bear's Jellystone Camp Resort** (56 Safari Drive, Greenwood, VA 22943, ☎ 540-456-6409) includes nature trails, a basketball court, soccer field, theater, swimming pool, grocery store, and rental trailers and cabins.

Appomattox Area

Even more grandiose than its counterpart near Charlottesville, **Yogi Bear's Jellystone Camp Resort** (PO Box 478, Paradise Lake, VA 24522, ☎ 804-993-3332) is about six miles west of Appomattox. In addition to basic campground amenities, you can go swimming in Paradise Lake, rent rowboats and paddleboats, ride a miniature train, play miniature golf, or listen to a country and western band on Saturday nights during the summer season.

Where To Eat

Richmond

 If you are looking for something quick and fast, almost any exit off I-64 or I-95 will yield a number of McDonald's, Burger King, Kenny Rogers, Dairy Queen, Arby's, Kentucky Fried Chicken, and numerous other such places. However, to really appreciate what the city has to offer, slow down a bit to partake of its diverse ethnic dining adventures.

Richmond was the capitol of the South during the Civil War, and for some good ol' Southern cooking head to the **Black-Eyed Pea** [$ to $$] (9498 West Broad St., Richmond, VA 23060, ☎ 804-762-4821), part of a small chain of restaurants. Roasted chicken, meat loaf, and pot roast are accompanied by well-cooked vegetables and fresh cornbread.

A few blocks away on the same street, **McCleans Restaurant** [$] (4001 West Broad St., Richmond, VA 23220, ☎ 804-358-0369) is busy with customers coming in for "The Biggest Breakfast in Town." Grits, buckwheat pancakes, country ham, biscuits, and even roe and eggs are served in large portions. Lunch and dinner feature meat loaf and bean soup.

Southern Culture [$ to $$] (2229 West Main St., Richmond, VA 23224, ☎ 804-355-6939) can take your culinary journey a little farther south with things Cajun, such as jumbalaya with chicken, shrimp, and andouille sausage. The menu also has a few Mexican and Caribbean entrées.

Just down the street is a mix that may exist nowhere else in the world, the **Texas-Wisconsin Border Café** [$] (1501 West Main St., Richmond, VA 23224, ☎ 804-353-6860). This intimate spot serves everything from Texas chili to German- and Polish-influenced Wisconsin keilbasa, bratwurst, and potato cakes.

In a former grain house in the downtown historic district, **Matt's British Pub** [$$] (109 South 12th St., Richmond, VA 23220, ☎ 804-644-0848) will take you across the Atlantic with items such as steak and mushroom pie.

It is easy to imagine yourself sitting at a sidewalk table looking up to the Eiffel Tower as you dine upon the quiches, crêpes, and savory and sweet tarts of the **Café de Paris** [$$] (7003 Chopt Road, Richmond, VA 23226, ☎ 804-673-7330).

Franco's Ristorante [$$ to $$$] (9031 West Broad St., Richmond, VA 23294, ☎ 804-270-9124) brings both Northern and Southern Italian cooking to the city. Besides the traditional fra diavolos, fettucines, and Parmigianas, there is an additional menu that varies with the seasons.

Authentic cuisine is the draw of **Passage to India** [$ to $$] (6856 Midlothian Turnpike, Richmond, VA 23225, ☎ 804-745-5291), a favorite with magazine and newspaper food critics. After specifying how hot or mild you want your curry, choose from pakoras, samosas, and roasted meats and tandoori-baked dishes served with basmati rice. A number of meatless entrées are available.

Vegetarians will also have a good time with the French-influenced Vietnamese **Indochine** [$ to $$] (2923 West Cary St., Richmond, VA 23221, ☎ 804-353-5799), where the extensive list of stir-fry items can be prepared sans meat. The entrées are a bit milder and more subtle than traditional Vietnamese fare.

Central Virginia

The original vegetarian spot in Richmond is the **Grace Place** [$ to $$] (826 West Grace St., Richmond, VA 23220, ☎ 804-353-3680). It's certainly not upscale dining, but the healthy rice, bean, and grain entrées, along with crisp salads, soups, and fresh-baked desserts, will keep your heart in good shape and ready to tackle your next adventure.

On the other end of the spectrum, quite upscale, a bit uptight, and maintaining a dress code, **The Tobacco Company** [$$ to $$$] (1201 Cary St., Richmond, VA 23220, ☎ 804-782-9431) attracts urban professionals and business travelers. Three levels inside an 1800s tobacco warehouse are decorated with Tiffany lamps and overstuffed sofas and chairs. Beef, seafood, and a thorough selection of salads are often accompanied with drinks from the bar.

Petersburg

About midway between Richmond and Petersburg, **Half Way House** [$$ to $$$] (10301 Jefferson Davis Highway, ☎ 804-275-1760) is in a 1760 manor house that was a stop on the Petersburg stagecoach line. It is not known if they ate the lobster, filet mignon, or the chicken and beef pot pies, but George Washington, Marquis de Lafayette, Thomas Jefferson, and Patrick Henry were all guests here. An extensive array of antiques add to the atmosphere.

Serving breakfast, lunch, and dinner in an older part of town, **Alexander's** [$] (101 West Bank St., Petersburg, VA 23803, ☎ 804-733-7134) has an Italian, Greek, and American menu featuring Athenian chicken and veal a la Greca.

A huge brick fireplace filled with hickory coals slowly smoking the beef and pork barbecue is the focal point of **King's Barbeque** [$ to $$] (3221 West Washington St., Petersburg, VA 23805, ☎ 804-732-5861). Have your barbecue minced or sliced, or choose fried chicken and/or homemade apple pie.

Close to a complex of motels by the interstate, **Pumpkin's Restaurant** [$ to $$] (12204 South Crater St., Petersburg, VA 23805, ☎ 804-732-4444) is family-oriented with a children's menu available.

Danville

A AAA three-diamond restaurant, **Stratford Inn** [$$] (2500 Riverside Drive, Danville, VA 24540, ☎ 804-793-2500) is a popular local spot, with a live Maine lobster tank, large salad bar, some Italian selections, and a Sunday brunch. Desserts are homemade; the date nut cream pie is outstanding.

As the name implies, **Bogie's** [$ to $$] (927 South Main St., Danville, VA 24541, ☎ 804-793-4571) is decorated with memorabilia from the days of Humphrey Bogart films. The bourbon-marinated steak is the evening special, while lunch is usually a bit lighter. A children's menu is also available in this casual dining spot near downtown.

Lynchburg

Consistently rated as one of the nicest restaurants in town, **Café France** [$ to $$$] (3225 Old Forest Road, Lynchburg, VA 24502, ☎ 804-385-8989) prepares a choice of daily specials using fresh vegetables, seafood, lamb, veal, and beef. The house specialty is pasta in a variety of forms. Excellent selection of wines.

Bull's Steakhouse [$$] (300 Graves Mill Center, Lynchburg, VA 24551, ☎ 804-385-7581) holds no surprises, but does well with its steak, prime rib, chicken, and fajitas.

Crown Sterling [$$ to $$$] (6120 Fort Ave., Lynchburg, VA 24502, ☎ 804-239-7744) also specializes in steaks, but theirs are charcoal cooked; fireplaces and candles add to an atmosphere that is a bit more upscale.

Getting away from heavy beef, the **East Side Crab Shack** [$$] (4716 Richmond Ave., Lynchburg, VA 24506, ☎ 804-528-0080) may make you think you have slipped off to the Eastern Shore when you try their Maryland-style steamed crabs.

Candlelight and food served with a French inspiration – such as tableside flambés and freshly prepared pastries – should make you forget that **Emil's** [$ to $$] (Boonsboro Shopping Center, Lynchburg, VA 24503, ☎ 804-384-3311) is in a shopping complex.

Just a few doors down, the gourmet pizzas at **Meriwether's** [$$ to $$$] (Boonsboro Shopping Center, Lynchburg, VA 24503, ☎ 804-384-3311) may make you vow never to call Domino's again. A great wine list complements other menu items like pastas and daily rotisserie specials.

Open only for lunch, **The Farm Basket** [$] (2008 Langhorne Road, Lynchburg, VA 24502, ☎ 804-528-1107) draws many of its fresh ingredients from the adjacent fruit and vegetable stand. Large picture windows overlook the outside deck which, in turn, sits above a bubbling small brook.

Charlottesville

Once a slave house, the dining room at **Historic Michie Tavern** [$] (683 Thomas Jefferson Highway, Charlottesville, VA 22902, ☎ 804-977-1234) serves a Colonial buffet of fried chicken, stewed tomatoes, black-eyed peas, green bean salad, biscuits, and apple cobbler from 11AM to 3 pm. To complement the atmosphere, plates and utensils are made of pewter and servers are dressed in period attire.

In addition to the usual heavy Swiss and German cuisines, **The Schnitzelhouse Restaurant** [$ to $$$] 2208 Fontain Ave., Charlottesville, VA 22903, ☎ 804-293-7185) has a number of healthy items on its menu.

Rococo's [$ to $$] (2001 Commonwealth Drive, Charlottesville, VA 22901, ☎ 804-971-7371) is not just a run-of-the-mill Italian eatery. In addition to the expected fettucine, ravioli, calzones, stromboli, and homemade pasta entrées, creative dishes – such as mesquite-grilled chicken marinated in balsamic vinegar and rosemary and a gourmet pizza topped with white cheese and pesto – are also offered.

Within the old downtown train depot, the **C&O Restaurant** [$$ to $$$] (515 East Water St., Charlottesville, VA 22901, ☎ 804-971-7044) has such a knowledgeable staff serving the innovative French cooking that it has been praised by food critics in *Bon Appetit* magazine.

Inside the Omni Hotel at the western end of the downtown pedestrian mall, **A Virginia Wine Country Restaurant** [$$ to

$$$] (235 West Main St., Charlottesville, VA 22902, ☎ 804-971-5500) has regional cuisine of grilled salmon, Black Angus beef, portobello mushrooms, and a well-respected crab soup.

North of Charlottesville in an old log building constructed by Hessian prisoners during the Revolutionary War, the **Silver Thatch Inn** [$$ to $$$] (3001 Hollymead Drive, Charlottesville, VA 22911, ☎ 804-978-4686) features a modern American cuisine of grilled meats and fish entrées served with healthy and eclectic sauces. Innovative vegetarian specials and homemade desserts are other attractions.

Wonderful vegetarian dishes are available from the authentic Indian menu at **Maharaja** [$$] (139 Zan Road, Charlottesville, VA 22901, ☎ 804-973-1110). The restaurant's Indian clay oven is also used to turn out curry and tandoori dishes of chicken, shrimp, and fish.

You would be hard-pressed to find a University of Virginia student who has not been to the **Blue Bird Café** [$ to $$] (625 West Main St., Charlottesville, VA 22902, ☎ 804-295-1166) for some fresh seafood, veal, or pasta accompanied by a choice of microbrewed beers.

Students are also often found just down the street for breakfast at **The Coffee Exchange** [$] (120 East Main St., Charlottesville, VA 22901, ☎ 804-295-0975). The popular baked goods are often sold out by midday.

Billing itself as Virginia's first restaurant/brewery, **Blue Ridge Brewing Co.**, [$$] (709 West Main St., Charlottesville, VA 22902, ☎ 804-977-0017) creates Hawksbill Lager, Piney River Lager, Afton Ale, and Humpback Stout on the premises. Thai pork chops, bourbon steak, and pesto lasagna are served for lunch and dinner.

Farmville

In a renovated warehouse overlooking the Appomattox River, **Charley's Waterfront Café** [$ to $$] (201 B Mill St., Farmville, VA 23901, ☎ 804-392-1566) has a children's menu, Sunday brunch, and a Wednesday night Italian buffet.

Who would expect that in out-of-the-way Farmville **The Silk Road Restaurant** [$ to $$] (2104 South Main St., Farmville, 23901, ☎ 804-392-8351) would feature a menu of American, Chinese, and Afghan dishes? Daily lunch and supper buffets permit you to sample a bit of everything.

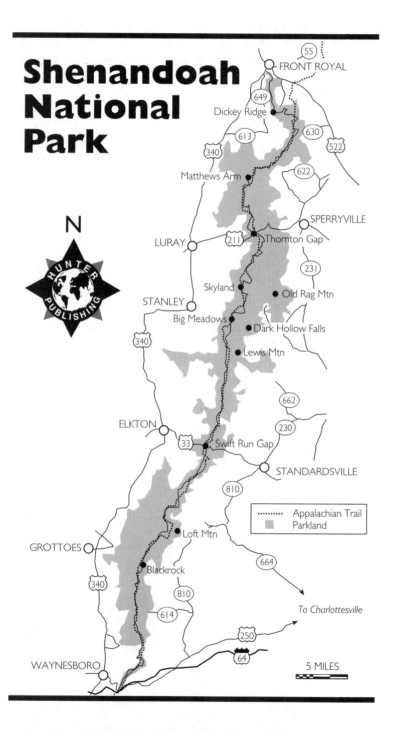

Shenandoah National Park

N

FRONT ROYAL
55
649
Dickey Ridge
613
630
340
522
Matthews Arm
622
SPERRYVILLE
LURAY
211
Thornton Gap
231
Skyland
Old Rag Mtn
STANLEY
Big Meadows
Dark Hollow Falls
340
Lewis Mtn
662
230
ELKTON
33
Swift Run Gap
STANDARDSVILLE
810
.... Appalachian Trail
Parkland
Loft Mtn
GROTTOES
664
Blackrock
340
810
To Charlottesville
614
250
WAYNESBORO
64
5 MILES

Shenandoah National Park

Encompassing the crest of the Blue Ridge Mountains and its hundreds of attendant spur ridges, Shenandoah National Park stretches from Rockfish Gap to Front Royal, a distance of almost 75 miles in an area of nearly 200,000 acres. Congress authorized the establishment of the park in 1926, but provided no funds for land acquisition. The Commonwealth of Virginia can be thanked for making the idea a reality. The Virginia Assembly appropriated one million dollars, and another 1.2 million dollars in donations (much of it from individual citizens) made possible the purchase of nearly 4,000 tracts of private land, which were deeded to the federal government in 1935.

Much of this land was not sold willingly and there is still deep-seated resentment of the government by some of the families who were relocated from their ancestral homes. While the loss experienced by these people should not be minimized, the many benefits that accrued from the park cannot be denied.

As the 20th century began, second- or third-growth forests, logged since the 1800s, covered much of what is now the park. Today, any signs left by lumbering, as well as by grazing and farming, have been largely erased through the regrowth of the forests. First came shrubs, pines, and black locusts; now 95% of the park is almost a mature forest of oak, hickory, yellow poplars, and other hardwoods. This forest growth is so complete that nearly 40% of the park was designated a wilderness area in 1976.

President Franklin Roosevelt officially dedicated the park in 1936, as the Civilian Conservation Corps busily built trails, shelters, fire roads, and various visitor facilities. The 105-mile Skyline Drive was essentially completed in 1939. This paved roadway, with its numerous overlooks and speed limit of only 35 mph, provides motorized access and a way to enjoy the scenery without much physical effort. Through the years, countless millions of Americans and international visitors have been able to enjoy these parklands which – based upon what has happened to other mountain areas of the East – would probably have been turned into housing developments or high-priced resorts if they had remained in private hands. Today, through law, the park cannot spend any funds to acquire new lands; sadly, short-sighted groups are presently spearheading a movement to limit even its acceptance of additional donated lands.

"Shenandoah"

There are many legends and stories about the origin of the word Shenandoah, but perhaps the most romantic and beautiful is that it is a derivative of a Native American word meaning Daughter of the Stars. When applied to Shenandoah National Park, those words seem more than appropriate, for the park is truly a stellar treasure in the system of public lands.

More than a dozen waterfalls tumble down the slopes, 200 species of birds – including 35 kinds of warblers – have been identified in the park, and over 1,100 different flowering plants can be found within its borders. Turkeys, bobcats, raccoons, and skunks inhabit the region in significant numbers, and there is the very real chance of seeing black bears. There are so many deer that it has become common knowledge in Virginia that if you want to see a deer, simply go to Shenandoah. The best feature of the park is that its network of more than 500 miles of trails makes its vast acreage easily accessible. Because most of the pathways are well marked, and many of them graded for gradual ascents and descents, the park is a good spot for those just introducing themselves to hiking, camping, and other outdoor activities. Within its borders are three lodging areas, a number of rustic cabins, four campgrounds, two visitors centers, seven picnic areas, and an information center.

You can enter the park with your car at four entrance points. One is in **Front Royal** at the northern end of Skyline Drive via US 340 and VA 55. US 211 between Luray and Sperryville passes through the park at **Thornton Gap** (Mile 31.5), while US 33 does so between Elkton and Stanardsville in **Swift Run Gap** (Mile 65.7). The southern end of the park may be reached on I-64 and US 250 between Waynesboro and Charlottesville. The entrance fee is presently $10 per vehicle or $5 per motorcyclist, bicyclist, or pedestrian.

The **Dickey Ridge Visitors Center** (Mile 4.6), the **Harry F. Byrd Visitors Center** (Mile 51), and the **Loft Mountain Information Station** (Mile 79.5) are staffed with park personnel able to answer just about any question you may have. Each has maps, guidebooks, and other interpretive materials for sale; the visitors centers also have exhibits and film presentations about the park.

Information Sources

Shenandoah National Park, 3655 US 211 E, Luray, VA 22835-9036, ☎ 540-999-3500

📖 Maps, guidebooks, and other interpretive information may be purchased from the **Shenandoah Natural History Association**, 3655 US 211 E, Luray, VA 22835-9036, ☎ 540-999-3582.

■ ■ ■

Adventures

■ On Foot

Self-Guided Nature Trails

The information learned on the park's five easy self-guided nature trails will add greatly to the enjoyment and understanding of your surroundings when you venture forth on longer hikes in the park. A circuit hike of 1.2 miles, **Fox Hollow Trail** (Mile 4.6) loops around an old homesite, a cemetery, and decaying fences. The 1.7-mile **Traces Nature Trail** (Mile 22.2) goes by overgrown fields, abandoned roadbeds, crumbling walls, and another homesite as it passes through a climax forest dominated by towering oaks. At about

1.8 miles, **Stony Man Nature Trail** (Mile 41.7) follows a section of the Appalachian Trail as it ascends through a spruce-fir forest to an Olympian 180° view. The two-mile **Story of the Forest Nature Trail** (Mile 51) and the 1.3-mile **Deadening Nature Trail** (Mile 79.4) explain the process of forest succession – how parklands sequentially changed from farms and open meadows to mature forests.

Waterfalls

The waterfalls of the park are popular destinations, and while the hikes are worthwhile anytime of year, the cascades will be at their most impressive in spring and early summer as the season's heavy rains wash down the mountainsides.

White Oak Canyon Trail is possibly the most spectacular waterfall hike in the park. From a parking area near Mile 43, the trail descends fairly gently to the first set of falls in a little over two miles. This 86-foot cascade churning its way down the nearly vertical slopes of the canyon is where a large percentage of people turn around, but if you feel energetic and are up to the challenge of negotiating some steep terrain, continue to descend. In doing so, you'll pass five more falls ranging from 35 feet to 62 feet in height. The final falls is reached at about four miles into the hike. On the return trip back up the same route, you should consider adding about a mile to your journey by looping onto the **Limberlost Trail**. Slow down along this pathway and take in the magnificence of the place, as there are few like it left anywhere in North America; many of the giant hemlocks in the virgin forest are believed to be 300 years old. The cry of a barred owl just adds to the romance of the woods. Addie and George Freeman Pollock, the founders of nearby Skyland Resort, gave the area its name because it reminded them of Gene Stratton Porter's *Girl of the Limberlost.*

Among the other waterfalls in the park, one of the most rewarding journeys is a 1.4-mile round-trip hike on **Dark Hollow Falls Trail** (Mile 50.7) to a 71-foot falls, while 81-foot **Lewis Falls** (Mile 51.2) may be reached via a two-mile round-trip hike. In the southern section of the park, 3.3 miles of round-trip walking permits views of two cascades along the **Dolye River Trail** (Mile 81.1). Forty-two-foot **Jones Run Falls** (Mile 84.1) makes the 3.4-mile round-trip journey, with a loss and gain of nearly 1,000 feet in elevation, worthwhile.

The Appalachian Trail

Some of the 101 miles of the Appalachian Trail in the park were built by the Civilian Conservation Corps in the 1930s. Using excellent trail-building techniques, the ascents and descents this group of hardworking men constructed here are some of the most gentle found throughout the length of the AT. This ease of walking – coupled with the fact that the trail crosses or comes in contact with Skyline Drive more than 30 times – makes the national park portion of the AT the perfect training ground for those new to backpacking, a bit out of shape, or hesitant to wander too far from civilization. In addition, the trail comes within a short walking distance of most of the restaurants, and every campground, camp store, and lodging area in the park, providing easy escape routes and opportunities to resupply or shower.

Some of the AT's major Skyline Drive crossings or contacts with developed areas are: **Elkwallow Gap** (Mile 23.9); **Thornton Gap** at US 211 (Mile 31.5); **Skyland** (near Mile 41.7); **Big Meadows Lodge and Campground** (near Mile 51); **Lewis Mountain Campground** (Mile 57.7); **Swift Run Gap** at US 33 (Mile 65.5); and **Loft Mountain Campground** (Mile 79.5).

The Best Longer Hikes

The best way to see, discover, and experience the park is to take an extended walk, but the AT is not the only trail available. Outings of several hours, days, or even weeks are possible by following and connecting together the dozens of park trails. In addition to the eight journeys described in detail in my book, *50 Hikes in Northern Virginia,* some of my favorite longer hikes in the park are described below.

The **Dickey Ridge Trail** begins at the park's northern entrance and continues for 9.2 miles to the Dickey Ridge Visitors Center. Although it stays close to Skyline Drive, the tranquil atmosphere around a small creek, the crumbling stone walls and old roads that are reminders of earlier days, and the pathway's rather gentle rate of ascent through lush vegetation put it in the "don't miss" category.

A wonderful overnight circuit of about 14 miles begins in Gravel Springs Gap (mile 17.7) by following the Bluff Trail for 1½ miles to make a right onto **Big Devils Stairs Trail**. The canyon you will be walking through is one of the most spectacular in the park; the trail traverses the tops of sheer cliffs overlooking cascades and waterfalls crashing over huge boulders inside the steep defile. Upon reaching the park boundary, turn around and return to the Bluff Trail. Make a right, eventually intersecting and bearing left onto the **Mount Marshall Trail**, seven miles into the journey. Gaining elevation at a gradual rate and crossing a couple of small streams, turn onto the **Jenkins Gap Trail**, soon crossing Skyline Drive. Intersect and bear left onto the **Appalachian Trail**, which brings you across North and South Marshall mountains for a couple of impressive views and back to Gravel Springs Gap.

An approximately 12-mile hike lets you cool off in a hemlock-shaded stream while shedding light on a bit of pre-park history. Leave your car at the Stony Man Mountain Overlook (Mile 38.6) and hike north on the AT for .3 mile to turn right onto **Nicholson Hollow Trail** and cross Skyline Drive. About two miles into the hike, bear right onto **Indian Run Trail**, parallel the headwaters of the Hughes River, and swing around Thorofare Mountain, making a left onto **Corbin Mountain Trail**. Rising to an overgrown homesite, descend steep switchbacks to bear left onto Nicholson Hollow Trail. Again gaining elevation now, cool your feet in the pools and rippling cascades of the Hughes River. An old road to the right leads to the ruins of **Aaron Nicholson's cabin**. According to Skyland founder, George Freeman Pollock, Nicholson and his family lived here before the establishment of the park and declared the hollow to be a "free state" and not subject to laws and taxes of Virginia. Continuing along the trail, you'll pass by other signs of former human inhabitation, recross Skyline Drive, and retrace your steps on the AT to return to your car.

There are a number of ways to reach **Old Rag Mountain**, one of the most popular destinations in the park. One of my favorite routes starts east along **Old Rag Fire Road** from Skyline

Drive, Mile 43. Two miles into the hike, bear left to descend Brokenback Run on the **Corbin Hollow Trail**; continue the descent, bearing left onto **Weakley Hollow Fire Road**. You'll soon come to a parking lot for those who are beginning their Old Rag experience at the park boundary along the **Ridge Trail.** When the exertion of climbing over and around the huge boulders becomes tiresome, I'm able to put fun back into the ascent by thinking of this as just a giant jungle gym. You are rewarded on the summit by unparalleled 360° views of the Piedmont to the east and the heights of the national park to the west. Return to your car by taking the **Saddle Trail**, and subsequently following the Old Rag Fire Road back to Skyline Drive – having hiked close to 15 miles. (Be aware that much of the land around Old Rag is a no-camping zone.)

A circuit hike of nearly 13 miles that brings you into one of the most remote sections of the park and across talus slopes begins in Browns Gap (Mile 83) by heading north along the **Appalachian Trail**. In about a half-mile, bear left onto **Big Run Loop Trail**, coming to a major intersection where you'll begin following **Rocky Top Trail**. Approximately 1½ miles into the hike, turn left onto rugged **Austin Mountain Trail** as it swings around the mountain's southern slope and descends steeply across a rocky hillside and under cliffs to arrive at **Madison Run Road,** five miles into the hike. Descend right to make a left for the long climb up **Furnace Mountain Trail**, with an optional side trail of a half-mile to a grand view of the Madison Run watershed. At the next major intersection, bear left onto **Trayfoot Mountain Trail**, soon to make another left onto **Blackrock Spur Trail**. Come onto the open talus slopes of Blackrock (named for the tripe which grows upon the rock) with nice views of the park's southern peaks. Bear left onto the AT to return to your car in Browns Gap.

The Best Shorter Hikes

If your time is limited, **Bettys Rock Trail** packs in a lot for an easy .6-mile round-trip walk. Wildflowers, such as pink moss phlox and cinquefoil, border the trail as it rises from the **Crescent Rock Overlook** at Mile 44.4. Mountain laurel bushes become loaded with pinkish-white flowers as June progresses.

Shenandoah Park

The panoramic view west from Bettys Rock takes in Hawksbill Mountain (the park's highest peak) and looks across the Shenandoah Valley to Massanutten Mountain's long ridgeline.

Another short hike (about 1½ miles round-trip) follows the **Appalachian Trail** south from **Beagle Gap** (Mile 99.5) to the open meadows atop **Bear Den Mountain**. In addition to the views, the windswept knob is a sunny, yet cool spot for a lazy afternoon of sunbathing.

■ On Wheels

Skyline Drive

The Drive has a lot to offer the cyclist. Pullouts to enjoy the fantastic views. Picnic areas supplying shaded resting spots and drinking water. Wildflowers by the thousands. Restaurants and grocery stores providing cold drinks and good food. Deer browsing by the roadside. No tractor trailers zooming by at 70 miles per hour. Campgrounds and lodge rooms for peaceful sleeps.

It certainly has its share of calf-burner climbs, but Skyline Drive may just be the best 105 miles worth of bicycle riding in all of Virginia.

Although continuous ups and downs make it hard to calculate just how much climbing you will be doing, elevations will give you an idea of what you'll be facing along the Skyline Drive.

It is definitely uphill for the first 21 miles as you rise from 1,300 feet at the park's northern entrance in Front Royal to nearly 3,400 feet at Hogback Overlook (Mile 21). The coast down to 2,300 feet in Thornton Gap (Mile 31.5) is succeeded by a haul up to Skyline Drive's highest point – 3,680 feet near Skyland (Mile 41.7).

Having gained the high spot, you're in for a bit of a reprieve in the central part of Skyline Drive as you'll never lose or gain more than 400 feet on the individual ups and downs. However, a roller coaster section begins with the drop from 3,125 feet at The Oaks Overlook (Mile 59.1) to 2,365 feet in Swift Run Gap (Mile

65.7), only to go up and down again through at least five more gaps to 2,980 feet at Wildcat Ridge Parking Area (92.1). From here the lay of the land tends in a downward direction to 1,909 feet in Rockfish Gap (Mile 105.4), the southern terminus of Skyline Drive.

Cycling Regulations

Cyclists in the park need to be aware of special regulations. While not encouraged by park staff because of safety concerns, bicycles are permitted on Skyline Drive and public roads in developed areas, but are prohibited on all trails and fire roads.

You must ride single file, stay well to the right of the road, and observe all applicable traffic regulations. Between sunset and sunrise, and in times of rain, fog, or other periods of low visibility, you must have a white light or reflector visible 500 feet to the front and a red light or reflector visible 200 feet to the rear. Be aware at all times that there is no shoulder to ride upon and that Skyline Drive is a narrow two-lane road with many curves.

■ On Horseback

Guided Trail Rides

Concentrating on the trails in the central portion of the park, guided trail rides of one hour and 2½ hours are available from **Skyland Stables** (☎ 540-999-2210) near Mile 47.7. Rides depart throughout the day from May through October. Since this is a popular activity, it is better to make reservations than just show up at the stables, especially if your riding time in the park is limited. Riders must be at least 4'10"; pony rides are available for smaller children.

Shenandoah Park

Horseback Riding Regulations

Throughout the park more than 150 miles of trails and fire roads are open to horseback riders. There are a number of strict regulations you must adhere to if you wish to do any backcountry horse camping, and even day riders will need to know where they are permitted to park trailers. Check with the folks at park headquarters or one of the visitors centers before departing on a ride. Horses are permitted only on trails marked with yellow blazes; those unmarked or with white or blue blazes are for foot travel only.

The Northern Region

There is a nice ride through a wide variety of terrain and environments making use of more than 12 miles of connecting fire roads and trails. **Lands Run Gap Road, Hickerson Hollow Trail, Jenkins Gap Trail, Springhouse Road, Compton Gap Fire Road, Compton Gap Horse Trail, Mount Marshall Trail, Jordan River Trail, Harris Hollow Trail**, and a portion of **Bluff Trail** are all open to horses.

The Central Region

In the central part of the park you can do well over 30 miles of riding by connecting **Hazel Mountain, Hazel River, Pine Hill Gap, White Rocks, Stony Man Horse, Furnace Spring, and Skyland/Big Meadows** horse trails with **Old Skyland, Weakly Hollow, Berry Hollow, Old Rag**, and **White Oak** fire roads.

The Big Run Area

With impressive rock formations, high cliff facings, viewpoints overlooking the Shenandoah Valley, and numerous free-running streams, Big Run is the park's largest wilderness area and has a great sense of isolation that is found nowhere else in the park. Close to 20 miles of trails and fire roads are open to horseback riders who want to explore this region's rugged beauty. The **Big Run Loop Trail** at Mile 81.2 provides access to Big Run Portal Trail, the main valley route through Big Run Canyon, which connects with other trails and fire roads.

■ On Snow

Cross-Country Skiing

 There are no developed downhill or cross-country facilities in the park. However, portions of **Skyline Drive** are not cleared for long periods of time after major snow storms, providing miles and miles of flat surface for cross-country skiing. Just remember to be alert for snow plows!

Most of the park's trails are too narrow and steep, but much of the **Appalachian Trail** from Bootens Gap (Mile 55.1) to Big Meadows Lodge (Mile 51.3) passes over fairly gentle terrain. Also, the **Passumaquoddy Trail** near Skyland (Mile 41.7) has a gentle grade and passes through a grove of giant hemlock trees that are absolutely gorgeous when draped in snow. Gliding along the undulating fields of **Big Meadows** is almost like skiing on a golf course. In addition, many of the fire roads, such as **Old Rag, Weakley Hollow**, and **Hazel Mountain**, are popular with local skiers.

■ In The Air

 There are several sites within the park from which you may launch a hang glider. Current regulations and permits can be obtained during weekday business hours from park headquarters in Luray.

Where To Stay

 At Mile 41.7 is **Skyland Lodge** [$$ to $$$], which George Freeman Pollock opened as the rustic Stony Man Camp in 1894. A carriage road from Luray wound up the western slope of the Blue Ridge carrying his guests to the

Shenandoah Park

resort sitting below Stony Man Mountain. Today's visitors have a choice of nearly 200 rooms and suites, some of which are in historic cabins.

Big Meadows Lodge [$$ to $$$] (Mile 51.3) was constructed in 1939 of chestnut from the park and stone from nearby Massanutten Mountain. It provides rooms, suites, and historic cabins overlooking the Shenandoah Valley.

Several rustic housekeeping cabins (with cooking done on an outside grill) are available at the **Lewis Mountain** [$] complex at Mile 57.5.

Information or reservations for all three of the above accommodations may be obtained by contacting **ARAMARK Virginia Sky-Line Company**, PO Box 727, Luray, VA 22835, ☎ 800-999-4714. Although dates can change from year to year, Skyland is usually open from March to December, while the other two facilities open sometime in May and close in October after the leaf color season.

For those looking to rough it a bit more, the **Potomac Appalachian Trail Club** (118 Park St. Southeast, Vienna, VA 22180, ☎ 703-242-0315) operates six enclosed backcountry cabins (pit toilets, no electricity, and water from nearby natural sources) scattered throughout the park near the AT. The cabins are locked, but you may obtain a key after making reservations.

■ Camping

All four of the park's developed campgrounds (**Mathews Arm** at Mile 22.2, **Big Meadows** at Mile 51.3, **Lewis Mountain** at Mile 57.5, and **Loft Mountain** at Mile 79.5) are open from sometime in May to mid-to-late October, and have tent and trailer sites, flush toilets, and showers (no showers at Mathews Arm). If you want a space on busy weekends you will need to arrive early, as the campgrounds are operated on a first-come, first-served basis. The exception is Big Meadows, which requires reservations from Memorial Day weekend to the last weekend in October. Reservations may be made up to five months in advance by calling ☎ 800-365-CAMP.

Camping Regulations

When hiking and camping in the backcountry, please be sure to obey regulations instituted by the park service in order to reduce the impact of tens of thousands of visitors a year. Wood fires are permitted only in fireplaces in developed campgrounds, picnic areas, and certain trail shelters. No fires are allowed in the backcountry, so bring your backpacking stove if you want any hot meals on your hikes. You must obtain a free backcountry camping permit (available at entrance stations, visitors centers, and some self-registering trailheads) before taking off on any overnight trips. No camping is permitted within sight of any trail, road, another group of campers, inside no-camping zones, within 25 feet of a stream, and within a half-mile of any park development such as a lodge, campground, or restaurant. The Old Rag Shelter and the Byrds Nest shelters are for picnics only and may not be used for overnight accommodations, except in extreme weather conditions. The huts along the Appalachian Trail are intended to be used only by long-distance hikers. All dogs must be kept on a leash, and are prohibited on certain trails. There are, of course, numerous other regulations – some of which change from time to time – and you will be given a list of the most pertinent ones when you receive your camping permit.

Where To Eat

 Elkwallow Wayside [$] (☎540-999-2253, Mile 24.1) offers counter service, with seating outside on the patio or on picnic tables and provides breakfast, sandwiches, and grilled items.

Panorama [$] (☎ 540-999-2265, Mile 31.5) has waitress service in the dining room and provides a varied menu, including soup, salad, pizza, and sandwiches.

Shenandoah Park

Big Meadows Wayside [$] (☎ 540-999-2251, Mile 51.3) has waitress service in the dining room and carryout service at the counter. The menu is a mixture of soup, salads, and sandwiches.

With picnic tables outside and counter service and tables inside, **Loft Mountain Wayside** [$] (☎ 804-823-4515, Mile 79.5) has a menu of sandwiches and grilled items.

All four of the above are open for breakfast, lunch, and dinner.

The dining halls at **Skyland Lodge** [$$] (☎540-999-2211, Mile 41.7) and **Big Meadows Lodge** [$$] (☎ 540-999-2221, Mile 51.3) provide a much more elegant dining experience, with picture windows overlooking the Shenandoah Valley. Always cooked with a country/mountain flair, items on the menus can change from year to year. Perennials for breakfast include large, calorie-laden Belgian waffles and tasty, artery-clogging four-cheese omelets. The blackberry ice cream pie for dessert can't be beat.

The Blue Ridge Parkway

Shenandoah and the Great Smoky Mountains national parks, two of America's most-visited and scenic parcels of public land, are linked via another beautiful and popular component of the national park system, the Blue Ridge Parkway (BRP). Meandering along the crest of the mountains for more than 469 miles, the Parkway provides an opportunity to become intimately associated with the natural and human histories of the southern Appalachian Mountains.

In 1933, President Franklin Roosevelt made an inspection tour of the first Civilian Conservation Corps camp to be established in Virginia. Roosevelt not only enjoyed the beauty of Shenandoah National Park, but was well pleased with the progress and potential of the Skyline Drive. Urged on by local politicians (who realized its economic benefits) and naturalists from Virginia, North Carolina, and Tennessee, Roosevelt approved the idea of the Parkway, and development began on September 11, 1935. With the construction of the Linn Cove Viaduct on the eastern flank of Grandfather Mountain in North Carolina in 1983 and several more years of joining together "missing link" sections, the task was accomplished. On September 11, 1987, a ceremony on the viaduct officially declared the completion of the Parkway, exactly 52 years after the project was started.

There are more than 40 park service trails and numerous forest service pathways that either connect to or come in close contact with Virginia's portion of the parkway – in other words, there are ample opportunities to experience and explore the mountains. In addition, the world-famous 2,100-mile Appalachian Trail parallels the parkway for more than 100 miles in Virginia.

The Blue Ridge Parkway may be reached by exiting either US 250 or I-64 in Rockfish Gap, a few miles east of Waynesboro. Follow highway signs for a very short distance and turn south onto the Parkway. In addition to many smaller roads intersecting the scenic route, other major highways that provide access are:

Blue Ridge Parkway

The Blue Ridge Parkway in Virginia

N

CHARLOTTESVILLE

WAYNESBORO

Staunton

Buena Vista

Lexington

LYNCHBURG

Bedford

ROANOKE

Appalachian Trail

Salem

Rocky Mount

Christiansburg

Blacksburg

Radford

Dublin

Pulaski

Wytheville

Galax

Sparta

Mt. Airy

VIRGINIA

NORTH CAROLINA

Wilkesboro

Boone

1. Rockfish Gap
2. Humpback Rocks/ Greenstone Trail
3. Whetstone Ridge
4. Otter Creek
5. James River Visitor Ctr
6. Peaks of Otter
7. Roanoke Mountain
8. Smart View
9. Rocky Knob
10. Mabry Mill
11. Fancy Gap
12. Cumberland Knob
13. Doughton Park
14. E.B. Jeffress Park

NOT TO SCALE

US 60 east of Buena Vista (Mile 45.6); US 501 west of
Lynchburg (Mile 63.7); US 221/460 north of Roanoke (Mile
105.8); US 220 south of Roanoke (Mile 121.4); US 58 west of Stuart (Mile 177.7); and US 52 in Fancy Gap (Mile 199.4).

Information Source

Blue Ridge Parkway, BB&T Building, One Pack
Square, Asheville, NC 22801, ☎ 704-298-0398.

■ ■ ■

Adventures

■ On Foot

Short Self-Guiding Trails

The parkway's self-guiding trails are good introduc-
tions to the natural and social history of the Blue Ridge
Mountains. The background information obtained on
these short pathways will greatly enhance your understanding
and appreciation of your surroundings while driving or hiking
along other sections of the parkway.

Mountain Farm Trail (Mile 5.9), half-mile round-trip, goes by
a number of reconstructed buildings depicting life on a pioneer
farmstead. A .2-mile circuit walk, **Greenstone Trail** (Mile 8.8)
passes through an oak-history forest exploring the volcanic ori-
gins of the northern Blue Ridge Mountains. With exhibits, a
well-preserved lock, and .4-mile round-trip, the **James River
Trail** (Mile 63.6) paints a vivid picture of 19th-century canal
systems. Branching off the James River Trail, the .4-mile circuit
walk **Trail of Trees** explains the life cycles of various plants
and trees. Interpretive signs identify plants and animals along
Elk Run Trail (Mile 85.9), a .8-mile circuit. Three interconnecting pathways comprise the one-mile round-trip **Roanoke
River Trail** (Mile 114.9), with notations on plants, animals,
and other bits of natural history.

Easy Indian Gap Trail (Mile 47.5) is not a self-guiding trail, but you don't need signs to appreciate the rhododendron tunnels and interesting rock formations along the .2-mile round-trip walk. Moderate **Fallingwater Cascades Trail** (Mile 83.1) is a lovely 1.6-mile round-trip trail taking in a series of tumbling falls. It was designated a National Recreation Trail in 1982. Only those in the best of shape should attempt the three-mile round-trip trek along **Sharp Top Trail** (Mile 86) to the top of the 3,875-foot Sharp Top for 360° views. (A park service concessionaire runs a seasonal bus to the summit for those unable or unwilling to do the hike.)

Sharp Top.

The Best Longer Hikes

For short day hikes or for long overnight backpacking journeys, the **Appalachian Trail** parallels the BRP from Rockfish Gap (Mile 0) to Blackhorse Gap (Mile 97.7). Sometimes within shouting distance of the BRP, sometimes swinging miles away to the east or the west, the AT comes in contact with the Parkway nearly two dozen times at places such as **Humpback Gap** (Mile

Rhododendron.

6), **Reeds Gap** (Mile 13.7), **Thunder Ridge Overlook** (Mile 74.7), and **Sharp Top Overlook** (Mile 92.5). You should inform a ranger or someone at a visitors center if you are going to leave your car overnight along the Parkway. The **Rock Castle Gorge Trail** (Mile 167.1) is the Parkway's longest pathway (10.6 miles, circuit) and winds along the heights of the mountains through open meadows, before dropping nearly 2,000 feet to the only authorized backcountry camping spot on BRP property in Virginia.

If you want further BRP trail information, *Walking the Blue Ridge: A Guide to the Trails of the Blue Ridge Parkway* contains detailed milepoint-by-milepoint descriptions about every trail along the full length of the parkway. Also included is information on where you may camp on forest service lands adjacent to the BRP, a parkway mileage log, and a roadside bloom calendar. Available in BRP Visitors Center or from University of North Carolina Press, PO Box 2288, Chapel Hill, NC 27515-2288, ☎ 800-848-6224.

Blue Ridge Parkway

■ On Wheels

For all practical purposes, the Blue Ridge Parkway is just a southern extension of Shenandoah National Park's Skyline Drive. There are no commercial trucks to contend with, the scenic highway stays to the crest of the mountains for grandstand views, and pullouts and picnic areas provide shaded resting spots and drinking water. Deer and other wildlife may be seen on a regular basis, while wildflowers bloom profusely by the roadside. Restaurants, camp stores, campgrounds, and lodges on BRP property make it convenient to refuel or rest for the night. (You should keep in mind, however, that these facilities are farther apart than those along Skyline Drive.)

Cycling Regulations

Cyclists on the parkway need to be aware of special regulations. Bicycles may be ridden only on paved road surfaces and parking areas, and are not permitted on any trails or walkways. You must ride single file, stay well to the right of the road, and comply with all applicable state and federal motor vehicle traffic regulations. Between sunset and sunrise, in times of rain, fog, or other periods of low visibility, and while traveling through a tunnel, you are required to have a white light or reflector visible at least 500 feet to the front and a red light or reflector visible at least 200 feet to the rear. You must ride at a speed reasonable for control with regard to traffic, weather, road, and light conditions.

The following chart (reprinted by permission of the Blue Ridge Parkway National Park Service with statistics courtesy of Tom DeVaughn of Roanoke, Virginia) helps provide an idea of the elevation changes you can expect while cycling various sections of the Parkway.

Major Elevation Changes			
SOUTHBOUND		**MAJOR UPHILLS**	
Mileposts	**Elevation Climbed (feet)**	**Mileposts**	**Elevation Change (feet)**
0-24	2,810	0-3	391
		4.7-8.5	1,100
		9.2-10.7	322
		18.5-23	785
24-48	1,742	37.4-38.8	229
		42-43.9	570
		47-48	177
48-63	250	48-49.3	228
63-76.7	3,305	63-76.7	3,305
76.7-96	1,360	89.1-91.6	569
		93.1-95.4	428
96-120.4	1,657	118.1-120.4	462
120.4	Mill Mtn Spur – length to summit 3.1 miles. Elevation climb from Parkway to summit, 580 feet; elevation climb from summit to Parkway, 330 feet.		
120.4-144	3,200	127-132.5	1,400
		134-134.9	195
		136.4-138.2	275
144-168	2,530	150.5-132.5	278
		157-157.6	200
		164.7-168	830
168-192	1,745	169.5-170.1	260
		176.2-177	212
		186.6-188.8	360
192-216	2,047	195-196.2	235
		197.6-198.7	210
		200.5-201.5	335
216.9	Virginia/North Carolina Border		
NORTHBOUND			
216-192	2,225	215.6-214	260
		210.6-209.4	222
		199.4-198.7	165

Blue Ridge Parkway

		189.4-188.7	220
192-168	2,445	175.1-171.9	575
		168.9-168	185
168-144	1,640	159.4-157.6	389
		150.6-149.8	226
		140.1-139.3	229
144-120.4	2,006	136-134.9	285
		124.6-123.1	320
		121.4-120.4	265
120.4	Mill Mtn Spur – Length to summit, 3.1 miles. Climb from Parkway to summit, 580 feet; climb from summit to Parkway, 330 feet.		
		115-113	280
120.4-96	2,680	106-103.6	500
		102.5-99.8	820
		93.1-91.6	374
96-76.7	2,865	89.1-87.3	
		85.6-84.7	230
		83.5-76.7	1,490
76.7-63	-		
		46.4-43.9	627
48-24	2,670	40-38.8	331
		37.4-34	951
		13.7-10.7	563
24-0	1,450	9.2-8.5	222
		4.7-3	300

(Statistics for cycling the North Carolina portion of the parkway may be obtained from any BRP visitors center.)

■ On Horseback

Guided horseback rides are unavailable along the Parkway, but a couple of excellent long-distance trails are open for those of you with your own horses.

The **Glenwood Horse Trail** is a cooperative effort between the US Forest Service and local equestrian groups. With well over 50 miles of pathway wandering beside rhododendron-lined brooks, along rocky ridgelines, and out to open viewpoints, the trail comes in contact with the Parkway at Miles 71, 80.5, and 93.1. However, trailers may not be left parked along the BRP, so you should contact the **Glenwood Ranger District**, PO Box 10, Natural Bridge Station, VA 24579 (☎ 540-291-2188) for authorized places on forest service lands.

The **Roanoke Valley Horse Trail** (Mile 110.6 to Mile 121.4) was conceived, and is maintained, by local equestrians. Although it does travel close to housing developments, paved roads, and private property, the route offers a mostly wooded ride that comes in contact with the Parkway at Miles 110.6, 112, 114.7, 116.4, 118, and 120.7.

The trail between Miles 114.7 and 116.4 has yet to be built, being stalled by the logistical problems of crossing the Roanoke River and providing a loading/unloading area on BRP property.

■ On Snow

Cross-Country Skiing

There are no developed downhill or cross-country facilities on BRP property. However, certain portions of the Parkway are not cleared for long periods of time after major snow storms, providing miles of flat surface for cross-country skiing. A long stretch of Parkway south of Roanoke is a local favorite as it is one of the first to be closed and one of the last to be plowed.

Most of the parkway's trails are too narrow and steep for cross-country skiing, but the open meadows along the **Rock Castle Gorge Trail** (Mile 167.1) have a fairly gentle slope and provide 360° views of the surrounding countryside. One-mile **Abbot Lake Loop Trail** (Mile 85.7) makes for some easy cross-country skiing, as does the one-mile **Otter Lake Loop Trail** (Mile 63.1). **Chestnut Ridge Trail** (Mile 120.5) is over five miles long and has a number of ups and downs, yet is an appropriate challenge for intermediate skiers.

Skiing at Wintergreen.

Less than two miles from the BRP at Mile 13.7 along VA 664, **Wintergreen Resort** (PO Box 706, Wintergreen, VA 22958, ☎ 800-325-2200) has been called by *Skiing Magazine*, "the South's best single ski resort." Possessing a 1,000-foot vertical drop, it has 17 slopes and trails featuring a variety of terrain for both downhill skiers and snowboarders, with a good mix of steep pitches, mogul fields, and cruising runouts. The longest runs are well over a mile.

■ In The Air

Hang gliding aficionados have been permitted to launch from various spots along the Parkway. However, sites and regulations (and outright bans) have varied through the years, so it would be irresponsible for this guidebook to name any particular places. You should contact the BRP main office (BB&T Buidling, One Park Square, Asheville, NC 22301, ☎ 704-298-0398) for the most current information.

Where To Stay

 Nestled in a small valley surrounded by its namesake mountains at Mile 86, **Peaks of Otter Lodge** [$$] (Virginia Peaks of Otter Company, PO Box 489, Bedford, VA 24523, ☎ 540-586-1081) is open year-round. Each room opens onto a private terrace or balcony from which you can enjoy the scenery. (On a personal note, Laurie and I were married in this marvelous setting.)

At Mile 179, **Rocky Knob Cabins** [$] (National Park Concessions, Inc., Meadows of Dan, VA 24120, ☎ 540-593-3503) are usually open from mid-May to Labor Day and offer rustic alternative accommodations. Built in the 1930s by the CCC, the cabins have electric kitchen facilities, but no source with which to provide heat on cold mountain nights. Showers and laundromat are located in a central bathhouse.

Not on BRP property, but less than a 30-second drive from Mile 189.2, **Doe Run Lodge** [$$$ to $$$$$] (PO Box 280, Fancy Gap, VA 24328, ☎ 800-325-6189) has deluxe accommodations ranging from suites with two bedrooms, two bathrooms, and a kitchen to townhouse-style, multi-floored villas. Single units with whirlpool baths or Jacuzzis, stereo systems, and natural stone fireplaces are also available. Located upon the extensive grounds are tennis courts, a swimming pool, a stocked pond, a short hiking trail, and views of the surrounding mountains dropping down to the Piedmont.

Blue Ridge Parkway

■ Camping

There are three park service campgrounds located along the BRP in Virginia. **Otter Creek** is at Mile 60, **Peaks of Otter** at Mile 86, and **Roanoke Mountain** is off the Mill Mountain Spur Road near Mile 120.4. The campgrounds are usually open from May through October, but one or the other may be available for winter camping, weather permitting. Drinking water, flush toilets, and dump stations are provided, but there are no electric hookups, showers, or laundry facilities. Sites are available on a first-come, first-served basis, with no reservations accepted.

The only place in Virginia where backcountry camping is permitted on BRP property is beside wonderfully isolated, lovely **Rock Castle Creek**. The benches, fire grates, and pit toilets of the primitive sites are reached either by hiking 3.25 miles along the **Rock Castle Gorge Trail** (Mile 167.1) or by a walk of .25 mile from VA 605, several miles west of Woolwine. The required free permits may be obtained from the **Rocky Knob Visitors Center** (Mile 169) or the ranger station at Mile 167 (☎ 540-745-9660).

Much of the BRP is surrounded by George Washington and Jefferson National Forests, where camping is permitted. However, as it is sometimes hard to tell where Parkway property ends and national forest begins, it is best to check at a BRP visitors center or consult *Walking the Blue Ridge: A Guide to the Trails of the Blue Ridge Parkway* before you decide to set up camp along a particular trail.

Where To Eat

Whetstone Ridge Restaurant (☎ 540-327-6397, Mile 29) [$] and **Otter Creek Restaurant** [$] (☎ 204-239-5862, Mile 60.7) serve country-style breakfasts, lunches, and dinners. They are usually open from the middle of April to the middle of November.

With picture windows overlooking Abbot Lake and Sharp Top Mountain, the dining hall at **Peaks of Otter Lodge** [$ to $$] (☎ 800-542-5827, Mile 86) is open year-round, offering breakfast, lunch, and dinner. The fare is decidedly Southern, with fried chicken, barbecued ribs, pan-fried trout, and prime rib figuring prominently on the menu. An adjoining coffee shop offers burgers, sandwiches, fries, and the like.

Mabry Mill Coffee Shop [$] (☎ 540-552-2947, Mile 176.1) is open most years from late April through October. The all-day menu includes breakfast, with pancakes made from flour ground at the mill a tourist favorite. Lunches and dinners feature burgers, salads, barbecue, and ham.

In a region where you often have to settle for overcooked vegetables and greasy fried entrées, a most unexpected dining pleasure along the Parkway is the **High Country Restaurant at Doe Run Lodge** [$$ to $$$] (☎ 800-325-6189, Mile 189.2). The seasonal menu has included such delights as she-crab soup, spicy Jamaican jerk chicken, spinach salad with shiitake mushrooms, Atlantic salmon with avocado butter, marinated tuna accompanied by kiwi salsa, and flame-grilled ribeye steak topped with herb garlic butter.

Shenandoah Valley Region

R ichly deserving its Shawnee name – Daughter of the Stars – the Shenandoah Valley Region is perfect for those seeking adventure. It is bounded on the east by Shenandoah National Park and the Blue Ridge Parkway, both federal entities founded to protect and facilitate access to the natural beauty of the Blue Ridge Mountains. Three hundred miles of the 2,100-mile Appalachian Trail wind through these mountains. To the west, the long ridgelines and rugged peaks of the Allegheny Mountains rise in increasing elevations of over 4,000 feet to establish the Virginia/West Virginia border.

Having lazily meandered around the eastern and western slopes of Massanutten Mountain – the massif which splits the valley in two – the waters of the North and South Forks of the Shenandoah River provide leisurely float trips as they come together at Front Royal.

Encompassing much of this land (and additional amounts in Southwest Virginia) is the more than 1,700,000 acres of the George Washington and Jefferson National Forests. Coursed through by scores of dirt roads and over 1,900 miles of pathways, the national forests are within a day's drive of nearly one-quarter of America's population. As a result, the forests play host to millions of hikers, bikers, and cross-country skiers each year. Dozens of rivers and streams lure canoeists and kayakers into their waters. Paddlers who are looking to test their skills often turn to the whitewater rapids along the Maury and Jackson rivers.

Here, too, are all four of the state's downhill skiing facilities: Bryce, hidden in a narrow Allegheny Mountains valley; Massanutten, within the confines of a large natural bowl at the southern end of its namesake mountain; Wintergreen, sitting atop the very crest of the Blue Ridge; and The Homestead, in the heart of the mineral spa region of the southern Appalachians.

Home to hunter-gatherers some 10,000 years ago, and later the Shawnee and other Native Americans, the Shenandoah Valley began attracting European settlers in the early 1700s. Lured by fertile soil, nearly free land, and the hopes of greater individual freedoms, Germans, Scots-Irish, English, and Welsh immigrants worked their way from northern states into this region by following the natural conduit of the Great Valley. This long swath of flat-to-rolling land – of which the Shenandoah Valley is a part – extends from New York through Virginia and on into the South.

Known as "The Breadbasket to the Confederacy," the rich earth of the Shenandoah Valley was the site of such intense fighting and so many battles during the Civil War that it sometimes feels as if the ghosts of those dark days can still haunt those who travel or live here. Museums, cemeteries, preserved battle-fields, and monuments are found even in the remotest corners of the region.

Although scorched, burned, and scarred more than a century ago, the land has healed itself and once again supports a rural, agrarian type of life. Interstate 81, which follows the general route of the old Indian pathways and settlers' wagon routes, has been described as one of the most scenic interstate drives in the United States. Rows of silky-green corn tassels and golden fields of hay border the highway, while long wooden sheds perched on hillsides house thousands of chickens and turkeys. On the interstate, you will often be passed by a speeding tractor trailer loaded 10 layers high with cages crammed full of poultry on its a way to numerous processing plants scattered throughout the valley.

Strung along I-81, college towns, such as Harrisonburg, Staunton, and Lexington, provide many of the region's cultural activities. At the southern end of the valley lies Roanoke, its largest city. Billing itself as the "Capitol of the Blue Ridge," the old railroad town-turned-commercial center has its own symphony, several theatrical troupes, and a former warehouse converted into an arts center housing three distinctly different museums.

Shenandoah Valley Region

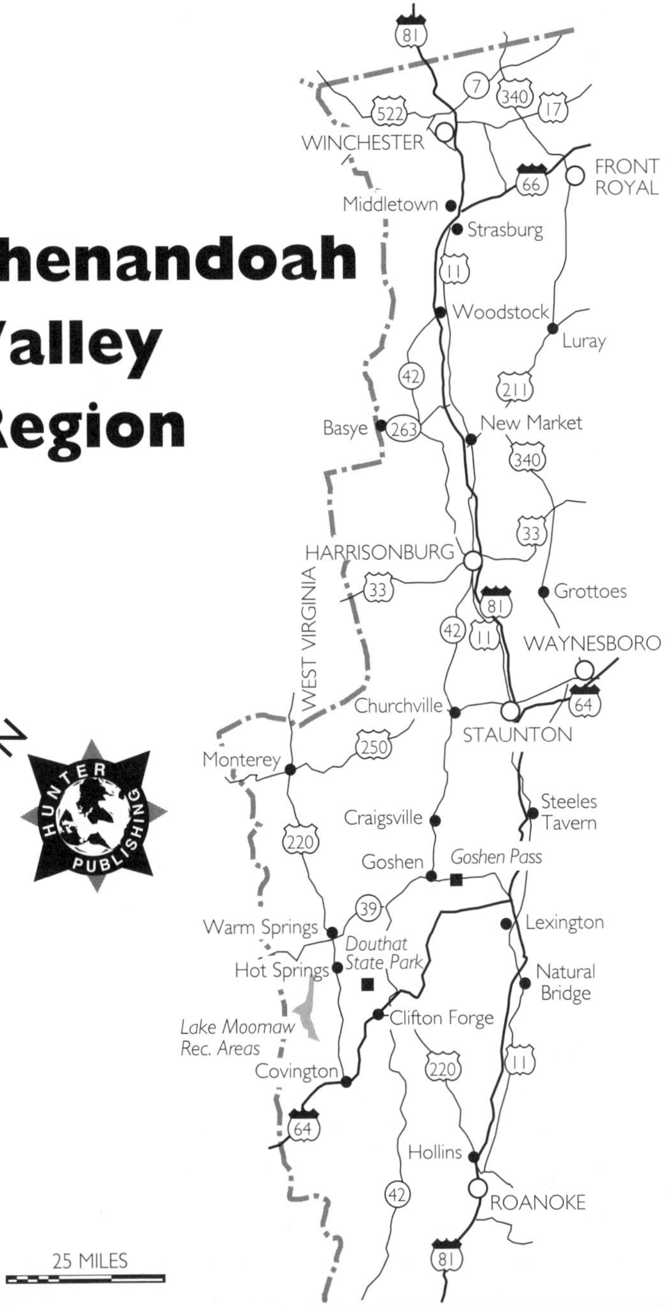
81
7
340
17
522
WINCHESTER
FRONT ROYAL
66
Middletown
Strasburg
11
Woodstock
Luray
42
211
Basye
263
New Market
340
33
HARRISONBURG
33
WEST VIRGINIA
81
Grottoes
42
11
WAYNESBORO
Churchville
64
STAUNTON
250
Monterey
Steeles Tavern
Craigsville
220
Goshen
Goshen Pass
39
Lexington
Warm Springs
Douthat State Park
Hot Springs
Natural Bridge
Clifton Forge
Lake Moomaw Rec. Areas
220
11
Covington
64
Hollins
42
ROANOKE
81
25 MILES

Information Sources

Shenandoah Valley Travel Association, PO Box 1040, New Market, VA 22844, ☎ 540-740-3132.

Front Royal-Warren County Visitors Center, 414 East Main St., Front Royal, VA 22630, ☎ 800-338-2576.

Harrisonburg-Rockingham County Convention & Visitors Bureau, PO Box 1, Harrisonburg, VA 22801, ☎ 540-434-2319.

Lexington Visitors Center, 106 East Washington St., Lexington, VA 24450, ☎ 540-463-3777.

Roanoke Valley Visitor Information Center, 114 Market St., Roanoke, VA 24011, ☎ 800-635-5535.

Staunton-Augusta County Visitors Center, 1250 Richmond Ave., Staunton, VA 24401, ☎ 800-332-5219.

Western Highlands Travel Council, 241 West Main St., Covington, VA, ☎ 540-962-2178.

Highland County Chamber of Commerce, PO Box 223, Monterey, VA 24465, ☎ 540-486-2550.

▪ ▪ ▪

Getting Around

There are several options if you want to reach the Shenandoah Valley region by air. **Dulles International Airport** (☎ 703-661-2700), served by many of the world's major airlines, is just outside Washington, DC and not much more than an hour's drive from the valley. Also on the eastern side of the Blue Ridge, but only 30 minutes or so from the Shenandoah Valley, is **Charlottesville-Albemarle Airport** (☎ 804-973-8341), served by Comair, USAir, and United Express. USAir and United Express also fly into the **Roanoke Regional Airport** (☎ 540-362-1999). Regularly scheduled commuter flights let you fly into the heart of the valley at the **Shenandoah Valley Regional Airport** (☎ 540-234-8304) in Wyers Cave.

On an east/west route, **Amtrak** (☎ 800-872-7245) makes stops in Staunton and Clifton Forge. A scheduled commuter train coming from Washington, DC makes a stop in Harpers Ferry, WV – 30 minutes northeast of Winchester.

Following the I-81 corridor down the length of the valley, **Greyhound** (☎ 800-231-2222) serves Winchester, Harrisonburg, Waynesboro, Staunton, Lexington, Buchanan, and Roanoke. You can also catch a bus or be dropped off in Clifton Forge and Covington.

In Winchester, Harrisonburg, Staunton, Lexington, and Roanoke you will be able to **rent cars** from national companies such as Avis, Budget, Dollar, Enterprise, and Hertz.

Touring

■ Winchester

Settled by Pennsylvania Dutch around the mid-1700s, and soon followed by a mixture of Germans, Irish, Scots, English, Welsh, and French, Winchester is considered the oldest city west of the Blue Ridge. Situated as it is on a crossroads at the northern entrance of the Shenandoah Valley, the area continues to draw new inhabitants, lured by rural surroundings and easy access to the Washington, DC area. Like other cities along major highways, it is beginning to suffer the bane of fast food restaurants, discount stores, and strip malls along its outer edges, but the center of town has managed to preserve much of its integrity and many of its historical structures and sites.

Abram's Delight (South Pleasant Valley Road, Winchester, VA 22601, ☎ 540-662-6519), the oldest home in the city, was constructed of native limestone in 1754. By stopping here you'll also be able to pick up brochures describing a couple of different walking tours of town. One tour visits the oldest part of town where 45 blocks have been placed on the National Register of Historic Places. The other tour takes in sites that figured into Patsy Cline's life while growing up in Winchester. One place

Shenandoah Valley

still in operation is Gaunt's Drug Store, where she worked after dropping out of high school. Although her career was cut short by a plane crash in 1963, Cline's "heartbreak" songs, such as *Crazy* (written by Willie Nelson) and *I Fall to Pieces*, helped bring country music to the attention of mainstream America.

George Washington, at the age of 16, arrived in Winchester in 1748 to begin his surveyor's apprenticeship. The log cabin he used as his office, and later as military headquarters while constructing Fort Loudoun during the French and Indian War, is now **Washington's Office-Museum** (☎ 540-662-4412) on the corner of Cork and Braddock streets.

Winchester

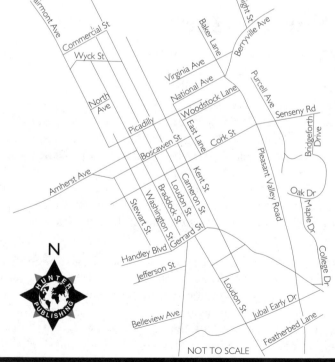

During the Civil War, the city's strategic location was of such importance that it changed hands more than 70 times. Some historians say 13 of those times occurred in a single day! Today, **Stonewall Jackson's Headquarters** (415 N. Braddock St., Winchester, VA 22601, ☎ 540-662-3242) is preserved in much the same condition as when General Jackson used it as a base of operations.

Nearby, the **Stonewall Cemetery** contains the graves of close to 4,000 men who died for the Confederate cause, while approximately the same number who fought to preserve the Union are buried in the National Cemetery.

Surrounded by orchards, Winchester is Virginia's largest producer of apples, and to celebrate its fame, the city hosts more than 250,000 visitors during the **Apple Blossom Festival** held each spring, with parades, music, and arts and crafts.

■ Middletown

Driving south on US 11, Middletown's antique shops, **Wayside Inn and Restaurant** (7783 Main St., Middletown, VA 22645, ☎ 540-869-1797), and acclaimed summer productions at **Wayside Theater** (Main St., Middletown, VA 22645, ☎ 540-869-1776) might be cause enough to spend an evening in the small village.

Belle Grove Plantation (PO Box 137, Middletown, VA 22645, ☎ 540-869-2028) was built in the late 1700s as the home of Major Isaac Hite, Jr., the brother-in-law of James Madison. With its pavilions, columns, Palladian-style front windows, and a hidden staircase, the building resembles other architectural works by Thomas Jefferson – who is said to have had a hand in designing Belle Grove. Now a National Trust Historic Site whose interior is furnished with period antiques, the plantation was occupied by Union General Philip Sheridan as he began his slash-and-burn campaign through the Shenandoah Valley in 1864. It was here that his Union troops defeated General Jubal Early's Confederate forces during the Battle of Cedar Creek.

Shenandoah Valley

■ Strasburg

A few miles south on US 11 will bring you to the **Strasburg Museum** (E. King St., Strasburg, VA 22664, ☎ 540-465-3175) in the old Southern Railway Depot where Stonewall Jackson brought the locomotives he had captured from the Union Army during a raid on Martinsburg, West Virginia. The museum is a potpourri collection of Native American artifacts, items from the Civil War, bits of railroad history, articles from Colonial days, and tools once used by coopers and blacksmiths.

■ Front Royal

Paralleling the North Fork of the Shenandoah River, drive east from Strasburg on VA 55 to swing around the northern flank of Massanutten Mountain as it splits the Shenandoah Valley in two and rises well over 1,000 feet above you. Once you're within the city limits of Front Royal, pick up a walking tour brochure at the **visitors center** (Main St., Front Royal, VA 22630, ☎ 540-635-3185), housed in an old railroad station. It will once again be hard to escape the specter of the Civil War.

Relocated to its present location, **Belle Boyd Cottage** (101 Chester St., Front Royal, VA 22630, ☎ 540-636-1446) is furnished to appear as it would have during the mid-1800s. For nearly two years during the War Between the States, Belle Boyd (described in one tourist pamphlet as a beautiful Southern aristocrat), stayed in the home and used her charms to extract military secrets from the Union forces that had occupied the town. Local lore says she invited General Nathaniel Banks to the home one evening and overheard him discussing upcoming maneuvers with his officers. That night she rode horseback 15 miles to apprise Stonewall Jackson of the situation. Marching through a gap in Massanutten Mountain, Jackson's troops surprised the Union forces on the morning of May 23, 1862, capturing nearly every soldier of the garrison.

Warren Rifles Confederate Museum (95 Chester St., Front Royal, VA 22630, ☎ 540-636-6982) contains memorabilia commemorating this and other events of the war.

At the edge of the city is the northern entrance to **Shenandoah National Park**, with nearly 200,000 acres of woodlands and mountains to explore via the 105-mile Skyline Drive and more than 500 miles of trail.

Just one mile south of Front Royal on US 340 is **Skyline Caverns** (PO Box 193, Front Royal, VA 22630, ☎ 800-296-4545). While not having quite the large numbers of stalactites and stalagmites as some of the other commercially operated limestone caverns spread throughout the Shenandoah Valley, it is one of the few known places in the world with an extensive array of anthodites. Seeming to defy gravity, these unique calcite formations grow down, out, and back up from the cavern ceilings in delicate flower-like forms.

Look at a highway map as you continue to drive south on US 340 and you'll see that you are now paralleling the many twists and turns of the Shenandoah River's South Fork. In order to enjoy the stream's placid beauty, make a right onto just about any roadway you pass, such as VA 613 or VA 663. You'll find that not only do these narrow country lanes deliver you to the banks of the river, but just about every one of them has an outfitter eager to rent you canoes, kayaks, tubes, or any other equipment you may need for day or overnight adventures floating downstream.

■ Luray

If you are going to go underground only once in Virginia, make sure it is **Luray Caverns** (Box 748, Luray, VA 22835, ☎ 540-743-6551). The largest cavern system in the East, it was discovered in 1878 and has been open to the public ever since. The vast display of colored stalactites, stalagmites, natural columns, underground pools, and huge rooms with ceilings more than 10 stories high, make these, by far, the most impressive and beautiful of all of the state's commercially operated caves. During a tour, the world's only "Stalacpipe Organ" produces a New Age sound by using rubber-tipped plungers to strike and resonate stalactites that are spread out over several acres.

It is visited by more than 500,000 people annually, so you should be prepared to wait in line to join one of the hour-long

Shenandoah Valley

conducted tours. Included in the price of admission is the Historic Car and Carriage Caravan, an exhibit of antique cars, carriages, coaches, and costumes dating from 1625.

To the east of Luray (whose name is believed to be a derivative of the French "Lorraine") is an entrance station to Shenandoah National Park on US 222. To the west of town, in New Market Gap, is the **George Washington National Forest Massanutten Visitors Center**. Forest Service employees and volunteers can provide information on the national forest's many opportunities for outdoor adventures. Nearby is the chance to paddle **Passage Creek** or hike the miles-long **Massanutten Mountain Trail**. Adjacent to the visitors center is the .2-mile wheelchair-accessible **Discovery Way Trail** and the half-mile **Wildflower Trail**, which retraces Stonewall Jackson's movements during his Shenandoah Campaign.

Before leaving the visitors center, pick up the free pamphlet describing the **Massanutten Mountain Motoring Tour**. One of the highlights along this driving tour is the opportunity to climb the **Woodstock Observation Tower** for a view of the world-famous horseshoe bends of the North Fork of the Shenandoah River. The meandering course of the river through the Shenandoah Valley between Edinburg and Strasburg is almost 50 miles, yet a straight distance between the two towns is only about 15 miles! You will also drive through aptly named **Fort Valley**. Hidden and surrounded by the eastern and western flanks of Massanutten Mountain, it would have been used by George Washington as a winter retreat had he been defeated by the British at Yorktown.

▪ Grottoes

Unlike highly commercialized Luray Caverns, **Grand Caverns** (PO Box 478, Grottoes, VA 24441, ☎ 540-249-5729) is so far off the average tourist's route (40 miles south of Luray on US 340) that you may have to wait up to 30 minutes before the guides decide no one else is going to show up and take you on your own personal tour. Complete with unique shield formations as well as flowstone, draperies, and the usual stalactites and stalagmites, the caverns contain chambers large enough that General Stonewall Jackson quartered his troops here. One of the largest rooms of any caverns in the East, Cathedral Hall is 280 feet long and over 70 feet high.

The caverns are within the confines of a regional park, which also offers hiking and biking trails, picnic shelters, and a swimming pool.

■ Waynesboro

From Grottoes, drive US 340 into Waynesboro, which thru-hikers (those walking the entire Appalachian Trail from Georgia to Maine) know as such a convenient place to outfit and/or resupply that they come into town in droves. The townsfolk are so friendly that the local YMCA permits the hikers to camp on its grounds and make use of its facilities.

Waynesboro is lucky enough to be situated next to the southern entrance of Shenandoah Park and the northern beginning of the Blue Ridge Parkway at Rockfish Gap. Fourteen miles south along the Parkway, just off VA 664, **Wintergreen Resort** has won numerous awards for the environmentally sensitive way it has developed its downhill ski slopes and attendant facilities.

Also within a short driving distance of Waynesboro are the forest service's **Sherando Lake Recreation Area** (complete with a swimming lake and campground) and **St. Mary's Wilderness**.

■ Staunton

Heading west from Waynesboro on US 250 brings you by the **Museum of American Frontier Culture** (PO Box 810, Dept. AFC, Staunton, VA, ☎ 540-332-7850), just off Exit 222 of I-81. The living history museum features costumed interpreters working on three authentic farms whose structures were brought over from Northern Ireland, England, and Germany – the homelands of many early valley immigrants. A fourth farm shows how these disparate influences blended together into a typical valley farm of the 1830s.

Shenandoah Valley

Downtown Staunton (be sure to pronounce the "au" in the first syllable more like stand than staunch or locals will immediately recognize you as a visitor) has five historic districts listed on the National Register of Historic Places. The **Woodrow Wilson Birthplace and Museum** (24 North Coalter St., Staunton, VA 24401, ☎ 540-885-0897) contains memorabilia tracing Wilson's life in Staunton, through his academic career at Princeton University, then as governor, and on into his two terms as the 28th President of the United States from 1913 to 1921.

For country music fans, the **Statler Brothers' Mini Museum** (501 Thornrose St., Staunton, VA 24402, ☎ 540-885-7297) is housed in the former middle school where Harold and Don Reid Statler were students.

Nearby, the original structure at the site of **Trinity Episcopal Church** (214 Beverly St., Staunton, VA 24401, ☎ 540-886-9132) was the Revolutionary capital of Virginia for 16 days in 1781.

Lexington

■ Lexington

Eschewing the speeding passenger cars and hordes of overloaded semis barreling down I-81, head south along US 11 to Lexington, which has been thrust into the limelight because of a recent US Supreme Court decision. Unlike private Mary Baldwin College in Staunton, **Virginia Military Institute** (☎ 540-464-7207) receives public funds, and the federal justices ruled that it must admit women in order to continue to do so. Breaking an all-male tradition that went back to 1839, the college accepted its first female cadets in 1997 and you can now watch the coed corps go through precision drills during one of the many formal dress parades.

Within the grounds of the institute is the **George C. Marshall Museum** (☎ 540-463-7103), commemorating the life and career of the former cadet whose post-World War II Marshall Plan helped rebuild Europe and earn him a Nobel Peace Prize. Also located here is the **VMI Museum** (☎ 540-464-7232). Among the displays of weapons, uniforms, and other memorabilia from those who attended the college, are, amazingly, the preserved remains of Stonewall Jackson's favorite horse, Little Sorrel.

The atmosphere undergoes a decided change as you walk from the military institute's campus onto that of **Washington and Lee University** (☎ 540-463-8400). Instead of sporting uniforms, closely cropped hair, and rigid postures, the students here resemble those at most other American colleges. All manner of dress, hair style, and an occasional tattoo or body-piercing ring may be seen.

This does not mean that tradition and history have been forgotten at the college once saved from bankruptcy by an endowment of $50,000 (which still generates dividends) from George Washington in 1796. After the Civil War, Robert E. Lee spent the final years of his life as college president and, along with members of his family, is buried below **Lee Chapel and Museum** (Lechter and Washington Sts., Lexington, VA 24450, ☎ 540-453-8768). The museum preserves Lee's office as he left it in 1870. Lee's beloved horse, Traveler, is interred in the adjacent grounds.

Lexington retains such an air of former times that it has been used as the set of major motion pictures. Ronald Reagan's Brother Rat *was filmed here, while the downtown district served as a location for the post-Civil War movie* Sommersby, *produced in 1993.*

The **Stonewall Jackson House** (8 East Washington St., Lexington, VA 24450, ☎ 540-463-2552), the only home owned by the Confederate general, has been restored to its mid-1800s appearance. Nearby on Main St., Stonewall Jackson Memorial Cemetery contains the graves of Jackson and more than 100 Confederate soldiers.

Having the remains of two famous horses within its city limits, it seems appropriate that Lexington is home to the 400-acre **Virginia Horse Center** (PO Box 1051, Lexington, VA 24450, ☎ 540-463-7060), with its annual shows of Arabian horses, US Ponies of America Association, the Miniature Horse Classic, and other equestrian events.

In springtime, when the vegetation on the mountainsides is that new neon-green color and the seasonal rains have swollen the waters of the Maury River, a trip along VA 39 just north of Lexington may just be the prettiest drive in all of Virginia. Beginning in open farmlands, the drive soon climbs into Goshen Pass where the vertical walls of the mountains close in and whitewater tumbles over huge boulders. This Class II-IV section of the river is popular with canoeists and kayakers, while later in the year when the water level has dropped, entire families float lazily down the river on inner tubes.

About a mile past the Maury River Overlook and Picnic Area, be on the lookout for an unsigned dirt road which leads right several hundred yards. Taking the swinging suspension bridge across the river permits you to saunter along restful pathways that parallel the stocked river both upstream and downstream. These routes also connect you to more than 25 miles of hiking and biking trails and dirt roads inside the **Goshen** and **Little North Mountain Wildlife Management areas**.

Continue driving upstream on VA 39 to the small crossroads hamlet of Goshen to take in the local color while having lunch in the **Mill Creek Café** or the **Cozy Corner Restaurant**.

■ Natural Bridge

Once owned by Thomas Jefferson, who purchased it in 1774 for 20 shillings (about $2.49), **Natural Bridge** (PO Box 57, Natural Bridge, VA 24578, ☎ 540-291-2121) is reached by following US 11 south from Lexington. Measuring 215 feet high, 90 feet long, and 150 feet wide in some places, the limestone arch is considered one of the Seven Natural Wonders of the World. (Although you could certainly think of a number of other places that deserve to be on the list, the other six are: Niagara Falls along the New York/Ontario border; The Garden of the Gods in Colorado; Yellowstone National Park in Montana and Wyoming; Valley of the 10 Thousand Smokes along the Alaskan Peninsula; The Blue Grotto of Italy's Isle of Capri; and Giant's Causeway in Dunlace, Ireland.) George Washington was so enamored by the bridge that he carved his initials – which are still visible – 23 feet up one of the sidewalls. Botanists take note:

Shenandoah Valley

along the pathway to the bridge are several arbor vitae trees believed to be over 1,600 years old.

Nearby **Natural Bridge Caverns** are more than 300 feet below the surface and contain three levels with flowstone cascade, hanging garden, and totem pole formations. The dark confines of the underground streams were once home to a population of blind fish, which are believed to have been killed by toxins from money thrown into the cavern's "wishing well."

■ Roanoke

Heading south on US 11, you will drive over the Natural Bridge before merging onto I-81. Continue on to Roanoke which, bounded on the east by the Blue Ridge Parkway and on the west by the Appalachian Trail, is the largest city of the region, situated at the southern end of the Shenandoah Valley.

Native Americans once hunted the animals which were attracted to the area's salt licks, giving rise to the town's original name of Big Lick. Scots-Irish and Germans from Pennsylvania began arriving in the 1700s, soon followed by English settlers from eastern Virginia. The city of Roanoke was incorporated in 1882 when tracks of the Norfolk and Western Railroad joined with those of the Shenandoah Valley Railroad, creating a major crossroads of transportation.

The **Farmers Market**, which was established at this time in downtown Roanoke, is still thriving, making it the one of the oldest in the country still operating in its original location.

Within the restored walls of a 1914 warehouse is the **Center in the Square,** adjacent to the Farmers Market. It is credited with having helped to revitalize the downtown area. In a unique cooperative effort, the building houses several disparate cultural organizations.

The **Art Museum of Western Virginia** (One Market Square, Roanoke, VA, ☎ 540-342-5760) features permanent and visiting exhibits of 19th- and 20th-century American art. Included are paintings, prints, photographs, sculptures, decorative ware, and a section on Southern Appalachian folk art. Admission is free, except during special visiting exhibits.

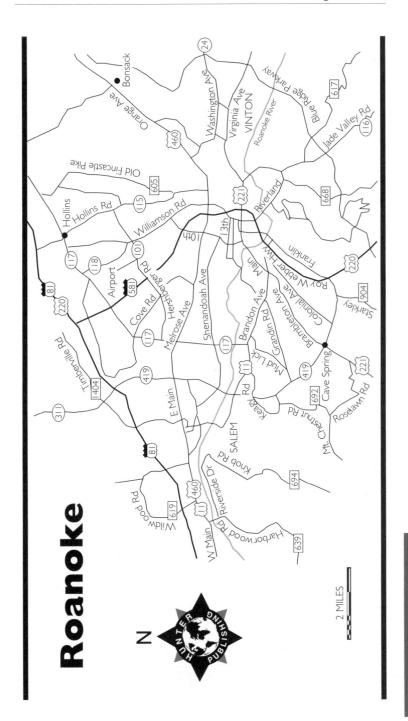

Roanoke

N

2 MILES

The **Science Museum of Western Virginia and Hopkins Planetarium** (One Market Square, Roanoke, VA 24011, ☎ 540-342-1240) takes an interactive approach geared toward small children and older students, but the presentations devoted to light, sound, color, anatomy, physiology, and computer science are engaging enough to keep adults interested too. A Chesapeake Bay Touch Tank, varying shows in the planetarium,-and visiting national exhibits all make a visit here worthwhile.

With displays ranging from prehistoric artifacts to exhibits about the effects of World War II on the valley's residents, the **Roanoke Valley History Museum** (PO Box 2008, Roanoke, VA 24008, ☎ 540-342-5770) illustrates the history of the region from the Stone Age to the present.

Mill Mountain Theater (One Market Square, Roanoke, VA 24011, ☎ 540-342-5745) brings professional productions to the city throughout the year, presenting a variety of musicals, new and experimental works, and old standards.

Housed in what was the first black public high school in western Virginia, the **Harrison Museum of African American Culture** (523 Harrison Ave., Roanoke, VA 24011, ☎ 540-345-4818) researches and preserves the achievements of African-Americans, especially as they relate to southwest Virginia. In addition to its galleries, the museum sponsors a number of festivals and celebrations throughout the year.

As befitting a city whose fortunes are closely tied to the railroads, the **Virginia Museum of Transportation** (303 Norfolk St., SW, Roanoke, VA 24016, ☎ 540-342-6898) displays vehicles from just about every mode of transit man has used. Included are vintage carriages, buses, trucks, fire engines, automobiles, aircraft, railroad cars, steam engines (which you are invited to board), and what the museum describes as the largest collection of diesel engines in the South. One of the more interesting exhibits is a miniature model of a traveling circus.

Roanoke may be the only city in the country that can claim a national park campground and pathway within its municipal boundaries. Providing a break from the hustle and bustle of downtown, the Blue Ridge Parkway's **Roanoke Mountain Campground** and the 5.3-mile **Chestnut Ridge Trail** are just a 10-minute drive away. The moderately easy pathway is a joy to walk in the spring when you'll discover a new bloom around every bend, be it azaleas, lady's slippers, or dogwood trees.

Located on this same ridgeline is the 100-foot-high **Mill Mountain Star**. Thought to be the largest neon star in the world, the electrical sculpture has attracted people, including Elvis Presley, for more than 45 years. In truth, the main attraction of the site is the magnificent view it provides over the city.

Within a five-minute walk of the star is the **Mill Mountain Zoological Park** (PO Box 13484, Roanoke, VA 24034, ☎ 540-343-3241). With more than 40 species of animals, the zoo has prairie dogs, hawks, a golden eagle, Asian reptiles, red pandas, a snow leopard, and a Siberian tiger.

Accessible from Milepost 115 of the Blue Ridge Parkway, **Virginia's Explore Park** (PO Box 8508, Roanoke, VA 24014-8508, ☎ 540-427-1800) allows you to walk through an early 19th-century western Virginia settlement and by a 1750s longhunters' open-faced cabin. (Longhunters spent extended periods of time in the wilderness in pursuit of game.) Costumed interpreters often invite guests to join in their activities, such as weaving on a loom, pumping a blacksmith's bellows, or helping a Native American construct a replica of an ancient lodge. Several miles of hiking trails wind into the gorge created by the Roanoke River and through the less disturbed sections of the park's 1,300 acres.

Just beyond the western boundaries of the city, VA 311 provides access to trails leading to Dragon's Tooth (4.6 miles round-trip) and McAfee Knob (seven miles round-trip) via the Appalachian Trail. From these points there are Olympian views stretching for more than 40 miles. The trailhead parking areas for both of these rugged hikes are clearly marked along the highway. As they are heavily visited areas, please help preserve their beauty by staying on the trail and camping only in designated sites.

Shenandoah Valley

■ Clifton Forge/Covington

Take leave of Roanoke by driving through the subdivided countryside in a northwestern direction along US 220. Soon, perpen-
dicular walls rising from the banks of the James River give you a
good idea of the scenery you would enjoy if you were paddling
down this stream. An excellent 15-mile Class I-II run with some
flatwater could be accomplished by putting in at the US 220
bridge near Lick Run and taking out at the US 220 bridge over
Craig Creek just above Eagle Rock.

Like Roanoke, Clifton Forge owes much of its existence to the
coming of the railroads. In this case, it was the Chesapeake and
Ohio Railway which contributed to the area's growth. The **C&O
Historical Society Archives** (312 East Ridgeway St., Clifton
Forge, VA 24422, ☎ 540-862-2210) preserves photographs, blue-
prints for engines and cars, conductor's uniforms, telegraph ap-
paratus, and books from railroading's early days.

Appropriate for a town that received its name for the production
of iron, the smoke stacks of the 19th-century Lucy Selina Furnace are still standing and can be seen along US 60 east of
Clifton Forge.

The highway also brings you by George Washington National
Forest Service's **Longdale Recreation Area,** which has a
small lake for swimming and connections to a large network of
pathways ascending North Mountain and into Rich Hole Wilderness.

In 1989, the forest service developed the nearby **Highland Scenic Tour**. The signed tour's 19 miles of dirt, gravel, and paved
roadways make it appropriate for explorations on a mountain
bike as well as by car. Because of the ease with which the route
delivers you onto forested slopes, next to rocky outcroppings,
and along grandstand pullouts with unfettered views across
waves of Allegheny Mountain ridgelines, I give it a "spectacular
– do not miss" rating. Wildlife sightings are also a real possibility. The last time I was there I saw more than 10 deer (including
two newly born fawns), soaring turkey vultures, and a black
snake so large it stretched across the width of the road. Additionally, rhododendron in full bloom in early June turns the
higher portions of the drive into a visual delight. Additional in-

formation on the recreation area and scenic tour may be obtained from **James River Ranger District**, 810A East Madison, Covington, VA 24426, ☎ 540-962-2214.

Swimming, boating, fishing, camping, and hiking on 40 miles of pathways are available north of Clifton Forge on VA 629 in **Douthat State Park** (Route 1, Box 212, Millboro, VA 24460, ☎ 540-862-8100). The park is one of oldest in the state's system, with many of its developments having been constructed by the Civilian Conservation Corps. In fact, the cabins for rent date from those days of the 1930s.

Made of hand-hewn oak held together with locust pins, **Humpback Bridge** is three miles west of Covington, just off I-64. The oldest of Virginia's few remaining covered bridges, the 100-foot-long structure is the only surviving curved-span bridge in the United States.

The look and feel of this tour begins to change as you head north from the bridge along VA 600. You'll be leaving behind divided highways, strip malls, and fast food restaurants. Driving into the heart of the Allegheny Mountains on winding two-lane roadways, the pace of the world around you slows down and your attention is drawn to more elemental things such as the waters impounded by Gathright Dam in 12-mile-long **Lake Moomaw**.

Although it is open to motorized boats which seem to be unable to go across the water at anything other than top velocity, the lake does have 43 miles of mountain-surrounded shoreline best explored by muscle and paddle power. In addition to two sandy beaches for swimming, marinas with rentals, and several boat ramps, the forest service has developed more than a dozen picnic and camping areas scattered along the southern and northern shores. All of the land surrounding the lake is public property, so you might want to consider paddling out to enjoy the sunset from your own private tentsite beside a quiet and hidden cove. Those without a boat can hike 3.3-mile-long **Greenwood Point Trail** to five designated primitive sites far removed from the other campgrounds.

Shenandoah Valley

■ Warm Springs/Hot Springs

From the northeastern end of the lake, drive gravel VA 603 through beautiful **Richardson Gorge**, formed by the erosive action of the Jackson River. The thick, leathery leaves of rhododendron and the thin needles of evergreen trees filter the sunlight in this narrow confine, creating bits of shadows and sparkles upon the river's cool water.

The 98° mineral waters in the small hamlet of Warm Springs have been attracting visitors for more than 200 years. Thomas Jefferson stopped by, while several decades later, Mrs. Robert E. Lee immersed herself in the springs to alleviate the pains of arthritis. Today, you can "take the waters" in much the same fashion as these folks did. The bathhouses at **Warm Springs Pools** (c/o The Homestead Hotel, Hot Springs, VA 24445, ☎ 540-839-5500) have changed little since they were constructed in 1761 and 1836.

The regularly scheduled chamber music concerts of the **Garth Newel Music Center** (PO Box 240, Warm Springs, VA 24484, ☎ 540-839-5018) might help further relax you.

About a five-mile drive south on US 220, **The Homestead** (Hot Springs, VA 24445, ☎ 800-838-1766) has all the attractions and trappings you would expect to find in a resort that has for decades consistently received four-star ratings. Famous for its mineral springs long before the United States won independence from England, the 15,000-acre retreat has tennis, swimming, golf, archery, cross-country and downhill skiing, carriage rides, and close to 100 miles of trails available for hiking, biking, and horseback riding. Inside, you can enjoy whirlpools, saunas, ice skating, bowling, exercise and weight rooms, and massages.

■ Monterey & Vicinity

Heading north from Hot Springs on US 220, you will drive deeper into the highlands of the Allegheny Mountains. The area is often referred to as "Little Switzerland," and Monterey is its unofficial capital. Just as the weather begins to warm a bit in early spring, this small village tucked into a high mountain valley plays host to the **Highland County Maple Festival** (☎ 540-468-2550). In addition to enjoying demonstrations on how maple syrup is made, you will find a myriad of items that started life as tree sap. If you are not here in springtime for the festival, visit the **Little Highland Maple Museum** (☎ 540-468-2550), south of town on US 220, for a complete history of syrup making from the olden days to the present.

Stop at the chamber of commerce (PO Box 223, Monterey, VA 24465, ☎ 540-468-2550) to obtain a walking tour brochure and spend some time exploring the town whose roots date back to the early 1700s.

Drive east from Monterey on US 250 to find **McDowell Battle-field** (☎ 540-468-2551), the location of the first victory in Stonewall Jackson's 1862 Valley Campaign. The nearby **McDowell Presbyterian Church** (☎ 540-468-2550) was used as a hospital during the Civil War. Further east on Shenandoah Mountain are the **Confederate Breastworks** constructed by troops as a defense during the war.

As you continue east along US 250, you pass by Ramseys Draft Wilderness (see page 289) and drop out of the mountains to make a left turn onto VA 42. You are now back into the fertile Shenandoah Valley and the region you are driving through is home to a large Mennonite population. At the **Farmers Market** in Dayton you can sample the fruits of their labors; don't pass up the delicious home-baked breads and goodies. It is common to see horses and buggies wending their way along the backroads as you continue on to Harrisonburg.

■ Harrisonburg

In an odd combination, higher education and poultry define the Harrisonburg of today.

The city is the county seat of Rockingham County, which has an annual production of more than 5,000,000 turkeys, most of them processed and frozen in regional packing plants. A turkey sculpture at the southern edge of town attests to the bird's importance for the local economy.

Within city limits, **James Madison University** (South Main St., Harrisonburg, VA 22801, ☎ 540-568-3621) offers guided tours of its 472-acre campus. Besides the attractive bluestone buildings dating from the school's founding in 1908, the programs presented in the university's **Miller Hall and Planetarium** (☎ 540-568-3621) are also of interest.

Seemingly small when compared to the 11,000 students of James Madison University, **Eastern Mennonite University and Seminary** (☎ 540-432-4000) nonetheless provides its 1,000-member student body, and the community, with an art gallery, natural history museum, planetarium, and an historical library containing books and memorabilia relating to the Mennonite religion.

Harrisonburg

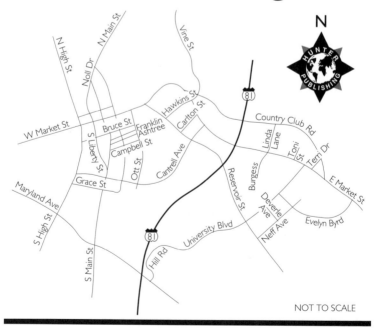

NOT TO SCALE

An electric relief map depicting Stonewall Jackson's Valley Campaign of 1862 is the main feature of the **Warren-Sipe Museum** (301 South Main St., Harrisonburg, VA 22801, ☎ 540-879-2681).

East of Harrisonburg and perched atop the southern tip of a mountain, the **Massanutten Resort** (PO Box 1227, Harrisonburg, VA 22801, ☎ 800-207-MASS) provides one of the four places in Virginia for downhill skiing.

■ New Market

Drive north of Harrisonburg on US 11 to the **New Market Battlefield State Historical Park** (PO Box 1864, New Market, VA 22844, ☎ 540-740-3101), operated by the Virginia Military Institute. On May 15, 1864, the entire student body of VMI marched from Lexington to play a role in defeating larger Union forces at this site. Almost next door is the privately operated **New Market Battlefield Military Museum** (9500 Collins Parkway, New Market, VA 22844, ☎ 540-740-8065), which has a collection of more than 3,000 military items and artifacts from 1776 to the present.

Millions of years ago water and carbon dioxide combined to make carbonic acid – which then flowed into the mountains, eating away at limestone and forming the **Endless Caverns** (PO Box 859, New Market, VA 22844, ☎ 540-896-2283). Guided tours explain the geology, history, and exploration of the caverns. Living up to its name, over five miles of the cave passage have been mapped, and no end has yet been found.

Less than 20 minutes away by car, the **Shenandoah Caverns** (Shenandoah Caverns, VA 22847, ☎ 540-477-3115) lets you become subterranean once more. The tour winds through chambers, great rooms, and towering ceilings, and by formations creatively dubbed Grotto of the Gods, Vista of Paradise, Rainbow Lake, and Bacon Hall.

Continuing the driving tour north on US 11, take a half-mile detour on VA 720 to **Meems Bottom Covered Bridge**, one of only several such bridges surviving in Virginia.

Shenandoah Valley

At Mount Jackson you can take a longer detour to **Bryce Resort** (PO Box 3, Bayse, VA ☎ 800-821-1444), in the mountains to the west. Although it is the smallest of the state's ski spots, the resort has some fun and challenging runs and provides an intimate family atmosphere.

■ Woodstock

Although strip malls and discount stores have come to Woodstock, it is still possible to see what this still-small town was before the interstate brought changes. The **Shenandoah County Courthouse** on Main St. was built in 1792 and is the oldest courthouse still in use west of the Blue Ridge Mountains. The inside has been restored to its original design. The **Woodstock Museum** (137 West Court St., Woodstock, VA 22664, ☎ 540-459-5518) has a collection of maps, tools, pottery, furniture, hardware, and other artifacts of local history and the life of early settlers.

There's no better way to end a tour of the Shenandoah Valley than by driving back south just a few miles to Edinburg and the **Shenandoah Vineyards** (3659 South Ox Road, Edinburg, VA 22824, ☎ 540-984-8699). Situated on 40 acres surrounded by the mountains, the valley's first winery has free daily tours and tastings of its Chardonnay, Cabernet Savignon, Cabernet Blanc, Shenandoah Ruby, and other palate-pleasing wines.

Adventures

■ On Foot

Front Royal Area

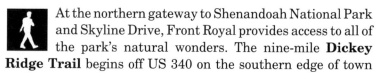 At the northern gateway to Shenandoah National Park and Skyline Drive, Front Royal provides access to all of the park's natural wonders. The nine-mile **Dickey Ridge Trail** begins off US 340 on the southern edge of town

stream. See the Shenandoah National Park chapter (above) for more information on the park.

MASSANUTTEN MOUNTAIN: Rising out of the middle of Shenandoah Valley, Massanutten Mountain's hundreds of acres of national forest land provide grand hiking, backpacking, and camping opportunities. There are so many miles of inter-connecting pathways that it is possible to spend days and even weeks exploring the mountain without ever retracing your steps. The best of those trails are described below.

An overnight journey begins after driving close to 11 miles from Front Royal to the forest service's **Elizabeth Furnace** picnic area on VA 678. Begin the hike from here and ascend 4½ miles along **Signal Knob Trail** [FS402] to a grandstand view onto the northern reaches of the Shenandoah Valley. During the Civil War, the Confederacy watched the movement of Union troops from this spot. By using a series of signaling flags, this information was relayed back to Richmond where strategies were planned.

From Signal Knob it is possible to hook up with the **Massanutten Mountain Trail North** [FS408] to do some ridgeline walking south for 17 miles to VA 675. Along the way you'll have a chance to climb the **Woodstock Observation Tower** to view the famous horseshoe bends of the North Fork of the Shenandoah River.

Hike the **Tuscarora Trail** [FS405] (still referred to on maps and other guidebooks by its older name of Big Blue Trail) for about two miles to join up with **Massanutten Mountain Trail East** [FS404]. With occasional views across the valley to the mountains of Shenandoah National Park, the rocky pathway continues south along the main crest of the mountains. With occasional views across the valley to the mountains of Shenandoah National Park, the rocky pathway continues southward along the main crest of the mountains. With a total distance of about 23 miles, it descends to end at the forest service's Camp Roosevelt Campground on VA 675.

At nine miles in length, the **Duncan Hollow Trail** [FS410] heads southward and upstream along Duncan Creek from the campground. Rising to cross over a ridgeline, the trail descends along the waters of Big Run to end on US 211, just east of the campground. Rising to cross over a ridgeline, the trail descends along the waters of Big Run to end on US 211, just east of the George Washington National Forest Massanutten Visitors Center.

Across US 211 from the Duncan Hollow Trail, the **Massanutten Mountain Trail South** [FS416] provides 19½ more miles of backpacking pleasure before coming to its southern terminus along FDR 65. (Gravel FDR 65 is most easily reached from the small town of Shenandoah via VA 602 and VA 636.)

Take a look at the George Washington National Forest Map and you'll realize that all of the above trails link together and could be followed for more than 50 miles of continuous hiking.

Waynesboro/Staunton Area

WINTERGREEN: Located south of Waynesboro off Milepost 13.7 of the Blue Ridge Parkway, Wintergreen (PO Box 706, Wintergreen, VA 22958, ☎ 800-325-2200) has developed a 30-mile system of marked trails coursing into the farthest reaches of the resort's 11,000 acres. A .4-mile round-trip jaunt, the **Plunge Trail** descends to an awe-inspiring view across the valley below and over to some of the higher peaks of the George Washington National Forest. A round-trip journey of three miles along the **Cedar Cliffs Trail** passes through a heath thicket of rhododendron, mountain laurel, and azalea. The Cedar Cliffs overlook the impressive **Shamokin Gorge** where waterfalls can be heard crashing through the chasm.

SHERANDO LAKE RECREATION AREA: With its large campground, picnic area, and sandy beach, Sherando Lake Recreation Area is popular with locals as well as travelers. You can reach the area by taking the Waynesboro & Lyndhurst exit of I-64 and following VA 624 to Lyndhurst. After a couple of miles, bear left onto VA 664 for a little more than seven miles to the entrance road.

The one-mile **Lakeside Trail** [FS300] is an easy loop around the lake. Branching off from this pathway, the **Cliff Trail** [FS301] provides higher elevation views of the lake for .7 mile. Ascending for 2½ miles, **White Rock Gap Trail** [FS480] connects the recreation area with the Blue Ridge Parkway by passing through an impressive gorge, complete with waterfalls and small wading pools along tree-lined Back Creek. **Blue Loop Trail** [FS507A] climbs from the campground to meet up with **Torry Ridge Trail** [FS507]. In addition to superb vistas across Kelly Mountain and into the Mill Creek watershed, this crestline pathway provides access to the trails of St. Mary's Wilderness – when combined with a short walk along FDR 162.

ST. MARY'S WILDERNESS: By car, St. Mary's Wilderness may be reached by following VA 606 east from the Raphine/Steeles Tavern exit of I-64/81 for 1½ miles to Steeles Tavern. Make a left onto US 11 for only .1 mile before turning right onto VA 56. After 1.1 miles there is a left turn onto VA 608. An additional 2½ miles brings you to FDR 41, which leads to the wilderness entrance parking lot.

The Wilderness Act

America achieved permanent protection for certain tracts of public land with the passage of the Wilderness Act in 1964. Within a few years, more than 90 areas and 11,000,000 acres had been preserved. However, the act was not as far-reaching as its proponents had hoped, as all but four of the areas were in the West. The law's definition of wilderness "the area generally appears to have been affected by the forces of nature, with the imprint of man's work substantially unnoticeable") prohibited almost any place in the East from being included in the system. Recognizing that this portion of America, with its earlier settlement and heavier population concentration, had more disturbed land than the West, a new law was passed in 1975. This permitted places where the evidence of human activity was being reclaimed by natural processes to be included.

Shenandoah Valley

St. Mary's is a prime example of an area which would have been excluded before 1975. Railroad tracks wound along the river valley and onto the mountains, permitting the removal of the manganese and iron ores that were mined during the early part of the 20th century. Additionally, surface mining began during World War II and continued to scar the land well into the 1950s. Vegetation has now begun to obscure much of the evidence of these activities, but hikers can still find ample reminders of these bygone days.

St. Mary's River Trail [FS500] heads upstream from the parking area. Most people follow it about 1½ miles and turn left onto **St. Mary's Falls Trail** [FS500B] for a half-mile to enjoy an afternoon of swimming and slumbering at the base of the 20-foot falls. The more adventurous continue up the main pathway to join with other wilderness trails and have the opportunity to explore the remains of the old surface mines – pits dug deeply into the earth, concrete and steel blocks, bits of iron slag, and small mounds of dirt covering old equipment.

 If you hike here – or in any other officially designated wilderness areas of Virginia – be aware that, in tune with the spirit of a true wilderness, the trails may not be as well maintained as other trails, and that the forest service is permitting the paint blaze markings to fade away.

Lexington/Clifton Forge/Covington

Owned by the VMI Foundation, but open to the hiking public, the seven-mile **Chessie Nature Trail** connects Lexington with Buena Vista to the east. Following a railroad grade along the Maury River, the route passes old locks, historic sites, steep cliffs, woodlands, and pastures. By obtaining the *Field Guide to the Chessie Nature Trail* (Rockbridge Area Conservation, PO Box 564, Lexington, VA 24450) available in local bookstores, you can turn this very pleasant and nearly level, easy walk into a family project to learn more about the history, geology, plants, and animals found along the way.

In addition to the Chessie Nature Trail, residents of Buena Vista can walk out their front doors and onto the **Elephant Mountain Trail System**. Beginning at the end of 12th St., **Reservoir Hollow Trail** [FS509A] provides several pleasant backcountry campsites as it ascends to pass by Elephant Mountain Trail in 1.7 miles, before ending at its intersection with Indian Gap Trail. Close to one mile and rising to 2,101 feet, **Elephant Mountain Trail** [FS509B] looks out onto the surrounding Garnet and Paxton peaks through breaks in the mountain laurel and pine trees. From the end of 21st St. in Buena Vista, the **Indian Gap Trail** [FS509] ascends through hemlock trees and blueberry bushes, connects with **Reservoir Hollow Trail** in 1½ miles, and continues to rise by mountain laurel, rhododendron, and bracken fern to terminate on US 60 in 2.6 miles.

Although it takes a bit of effort to reach, waterfall lovers should seek out the **Panther Falls Trail** [FS508]. Drive east from Buena Vista on US 60, go under the Blue Ridge Parkway, turn right onto FDR 39 for about three miles, and you will come to the trailhead parking area. A walk of approximately one mile brings you to the multi-level falls, whose waters froth and churn through a narrow passageway and into watercarved pools and bowls.

South of Buena Vista on US 501, the **Appalachian Trail** passes through the 9,000-acre **James River Face Wilderness**, with its multiple miles of interconnecting pathways. One of the best is the **Belfast Trail** [FS9] which, in its 2.8 steep and difficult miles, goes by Devil's Marbleyard, a large outcrop of loose boulders.

Off US 60 between Lexington and Covington, the **North Mountain Trail** [FS467] winds up to the crest of North Mountain from Longdale Furnace Recreation Area. Hikers are rewarded with bubbling streams, fascinating rock formations, and a variety of forest environments. There are views of the surrounding countryside, Lake Roberston, and the far-off Peaks of Otter along the Blue Ridge Parkway. In a little more than nine miles,

Shenandoah Valley

the trail connects with FDR 447, which is part of the Highland Scenic Tour for automobiles.

Warm Springs/Hot Springs

THE HOMESTEAD: Guests of The Homestead in Hot Springs have 100 miles of pathways to explore in the resort's 15,000 acres.

Just a short drive up dirt and gravel VA 658 from The Homestead, the **Little Mare Mountain Trail** [FS714] and the **Brushy Ridge Trail** [FS456] connect to provide close to 10 miles of hiking. Wildflowers such as bluets, trillium, and azalea are particularly beautiful along these pathways in the spring. Also be on the lookout for wild turkey, deer, and an abundance of squirrels and chipmunks; turkey vultures are often spotted from numerous rock outcroppings.

LAKE MOOMAW: In addition to the **Greenwood Point Trail** [FS720] already described above (page 277), Lake Moomaw has other walking opportunities to offer. From the Bolar Mountain Recreation Area, the 1.8-mile **Grouse Point Loop Trail** [FS721] leads to two outstanding views of the lake. Near the Fortney Branch Boat Launch on FDR 604, the **Oliver Mountain Trail** [FS469] and **Jackson Trail** [FS469A] combine for four miles through a forest of oak, hickory, and mountain laurel along moss-lined pathways.

Monterey

LOCUST SPRINGS RECREATION AREA: This recreation area provides a chance to walk through a bit of New England while still in Virginia. Red Spruce, red pine, and birch thrive, interspersed with sugar maple and oak. Beaver ponds flood mountain valleys, creating the bogs that are so much associated with states farther north. The area is also home to snowshoe hares and is one of the few places in Virginia with a known population of northern flying squirrels. This isolated and not-well-visited spot may be reached by driving US 220 north of Monterey to Forks of Water, where a left turn onto rough-surfaced VA 642 will eventually lead you to the recreation area. The **Laurel**

Fork Trail [FS450], at 6½ miles, follows the lovely waters of its namesake, providing access to over 20 more miles of pathways. Hiking and backcountry camping in Virginia don't get much better than what you will find here.

Beaver Pond at Laurel Fork.

RAMSEYS DRAFT WILDERNESS: East of Monterey on US 250, Ramseys Draft Wilderness has over 6,500 acres of mountainous terrain which reaches heights of more than 4,200 feet. Treks of several days are possible, making use of close to 30 miles of interconnecting pathways and camping under hemlock trees estimated to be at least 300 years old. Despite having been inundated and washed out by flash floods in the last few decades – resulting in a somewhat arduous walk along a rough pathway which crosses the stream a number of times – seven-mile **Ramseys Draft Trail** [FS440] is still the main route into the wilderness.

Harrisonburg Area

The city of Harrisonburg occupies an enviable position, roughly two hour's drive from everything described in this chapter on the Shenandoah Valley Region. So, if you base yourself here for a few days, your options are many.

Close by, the forest service maintains developed recreation areas at Hone Quarry, Shenandoah Mountain, Todd Lake, and North River – all within a 30-minute drive of each other. Emanating from or near these places are so many interconnecting trails that it would take a week or more to hike all of them.

Among the best of these is the **Cliff Trail** [FS440], which climbs from the Hone Quarry Campground to the top of Oak Knob. The impressive views of Shenandoah Mountain, Slate Springs Mountain, and Hone Quarry Lake make the 1,500 feet of elevation gain worth the effort.

Nearly eight miles in length, the **Timber Ridge Trail** [FS 431] climbs over 2,600 feet from FDR 101 near Hearthstone Lake to a 360° viewpoint atop Reddish Knob on Shenandoah Mountain.

Between the Shenandoah Mountain and Todd Lake recreation areas along FDR 95, you may have to ford North River to begin the **Bald Knob Trail** [FS716]. However, once you've gotten your feet wet and ascended for over three miles, you're going to have a most spectacular view. To the northeast is Massanutten Mountain; on clear days it is even possible to see the mountains of Shenandoah National Park. To the west is the undulating ridgeline of Shenandoah Mountain, while beyond are the higher spires of the Allegheny Mountains of West Virginia. If you have the time, make camp here; the sunrises and sunsets can be awe-inspiring.

Woodstock

In an out-of-the-way spot along the Virginia/West Virginia border on VA 675 west of Woodstock, the **Tibbet Knob Trail** [FS578] ascends through a mixed forest of hardwoods and pines for 1½ miles to 2,925 feet in elevation on Tibbet Knob, for views onto the Allegheny Mountains of West Virginia. Continuing for another mile, the trail ends on VA 691, which can be walked west for three miles to the beginning of the **North Mountain Trail** [FS1009]. Staying along the Virginia/West Virginia border, this 6½-mile pathway covers steep and rocky terrain with overlooks and outcroppings providing views of the Shenandoah

Valley and Blue Ridge Mountains to the east and the Allegheny Mountains to the west. The route's southern trailhead is along VA 720.

Camping Equipment Outfitters

Wilderness Voyagers, 1544 Market St., Harrisonburg, VA 22801, ☎ 540-434-7234.

Rockfish Gap Outfitters, 1461 Main St., Waynesboro, VA, ☎ 540-943-1461.

Backcountry Ski & Sports, 1931 Apperson Drive, Salem, VA 24153, ☎ 540-389-8602.

Blue Ridge Outdoors, Tanglewood Mall, Roanoke, VA 24014, ☎ 540-774-4311.

■ On Wheels

Mountain Biking

Front Royal/Luray

 By combining lightly traveled paved roads, gated dirt roads, and forest service trails, the riding possibilities are nearly endless for mountain bikers in the Massanutten Mountain area west of Front Royal and Luray.

MASSANUTTEN MOUNTAIN NORTH: On the northern end of the mountain, **Elizabeth Furnace Recreation Area** provides the starting point for a number of rides.

Directly across VA 678 from the recreation area, **FDR 1350** has a moderately easy seven-mile round-trip ride on a dirt and gravel roadway.

A more challenging and strenuous 10½-mile ride can be accessed just north of the recreation area from VA 678. From the signed Signal Knob parking area, take the yellow-blazed **Signal Knob Trail** [FS402], leaving the parking lot to the right. The climbing begins almost immediately along switchbacks. An overlook at 1½ miles provides a glimpse of Buzzard Rocks, a prominent outcropping to the east; the mountains of Shenandoah National Park are to the southeast. Continue following yellow blazes to 2,106-foot Signal Knob for commanding views of the northern reaches of the Shenandoah Valley. From the knob, locate and follow the orange blazes of the **Massanutten Mountain West Trail** [FS408], which will bring you to the headwaters of Little Passage Creek, 5.1 miles into the ride. At 5.7 miles, make a left onto the blue-blazed **Bear Wallow Trail** [FS405]. Ascend to the main crest of the mountain before a quick descent returns you to the parking area.

MASSANUTTEN MOUNTAIN SOUTH: On the southern portion of Massanutten Mountain, a long ride of close to 40 miles begins at the Catherine Furnace Recreation Site near the junction of FDR 375 and FDR 65. Take FDR 375 west for more than one mile to make a left and follow the full length of the **Massanutten Mountain South Trail** [FS 416] to its terminus on FDR 65. Turn left on this gravel roadway to return to Catherine Furnace. This ride has it all: single track, double track, dirt and gravel roads, rocks and boulders, rough and rocky terrain, stream crossings, views, and more.

Do not underestimate the time required to complete the above full loop; there are numerous places you'll end up walking or carrying your bike across.

Waynesboro/Staunton

SHERANDO LAKE CAMPGROUND TRAILS: The trails close to the Sherando Lake Campground attract increasing numbers of mountain bikers every year.

Especially popular – because they all join up with FDR 162, FDR 162A, and FDR 162B in an area known as Big Levels – are six-mile **Torry Ridge** [FS507], seven-mile **Mills Creek** [FS518], and three-mile **Kennedy Ridge** [FS479].

Be aware these trails and roadways can connect you with those of St. Mary's Wilderness and the Blue Ridge Parkway, which are closed to bikes.

GREAT NORTH MOUNTAIN: A different **North Mountain Trail** [FS443] than the ones discussed in the *On Foot* section above enables you to ride the crest of Great North Mountain for more than 14 miles in one direction. The northern trailhead is reached by driving VA 254 west from Staunton for about eight miles to Buffalo Gap, where you continue straight on VA 42 for a short distance to turn right onto VA 688. Be alert as the trailhead is an unmarked parking area on the left side of the road in Dry Branch Gap.

The ride begins along an old road, but soon ascends along a single track route. Be prepared, as you'll ascend more than 2,000 feet in 4.7 miles to Elliot Knob, the highest point of the George Washington National Forest. The vista makes the effort worth it as you gaze upon what will be the rest of this ride along the ridgeline of Great North Mountain. Shenandoah Mountain is to the west. To the east, across Little Calfpasture Valley, is the Virginia Department of Game and Inland Fisheries' Wildlife Management Area on Little North Mountain. (The management area's dirt roads make up an excellent 25 miles of isolated riding.)

From Elliot Knob, North Mountain Trail continues along the ridge, crossing FDR 82 at 8½ miles, goes over a series of knobs, and makes a two-mile descent along an old woods road to end on VA 687 at 14½ miles. You can drive to this southern trailhead by going south on VA 42 from Buffalo Gap to Craigsville. About two miles from the small town, make a right onto VA 687 to a parking spot on the top of the mountain.

Roanoke

CARVIN COVE: A trail system open to mountain bikes has been developed around Carvin Cove, a reservoir serving as part of the city's water supply. There are so many miles of connecting pathways and fire roads that it would take a couple of days to explore all of them. An easy ride of about 90 minutes follows dirt road **Carvin's Trail** along the edge of the reservoir from the boat dock to the picnic area. A more technical ride of several hours includes Carvin's Trail, a 1,000-foot climb on **Fire Road**, a quick descent along the **Hi-Dee-Hoe Trail**, and a right turn onto paved VA 740 to return to Carvin's Trail and the boat dock.

There are several trailheads for the Carvin Cove Trail system, but the easiest way to reach the boat dock is to drive I-81 to the Hollins exit, head north on US 11 for two miles, and make a left onto VA 649 (Reservoir Road). Free trail system maps are available from **Blue Ridge Outdoors** (☎ 540-774-4311) in Tanglewood Mall.

THE DRAGON'S BACK: About 10 miles west of Roanoke on US 311 is a system of forest service trails local mountain bikers refer to as The Dragon's Back. In conjunction with FDR 224 (Wildlife Road), **Deer Trail** [FS186], **Grouse Trail** [FS188], **Turkey Trail** [FS 187], and **North Mountain Trail** [FS263] present such a challenge that they have been used for officially sanctioned mountain bike races.

Lexington/Clifton Forge/Covington

SOUTH PEDLAR ATV TRAIL SYSTEM: Although you have to share the woodlands with motorized vehicles, the South Pedlar ATV Trail System has a looping 25-mile network of trails from which to enjoy an abundance of mountain laurel blossoms and panoramas of the James River Valley. Some of the trails are wide and easy, others narrow, twisting, and quite inclined. You may access the trail system by driving east from Lexington on US 60 to Buena Vista, where you'll turn south on US 501. About one mile beyond the US 501/VA 130 intersection, make a left onto FDR 564 to arrive at the trailhead parking lot.

LONGDALE RECREATION AREA: Just off US 60 west of Lexington, Longdale Recreation Area makes a great base camp for a number of trips. **YACCer's Run Trail** [FS 658] encircles the area for an easy three-mile loop. For a much longer and moderately strenuous ride, follow the route of the spectacular and highly recommended **Highland Scenic Tour,** described on page 276. Those with good technical skills might want to try a 12-mile circuit across I-64 from the recreation area. Rising on

FDR 108, you'll come to the site of a former fire tower with views into the Cowpasture River Valley and onto Rough and Beards mountains. The ride gets interesting as you negotiate the **White Rock Tower Trail** [FS466] on a rough and rocky tread-way past occasional vistas and a steep descent with switchbacks to a left turn onto gravel FDR 333. This, in turn, returns you to pavement and the starting point of the ride.

FDR 55: Clinging to the Virginia/West Virginia border, FDR 55 begins in Gathright Wildlife Management Area (close to Lake Moomaw north of Lexington) off VA 600. From here it is possible to make a moderately easy ride of more than 25 miles (sharing the road with an occasional logging truck) to isolated VA 84, west of Mill Gap.

Warm Springs/Hot Springs

HIDDEN VALLEY: Hidden Valley has changed so little from the mid-1800s that the area was used to film the 1993 post-Civil War movie *Sommersby*. Wherever you gaze, there are no utility lines, communications towers, or microwave dishes to mar the ridgelines. The forest service's **Hidden Valley Campground** provides a base from which to explore. Drive to the campground from Warm Springs by following VA 39 west for 1½ miles to make a right onto VA 621. In one mile, turn left onto FDR 241 to the campground on the left side of the road. An easy loop ride of 5½ miles along the Jackson River can be accomplished by combining **FDR 241**, the **Hidden Valley Trail** [FS 481], and the **Jackson River Gorge Trail** [FS481D]. Along the way, you'll pass by historic Hidden Valley Bed and Breakfast (see *Where To Stay*, below). Numerous dirt roads and other trails make the Hidden Valley area a place you will want to explore again and again.

A few miles north of Warm Springs on US 220, dirt **FDR 124** ascends about five miles to 3,839-foot **Duncan Knob** for grand vistas of the mountains of Virginia and West Virginia.

Guests of The Homestead in Hot Springs have 100 miles of pathways available to them on which to explore the resort's 15,000 acres by bike.

Monterey

HIGHLAND WILDLIFE MANAGEMENT AREA: Accessible from VA 678, Highland Wildlife Management Area has more than 14,000 acres and 20 miles of dirt and gravel roadways to explore on bike. All of these roads (and the area's footpaths) are unsigned and unblazed, so be prepared with a good map, a compass, and a working knowledge of how to use them. An especially rewarding journey is to take the side road up to **Sounding Knob Lookout** for a view down onto the placid Bullpasture River Valley.

SHENANDOAH MOUNTAIN TRAIL: East of Monterey on US 250 is the Shenandoah Mountain Trail (South) [FS 447], whose highlights include many panoramic vistas, rock outcroppings, pleasant backcountry campsites, good springs, and numerous side roads and pathways to explore. Built by the Civilian Conservation Corps in the 1930s, the route begins across from the Confederate Breastworks on US 250 by following dirt FDR 336 for about three miles. Single track begins and you will enjoy riding the main crest of the ridge for another 18 miles to the route's end on VA 627 (which may be accessed from VA 629 north of Green Valley).

Harrisonburg

HONE QUARRY RECREATION AREA: Within a 30-minute drive of downtown, trails of the Hone Quarry Recreation Area have become a mountain biking Mecca for residents of Harrisonburg. From the city, drive VA 42 to Dayton, where you'll turn right onto VA 257 for 11 miles to FDR 62. The recreation area is three miles further.

A moderately difficult ride begins across the road from the recreation area by climbing over 1,500 feet on the **Cliff Trail** [FS 429] to intersect and turn left onto the **Slate Springs/Meadow Knob Trail** [FS428] at the summit of Oak Knob. Continue to climb, arriving on Pond Knob at 4½ miles. From here you should take a side journey (still following the Slate Springs/Meadow Knob Trail) of a little more than a half-mile to the bald summit of Meadow Knob for a grandstand view of the mountains and ridgelines to the north. Returning to Pond Knob, turn right and make a fast and steep (make sure your brakes are in good shape!) descent along the **Pond Knob Trail** [FS428B] to FDR 62. A left turn along the roadway returns you to the recreation area and brings an end to this approximately 10-mile loop.

A ride of moderate difficulty going up, but requiring agility and quick thinking descending, also begins in the recreation area. Follow **FDR 62** uphill for a half-mile to a left turn onto **Big Hollow Trail** [FS 430] ascending to **Hone Quarry Ridge Trail** [FS435], which is, in actuality, a jeep road. Bear right through mountain laurel and blueberry bushes, continuing to ascend. Somewhere along the way, the designation for the route changes from pathway to **FDR 539**. At 6.4 miles into the ride, turn right on **FDR 85** for a short distance before making another right on **FDR 85A** to arrive at Flagpole Knob, at 9½ miles. Just beyond the knob, turn right to follow the orange blazes of the **Slate Springs Trail** [FS428A] for two extremely steep miles, before making a left onto FDR 62 and returning to the recreation area at 12.3 miles.

 This is a great ride, but do not underestimate the steepness and difficulty of descending along the Slate Springs Trail.

TODD LAKE RECREATION AREA: South of Hone Quarry, the Todd Lake Recreation Area has two rides worth checking out. Across FDR 95 from the lake, **Trimble Mountain Trail** [FS 375] is a 3.8-mile loop trail of moderate difficulty. Fossils found at some of the rock outcroppings along the trail show the outlines of plants that were growing on the mountain as it was formed about 300,000,000 years ago during the Paleozoic era. A short drive from the lake, the **North River Gorge Trail** [FS538] is an easy ride of 4½ miles between FDR 95B and FDR 95. Nine stream fordings keep this an interesting ride, while an abundance of wildflowers add to the beauty of the bottomland through which you are passing.

THE ROCKY RUN ATV COMPLEX: This is a 12-mile system of loop routes encircling the headwaters of Rocky Run. Although open to ATV's, motorcycles, and even four-wheel-drive vehicles in some places, the trails are such a rough and rugged

Shenandoah Valley

challenge that local mountain bikers can't resist them. The system's signed trailhead is about 10 miles west of Harrisonburg along US 33.

Woodstock

Get on your bike and take **VA 758** east out of town, entering the rich, green, fertile landscape that has given the Shenandoah Valley much of its fame. Stay on VA 758 through several intersections, soon crossing the North Fork of the Shenandoah River. Remember what the river looks like close up, for soon you'll be treated to an aerial view taking in many miles of its course. The road eventually turns to dirt and makes numerous switchbacks up to the highest reaches of Powell Mountain. Once on the ridgeline, walk .2-mile to the Woodstock Mountain Lookout and its famous view of the horseshoe bends of the river. Continuing on VA 758 drops you down into Fort Story Valley and provides access to all of the rides described in the Front Royal/Luray section above.

Mountain Biking Regulations

All trails in Congressionally designated wilderness areas, the entire Appalachian Trail, and a few other trails on national forest lands are closed to bikes. Yet, because the George Washington and Jefferson National Forests have taken a very broadminded approach, there are thousands of miles of dirt roads and trails open to mountain bikers. You may ride your bike on any forest road or trail unless it is specifically closed to mountain bike use; the routes closed are usually well signed. Although prohibitions are few, it is recommended you contact the forest service if you are in doubt about a particular trail. Sadly, signs are vandalized or removed; it is your responsibility to know the restrictions and regulations.

Road Biking

The TransAmerica Bicycle Route

Close to 120 miles of the 4,100-mile TransAmerica Bicycle Route are located within the Shenandoah Valley Region. Marked by "Bike-76" signs along the highways, the route enters the southern portion of the valley near Roanoke. Making use of lightly traveled roads, it heads northeast, passing through or coming close to the cities and towns of Catawba, Daleville, Troutville, Buchanan, Natural Bridge, and Lexington. From Vesuvius, the route climbs to the Blue Ridge Parkway, which it follows north to Rockfish Gap east of Waynesboro. Here it leaves the Shenandoah Valley Region and drops quickly into the Piedmont.

US 11

From Winchester to Roanoke – a distance of about 170 miles – US 11 parallels I-81, making a grand tour of the entire Shenandoah Valley. Although it is a major roadway, the mostly local traffic is fairly light and much of the route is four-lane, providing ample room for cars to pass.

Front Royal/Luray

VA 678: West of Front Royal, VA 678 is a lightly traveled roadway whose 18 miles traverse the full length of Fort Valley, which is enclosed by the towering eastern and western ridgelines.

If you don't mind a bit of traffic, VA 678 could be incorporated into an excellent full day's ride. From Front Royal, head west on VA 55 for about seven miles to the left turn onto VA 678. When you turn left onto VA 675, you will pass by Camp Roosevelt Campground and have a bit of a climb to cross over the eastern flank of Massanutten Mountain before a pleasant descent to the Shenandoah River. About two miles past the river, make a left on VA 654. (Continuing straight on VA 675 for two miles delivers you into Luray, with an opportunity to visit Luray Caverns.)

VA 654 intersects well-traveled US 340, which you'll follow north back to Front Royal. Along the way you might want to take one of the numerous roadways to the left to rent a canoe from an outfitter and enjoy a paddle along the South Fork of the Shenandoah River.

PAGE VALLEY: An enjoyable ride through the farmlands of Page Valley, beside the South Fork of the Shenandoah River and along the eastern edge of Massanutten Mountain, begins in Luray. Head south from town on VA 616 for seven miles to intersect and turn left onto US 340 for just a short distance before another left onto VA 650. Riding beside the river, make a left onto VA 602, cross US 340 and the river, and come to the end of the ride at US 33. (A couple of miles west on US 33 brings you to The Boarding House, a bed & breakfast operated in conjunction with Pineapple Pedalers – see *Where To Stay*, below.)

Waynesboro/Staunton

GROTTOES: A moderately easy ride of about 10 miles begins in Grottoes, 14 miles north of Waynesboro. During the trip you will be brought to the edge of Shenandoah National Park and have the chance to explore some underground caverns. From the small town, head east on VA 661, gaining about 350 feet in elevation over four miles, to make a right turn and descend along VA 778. (Staying straight at the intersection will put you onto an unimproved roadway, but, in approximately one mile, it also brings you in contact with the Trayfoot Mountain and Paine Run hiking trails of Shenandoah National Park.) In the small settlement of Harriston, turn right onto US 340, but almost immediately make a left back onto VA 778, which brings you to a right turn onto VA 825. This small road along the South River returns you to Grottoes, where Grand Caverns are located on the edge of town.

STAUNTON: A full day's ride from Staunton begins by heading south on US 11, soon making a left onto VA 635, where a short half-mile side-trip allows you to visit the Museum of American Frontier Culture (see page 283). Continue on VA 635, cross I-81, and – a little over five miles from the museum – bear right onto VA 608. The smell of chocolate from the Hershey factory permeates the air as you enter Stuart's Draft. Just before crossing US 340, The Candy Store gives you a chance to purchase some of the factory's products. Continue on VA 608 along the edge of George Washington National Forest to make a right onto VA 662. Cross US 11 and I-81 to make a right onto VA 613 and return to Staunton.

Roanoke/Salem

Roanoke's adjacent city, Salem, has a 16-mile marked bike route coursing up and down and into some of its prettiest and most interesting neighborhoods.

THE TRANSAMERICA BICYCLE ROUTE: An especially enjoyable 19-mile stretch of the TransAmerica Bicycle Route begins north of Roanoke at the junction of US 11 and VA 779 in Troutville. Ride VA 779 west under I-81, make a right onto US 220, and a left in .1 mile to continue on VA 779. Passing by numerous intersections, you will stay on this route through achingly beautiful and bucolic Catawba Valley, running within the shadows of Tinker, Catawba, and North mountains. The ride ends on VA 311 in the small hamlet of Catawba, where one of the best restaurants in the region, The Homeplace, is located (see *Where To Eat*, below).

Lexington/Clifton Forge/Covington

GOSHEN PASS: In the springtime, VA 39 through Goshen Pass is one of the prettiest rides in western Virginia. (See the Lexington/Clifton Forge *Touring* section, above.)

A much longer – close to 50 miles – and much more strenuous loop version of the above journey may be accomplished by heading north from the center of Lexington on US 11, crossing the Maury River and bearing left onto VA 631. Soon you'll begin rising in elevation, paralleling Kerrs Creek, making a right onto US 60, and quickly bearing left onto VA 850. Cross I-64 and avoid the first left onto VA 780 to make the next right onto VA 780, which you will follow along Barton's Run to a right turn onto VA 39. This route brings you through Goshen Pass and onto US 11, which is followed south to the starting point. Do not underestimate the ups, downs, and difficulties of this ride – even for those in the best of shape.

Shenandoah Valley

CLIFTON FORGE: Another hard, but very rewarding ride has two forest service campgrounds along its route and a bed & breakfast accessible by a short detour – which is good, as you should definitely not attempt this ride in one day. Begin off the I-64 Lowmoor Exit west of Clifton Forge by riding south along Karnes Creek on VA 616. Pass by several intersections to make a left onto VA 617. You'll be riding along the edge of Barbours Creek Wilderness where the **Pines Campground** gives you an opportunity for a break or a stopping spot for the night. Continuing along VA 617, make a left and descend VA 611 to make another left onto VA 615. (Staying straight at this intersection would bring you to New Castle for refreshments at the small grocery store and soft beds if you decide to stay at The Inn B&B, PO Box 351, New Castle, VA 24127, ☎ 540-864-5715.)

Continuing northeast on VA 615, you will be riding through **Craig Creek Valley**, where rural scenery may make it hard for you to keep peddling. Consider making the short side-trip to the **Craig Creek Campground** for a break, a wade in the stream, or rent a tentsite. Several miles beyond the campground, bear left onto VA 621, do some very serious climbing over **Rich Patch Mountain**, and make a right onto VA 616 to return to the starting point of this wonderful journey. Suitable only for those with stamina and experience.

Warm Springs/Hot Springs

An easy ride of approximately 10 miles begins at the spa in Warm Springs, heads west along VA 39 for three miles to make a right onto VA 629. Rising along this road, you have the option of taking a short side-trip into Hidden Valley. Continuing on VA 629, come to US 220, make a right and descend back into Warm Springs for a relaxing soak in the spa.

Monterey

BULLPASTURE RIVER VALLEY: Beginning on US 250 in McDowell east of Monterey, lovely Bullpasture River Valley is a downstream ride of nearly 10 miles along VA 678 to Williamsville. If you have the stamina and the time for a day's worth of riding, it is possible to continue on VA 678 to Green Valley, where you will bear left onto VA 629 and ride northeast to US 250 at West Augusta. Although US 250 could bring you back to the starting point, it is strongly suggested you have someone meet you and end the journey here. It is a hard climb over Shenandoah Mountain, and traffic along the narrow and twisting roadway only adds to the misery of the ascent.

Harrisonburg

An afternoon's loop ride through Mennonite farmland begins by riding west from Harrisonburg on VA 763 for several miles to turn north onto VA 613. In the hamlet of Singer's Glen, keep to the right onto VA 721, which brings you past Edom and VA 42 to a south turn onto VA 753. From here it is a little over three miles back to Harrisonburg.

One of the very few companies offering cycling tours in the state that is actually based in Virginia, **Pineapple Pedalers** (RR 1 Box 15, McGaheysville, VA 22840, ☎ 800-893-2516) has inn-to-inn packages available, or will custom-design a tour for you. These folks also put together mountain biking, hiking, and canoeing trips. In just a few years, founder Steve Poulson has developed Pineapple Pedalers into one of the state's premier outdoor adventure organizations.

Bicycle Outfitters

Blue Ridge Cycleworks, 774 East Market St., Harrisonburg, VA 24011, ☎ 540-432-0280. In addition to sales and service, this is where the Shenandoah Mountain Bike Club gathers for weekly mountain rides.

Mark's Bike Shop, 1570 South Main St., Harrisonburg, VA 24011, ☎ 540-434-5151.

Mole Hill Bikes, 440 North Main, Dayton, VA 22821, ☎ 800-MOLEHILL.

Cardinal Bicycle, 2901 Orange Ave. Northeast, Roanoke, VA 24012, ☎ 540-344-2453.

East Coasters Cycling & Fitness, 4341 Starkey Road, Roanoke, VA 24014, ☎ 540-774-7933.

■ On Horseback

Front Royal/Luray

 Nestled in between the eastern and western arms of Massanutten Mountain, **Fort Valley Riding Stable** (229 South Fort Valley Road, Fort Valley, VA 22652, ☎ 540-933-6633) has guided rides from one hour to half-day trips to overnight excursions into the mountain's higher elevations.

South of Luray, **Jordan Hollow Farm Inn** (326 Hawksbill Park Road, Stanley, VA 22851, ☎ 888-418-7000) offers guided trail rides of varying lengths. All-day rides course through the Blue Ridge and Massanutten mountains. Guests staying at the inn are encouraged to bring their own horses.

In the same vicinity, **River's Bend Guest Ranch** (397 Riversbend Drive, Stanley, VA 28851, ☎ 800-672-7726) has riding adventures that include an introduction to horses and guided trail rides along the South Fork of the Shenandoah River. The rides are Western style on American quarter horses, paints, and appaloosas.

Waynesboro/Staunton

Within the extensive grounds of Wintergreen Resort, the experienced guides of **Rhodes Farm Stables** (Wintergreen Resort, Wintergreen, VA 22958, ☎ 804-325-8260) provide trail rides daily (except Wednesdays) from mid-March through November. In addition to these trips using English saddles, there are also pony rides for children, sunset trail rides, riding lessons, vaulting lessons, and private and advanced rides.

Roanoke

In Craig County west of Roanoke, the **Ferrier Trail** [FS 189], **FDR 5026**, and **Lick Branch Trail** [FS 262] connect with each other for more than 10 miles of quiet backcountry riding. Because these trails were quite overgrown the last time I was on them, I suggest making an inquiry as to present conditions at the **New Castle Ranger District Office** a few miles north of New Castle on VA 615 (PO Box 246, New Castle, VA 24127, ☎ 540-864-5195).

Lexington/Clifton Forge/Covington

The 400-acre **Virginia Horse Center** (PO Box 1051, Lexington, VA 24450, ☎ 540-463-7060) is a year-round facility for horse-related activities with shows, clinics, auctions, and festivals. Information on riding opportunities in the region is also available.

If you've brought your own horse and have forgotten or lost some equipment, **Lexington Horse and Country** (11 West Washington St., Lexington, VA 24450, ☎ 540-464-9500) should be able to help you replace it.

For some isolated riding on infrequently used hunter trails and dirt forest service roads, drive from Lexington on VA 39 through Goshen Pass. In the crossroads settlement of Goshen, turn west on VA 42, soon to make a right onto VA 640, which leads you to a right turn onto FDR 61. This narrow road gives you access to **Mill Mountain Trail** [FS 492], **Jerrys Run Trail** [FS659], **Back Draft Trail** [FS 546], and gated **FDR 387** – all of which can be connected for a full day's (or more) worth of riding.

Near the Fortney Branch boat launch on FDR 604 in the Lake Moomaw area north of Covington, **Brushy Lick Loop Trail** [FS502] and **Oliver Mountain Trail** [FS469] are open to horses and connect for close to nine miles of riding.

Maintained by a local riding club, 14-mile **Fore Mountain Trail** [FS 473] begins at the forest service's Dolly Anne Work Center off Valley Ridge Road in Covington. Rising for two miles, the trail stays close to the crest of the mountain, with occasional views to the east and the west. Dropping to ford Smith Creek, the trail rises again, crosses VA 606, and meets up with the **Middle Mountain Trail** [FS473.1; older maps show this as FS 458], for additional miles of riding.

Shenandoah Valley

Outfitters

Virginia Mountain Outfitters (Route 1, Box 244, Buena Vista, VA 24416, ☎ 540-261-1910) offers riding trips with overnight accommodations and meals at the working Lavender Hill Farm. Multi-night pack trips from inn to inn or rustic camping adventures with everything supplied but sleeping bags can also be arranged.

Warm Springs/Hot Springs

Guests of **The Homestead** in Hot Springs can explore the resorts 15,000 acres on 100 miles of pathways.

In addition to hour-long and half-day trail rides, **River Ridge Guest Ranch** (Route 1, Box 119, Millboro, VA 24460, ☎ 800-221-0635) has hay wagon rides complete with an outdoor dinner atop a high-elevation ridgeline.

Monterey

LOCUST SPRINGS RECREATION AREA: Isolated Locust Springs Recreation Area may be reached by driving US 220 north of Monterey to Forks of Water, where a left turn on rough-surfaced VA 642 will eventually lead you to the recreation area. **Laurel Fork Trail** [FS450], at 6½ miles, follows the lovely waters of its namesake, providing access to over 20 more miles of pathways open to horses. You will be wandering through a landscape more like New England than Virginia.

SHENANDOAH MOUNTAIN EQUESTRIAN TRAILS: East of Monterey on US 250 are the Shenandoah Mountain Equestrian Trails, a system of 25 miles of old forest roads, hiking trails, open roads, and constructed horse trails marked by yellow plastic diamonds for horse users. Two sites designated by the forest service as horse camps provide access to this system. One camp is on VA 616, the other along FDR 396 at the top of Shenandoah Mountain.

Nearby, on VA 616 close to the settlement of Head Waters, **Shaws Ridge Trail** [FS 652] gives you an option for six more miles of riding.

Harrisonburg

Mountaintop Ranch (Route 1, Box 402, Elkton, VA 22827, ☎ 540-298-9542), located east of Harrisonburg, runs hour-long to two-day trips through its property, which is bounded on three sides by Shenandoah National Park.

WILD OAK NATIONAL RECREATION TRAIL: Steep ascents, miles of trail at high elevation, good water sources few and far between, two major river fords, and a rough and rocky treadway in many places – descriptions such as this may scare off timid riders. However, if you are experienced and view these challenges as reasons to ride, the Wild Oak National Recreation Trail [FS 716] can be a great escape from the crowds. Spur trails – **Bald Ridge** [496], **Dowells Draft** [FS650], and **White Oak Draft** [FS496] – connect with the main route, giving you more than 40 miles of backcountry to explore.

 Be aware that water is scarce, so carry plenty for you and your mount. In addition, be prepared to meet mountain bikers who are also attracted to the rigors of this ride.

The main trailhead for the Wild Oak National Recreation Trail is reached by driving west from Harrisonburg on VA 42 to make a right onto VA 747 at Mossy Creek. In several miles, bear right onto VA 730, which is followed to the signed trailhead parking on FDR 95.

Woodstock

T. Jay Stables (Bayse, VA 22810, ☎ 540-856-8100) at Bryce Resort has daily (except Wednesday) one-hour guided trail rides around Lake Laura from Memorial Day Weekend to Labor Day Weekend.

Shenandoah Valley

Equestrian Equipment Outfitters

Lexington Horse and Country, 11 West Washington St., Lexington, VA 24450, ☎ 540-464-9500.

Jay's Saddle & Tack Shop, 2800 West Main St., Salem, VA 24153, ☎ 540-387-0150.

■ On Water

Winchester

 OPEQUON CREEK: Kept relatively clear by the numerous springs that feed it, Opequon Creek east of Winchester is a moderately easy alternative through pleasant farmland for those who wish to avoid the crowds along the Shenandoah River. North from US 50 to the West Virginia line provides close to 20 miles of stream to paddle, with numerous road crossings for put-in and take-out points.

 Be on the lookout for a low water bridge and dam that need to be portaged.

SHENANDOAH RIVER: Further east, world famous Shenandoah River has evoked praise from generations of paddlers. Bounded on the west by fertile farmland with the Blue Ridge Mountains rising to the east, the scenery could not be any prettier. Unless the water is extremely high, the river provides a wonderful 20-mile experience for beginners and families from its beginnings near Front Royal to the West Virginia line. There are trailerable launch sites at river crossings on VA 624, US 17/50, along VA 621 near Lockes Landing, and on VA 7.

CEDAR CREEK: Those with just a bit more experience will enjoy the Class I-III trip on Cedar Creek, south of Winchester. With caves, cliffs, historic structures, and a waterfall coming in from a side waterway, do not be so distracted that you neglect to portage around a number of low water bridges.

Front Royal

PASSAGE CREEK: Draining isolated Fort Valley between the eastern and western ridgelines of Massanutten Mountain, north-flowing Passage Creek is appropriate for a variety of skill levels. The upper portion of the stream down to the Elizabeth Furnace Recreation Area alternates flowing through open farmland and heavy forest, with just a few small rapids. On the other hand, the lower stretch roars through a gorge as the creek drops out of the mountains to meet up with the North Fork of the Shenandoah River near VA 55.

 On both sections you need to watch for trees in the stream, several low water bridges, and dams.

SOUTH FORK OF THE SHENANDOAH RIVER: Possibly the most family-suitable waterway in all of Virginia, the South Fork of the Shenandoah River meanders through outrageously beautiful Old Dominion scenery of farmland, mountains, and forests. Starting near Port Republic, more than 100 miles of the river are runable during the season. Most people concentrate on the lower 50 miles or so between Newport and Karo Landing, which has mostly flatwater paddling, with an occasional Class I-II rapid. Many folks tube the river during the summer and early fall. The forest service's **High Cliff Canoe Camp** provides picnic tables, grills, and pit toilets for those who want to undertake an overnight journey.

Outfitters

Front Royal Canoe Company (PO Box 473, Front Royal, VA 22630, ☎ 540-635-5440) rents canoes, flatbottom boats, and tubes for day or overnight trips – in addition to supplying shuttle services, even for those with their own boats.

Located next to the river, **Downriver Canoe Company** (Route 1, Box 256-A, Bentonville, VA 22610, ☎ 540-635-5526) also provides canoe rentals and shuttles. Their free handout map gives an excellent overview of the river.

Shenandoah Valley

Basically next door, **River Rental Outfitters** (PO Box 145, Bentonville, VA 22610, ☎ 800-RAPIDS1) not only has canoes, kayaks, rafts, and tubes for rent, but will also customize paddling, biking, or hiking trips and supply all of the necessary equipment.

A bit further south, **Shenandoah River Outfitters** (6502 South Page Valley Road, Luray, VA 22835, ☎ 800-6CANOE2) has canoes for sale as well as for rent.

Waynesboro/Staunton

THE SOUTH RIVER: While watching out for an occasional downed tree, moderately skilled paddlers will find that the South River provides a fairly easy journey all the way from a trailerable put-in at Waynesboro to a take-out at Port Republic. The mountains of Shenandoah National Park form the backdrop to the east, while farmland and livestock pastures are seen along the western bank.

Roanoke

CATAWBA CREEK: When the water is up, there is no prettier whitewater stream in the southern portion of the Shenandoah Valley region than Catawba Creek. With its headwaters west of Roanoke along the slopes of Catawba Mountain, the creek twists and turns north through open farmland, limestone gorges, and by towering hillsides to its meeting with the James River south of Clifton Forge.

 Low water bridges, fences across the stream, a number of dams, and no trailerable ramps make this a journey only for those with experience in dealing with such obstacles.

POTTS CREEK: Further west of Roanoke, the same warnings apply to Potts Creek from Paint Bank to its confluence with the Jackson River near Covington. However, if you are up to the challenge of making some quick, expert moves in several spots, you will be paddling through one of the most bucolic valleys in all of Virginia. In addition to cattle-dotted pastures, rock outcroppings, and clear water, the mountains rise up on both sides of the valley to frame the sky above. The forest service's **Steele Bridge Campground** enables you to make this an overnighter.

Outfitters

If you are new to paddling, unsure of yourself in the water, or just want to improve your skills, the ACA-certified instructors at **Back Country Ski & Sports** (1931 Apperson Drive, Salem, VA 24153, ☎ 540-389-8602) can help you.

Lexington/Clifton Forge/Covington

THE MAURY RIVER: As it flows through the steep sidewalls of Goshen Pass, the Maury River is one of the most popular stretches of whitewater in Virginia. The Devil's Kitchen, Sliding Rock, Undercut Rock, and other Class II-IV rapids make this a run only for expert kayakers and canoeists, yet later in the summer when the water is down, many folks take lazy tubing trips downstream. Most people put in along VA 39 above the pass and take out on VA 39 at Rockbridge Baths.

THE JAMES RIVER: From its beginnings near Clifton Forge, the James River has many, many miles of wonderful paddling for novices and experts alike. An especially beautiful 30-mile stretch with Class II-IV rapids is from Springwood to Snowden, where the river cuts through the Blue Ridge Mountains.

Outfitters

For those who don't have their own watercraft, **James River Basin Canoe Livery** (RFD 6, Box 125, Lexington, VA 24450, ☎ 540-261-7334) rents (and sells) everything you need for a safe trip – kayaks or canoes, paddles, life jackets, river maps, orientation, instruction, and shuttle service. In addition to offering package trips on the lower Maury River and along many miles of the James River, they will put together customized hour, day, or overnight trips for you.

> **Wilderness Canoe Company** (US 11 & VA 130, Natural Bridge, VA 24578, ☎ 540-291-2295) has a 50-acre wilderness base camp from which they coordinate paddling, hiking, and biking trips.

THE JACKSON RIVER: From Lake Moomaw's Gathright Dam to a take-out above Covington, the Jackson River has close to 15 miles of Class I-II rapids appropriate for those with intermediate skills. The high bluffs and cliffs, open valley, and green farmland add to the serenity of the surroundings. Public access points are below the dam spillway and at the river crossings of VA 687, VA 721, and VA 687. Be aware that land on both sides of the river is private property.

Warm Springs/Hot Springs

THE JACKSON RIVER ABOVE LAKE MOOMAW: If you want to do some backcountry camping while on a paddling trip, check out the Jackson River above Lake Moomaw. From the put in along US 220 north of Warm Springs to a take-out beside FDR 241, the river passes through heavily wooded forest service land in Hidden Valley, which is bounded by the rising heights of Warwick Mountain and Little Mountain. Those with moderate skill levels should be able to accomplish these eight to 10 miles with no difficulties.

Monterey

BULLPASTURE RIVER: Just as cyclists like riding along the Bullpasture River east of Monterey, so too will paddlers with Class II-IV experience enjoy the 15 or so miles of the river from US 250 to Williamsville. Especially pretty, but also the most difficult, are the few miles through the Bullpasture Gorge.

Harrisonburg

THE NORTH RIVER: For another gorge experience, drive west from Harrisonburg on VA 42 to make a right onto VA 747 at Mossy Creek. In several miles, bear right onto VA 730, which becomes FDR 95. Follow this dirt road to a left onto FDR 95B

The put in is next to the forest service campground. After doing some scouting along the North River Trail, advanced paddlers will probably have no time to enjoy the stunning scenery as they will be busy with nearly constant rapids, rock gardens, ledges, and possible downed trees across the narrow stream.

Woodstock

NORTH FORK OF THE SHENANDOAH RIVER: Like the South Fork, the North Fork of the Shenandoah River has close to 100 miles of runable water, with most of it appropriate for those just beginning to test their skills. With its headwaters high in the mountains of Rockingham County, the meandering river crosses the width of the Shenandoah Valley, passing under I-81 north of New Market. Paddlers enter the Seven Bends of the North Fork near Edinburg, while the stretch from Mauertown to Strasburg is the most family-friendly.

Canoe & Kayak Equipment Outfitters

Village Store, Routes 659 & 605, Port Republic, VA, ☎ 540-249-3096.

Backcountry Ski & Sports, 1931 Apperson Drive, Salem, VA 24153, ☎ 540-389-8602.

Appalachian Adventures, Inc., 1122 Wasena Ave. Southwest, Roanoke, VA 24015, ☎ 540-342-2858.

■ On Snow

Massanutten

 Located within the confines of a large natural bowl at the southern end of its namesake mountain, Massanutten (PO Box 1227, Harrisonburg, VA 22801, ☎ 800-207-MASS) has a 1,100-foot vertical drop – the largest in Virginia. The longest of its 14 slopes is 4,100 feet and one of the most difficult runs is reserved exclusively for snowboarders. The Massanutten Adaptive Ski School promotes alpine skiing instruction to help individuals overcome a variety of physical challenges and its instructors follow programs as defined by National Handicapped Sports.

Wintergreen Resort

Wintergreen Resort (PO Box 706, Wintergreen, VA 22958, ☎ 800-325-2200) has 17 downhill ski slopes, the majority of which are lit for night skiing. The resort has won numerous awards for the environmentally sensitive way it has been developed. More than half of its 11,000 acres have been set aside as a woodlands preserve, never to be developed. Most of the condominiums and private homes have been clustered around the slopes, so that, even within the developed area, as much of the forest as possible was left standing. Although the environment would be best served by no further development in the world, if we must disturb the land, architects and planners would do well to emulate Wintergreen's example.

The Homestead

Situated in the heart of the mineral spa region of the Southern Appalachians, The Homestead (Hot Springs, VA 24445, ☎ 800-838-1766) may be known as an upscale, four-star retreat, yet lift tickets to its nine slopes (with a 900-foot drop) are among the lowest cost in the state. In addition, the resort's 15,000 acres present ample opportunity for some cross-country skiing.

Bryce Resort

The smallest of the state's ski spots, family oriented Bryce Resort (PO Box 3, Bayse, VA ☎ 800-821-1444) does an excellent job of accommodating skiers of all skill levels. Covering more than 20 acres, eight slopes drop 500 feet into a narrow mountain valley occupied by a golf course, condos, and individual homes. During the off-season, Bryce is the only place in Virginia where you can learn how to grass ski, a sport best enjoyed by the young and agile.

Shenandoah Mountain Trail

Following a route first dug by the Civilian Conservation Corps in the 1930s, Shenandoah Mountain Trail [FS447] heads north from US 250 east of Monterey. Unlike other ridgeline trails which seem to go up and over every knob and knoll, this pathway skirts these natural fluctuations, resulting in a 10-mile route with little change in elevation. In addition, frequent, heavy snows make this a great cross-country ski route (with options for backcountry camping).

Chessie Nature Trail

Although snowfall is less in the valley, there are a number of days each winter that cross-country skiers are able to enjoy gliding along the Chessie Nature Trail's old railroad grade for seven miles between Lexington and Buena Vista.

■ In The Air

 In recent years, hang gliding enthusiasts have been using **Massanutten Mountain** near the Woodstock Lookout Tower as a launch site to ride the thermals rising from the Shenandoah Valley. Regulations and conditions change from time to time, so it is best to contact the forest service for the most current information. George Washington and Jefferson National Forests, 5162 Valleypointe Parkway, VA 24019, ☎ 540-265-6054.

Scenic airplane flights of varying lengths over the valley and the Blue Ridge Mountains are offered at the **Warren County Airport** (229 Stokes Airport Road, Front Royal, VA 22630, ☎ 540-635-3570), and from the Woodrum Airport in Roanoke by **Bill Saker Flying Service** (☎ 540-362-5331). Most folks who have done so say that just after sunrise and before sunset are the best times to enjoy these aerial ventures.

You can take a breathtaking flight over scenic McAfee Knob and the other mountains surrounding Roanoke by contacting **Sky Shots Helicopter Service** (41B West Main St., Salem, VA 24153, ☎ 540-387-3379).

McAfee Knob.

Making use of a meadow as a landing field in Craig County west of Roanoke, the **Blue Ridge Soaring Society** (HC34 Box 54, New Castle, VA 24127, ☎ 540-864-5542) sponsors an annual race in late summer/early fall, which attracts glider devotees from around the world.

You can experience the thrill of soaring through the air without a motor by taking flying lessons with **Shenandoah Valley Soaring** (Eagle's Nest Airport, Waynesboro, VA 22980, ☎ 540-293-5997). Children as young as 14 can take lessons and you can obtain a license by the age of 16!

One of the best (and most romantic) ways to welcome the day is to make reservations for **Shenandoah Balloon Adventures** (PO Box 388, Bayse, VA 22810, ☎ 540-856-3337) to take you on an early morning flight over the northern Shenandoah Valley. Floating along – almost as silently as the drifting fog – you will be above the rest of the world, able to watch deer and other wildlife wake to greet the sun as it rises over the heights of the Shenandoah Mountains. A brunch of champagne and finger food delicacies caps the experience.

■ Ecotours

As a part of its commitment to environmental awareness, **Wintergreen** (PO Box 706, Wintergreen, VA 22958, ☎ 800-325-2200) sponsors a number of ecotourism weekends each year. The programs, led by the staff of the Wintergreen Nature Foundation and academic guest lecturers, feature slide presentations, guided field or canoe trips, and group discussions. Topics in the past have included Early Spring in the Blue Ridge, Wildflower Identification, Birds of the Blue Ridge, and Geology of the Appalachians.

Have you ever wondered if you could find enough to survive if you were stranded in the wilderness? Foraging classes led by **Highland Adventures** (PO Box 151, Monterey, VA 24465, ☎ 540-468-2733) will teach you how to live off the land. The one-day classes are designed to provide a solid background on the subject, while the multi-day classes are rigorous and experiential – you eat only what you find. Highland Adventures' staff is also adept at teaching the skills needed for caving, rappelling, rock climbing, and mountain biking. Programs can be custom-tailored for individuals or groups.

Where To Stay

Winchester & Vicinity

Many of the town's motels, of course, are clustered around the I-81 exits. **Days Inn** [$] (1601 Martinsburg Pike, Winchester, VA 22603, ☎ 540-667-2818) has a swimming pool and an adjacent restaurant. Also low cost is **Bond's** [$] (2930 Valley Ave., Winchester, VA 22601, ☎ 540-667-8881), providing complimentary morning coffee.

The **Travelodge** provides a free continental breakfast, heated pool, and accepts pets [$$] (160 Front Royal Pike, Winchester, VA 22602, ☎ 540-665-0685).

Southeast of Winchester, the 10 rooms of **L'Auberge Provencale** [$$$$ to $$$$$] (PO Box 119, White Post, VA 22663, ☎ 800-638-1702) were once on a sheep farm owned by Lord Fair-

Shenandoah Valley

fax in the mid-1700s. Bellhops and a complimentary full break-fast are part of the experience. Biking and horseback riding are also offered.

South of Winchester, the building housing the **Wayside Inn** [$$$ to $$$$] (7783 Main St., Middletown, VA 22645, ☎ 540-869-1797) has been in the business of catering to travelers since the end of the 18th century. Each of the restored 24 rooms is decorated with antiques, fine art, and memorabilia.

Front Royal/Luray

Being the northern gateway to Shenandoah National Park, Front Royal has more accommodations than other towns its size. Most are located on the southern end of town, close to the park entrance.

Some of the 107 rooms at the **Quality Inn Skyline Drive** [$$] (10 Commerce Ave., Front Royal, VA 22630, ☎ 540-635-3161) have refrigerators and microwaves, and all are decorated with pleasing touches.

Providing basic, but clean rooms are the **Scottish Inn** [$] (535 South Royal Ave., Front Royal, VA 22630, ☎ 800-251-1962) and the **Twin Rivers Motel** [$] (1801 Shenandoah Ave., Front Royal, VA 22630, ☎ 540-635-4101).

Located near the center of town, **Chester House B&B** [$$ to $$$$$] (43 Chester St., Front Royal, VA 22630, ☎ 540-636-8695) sits on two acres of formal English gardens. The 1905 Georgian home has seven rooms available for guests.

South of Front Royal on US 340 you could hike all day and never have to leave the 100 acres of **Cedar Point Farmhouse** [$$ to $$$] (221 Good Mill Road, Rileyville, VA , ☎ 540-743-3408).

Near the caverns in Luray, **Luray Caverns Motel East** and **Luray Caverns Motel West** [$$] (PO Box 748, Luray, VA 22835, ☎ 540-743-4531) provide basic family-oriented accom-modations.

Ramada Inn [$$ to $$$] (PO Box 389, Luray, VA 22835, ☎ 800-2RAMADA) is a bit more upscale, with swimming and wading pools, horseshoes, volleyball, and an outdoor fitness course.

A stay at the truly upscale **Woodruf House B&B** [$$$$] (320 Mechanic St., Luray, VA 22835, ☎ 540-743-1494) includes a full breakfast, afternoon tea, and a multi-course "fine dining" evening meal. A heated Jacuzzi is surrounded by manicured gardens, while canoes and bicycles are available for guest use.

Close to Shenandoah National Park, **The Cabins at Brookside** [$$ to $$$$] (2978 US 211E, Luray, VA 22835, ☎ 540-743-5698) allow you to be rustic and luxurious at the same time.

Seven miles south of Luray, **Milton House B&B** [$$$] (PO Box 366, Stanley, VA 22851, ☎ 540-778-3451) pampers guests with an included candlelight dinner, a full breakfast, private baths, and an outdoor Jacuzzi.

Waynesboro/Staunton

Within the same price range are the **Budget West Lawn Motel** [$ to $$] (2240 West Main St., Waynesboro, VA 22980, ☎ 540-942-9551) and the **Comfort Inn Waynesboro** [$ to $$] (640 West Broad St., Waynesboro, VA 22980, ☎ 540-942-1171).

The lowest rates in town are usually found at the **Deluxe Budget Motel** [$] (2112 West Main St., Waynesboro, VA 22980, ☎ 540-949-8253).

Built in 1991, the guest rooms of the cedar and brick **Iris Inn B&B** [$$ to $$$] (191 Chinquapin Dr., Waynesboro, VA 22980, ☎ 540-943-1991) are attractively decorated with antiques or reproductions and have wildlife or nature themes. Wraparound porches on both the first and second floors provide restful views of the 20-acre tract on the western slope of the Blue Ridge Mountains.

Located south of Waynesboro off Milepost 13.7 of the Blue Ridge Parkway, the ski resort of **Wintergreen** (Wintergreen Resort, Wintergreen, VA 22958, ☎ 804-325-8260) has all manner of accommodations – from motel-type rooms, to condos, to private homes – available at a wide range of prices. Within the resort grounds is the **Trillium House** [$$$] (PO Box 280, Nellysford, VA 22958, ☎ 800-325-9126), a country inn known far and wide for its relaxing atmosphere, large rooms, and the quality and quantity of its full breakfast. Guests receive preferred rates for many of Wintergreen's attractions.

Just off I-81 at Staunton and close to the Museum of American Frontier Culture, the **Comfort Inn** [$$] (1302 Richmond Ave., Staunton, VA 24401, ☎ 800-221-2222) and the **Holiday Inn Staunton** [$$ to $$$] (PO Box 3209, Staunton, VA 24402, ☎ 800-932-9061) provide the usual amenities most of us expect from these chains.

Within the center of town and accented by a relaxing herb and flower garden, five connected townhouses of Greek Revival design comprise the historic **Frederick House B&B** [$$ to $$$] (28 North New St., Staunton, VA 24401, ☎ 540-885-4220). The hosts here can help your plan day outdoors.

Also near the center of town is the **Belle Grae Inn B&B** [$$ to $$$$] (515 West Frederick St., Staunton, VA 24401, ☎ 540-886-5151). It has several separate buildings as well as the main house. Guests are greeted with tea and cookies, there is afternoon tea and sherry, and evening drinks are provided in the main parlor.

The Buckhorn Inn [$$] (HCR 33 Box 139, Churchville, VA 24421, ☎ 800-693-4242) sits at the base of the Allegheny Mountains 12 miles west of Staunton. In addition to lodging in a restored 1811 structure, the inn features country buffets and hearty family-style meals.

Lexington

On a hillside location with a scenic view, the **Keydet General Motel** [$ to $$] (RFD 6 Box 31, Lexington, VA 24450, ☎ 540-463-2143) accepts pets and has free movies and cable TV. The **Best Western Inn at Hunt Ridge** [$$ to $$$$] (Route 7 Box 99A, Lexington, VA 22450, ☎ 540-464-1500) also has a view overlooking the Blue Ridge Mountains, plus indoor and outdoor pools. The 100 rooms have a country decor, coffemakers, and free movies.

In the heart of Lexington, **Llewellyn Lodge B&B** [$$ to $$$] (603 South Main St., Lexington, VA 24450, ☎ 800-463-3225) will not only put you up in comfort, but will provide advice and trail maps for hiking and biking in the area. They will also put together customized outdoor adventure packages.

If you wish to be close to the Virginia Horse Center, check in at the nearby **Comfort Inn** [$$ to $$$] (PO Box 905, Lexington, VA 24450, ☎ 540-463-7311), which has an indoor pool, coffemakers, free movies, and a complimentary continental breakfast.

Almost next door to the horse center is the **Fassifern** [$$ to $$$] (Route 5 Box 87, Lexington, VA 22450, ☎ 540-463-1013), a country inn set in a restored 1867 home. Each of the five guest rooms has a private bath. Although the included meal is called a continental breakfast, most guests agree that fresh fruit, freshly squeezed orange juice, croissants, ham, spreads, and homemade cereals deserve to be called a bit more than that.

Roanoke/Salem

As is befitting of the largest city in the Shenandoah Valley Region, the number of places to stay here is almost overwhelming, ranging from low-cost motels to pleasant bed and breakfasts and luxury hotels.

If you are simply looking for a clean and comfortable place to spend the night, the **Budget Host Blue Jay Motel** [$] (5399 West Main St., Salem, VA 24153, ☎ 800-283-2080) at I-81 Exit 132 should suffice.

Knight's Inn [$] (310 Wildwood Road, Salem, VA 24153, ☎ 800-843-5644) off I-81 Exit 137 will also provide you a night's sleep in simple, but clean rooms.

Clustered around the Roanoke County Airport are a host of national chain motels, including the **Hampton Inn** [$$] (6621 Thirlane Road, Roanoke, VA 24019, ☎ 540-265-2600) and the **Holiday Inn** [$$] (6626 Thirlane Road, Roanoke, VA 24019, ☎ 800-HOLIDAY).

The huge **Marriott-Roanoke Airport** [$$ to $$$$] (2801 Hershberger Road, Roanoke, VA 24017) has 320 rooms, two pools, whirlpool, sauna, lighted tennis courts, and an exercise room.

Shenandoah Valley

Hotel Roanoke & Conference Center [$$$ to $$$$] (110 Shenandoah Ave., Roanoke, VA 24016, ☎ 800-222-8733) provides luxury accommodations in the heart of town. It has vaulted ceilings, frescoes, and marble floors. The owners were able to renovate it recently, in part, because of donations. Due to a vigorous publicity campaign, local governments, private citizens, and even school children became convinced that the 1880s structure was vital to the downtown area's revitalization.

On the National Register of Historic Places, the **Radisson Patrick Henry Hotel** [$$$ to $$$$] (617 South Jefferson St., Roanoke, VA 24011, ☎ 800-833-4567) has been welcoming visitors to the downtown district and its large, beautifully appointed lobby since 1925. Rooms furnished with four-poster beds, TVs hidden in cabinets, and closets almost big enough to live in add to the overall days-gone-by feel.

Across the street, simple rooms at the **Jefferson Lodge** [$ to $$] (616 South Jefferson St., Roanoke, VA 24011, ☎ 800-950-2580) are an alternative for those who want to stay downtown without spending all of their vacation dollars. Also consider the **Days Inn Civic Center** [$$] (535 Orange Ave., Roanoke, VA 24016, ☎ 800-329-7466).

The **Mary Blandon House B&B** [$$ to $$$] (381 Washington Ave. SW, Roanoke, VA 24011) is in the heart of the historic Old Southwest District. Bill and Sheri Bestpitch, the hosts of this 1890s Victorian Home with a wraparound porch, can direct you to a wide variety of nearby outdoor activities.

Located 15 minutes west of Roanoke – where the Appalachian Trail and the TransAmerica Bicycle Route meet – **Crosstrails Bed & Breakfast** [$$] (5880 Blacksburg Road, Catawba, VA 24070, ☎ 540-384-8078) is operated by retired *Roanoke Times* outdoor writer Bill Cochran and his wife Katherine. They will provide shuttles to nearby locations for hiking, biking, canoeing, kayaking, or other outdoor activities. If you exhaust their extensive knowledge of local spots, their library contains a large collection of hiking and outdoor-oriented books. Road bikes and cross-country ski equipment are available for guests. Tranquil evenings may be spent relaxing in the outdoor hot tub overlooking the 15-acre property, which is joined on three sides by national park lands.

Clifton Forge/Covington

Longdale Inn B&B [$ to $$$] (6209 Longdale Furnace Road, Clifton Forge, VA 24422, ☎ 800-862-09386), once the mansion of the owners of the Longdale Furnace, is quite a sumptuous base from which to explore nearby national forest and state park lands.

Even though I-64 runs next to them, Clifton Forge and Covington have only a few motels from which to choose.

Comfort Inn [$$] 203 Interstate Drive, Covington, VA 24426, ☎ 800-221-2222) accepts pets and has a pool, whirlpool, and sauna.

Mountain View [$$ to $$$] (820 East Madison St., Covington, VA 24426, ☎ 540-962-4951) lives up to its name, perched on a hillside overlooking the interstate and surrounding mountains. It also accepts pets and has swimming and wading pools.

Knights Court [$$] (908 Valley Ridge Drive, Covington, VA 24426, ☎ 540-962-7600) lacks the pool, but does accept pets and will take fewer of your dollars for a night's sleep.

The most pleasant stay in the area may be the **Milton Hall B&B** [$$$] (207 Thorny Lane, Covington, VA 24426, ☎ 540-965-0196). A rarity for B&Bs in that it accepts pets, the 1870s country manor house sits on more than 40 acres adjacent to George Washington National Forest.

Warm Springs/Hot Springs

The Homestead [$$$$$] (The Homestead, Hot Springs, VA 24445, ☎ 800-838-1766) has all the attractions and trappings you would expect to find in a resort that has, for decades, consistently received four-star ratings. Famous for its mineral springs long before the United States won independence from England, the 15,000-acre retreat has facilities for tennis, swimming, golf, archery, cross-country and downhill skiing, and carriage rides. There are close to 100 miles of trails for hiking, biking, and horseback riding. Inside activities include whirlpools, saunas, ice skating, bowling, exercise and weight rooms, and massages.

Shenandoah Valley

Golf at The Homestead.

At the other end of the rate spectrum, the **Rosloe Motel** [$] (PO Box 590, Hot Springs, VA 24445, ☎ 540-389-5373) permits you to have a low-cost base in the vicinity of The Homestead and enjoy many of the resort's attractions, which are open to the public for a fee.

In between the above two in price is the **Vine Cottage Inn** [$$ to $$$] (PO Box 918, Hot Springs, VA 24445, ☎ 540-389-2422). Built around 1900, it has 12 rooms and offers golf and ski packages in conjunction with The Homestead.

Within walking distance of the Warm Springs pools, **Inn at Gristmill Square** [$$$] (Box 359, Warm Springs, VA ☎ 540-389-2231) has 16 rooms in four buildings, decorated with antiques and period reproductions.

On a 3,200-acre estate, the **Fort Lewis Lodge** [$$$ to $$$$] (HCR 3 Box 21A, Millboro, VA 24460, ☎ 540-925-2314) joins the Inn at Gristmill Square in offering inn-to-inn, overnight hikes through beautiful Bath and Highland counties backcountry. Trekkers are joined by a naturalist for part of the journeys.

Close to 20 miles of hiking trails and two miles of the Jackson River wind through 1,600 acres at **Meadow Lane Lodge** [$$$

to \$\$\$\$] (HCR 01 Box 110, Warm Springs, VA 24484, ☎ 540-839-5959).

 It's nice to know that the Meadow Lane Lodge acreage has been placed under a conservation agreement, meaning it will always be preserved in its natural state.

In 1788, Jason Warwick obtained property in the Hidden Valley a few miles northwest of Hot Springs. The land was passed on to his grandson, Judge James Warwick. Using the labor of slaves, the judge had a mansion built out of bricks formed from the mud of the Jackson River. In 1993, the mansion was part of the set for the post-Civil War film *Sommersby*. Today, it has been restored and, under an agreement with the forest service, is open to the public as a bed and breakfast. In addition to enjoying the quiet solitude of the Hidden Valley, guests at the **Hidden Valley B&B** [\$\$\$] (Hidden Valley Road, Warm Springs, VA 24484, ☎ 540-839-3178) are sleeping in the same building that served as Richard Gere's and Jody Foster's home in the movie.

Monterey

Montvallee [\$] (Box 25, Monterey, VA 24465, ☎ 540-468-2500) is the only motel in this small mountain village.

On the National Register of Historic Places is **Highland Inn** [\$\$] (Main St., Monterey, VA 24465, ☎ 540-468-2143), a large Victorian country home built in 1904.

The Victorian-style **Curry Alexander B&B** [\$\$ to \$\$\$] (PO Box 68, Monterey, BA 24465, ☎ 540-468-2055) has a tea room and a bakery open to the public Tuesday through Friday.

Harrisonburg & Vicinity

Finding a motel or other accommodations to your liking is an easy task in Harrisonburg. It caters to visitors at three institutions of higher learning and the travelers moving along I-81. Motels just off the interstate include:

Comfort Inn [\$\$] (1440 East Market St., Harrisonburg, VA 22801, ☎ 800-221-2222); **Ramada Inn** [\$\$] (1 Pleasant Valley

Road, Harrisonburg, VA 22801, ☎ 800-434-7456); **Sheraton Hotel** [$$ to $$$] (1400 East Market St., Harrisonburg, VA 22801, ☎ 540-433-2521); and **Super 8 Motel** [$ to $$] (3330 South Main St., Harrisonburg, VA 22801, ☎ 540-433-8888).

Providing basic rooms less than one mile from I-81 is **Rockingham Motel** [$] (4035 South Main St., Harrisonburg, VA 22801).

HoJo Inn [$$] (605 Port Republic Road, Harrisonburg, VA 22801, ☎ 540-434-6771) is directly across from James Madison University. Its 134 terraced rooms are larger than what you would expect and have cable TV.

North of Harrisonburg, the seven acres and five antique-filled bedrooms of the 1830s **Widow Kip's County Inn B&B** [$$ to $$$] (355 Orchard Drive, Mount Jackson, VA 22842, ☎ 800-478-8714) are a favorite with cyclists and skiers.

Guests converse while relaxing in rocking chairs on the verandah at reasonably priced **Red Shutter Farmhouse B&B** [$$] (New Market, VA 22844, ☎ 540-740-4281).

East of Harrisonburg, **The Boarding House B&B** [$$] (RR 1 Box 15, McGaheysville, VA 22840, ☎ 800-893-2516) and **Patrick Manor B&B** [$$] (PO Box 6, Port Republic, VA 24471, ☎ 540-249-3156) serve as the home base for Pineapple Pedalers (see page 303). Meals served in both homes reflect the hosts' commitments to healthy living.

Woodstock

The construction of I-81 changed Woodstock from a sleepy Shenandoah Valley village to a busy fast food/motel exit off the interstate.

With three stories and more than 120 rooms, **Ramada Inn** [$$] (1130 Motel Drive, Woodstock, VA 22664, ☎ 800-2RAMADA) dominates the market. A swimming pool appeals to guests in the summer, while ski packages in conjunction with nearby resorts help entice them back in winter.

Budget Host Inn [$] (1290 South Main St., Woodstock, VA 22664, ☎ 540-459-4086) has a pool and will let you bring Fido into your room.

On a totally different level – and one of the most enjoyable places to stay in the Shenandoah Valley – is **The Inn at Narrow Passage** [$$$] (PO Box 608, Woodstock, VA 22664, ☎ 540-459-8000). The oldest section of this early American log inn has been welcoming travelers since 1740; Stonewall Jackson used the inn as his headquarters during the Valley Campaign of 1862. The staff is partial to those pursuing outdoor activities and might even help launch your canoe into the North Fork of the Shenandoah River, which flows along the edge of the inn's five acres.

Situated on one of the famous seven horseshoe bends along the North Fork of the Shenandoah River, **Victorian River D'Inn** [$$$ to $$$$] (Route 1 Box 217-A1, Woodstock, VA 22664, ☎ 540-459-5369) has a wraparound porch looking out onto its 25 acres.

■ Camping

There is no lack of camping opportunities in the Shenandoah Valley Region. National forests provide nearly half of the public campgrounds in the United States, and more than a dozen of these are scattered throughout the area. With few exceptions, backcountry camping is allowed on all national forest lands, while there are literally hundreds of pretty spots along forest service roads where you are permitted to pull off and set up camp. In addition, commercial campgrounds abound, both close to the interstate and in more isolated areas. Note: Individual Forest Service campgrounds are run on a first-come, first-served basis; no telephones are available.

Winchester

South of Winchester in Middletown, and convenient to I-81 and I-64, **Battle of Cedar Creek Campground** (8950 Valley Pike, Middletown, VA 22645, ☎ 800-343-1562) is open year-round. It offers full hookups, dump station, and a laundromat.

Front Royal/Luray

There are four forest service campgrounds in the Massanutten Mountain area. **Camp Roosevelt** on VA 675 and **Little Fort** on VA 758 are primitive sites with drinking water and pit toilets. You will need to bring your own water to **High Cliff**, next to the South Fork of the Shenandoah River off VA 684. **Elizabeth Furnace** on VA 678 is a bit more deluxe, with drinking water, flush toilets, and showers. All are administered on a first-come, first-served basis.

More luxurious, and one mile south of Front Royal on US 340, **Front Royal KOA** (PO Box 274, Front Royal, VA 22630, ☎ 800-635-2741) has all the trappings people have come to expect from this national chain – full hookups, heated pool and hot tub, and KOA's trade-marked Kamping Kabins.

Poe's South Fork Campground (Riverside Drive, Front Royal, VA 22630, ☎ 540-645-5887) has 35 riverfront sites, full hookups, a boat ramp, and hot showers.

Yogi Bear's Jellystone Park (PO Box 191, Luray, VA 22835, ☎ 800-420-6679) is more a resort than a campground. There is a swimming pool, fishing pond, mini golf, camp store, laundromat, full hookups, housekeeping cabins, and planned activities for the kids.

Waynesboro/Staunton

In addition to providing swimming along a sandy beach, the forest service's **Sherando Lake** has tent and trailer sites, a dump station, and warm showers.

Full hookups for your RV are available at **Waynesboro North 340 Campground** (Route 3 Box 333, Waynesboro, VA 22980, ☎ 540-943-9573).

A bit farther south, **Shenandoah Acres Family Resort** (PO Box 300F, Stuarts Draft, VA 24477, ☎ 540-337-1911) is a huge complex with 150 tent and RV sites. There is mini golf, lake swimming, a camp store, dump station, laundromat, and hot showers. You do not even have to leave the grounds to walk a trail or ride a horse.

Off I-81 Exit 217 south of Staunton is **Walnut Hills Campground** (391 Walnut Hills Road, Staunton, VA 24401, ☎ 540-337-3920) with swimming, laundry, dump station, camp store, and full hookups. Cabins and RVs are available for rent if you want to rough it easy.

Lexington

Lake A. Willis Robertson Recreation Area (RFD 2, Box 251, Lexington, VA 24450, ☎ 540-463-4164) is 14 miles from Lexington on VA 770. Activities and facilities are centered around a 31-acre lake popular with canoeists and anglers. More than 50 campsites, hot showers, a swimming pool, tennis courts, ball fields, and hiking trails may make you feel you are in a commercially run resort rather than a state facility.

The **Campground at Natural Bridge** (PO Box 266, Natural Bridge Station, VA 24579, ☎ 540-291-2727) is east of Lexington on VA 782. The site's 116 acres offer full hookups, a swimming lake, camp store, and a paddock for those of you who travel with your horse.

Natural Bridge KOA (Box 148, Natural Bridge, VA 24578, ☎ 800-KOA-8514) is a full-service campground in the same vicinity.

Roanoke

In Craig and Botetourt counties west of Roanoke, the forest service has developed three campgrounds. **The Pines** on VA 617 and **Steel Bridge** near Paint Bank have pit toilets and drinking water. No potable water is available at **Craig Creek** north of New Castle off VA 615.

In addition to providing the chance to go underground, **Dixie Caverns Campground** (5753 West Main St., Salem, VA 24153, ☎ 540-380-2085) south of Roanoke has the usual facilities you find in a campground located next to an interstate.

Shenandoah Valley

Clifton Forge/Covington

Douthat State Park (Route 1, Millboro, VA 24460, ☎ 540-862-8100) is just a few minute's drive from I-64 and Clifton Forge. Campsites, several with water and electric hookups, as well as some rustic cabins, may be reserved by calling ☎ 800-933-PARK.

Along the northwestern shore of Lake Moomaw (north of Covington), there are couple of campgrounds at **Bolar Mountain**. Rather deluxe when compared to other forest service facilities, these have drinking water, flush toilets, showers, and dump stations.

Reservations may be made for sites at **Morris Hill Campground** (near the southern end of the lake) by calling ☎ 800-280-CAMP. You will find amenities here similar to those at Bolar Mountain.

Warm Springs/Hot Springs

Hidden Valley and **Blowing Springs** are forest service campgrounds with drinking water, pit toilets, and dump stations. Both are accessible from VA 39 west of Hot Springs.

Monterey

East of Monterey the forest service has designated two sites for horse campers. One is on VA 616, the other along FDR 396 at the top of Shenandoah Mountain.

Harrisonburg

In the national forest west of Harrisonburg, **North River** (along FDR 95B) and **Hone Quarry** (on FDR 62) have drinking water and pit toilets. Beside a popular swimming spot in the mountains, **Todd Lake** adds warm showers to its attractions.

There are electric and water hookups on some of the 136 sites at **Natural Chimneys Regional Park** (Route 1, Mount Solon, VA 22843, ☎ 540-350-2510) west of Harrisonburg. Within the grounds are hiking and biking trails, hot showers, laundromat, and a swimming pool.

To the east of Harrisonburg, the **Swift Run Campground** (Elkton, VA, ☎ 540-298-8086) is less than four miles from Skyline Drive in Shenandoah National Park.

Open all year north of Harrisonburg is the **Rancho Campground** (Route 1 Box 404, New Market, VA 22844, ☎ 540-740-8313). Full hookups, dump station, camp store, and laundromat are available.

Woodstock

On the Virginia/West Virginia border at high elevations on Great North Mountain on VA 675, the forest service runs the **Wolf Gap Campground**. It has drinking water and pit toilets.

Orkney Springs Campground (28 Orkney Springs Campground Road, Orkney Springs, VA 22845, ☎ 540-856-2585) offers wooded sites, hot showers, camp stores, laundromat, and a swimming pool. It is open all year for those of you interested in skiing at nearby Bryce Resort.

Where To Eat

Winchester

There are the usual fast food chains along I-81, but there is quite an eclectic choice here if you are willing to put a bit of distance between you and the four-lane.

Located within the city's historic district and housed in an early 1900s structure that once served as a post office, **The Old Post Office Restaurant & Lounge** [$] (200 North Braddock St., Winchester, VA 22601, ☎ 540-722-9881) offers up American fare of gourmet sandwiches and salads for lunch, with veal and seafood being favorites for dinner.

Also in the historic district, **Cork Street Tavern** [$ to $$] (8 West Cork St., Winchester, VA 22601, ☎ 540-667-3777) is famous for its barbecue.

Ethnic offerings are abundant for a city the size of Winchester.

China Gourmet Restaurant [$ to $$] (210 Millwood Ave., Winchester, VA 22601, ☎ 540-722-3333) has house specialties of seafood and Peking duck.

Certainly not elegant dining, yet fairly authentic in its food, **El Dorado** [$] (1919 Valley Ave., Winchester, VA 22601, ☎ 540-662-6488) is the place to head for a Mexican meal.

Close by, **Café Sofia** [$$] (2900 Valley Ave., Winchester, VA 22601, ☎ 540-667-2950) serves the only Bulgarian-Slavic food to be found in the Shenandoah Valley.

Without a doubt, your taste buds will thank you for driving about nine miles east of Winchester to **L'Auberge Provencale** [$$$$+] (US 340, White Post, VA 22663, ☎ 540-837-1375). The nouvelle and classical French cuisine, with specialties such as *lapin fumé aux champignons* (smoked rabbit with mushrooms) and *veau au porto* (veal in port), is so delicious that it draws crowds of diners from Washington, DC – more than an hour's drive away.

Front Royal/Luray

There are the usual fast food, diners, and chain restaurants in Front Royal, but the most pleasurable meals will be had at **The Feed Mill** [$$] (500 East Main St., Front Royal, VA 22630, ☎ 540-636-3123). Housed in a refurbished warehouse, the rustic elegance of the decor adds to the enjoyment of the varied menu.

East of Luray on US 211, buffets of all-you-can-eat country cooking food and divine peach cobblers make **Brookside Restaurant** [$ to $$] (2978 US 211E, Luray, VA 22835, ☎ 540-743-5698) a favorite with the locals.

A *Wine Spectator* award winner, **Parkhurst Restaurant** [$$ to $$$] (2547 US 211W, Luray, VA 22835, ☎ 540-299-2655) has a casual atmosphere, but elegant table settings. Menu choices range from escargot to veal Oscar and roast duck.

Waynesboro/Staunton

Just an ordinary-looking diner, **Weasie's Kitchen** [$] (130 East Broad St., Waynesboro, VA 22980, ☎ 540-943-0500) serves such delicious home-cooked food that you may have to wait a while for a table. Appalachian Trail thu-hikers flock here for the large portions at breakfast, especially the biscuits and gravy and the all-you-can-eat hiker pancake special. One warning: your lungs will get more than their quota of second-hand smoke during your meal.

Scotto's Italian Restaurant & Pizzeria [$ to $$] (1412 West Broad St., Waynesboro, VA 22980, ☎ 540-982-8715) has refreshingly tasty and authentic Italian cuisine in a town otherwise dominated by bland pizza chain restaurants.

With an English pub atmosphere and decor, **The Fox and Hounds** [$$ to $$$] (533 West Main St., Waynesboro, VA 22980, ☎ 540-946-9200) occupies a building dating from the 1830s that was used as a hospital during Civil War. There is a choice of more than 30 beers and malts to accompany a continental menu of chicken cordon bleu, lamb chops, and fresh trout.

At first glance, the **Beverly Restaurant** [$] (12 East Beverly St., Staunton, VA 24401, ☎ 540-886-4317) appears to be just a small diner serving good country breakfasts, lunches, and dinners in the heart of historic Staunton. Yet, a sophisticated and genteel side is revealed on Wednesday and Friday afternoons when traditional English tea is served, complete with cheeses, scones, and other delicacies.

Also in the historic district, the **Pampered Palate Café** [$] (26 East Beverly St., Staunton, VA 24401, ☎ 540-886-9463) is a great lunch spot for sandwiches with interesting ingredients (such as brie and meat combinations), cold salads, and gourmet coffees and teas.

The Depot Grille [$ to $$] (42 Middlebrook Ave., Staunton, VA 24401, ☎ 540-885-7331) is in the same building as the Amtrak station and has steaks and seafood, with lighter entrées available.

Shenandoah Valley

In a cozy log cabin off I-81 Exit 213 south of Waynesboro and Staunton, the **Edelweiss Restaurant** [$$] (US 11 & US 340, Greenville, VA 24440, ☎ 540-337-1203) serves traditional German cooking from the Black Forest region. A wide assortment of beers complement entrées such as sauerbraten, rindsouladen, schnitzel, and huhnerbrust. Of the many desserts, Black Forest cake, of course, is the house specialty.

Lexington

As befitting a town with two colleges, there are a number of small cafés and bistros catering to students. Serving a light breakfast, lunch, and dinner, **Harb's** [$ to $$] (19 West Washington St., Lexington, VA 24450, ☎ 540-464-1900) has a rotating menu that includes sandwiches, gourmet soups, salads, pastas, and fresh baked breads and sweets. There is always at least one vegetarian dish available.

Converted from a Victorian ice cream parlor, **The Palms** [$ to $$] (101 West Nelson St., Lexington, VA 24450, ☎ 540-463-7911) is also popular with the local and college crowd who come to enjoy friendly conversation and freshly prepared soups, meats, and chicken.

Within Lexington's historic downtown district and housed in an 1820s Greek Revival house furnished with antiques, the food at the **Wilson-Walker House Restaurant** [$$] (30 North Main St., Lexington, VA 24450, ☎ 540-463-3020) has been described as "gourmet American cuisine." The choice includes pasta, veal medallions, chicken, and the specialty, seafood.

Roanoke

The greater metropolitan area of Roanoke has a population of close to 250,000, which is reflected in the number of restaurants. There are, of course, countless fast food spots and chain restaurants, such as Hardee's, Denny's, and Shoney's, found off interstate exits and throughout town.

If you want something a little more imaginative, yet fairly quick and low cost, head to the **Roanoke City Market Building** in the center of downtown. In what was once a meat processing plant, you'll find the International Food Court and a wonderful blend of aromas. Among the many stalls here, **The Saigon Café** [$] (☎ 540-345-5593) serves up broccoli and cauliflower cheese casseroles, croissant sandwiches, and garlic and chili shrimp. **Kim's Seafood and Deli** [$] (☎ 540-343-0516) specializes in fried fish, such as codfish nuggets or butterfly shrimp. **Paradiso Cuban Cuisine** [$] (☎ 540-309-2199) has just what its name implies – black bean soup, *ropa vieja* (well-simmered meat that shreds apart), and fried meat-stuffed potatoes. In the absence of any other really good Mexican restaurants in town, **Red Coyote Mexican Grill** [$] (☎ 540-345-2180) is the place to go for things Southwestern. One burrito is large enough to keep you feeling full all day, while the grill's spicy vegetarian dishes prove that healthy can also be tasty.

Still in the heart of downtown, but a bit more upscale, **Carlos Brazilian International Cuisine** [$$] (312 Market St., Roanoke, VA 24015, ☎ 540-345-7661) is quite reasonably priced. It serves superb Spanish, French, and Brazilian food. Again, the vegetarian dishes here are good. Be ready to wait for a table at lunch time.

Located in an unassuming strip mall, **The Library** [$$ to $$$] (3117 Franklin Road, Roanoke, VA 24014, ☎ 540-985-0811) consistently receives *Roanoker* magazine's award as one of the most elegant and exclusive restaurants in the city. Traditional French dishes of veal princess, Dover sole, rack of lamb, and a tableside preparation of cherries jubilee keep Roanokers coming back whenever they have a special occasion to celebrate.

Wildflour Café [$] (Towers Mall, ☎ 540-344-1514) is so popular with the locals that it recently opened a second restaurant (1212 4th St. Southwest, Roanoke, VA 24015, ☎ 540-343-4543) in the residential Old Southwest District. Both places will serve you some of the freshest salads, soups (try the white bean chicken chili), sandwiches, and vegetarian dishes to be found anywhere. Pick up a loaf of their freshly baked breads to take out on the road with you.

Almost-hip without even realizing it, **Hurley's** [$] (1540 Grandin Road Southwest, Roanoke, VA 24015, ☎ 540-344-9483) is also in a residential part of town. A resourceful mix of sand-

Shenandoah Valley

wiches, soups, salads, burgers, and pasta dishes keep the place busy serving locals.

Once travelers on the Blue Ridge Parkway find **Buck Mountain Grill** [$ to $$] (5002 Franklin Road, Roanoke, VA 24014, ☎ 540-776-1830) it doesn't take much for them to come up with an excuse to return for another serving of pasta with crab and pesto or one of the restaurant's vegetarian features.

In a rambling old farmhouse 15 minutes west of town on VA 311, **The Homeplace** [$] (VA 311, Catawba, VA 24070, ☎ 540-384-7252) serves dinner only from Thursday to Sunday. Yet, its green beans, mashed potatoes, fried chicken, roast beef, ham, pinto beans, and other country-cooked items served family-style are so popular that a wait of an hour or more is not uncommon. Thru-hikers on the Appalachian Trail – which passes less than a mile away – say the food and service here are the best to be found from Georgia to Maine.

Clifton Forge/Covington

Seemingly out of place in a small Allegheny Mountains town, **Michel Café and French Restaurant** [$$ to $$$] (424 East Ridgeway St., Clifton Forge, VA 24422, ☎ 540-862-4119) relies on seasonally available ingredients to make up its daily specials. Always on the menu are crab cakes, fresh trout, and pepper steak.

In a departure from the bland fare of most motel-affiliated restaurants, **Comfort Center Restaurant** [$ to $$] (203 Interstate Drive, Covington, VA 24426) has a menu specializing in steaks and seafood that is good enough to have earned it a three-diamond rating.

Warm Springs/Hot Springs

Part of the Inn at Gristmill Square, **Waterwheel Restaurant** [$$ to $$$] (Box 259, Warm Springs, VA 24484, ☎ 540-389-2231) occupies a portion of the restored mill, providing a rustic, cozy ambiance. Meals of local trout, veal, and pasta are accompanied by homegrown vegetables. Diners are encouraged to visit the wine cellar, where they can choose from an extensive collection.

Harrisonburg

With several major interstate exits, Harrisonburg is a mecca of fast food and chain restaurants. McDonald's, Hardee's, Pizza Hut, Shoney's, Taco Bell, Dairy Queen, and others are well represented.

Surprisingly, a motel restaurant provides a nice alternative. In a scenic setting, the **Village Inn Restaurant** [$ to $$] (Route 1 Box 76, Harrisonburg, VA 22801, ☎ 540-434-7355) serves solid home-cooked meals, as do **Evers Family Restaurant** [$] (I-81 Exit 240, ☎ 540-433-0993) and **Pano's** [$] (I-81 Exit 243, ☎ 540-434-2367).

J. Willoby's Roadhouse [$ to $$] (1221 Forest Hill Road, Harrisonburg, VA 22801, ☎ 540-574-36444) features mesquite-grilled steak, chicken, and seafood.

Inside a Victorian home that was once a fraternity house for James Madison University students, **Joshua Wilton House** [$$$$+] 9201 South Holliday St., Harrisonburg, VA 22810, ☎ 540-465-9191) has quite an eclectic bill of fare compared to other Harrisonburg establishments. You will have a choice of trout with ham cream sauce, grilled tenderloin with smoked oysters, quail, duck, salmon, or veal.

Woodstock

South of Woodstock in New Market, the Newland family has been serving such good home cooking since 1955 that tour buses make meal stops at **Southern Kitchen** [$ to $$] (US 11, New Market, VA 22844, ☎ 540-740-3514).

In a log cabin chock full of early American antiques, the **Spring House** [$ to $$] (325 South Main St., Woodstock, VA 22664, ☎ 540-459-4755) serves breakfast, lunch, and dinner.

River'D Inn [$$$$+] (1972 Artz Road, Woodstock, VA 22664, ☎ 540-459-5369) fulfills the fine dining needs for this part of Virginia. Reservations are required as there is room for only 10 guests, and dinner is served only on Wednesday through Sunday. Filet mignon, chicken cordon bleu, and other gastronomical delights are brought to tables adorned by candlelight and fresh flowers.

Shenandoah Valley

Southwest Virginia

So far removed from the major population centers in the eastern part of the state, Southwest Virginia is often overlooked or dismissed as a destination area. Yet, here are some of the best places in the Commonwealth for adventuring.

Between them, the New River Trail and the Virginia Creeper Trail have almost 100 miles of pathways following old railroad grades beside mountain streams and through sumptuous scenery. More than 200 miles of the 2,100-mile Appalachian Trail wind through these mountains. Close to the North Carolina border rises the state's highest point, Mount Rogers, surrounded by lofty ridgelines. With its alpine vegetation and rugged terrain, the area has been likened to the Continental Divide in Montana, Idaho, and Wyoming.

Well over 1,000 miles of trails course through the more than 700,000 acres of the Jefferson National Forest, luring hikers, bikers, and horseback riders. The New River has close to 150 miles and the Clinch River about 100 miles that can be paddled year-round. In later winter and early spring, canoeists and kayakers head to the smaller mountain streams that are flush with snow melt and seasonal rains.

South of Radford and west of I-81, the area I call far-Southwest Virginia is a world unto its own. Although it was the gateway through which Daniel Boone and early settlers passed on their way to the western lands beyond the Cumberland Gap, it was the last area in Virginia to be settled. Isolated from the rest of the state, residents here developed the attitude that if anything was going to get accomplished, they would have to do it themselves. That rugged approach continues to this day, with people looking to each other and not to the state government in Richmond to solve any of the region's problems.

Things are still a little rough around the edges in far-Southwest Virginia. And that is its allure. Malls and supersized discount stores are few and far between. Large luxury resorts are nonexistent, the restaurants serve home-style cooking, and mom and pop enterprises are the norm. The mountains here are more rugged than those east of I-81, rising more in jumbles than in long ridgelines. This is Virginia's coalfield and, while driving on the narrow roadways, you will often look into the rear view mirror to see the grill of an overloaded coal truck barreling down the mountain just inches from your bumper.

Much of this may change. There are plans to open the region to "economic development," with construction of a four-lane highway coming in from West Virginia and upgrading of the entire length of US 58 to four lanes. The time to visit far-Southwest Virginia is now, before it loses its rough edges, before its roadsides are littered with the parking lots of fast food restaurants. Go now, before other folks learn of the charms of this place and come flocking to an area that is just waiting to be discovered. Go now, while the trails of the Clinch Ranger District of the Jefferson National Forest and the Cumberland Gap National Historical Park are little visited.

Information Sources

Abingdon Convention and Visitors Bureau, 335 Cumming St., Abingdon, VA 24210, ☎ 800-435-2440.

Big Stone Gap-Wise County Tourist Information Center, PO Box 236, Big Stone Gap, VA 24219, ☎ 540-523-2060.

Bristol Convention and Visitors Bureau, PO Box 519, Bristol, VA 24203, 423-989-4850.

City of Galax Downtown Association, PO Box 544, Galax, VA 24333, ☎ 540-236-0668.

Giles County Chamber of Commerce, 101 South Main St., Pearisburg, VA 24134, ☎ 540-921-3892.

Grayson County Tourist Information Center, PO Box 336, Independence, VA 24348, ☎ 540-773-3711.

Southwest Virginia

25 MILES

N

KENTUCKY

Cumberland Gap Nat'l Hist. Park

Katlan State Park

32

58

Jonesville

Appalachia

ALT 58

119

North Fork Pound Lake Rec. Area

Wise

Norton

23

23

Big Stone Gap

Duffield

Natural Tunnel State Park

23

TENNESSEE

John W Flannagan Dam & Reservoir

Breaks Interstate Park

Grundy

83

Pound

63

Pounding Mill

Richlands

460

19

St. Paul

71

Hiltons

BRISTOL

81

Abingdon

Damascus

South Holston Lake

WEST VIRGINIA

16

Tazewell

Burkes Garden

Hungry Mother State Park

91

Mt. Rogers (5,729 ft.)

Grayson Highlands State Park

Princeton

19

460

BLUEFIELD

77

Bland

Marion

16

58

Narrows

Radford

42

Pulaski

Wytheville

21

81

BLACKSBURG

81

Newport

Christiansburg

8

Floyd

Claytor Lake State Park

Hillsville

77

Heart of Appalachia Visitor Information Center, 17505 Lee Highway Suite 2, Abingdon, VA 24210, ☎ 888-267-6867.

Highlands Gateway Visitors Center, Factory Merchants Mall of Fort Chiswell, Box 12B, Max Meadows, VA 24360, ☎ 800-446-9670.

Patrick County Chamber of Commerce & Visitors Center, PO Box 577, Stuart, VA 24171, ☎ 540-694-6012.

Pulaski Tourism Information, PO Box 660, Pulaski, VA 24301, ☎ 540-980-5432.

Smyth County Chamber of Commerce, 124 West Main St., Marion, VA 24354, ☎ 540-783-3161.

Virginia Coalfield Regional Tourism Development Authority, PO Box 639, Castlewood, VA 24224, ☎ 540-762-3946.

Washington County Chamber of Commerce, 179 East Main St., Abingdon, VA 24210, ☎ 540-628-8141.

Wytheville Area Convention and Visitor Bureau, PO Box 533, Wytheville, VA 24382, ☎ 540-223-3355.

■ ■ ■

Getting Around

The best and really the only way to fly into Southwest Virginia is via **Roanoke Regional Airport** (☎ 540-362-1999), which is served by USAir and United Express.

Following the I-81 corridor, **Greyhound** (☎ 800-231-2222) services Christiansburg, Radford, Dublin (a flag stop), Pulaski, Wytheville, Marion, Abingdon, and Bristol. Along I-77, the bus makes stops in Bland and Hillsville. In what is surely a commentary on the sad state of mass transportation in the US, there is no bus service west on I-81 in far-Southwest Virginia and no passenger rail service anywhere in Southwest Virginia.

In Blacksburg, Christiansburg, Radford, Wytheville, Abingdon, and Bristol you will be able to **rent cars** from national companies such as Avis, Budget, Dollar, Enterprise, and Hertz.

Touring

■ Radford/Pulaksi

 The tour of Southwest Virginia begins in Radford, home of **Radford University** (PO Box 6965, Radford, VA 24142, ☎ 540-831-5754), which serves as the town's cultural center. The **Flossie Martin Art Gallery** presents changing exhibits with an emphasis on regional, national, and international contemporary visual arts. Next to the gallery, the **Corinna de la Burde Sculpture Court** is an open-air experience with changing and permanent displays of contemporary large-sized sculpture. While on campus, head over to the **Dedmon Center** just to see its air-supported fabric roof over the gymnasium.

The Ingles Story

Radford was at the very western edge of Virginia's frontier in 1755 when Mary Draper Ingles and several members of her family were kidnapped by Shawnee Indians. Forced to travel west to the Native Americans' village near present-day Portsmouth, Ohio, Mary made a daring 45-day, 850-mile escape back to Virginia. Her heroic tale is retold in the outdoor drama, *The Long Way Home* (PO Box 711, Radford, VA 24241, ☎ 540-639-0679), presented each year from mid-June through August. A great read, *Follow the River* by James Alexander Thom is an historical novel based on Mary's escape.

Following I-81 south from Radford, take a short detour to visit **Claytor Lake State Park** (Route 1 Box 267, Dublin, VA 24804, ☎ 540-674-5492), centered around the 21-mile lake, with more than 100 miles of shoreline. In addition to a couple of hiking trails, a bathing beach, picnic areas, campground, rental cabins, and a marina, the historic **Howe House** features exhibits about the life of early settlers in the region.

South of Radford in Pulaski is the northern terminus of the 57-mile **New River Trail** (Route 2 Box 126 F, Foster Falls, VA 24360, ☎ 540-699-6778). When Norfolk Southern donated a right-of-way from Pulaski to Galax, the Commonwealth established a state park and developed the former railroad bed into a hiking, biking, and horseback riding trail, with a short spur route leading to the small town of Fries. With more than 40 miles of trail along the banks of the New River, several different landscapes are traveled, from steep rock cliffs to rolling pastureland. The physical features of the route are as much of an attraction as the scenery. More than 30 bridges – one over 1,000 feet – and numerous tunnels nearly 200 feet long, enable you to keep going forward without any obstacle. Numerous access points let you decide just how long you want to make your journey in this linear state park. Launch sites in several places also provide access to the river for canoes, kayaks, and inner tubes.

■ Wytheville

South of Pulaski, Wytheville was once a sleepy little village in the Great Valley. All that changed with the construction of I-77 and I-81, which cross each other within the city limits. Today, huge complexes of motels, fast food restaurants, truck stops, and even an outlet mall line the four-lane roadways. However, a couple of places in the inner part of town have escaped the rampant development and are worth a visit to catch a glimpse of yesteryear.

The native gray limestone structure that houses the **Rock House Museum** (Corner of Tazewell and Monroe Sts., Wytheville, VA 24382, ☎ 540-233-3330) was constructed in the 1820s and purchased by Dr. John Haller, the town's first resident physician. As it seems to be with almost every Virginia house, barn, building, or structure that was standing in the 1860s, the Rock House was used as a hospital during the Civil early farming and mining equipment, as well as items from the Civil War and both World Wars.

Southwest of Wytheville via I-81 is **Hungry Mother State Park** (Route 5, Box 109, Marion, VA 24354, ☎ 540-783-3422), with more than eight miles of hiking trails, a riding stable, campground, rental cabins, restaurant, and swimming and boating in a small lake.

Historians generally agree the park's name is derived from an incident when a mother and her child escaped from their Indian captors. Wandering through the forest with only berries to eat, the mother finally collapsed. When the child was found, the only words she could utter were, "Hungry mother."

■ Mount Rogers Area

As you drive south from Marion on VA 16 you will be entering the state's highest mountain region and one of its best outdoor recreational areas. The Appalachian Trail and hundreds of miles of forest service trails open to hikers, bikers, and horse-back riders snake through the mountain laurel, hemlock, and high open meadows of **Jefferson National Forest** and the **Mount Rogers National Recreation Area**.

Grayson Highlands State Park

At the small settlement of Volney, you will bear to the right, following US 58 west to Grayson Highlands State Park (Route 2 Box 141, Mouth of Wilson, VA 24363, ☎ 540-579-7092). Amid the most spectacular alpine scenery in the Commonwealth, the park has a campground, picnic area, and stable facilities. The trails not only wander over park property, but also connect with forest service pathways – including more than 60 miles of trails open to horses. By connecting several of these routes, you can work your way up to 5,729-foot **Mount Rogers**, the Commonwealth's highest point.

forest service pathways – including more than 60 miles of trails open to horses. By connecting several of these routes, you can work your way up to 5,729-foot **Mount Rogers**, the Commonwealth's highest point.

■ Damascus

Continuing west on US 58 you will come into Damascus. Billing itself as "The Friendliest Town on the Trail," the town plays host to Trail Days every year in May. Conceived in 1987 as a way to celebrate the 50th anniversary of the Appalachian Trail's completion, the event now attracts hundreds of hikers, locals, and visitors for a week-long series of events focusing on the trail.

The town had its beginnings in 1821, when a settler from North Carolina arrived to establish Mock's Mill. In 1886, John D. Imboden promoted a rail line from Abingdon and began extracting the area's timber and mineral wealth. Because of the abundance of manganese, iron ore, coal, water, and timber, he named the area (so folklore says) for Damascus, the ancient capitol of Syria.

Passing through the center of town is the **Virginia Creeper Trail** (c/o Mount Rogers National Recreation Area, Route 1, Box 303, Marion, VA 24354, ☎ 540-783-5196). Beginning as a Native American footpath, the trail was later used by European pioneers, including Daniel Boone. By 1900, a rail line followed the route of the pathway from Damascus to Abingdon, hauling lumber, iron ore, supplies, and passengers. Its steam locomotives struggled so slowly up the steep mountain grades that the line earned the Virginia Creeper nickname. The Great Depression brought economic hardships from which the line never really recovered. The Creeper made its last run in 1977.

Through a cooperative effort among the US Forest Service and the towns of Damascus and Abingdon, a 33-mile stretch of the railbed has been opened to hikers, bikers, and horseback riders. Running through river gorges, beside crashing waterfalls, over more than 100 bridges and trestles, and cresting at 3,600 feet above sea level, the trail has been hailed as one of the most beautiful and successful of the country's rail-trails.

■ Abingdon/Bristol

Drive west on US 58 from Damascus to Abingdon, where Robert Porterfield founded the **Barter Theatre** (PO Box 867, Abingdon, VA 24212, ☎ 540-628-3991) in 1933, at the height of the Great Depression. Convincing a group of starving Broadway actors to come to Virginia, Porterfield offered tickets to local residents in exchange for chickens, ham, milk, and other food items. Since then, some of America's best-known actors, including Mary Martin, Gregory Peck, and Helen Hayes, have performed on its stage. Open all year, recent presentations have included *Camelot*, *Travels With My Aunt*, and original productions.

Drive south on I-81 from Abingdon to Bristol, a city half in Virginia and half in Tennessee. On the Virginia side in downtown Bristol is the **Train Station Marketplace** (State St., Bristol, VA 24201, ☎ 423-989-4850), originally built as the Norfolk and Western Station in 1847. Today, the restored building houses restaurants and small shops.

■ Scott County

Driving west on US 58 from Bristol you will be following the same route that Daniel Boone and other early explorers and settlers traveled. You will also escape the influence that interstates have over the lands and the lives of the people around them. Fast food restaurants, malls, and supersized discount stores are fewer and farther between, becoming almost nonexistent the further west you go.

If you happen to be in this area on Saturday night, take a side-trip via VA 709 and VA 614 to Maces Spring and the **Carter Family Fold** (PO Box 111, Hiltons, VA 24258, ☎ 540-386-9480). Officiated by Janette Carter, the youngest daughter of A.P. and Sarah Carter, the sounds of traditional acoustic music flow over the audience and out of the open sides of the unique auditorium. The "Fold" has huge plywood walls that are folded up to let cool summer breezes in or are put down to keep out the cold of winter. The benches are carved out of the hillside and audience members sit on seats salvaged from school buses. Of course, when the music starts, the seats do not get much use. It seems that just about everyone – from old geezers to grade school youngsters – can not resist jumping up to do some clogging or buck dancing. This is an old time mountain music experience not to be missed.

Natural Tunnel State Park

Natural Tunnel.

Continuing to the west several miles past Gate City, make a right onto VA 871 to the Natural Tunnel State Park (Route 3, Box 250, Duffield, VA 24244, ☎ 540-940-2674). Dubbed the "Eighth Wonder of the World" by William Jennings Bryan in the late 1800s, the tunnel is believed to be one million years old. Like the limestone caverns of the Shenandoah Valley, the tunnel began when water containing carbonic acid percolated through cracks and crevices and slowly dissolved the surrounding limestone and dolomitic bedrock. As the cracks widened, the water table dropped and Stock Creek was rerouted into its existing valley. The erosive action of the stream created the tunnel you see today.

You can reach the tunnel by either taking a 530-foot chairlift into the gorge or by hiking along the moderately strenuous .6-mile round-trip **Tunnel Hill Trail**. (The most impressive view of the tunnel is along this pathway.) Other attractions in the park include six other trails, a campground, swimming pool, and picnic areas.

■ Cumberland Gap

Karlan State Park

From the tunnel, return to and resume driving west on US 58 (which is now two lanes for long stretches). About five miles west of Ewing is one of the Commonwealth's newest recreational facilities, Karlan State Park (Route 2 Box 78, Ewing, VA 24248, ☎ 540-445-3065). Purchased in 1993, the park is still under development, but its 200 acres are presently a day-use area open for picnics and hikes. One of the most exciting aspects of the park is the **Wilderness Road Trail** that passes through it. This hiking and biking pathway, constructed by the Virginia Department of Transportation, stretches from its western trailhead in the Wilderness Road Campground of the Cumberland Gap National Historical Park to its eastern terminus at Chadwell Gap on VA 688 (reached by taking VA 690 through Caylor from US 58).

Cumberland Gap National Historical Park

At the westernmost point of the state, the Cumberland Gap National Historical Park (Box 1848, Middlesboro, KY 40965, ☎ 606-248-2817) sits atop the crest of the ridgelines on the Virginia/Tennessee/Kentucky border. Long before its most famous traveler, Daniel Boone, came through in 1769, the gap provided a natural passageway for Native Americans who had learned of it by following the buffalo. By 1800, more than 300,000 people had crossed it in the hopes of establishing new lives in the lands to the west, and as many head of livestock were annually driven over it to eastern markets.

The park has about 50 miles of hiking trails, ranging from short self-guided nature hikes to longer overnight journeys. Two of the most popular pathways are the two-mile round-trip **Tri-State Peak Trail** (leading to an Olympian view of the three states) and the 16-mile **Ridge Trail** (running nearly the full length of the park).

On the Kentucky side of the park, one of the most popular destinations is the site of the **Hensley Settlement**, which flourished for nearly five decades. Established in 1904, it reached a peak of about 100 people before being abandoned in the 1940s and 1950s. The park service has restored three of the farmsteads with their houses, barns, fences, and fields, as well as the schoolhouse and cemetery. A hike to this spot in an isolated corner of the park is well worth it to learn what a hardy lot our forebears were. Those unwilling or unable to walk here can make reservations for scheduled van trips at the park's visitors center, located just across the state line in Kentucky.

In addition to looking over the displays and videos concerning the history of the gap, you can obtain the required (free) backcountry camping permits in the visitors center if your travels include an overnight hike. The park also has a campground with running water and flush toilets.

■ Big Stone Gap

Retrace your route along US 58 from the park, making a turn north onto Alternate US 58 in Jonesville. Driving through the settlements of Ben Hur, Pennington Gap, and Dryden, arrive in Big Stone Gap. Small though it may be, the town has served as the cultural center of this region for more than 100 years. A walking tour brochure available from the visitors center (located inside an 1870 rail car) points you in the right direction to explore this town in Virginia's coal fields.

Big Stone Gap's "boom and bust" days are featured on the first floor of the **Southwest Virginia Museum** (Box 742, Big Stone Gap, VA 24219, ☎ 540-523-1322). Having discovered the region's extensive coal and iron ore deposits in the late 1800s, northern businessmen dreamed of turning the town into the "Pittsburgh of the South." Although the boom days lasted only a few years, much money was made here and the museum is housed in the mansion originally built by a Virginia attorney general, Rufus Ayers. Other floors and displays in the museum depict the exploration and development of Southwest Virginia and the lives of the men and women who settled the area.

The **John Fox, Jr. Museum** (Shawnee Ave. East, Big Stone Gap, VA 24219, ☎ 540-523-4950) contains the memorabilia of one the town's most famous residents and the author of *The Trail of the Lonesome Pine*. Based in part on fact, the book was the first novel in America to sell a million copies and portrays the love story between a young local girl and a mining engineer from the East. Set in the boom days, it clearly depicts the drastic ways in which "progress" changed the lives of the mountain people.

For more than 30 years, *The Trail of the Lonesome Pine* (Drawer 1976, Big Stone Gap, VA 24219, ☎ 800-362-0149) has told the story as a summer outdoor drama presented by an ever-changing cast of local volunteers and actors. The play will introduce you to characters such as the not-quite-right preacher Red Fox, family patriarch Devil Judd Tolliver, and mountain neighbors Uncle Billy and Old Hon Beam.

Big Stone Gap

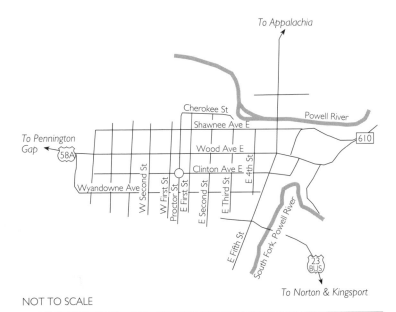

NOT TO SCALE

Next door to the theater is the **June Tolliver House** (Drawer 1976, Big Stone Gap, VA 24219, ☎ 540-523-2747), named for the Trail of the Lonesome Pine heroine. Her character is based on a young girl who actually lived in the house when she came out of the mountains to attend school. The home contains a 19th-century parlor and "June's" bedroom.

The **Harry W. Meador, Jr. Coal Museum** (East 3rd St. & Shawnee Ave., Big Stone Gap, VA 24219, ☎ 540-523-4950) traces the history of the coal industry from its beginnings in Southwest Virginia to the present. The museum does a good job of portraying the job of a coal miner, but there is scant reference to the conflicts and deaths that arose when miners tried to organize a union.

Still very much a part of the daily life of the region, coal is not quite the king it once was. Driving north from Big Stone Gap on US Alternate 58/Business 23, you will pass by the huge **Bullit Mine Complex** owned by Westmoreland Coal Company. At its zenith the company had more than 55,000 employees, before laying all of them off and turning to lower-cost strip mining in the West.

The town of **Appalachia** sprang up during the boom days after the Louisville and Nashville Railroad and the Southern Railroad made a junction here in 1890 to take advantage of the coal reserves.

North of Appalachia via VA 78 is a chance to visit the remnants of a few coal camps that were built by early 20th-century mining barons for their employees. Most of the original homes in **Derby** are still occupied, as they are built of red tile instead of the wood and tar paper used for most coal camp homes.

Return to Appalachia and drive east along US 23 to Norton, turning right onto VA 609. Entering national forest land, the roadway becomes FDR 2416 and leads you to **High Knob**. The superbly constructed lookout tower on the top of the 4,162-foot summit provides a spectacular 360° vista across the surrounding mountains and valleys of Virginia, North Carolina, Tennessee, Kentucky, and West Virginia. A wonderful 16-mile hike, via a number of forest service trails also begins here. See the *On Foot* section below for details.

■ Breaks Interstate Park Area

Return to Norton, drive US 23 north through Wise and turn east onto VA 83 in Pound. So that you can enjoy even more of what this area has to offer, bear left onto VA 631 in Clintwood. Crossing the Pound River, make a right onto VA 611 to drive through woodlands, meadows, and farmlands perched along the eastern flank of Cumberland Mountain. Look for the sign directing you down a half-mile side road through hemlocks and hardwoods to the **Branhams Farm Wildlife Area**. An easy walk of just a few minutes along a grassy road brings you to pleasing views of the Flannagan Reservoir.

The **John W. Flannagan Dam and Reservoir** (Route 1 Box 268, Haysi, Virginia 24256, ☎ 540-835-9544) is reached by way of VA 739, another side road off VA 611. The lake was created in 1964 to provide flood and water pollution control, low-flow augmentation of downstream waters, and a reliable supply of drinking water for local communities. With three campgrounds, picnic areas, boat ramps, a commercial marina, and hiking trails, the lake has become a popular recreation destination, especially with powerboaters, skiers, and anglers.

Continuing on VA 611 to a place known as Bartlick, you will come to a spot that is a favorite put-in for rafters and kayakers of the **Russell Fork River**. During the four weekends in October when the Flannagan Dam is releasing water, the river becomes the most technical and challenging commercially rafted stream in the East. Descending at a record gradient of 200 feet per mile with nearly five miles of continuous Class V+ whitewater, running its steep plunging drops has become a right of passage for the country's boldest paddlers.

Breaks Interstate Park

When VA 611 comes to an end, make a left onto VA 80, climbing uphill to Breaks Interstate Park (PO Box 100, Breaks, VA 24607, ☎ 800-982-5122). In my opinion, the park has, by far, the most beautiful and dramatic setting of all the state-run recreational facilities inside the boundaries of the Commonwealth.

Blessed with an abundance of hemlocks and rhododendrons, it is perched along the edge of the **Russell Fork Gorge**, whose vertical walls drop 1,600 feet into the largest canyon east of the Mississippi River. Not only do the hiking trails lead to exciting vistas, but even the restaurant and lodge rooms have picture windows overlooking the five-mile-long gorge. This is far-Southwest Virginia's premier attraction; if your time in this region is limited, you should bypass everything else and spend your time here. In addition to the scenery and hiking trails, the park has a mountain bike route, horseback riding, campsites, rental cottages, lodge rooms, swimming pool, and a hard-surfaced nature drive. If I had my way, I would spend my whole summer here.

A view of the Russell Fork River from Breaks Interstate Park.

■ Tazewell

The interstate park is the turnaround point of the driving tour and you will now follow twisting VA 609 east to Grundy, where you make a right onto US 460. You are now back into the heart of coal country. Be sure to give those overloaded coal trucks the right of way as they come lumbering down this narrow roadway at speeds that are surely unlawful and certainly unsafe. Just tell yourself that this is part of the "cultural experience" of far-Southwest Virginia.

Thankfully, the highway becomes four lanes as you go by Richlands and turn to the northeast along US 19/460 to visit the **Crab Orchard Museum and Pioneer Park** (Route 1 Box 194, Tazewell, VA 24651, ☎ 540-988-6755), an interesting reconstruction of an early 1800s settlement with 13 historic log and stone buildings and artifacts from days gone by. A fossil collection includes mastodon tusks and teeth unearthed on nearby Clinch Mountain.

Leave the museum on US 19/460, coming into the town of Tazewell and continuing to the east on VA 61. A few miles later, make a right onto VA 623, climb over Rich Mountain and drop into other-worldly **Burkes Garden**. Enclosed by Garden Mountain, this circular mountain valley looks like the crater floor of a volcano. The best way to explore it is by bicycle, taking your time to savor the long, rolling croplands slowly rising to the forested hillsides. A more rural, pastoral setting would be hard to find.

■ Blacksburg

Returning to VA 61, continue to the northeast through farmland and mountain scenery, cross I-77 at Rocky Gap, and turn to the east along US 460 at Narrows. Hiking opportunities abound off this highway:

The **Appalachian Trail** crosses the four lanes at the New River Bridge. Hiking south on the trail for just a few miles brings you to **Angels Rest**, a grand viewpoint overlooking the river's twists and turns. Walking north along the AT from the New River brings you to the crest of **Peter's Mountain**, where you can follow the trail with little change in elevation for more than 10 miles.

East of Pearisburg in the small town of Pembroke you can drive VA 623 to the beginning of the **Cascades National Recreation Trail**. Paralleling the ripples of Little Stony Creek, the four-mile round-trip trail leads you to a 60-foot waterfall dropping out of the heights of the mountain. This is such a popular journey that you may share it with literally hundreds of other people on a pleasant weekend day.

A few miles east of Pembroke, you can make a left onto VA 700 and drive seven miles to the **Mountain Lake Resort** (VA 700, Mountain Lake, VA 24136, ☎ 800-346-3334), overlooking one of only two natural freshwater lakes in all of Virginia. (The other one is Lake Drummond in the Tidewater area.) The greystone lodge with a red roof would fit right in with the mountain chalets of Switzerland. Many miles of trails, some open to mountain bikes, wind through the resort's 11,000 acres of high mountain scenery. Although the management prefers that you be a guest, you would probably be granted permission to hike the trails if you ask. (If for some reason you are not given permission or feel uncomfortable walking on private property, just continue driving beyond the resort on VA 613, eventually coming to trailheads for the War Spur and Appalachian trails on forest service lands.)

Return to US 460 and continue driving east to Blacksburg, home to **Virginia Polytechnic Institute and State University**. This largest university in the state (with over 24,000 students and a 2,600-acre campus) dominates the cultural life of the community. Its museums and galleries, such as the **Armory Art Gallery**, the **Museum of Natural History**, and the **Museum of Geological Sciences**, are open to the public.

On the edge of campus is the **Smithfield Plantation House** (1000 Smithfield Plantation Road, Blacksburg, VA 24060, ☎ 540-231-3947), built on the grounds of a 1,900-acre estate in 1772 by Colonel William Preston. Although the growth of the city has taken away most of the grounds, the house has been restored and is considered a Virginia Historic Landmark. Two of Virginia's governors, James Patton Preston and John Buchanan Floyd, were born here, and a third, John Floyd, Jr. lived here for a while.

Your driving tour of Southwest Virginia, which has taken you from the foothills of the Blue Ridge to the Cumberland Mountains along the Kentucky border, comes to an end as you drive US 460 east to I-81, which can be followed north to Roanoke.

Adventures

■ On Foot

The Appalachian Trail

More than 200 miles of the Appalachian Trail course through Southwest Virginia. Entering the state at Damascus, the trail climbs to 5,000 feet, crossing the slopes of **Whitetop Mountain** and entering the **Mount Rogers National Recreation Area**. Traversing some of the Commonwealth's highest mountains, the trail eventually swings west, making use of old roads and railroad grades left behind by logging activities in the early part of the 20th century and by strip-mine operations for manganese during World War II. Crossing the Great Valley of Virginia and Interstate 81, the AT enters **Crawfish Valley**. Extensively farmed and logged in the 1880s to 1920s, the spot is now a quiet, isolated valley far from any signs of civilization.

Having left the Blue Ridge for the Allegheny Mountains, the trail goes over **Big Walker** and **Garden mountains**. Besides overlooking beautiful **Burkes Garden**, the trail along this section provides a chance to search for trace fossils more than 400 million years old. Tracks in the rock show where animals, probably worm-like creatures, burrowed along sand bed surfaces, leaving labyrinths several inches long and nearly one-inch wide. Descending Garden Mountain, northbound hikers may encounter evidence of beavers in the isolated **Hunting Camp** and **Little Wolf Creek valleys** before arriving in **Lickskillet Hollow**.

From Lickskillet Hollow, the AT traverses **Pearis Mountain**, crosses the **New River**, and follows the Virginia/West Virginia border for more than 13 miles along **Peters Mountain**. Heading east, the trail goes by what has been called Virginia's "Triple Crown" of viewpoints. The monolith of 3,050-foot **Dragon's Tooth** gazes out upon Catawba Valley, Big Tinker Mountain, and Peaks of Otter, while the view from **McAfee Knob** on

Catawba Mountain is considered by many to be the best vista in all of Virginia. Overlooking both the Catawba and Roanoke valleys, the knob permits hikers to look north, tracing the route of the trail for more than 80 miles. Just six miles to the north, **Tinker Cliffs** is a half-mile-long precipice with views into Catawba Valley, out across North and Potts mountains, and back onto McAfee Knob.

Recrossing the Great Valley of Virginia and I-81, the trail returns to the Blue Ridge Mountains in Black Horse Gap.

Radford/Pulaski

CLAYTOR LAKE STATE PARK: There are only two short trails in Claytor Lake State Park, but they do provide an opportunity for you to stretch your legs if you become tired of swimming or sitting around the campground. The .6-mile-loop **Sandy Ridge Trail** is a natural history interpretive route with numbered stops keyed to a brochure. The moderately easy 1.6-mile **Claytor Lake Trail** begins near the marina and makes a few quick ups and downs as it loops through a forest of hickory, locust, pine, and sycamore. There are several nice views of the lake along the way.

NEW RIVER TRAIL STATE PARK: The New River Trail State Park, stretching for 57 miles from Pulaski to Galax, is one of the most popular rails-to-trails routes in the country. See the mountain biking portion of the *On Wheels* section below for details.

Wytheville/Mount Rogers Area/Abingdon

OLD TOWN ABINGDON: Situated in rolling hills, Old Town Abingdon has restored homes bordered by brick walls and framed by growths of mountain laurel and rhododendron. A walking tour brochure is available from the visitors center.

BRISTOL: For years there were intense arguments over the state boundary line within the city of Bristol. Finally, in 1881, it was decided the line would be along the exact center of State St. and brass markers now serve as monuments to the settlement.

A brochure of a walking tour, which will take you from one state to another in just one step, is available from the town visitors bureau.

MOUNT ROGERS NATIONAL RECREATION AREA: The towns of Wytheville, Marion, and Abingdon are all gateways to the Mount Rogers National Recreation Area.

Established by an act of Congress in 1966, the more than 100,000-acre area is full of natural and scenic wonders and has become one of the most popular hiking destinations in Virginia. Below spruce- and fir-covered Mount Rogers are thousands of acres of open grasslands reminiscent of the Continental Divide in Montana and Wyoming.

Adding to the feel of being in the West are the abundant wild ponies roaming through the recreation area and **Grayson Highlands State Park**. Much like the famous ponies of Assateague Island in eastern Virginia, the ponies here are descendants of animals that escaped domestication generations ago. Running free throughout most of the year, they are rounded up in the fall, when some are auctioned. A portion of the money raised goes toward local efforts to keep the rest of the herd healthy and running wild. Also plentiful are the more than 150 birds that have been sighted here. In addition, bear, deer, foxes, bobcats, raccoons, red squirrels, chipmunks, and woodchucks all make homes within the recreation area.

Hundreds of miles of trails run through the recreation area, so you could easily spend weeks walking here without covering the same ground. Several of the pathways could be destinations in and of themselves. Running almost the full length of the recreation area, the **Iron Mountain Trail** [FS301] is over 50 miles, while more than 60 miles of the **Appalachian Trail** [FD1] are within its borders. The longest single trail is the 67-mile **Virginia Highlands Horse Trail** [FS337]. More than 16 miles of the **Virginia Creeper Trail** [FS 4575] are also in the recreation area.

The hiking possibilities are almost limitless and you are urged to obtain a forest service map and go off and do some exploring. To get you started, some of my favorite journeys are described below.

WILBURN RIDGE & MOUNT ROGERS: One of the most popular ways to the summit of Virginia's highest point begins in Grayson Highlands State Park. Take the blue-blazed **Rhododendron Trail** (which is basically a state park service dirt road) from the parking area through open meadows to meet the **AT** [FS1] in half a mile. Bearing left to follow white blazes, you will soon leave the state park, enter national forest lands, and come to the junction with the **Wilburn Ridge Trail** [FS4597], which goes right to the highest points of Wilburn Ridge. (You can use this pathway as an alternate route if you wish; it rejoins the AT in 1.4 miles.)

High open meadows, 360° views, mountain air blowing across your face – hiking doesn't get much better than this. Enjoy the vistas spread out before you. Above you and to the west is the spruce- and fir-covered summit of Mount Rogers. Behind are the rolling grasslands you traversed to reach here and the summits of Haw Orchard and Stone mountains, while far to the south are the mountain peaks of North Carolina, with Grandfather and Sugar mountains rising prominently.

Continue to follow white blazes when you come to the intersection at 3.1 miles. In just a few minutes, bear right to ascend the **Mount Rogers Spur Trail** [FS4590], reaching the 5,729-foot summit at 3.6 miles. You can either return to your car by retracing your steps or by getting out the forest service map and plotting a new course.

PINE MOUNTAIN: A long day or an excellent overnight hike also begins at the parking area in Grayson Highlands State Park by ascending the blue-blazed **Rhododendron Trail**. This time when you come to the **AT** [FS1] after a half-mile, bear right and rise to the open, rocky heights of Wilburn Ridge. Eventually you will descend and cross Quebec Branch (at 1.8 miles), Little Wilson Creek, and the East Fork of Big Wilson Creek. Merging onto an old railroad grade at 3.3 miles, you will soon leave it to walk by a spring at four miles. Walking through fields to the meadowlands on the top of Stone Mountain, descend to cross the fences of "The Scales" (a one-time cattle weighing area) at 5½ miles. Continuing in open country, bear left onto the blue-blazed **Pine Mountain Trail** [FS4595] at 6.9 miles. Crossing the crest of Pine Mountain, make a left onto the white blazes of the **AT** [FS1] at 9.1 miles. Leaving national forest lands and re-entering the state park, turn right onto the Rhododendron Trail and descend to your car, completing the journey at 11.6 miles.

THE WEST END CIRCUIT: If you are looking for a long week-end trek that takes in the best of what the area has to offer, try what is known as the West End Circuit, which begins at a parking lot for the AT on VA 603, about four miles west of Troutdale.

Rising to the south on the **AT** [FS1], you will come to the **Old Orchard Shelter** at 1.7 miles; take a break and enjoy the view of the surrounding mountains. Continuing to rise, turn right onto the **Pine Mountain Trail** [FS4595] at 3.2 miles, bearing right onto the **AT** [FS1] at 5.1 miles. With glorious 360° views provided by the open fields through which you are walking, pass by the Thomas Knob Shelter and the half-mile side trail to the summit of Mount Rogers.

Dropping to cross VA 600 at 10.3 miles, rise to swing around the forested slopes of Whitetop Mountain to come to **Buzzard Rocks**, one of the best viewpoints of the journey. North are the heights of Mount Rogers, while south your gaze will be drawn to the mountains of North Carolina. The trek passes by Lost Mountain Shelter and drops quickly to join the **Virginia Creeper Trail** [FS4575]. Cross a 500-foot trestle at 20.1 miles.

Soon the AT veers to the right and you will remain on the Creeper Trail, following it for three miles through a gorge complete with cascades, towering cliffs, and a series of bridges enabling you to cross Whitetop Laurel Creek a number of times. Watch for a blue-blazed trail to the right at 24.9 miles that you will turn onto, soon making a left onto the **AT**. Following the white blazes, you will be paralleling the Creeper Trail, but higher up on the hillside.

After crossing US 58, turn to the right and gain elevation as you begin to traverse the **Feathercamp Trail** [FS169] at 27.9 miles. Swinging around the southern side of the mountain, intersect and bear right onto the **Iron Mountain Trail** [FS301] at 29.3 miles. Passing by Sandy Flats Shelter, there are small ups and downs as you stay to the ridgeline – which provides an occasional view. Soon after going by Straight Branch Shelter, make a right onto VA 600, walking along it for less than a mile to make a left and continue along the Iron Mountain Trail at 36.2

miles. Skirting Hightop and Doubletop mountains and the headwater area of Little Laurel Creek, come onto FDR 84 and bear right for almost a mile, making another right back onto Iron Mountain Trail at 38.8 miles.

Beyond the Cherry Tree Shelter you need to make a right onto FDR 828, but quickly turn left to continue following the Iron Mountain Trail. Upon reaching the **AT**, bear right and descend on a series of long switchbacks to end the trek and return to your car at 44.2 miles.

COMERS FALLS: For a moderately easy and pleasant .6-mile round-trip walk to a waterfall, drive VA 16 south from I-81 Exit 145 (at Marion) for 16½ miles to make a right onto VA 741. In a half-mile look for a small parking area on the right side of the road. Following the white blazes of the **AT** [FS1] to the south, you will pass through an emerging forest before dropping down to small, but eye-pleasing Comers Falls.

In the late 1990s, the Virginia Department of Transportation had planned to turn this lovely spot into a concrete culvert so they could make US 58 into a four lane highway. So many citizens voiced opposition through public meetings and a letter-writing campaign that the idea was canceled.

Forest Service Campground Trails

If you are going to be spending any time in the forest service campgrounds (see *Camping* below for driving directions), there are several short trails worth checking out:

RAVEN CLIFF FURNACE TRAIL: In the eastern end of the recreation area, the Raven Cliff Furnace Trail [FS 4616] begins in the Raven Cliff Campground and follows Cripple Creek to arrive at the old **Raven Cliff Iron Furnace**. From the 1800s to the early 1900s, the furnace was used to heat a mixture of iron ore, limestone, and charcoal. The resulting pig iron was then shipped to factories to be alloyed and made into cast iron and steel. You return to the campground by retracing your steps for a total walking distance of not quite one mile.

DICKEY KNOB TRAIL: In about the middle of the recreation area, the Dickey Knob Trail [FS346] emanates from the Raccoon Branch Campground. Making use of foot bridges to cross a number of small creeks, the narrow pathway climbs to the cliffs on 3,649-foot **Dickey Knob** for great views north of the Rye Valley, Sugar Grove, and Brushy Mountain. Retrace your steps back to the campground to complete the approximately five-mile round-trip journey.

HURRICANE KNOB NATURE TRAIL: A little further west is the Hurricane Knob Nature Trail [FS 4517]. The 1.1-mile loop begins in the Hurricane Campground by paralleling Hurricane Creek. Crossing the stream a couple of times on footbridges, make a fairly easy rise to **Hurricane Knob**. There are no great views here, but you will be walking through a nicely wooded forest. The trail descends from the knob to return to the campground.

Outfitters

Allowing you to savor the beauty of the recreation area without having to carry a backpack is **Treasure Mountain Farm Llama Trekking** (10436 Echo Lane, Glade Springs, VA 24340, ☎ 540-944-4674). Llamas make especially good pack animals in the mountaintop ecosystem because their feet do not impact the sensitive soils. With the llamas carrying everything in saddlebags, you are free to hike and enjoy the scenery. Day trips and overnight journeys are both available.

Virginia Highland Llamas (Route 1, Box 41, Bland, VA 24315, ☎ 540-688-4464) offers all-day leisurely hikes following a pioneer trail to a scenic high rock on top of Big Walker Mountain. They will even let you lead a llama during the walk.

Scott County/Natural Tunnel State Park

The seven trails in Natural Tunnel State Park add up to a total of only 3.2 miles of pathways, but they lead to such great spots that you should consider walking every one of them.

TUNNEL TRAIL: This .6-mile round-trip uses a series of switchbacks to drop into the gorge and come to an observation deck looking into the mouth of the tunnel. It's too dangerous to walk into the tunnel (trains still come roaring through it). However, just standing here, you can't help but be impressed by the erosive powers of Stock Creek.

LOVER'S LEAP TRAIL: Use caution as you follow the Lover's Leap Trail, which begins at the visitors center and rises .4 mile to a breathtaking view into the deep gorge where the tunnel is located. Wire fences, stone walls, and signs are warnings that other folks have had mishaps on this route.

TUNNEL HILL, LOVER'S LEAP & GORGE RIDGE TRAILS: The .7-mile Tunnel Hill Trail connects the picnic and swimming area with the Lover's Leap Trail, while the .3-mile Gorge Ridge Trail starts at the campground to meet up with the Lover's Leap Trail. The .2-mile Center Trail is a connector between the Tunnel Hill Trail and the Gorge Ridge Trail.

PURCHASE RIDGE TRAIL: The longest pathway in the park is the 2.2-mile round-trip Purchase Ridge Trail, which rises along the edge of the gorge coming to a knob with a scenic overlook into the deep cleft. This hike is especially pretty in early spring when the umbrella-like leaves of the mayapple carpet the forest floor.

SPRING HOLLOW TRAIL: The Spring Hollow Trail is a .4-mile round-trip walk that begins along VA 646 and drops to Stock Creek and the northern entrance of the Natural Tunnel.

Cumberland Gap

A network of approximately 50 miles of trails penetrate the 20,270 acres of the Cumberland Gap National Historical Park. Ranging from short self-guided nature trails to longer overnight treks, the pathways are not blazed, but are well maintained and are signed at intersections and trailheads.

RIDGE TRAIL: Running almost the full length of the park, the 16-mile Ridge Trail is its main route. Beginning at the Pinnacle Overlook parking area, the trail follows the crest of Cumberland Mountain through a predominantly hardwood forest as it swings back and forth into Kentucky and Virginia. Connecting with nearly every other trail in the park, it also provides access to the four designated backcountry campsites and has a number of views into both states from large rock outcroppings. Its eastern terminus is the boundary of the park and can reached by ascending the strenuous 2.4-mile **Ewing Trail** from the parking area at Civic Park. (This parking area is located on VA 724, one mile from US 58 at the small village of Ewing.)

CIRCUIT HIKE: The only easily accomplished circuit hike begins by ascending 4.8-mile **Gibson Gap Trail** from a parking area on US 58 near the Wilderness Road Campground. Rising by a series of switchbacks, it crosses Station Creek three times before coming to the Gibson Gap backcountry campsite and the crest of Cumberland Mountain. Bearing left onto the **Ridge Trail**, enjoy an occasional view and maybe spot a deer or two before making a left at 8.2 miles to descend along the **Skylight Cave Trail**. The cave is a good spot to take a break before continuing to the picnic area and the campground. The campground has access to the **Gibson Gap Trail**, which will return you to your car as you complete this 10.3-mile journey.

THE HENSLEY SETTLEMENT: The shortest route to the Hensley Settlement – where the park service has partially restored a mountain community that existed from 1904 to the 1950s – begins on the **Chadwell Gap Trail**. (Its trailhead may be reached by following US 58 east from the Wilderness Road Campground for 11 miles to make a left onto VA 690, which brings you to the parking area on VA 688.) Rising on a long series of switchbacks, turn left onto the **Ridge Trail** at two miles. Bypassing a side trail to the Martins Fork campsite, go by the Chadwell Gap campsite and take the trail to the right which descends steeply to the settlement at 3.4 miles. Retrace your steps to return to your car.

OTHER PATHWAYS IN THE PARK:

- The two-mile **Sugar Run Trail** ascends from a picnic area in Kentucky to the Ridge Trail.

- The **Tri-State Peak Trail** ascends from US 25E for almost one mile to the 1,990-foot summit for a grandstand view of Virginia, Kentucky, and Tennessee.

- Continuing beyond Tri-State Peak, the **Cumberland Trail** is a long-distance trail which heads out of park lands following the Tennessee and Kentucky border.

- Not quite one mile, the **Wilderness Trail** descends from the Tri-State Peak Trail to the old Iron Furnace in the small town of Cumberland Gap, Tennessee.

- The one-mile **Honey Tree Trail** and the .7-mile **Green Leaf Nature Trail** are both located beside the Wilderness Road Campground.

Big Stone Gap

STONE MOUNTAIN TRAIL: The 14-mile Stone Mountain Trail [FS207] is, without a doubt, one of the most scenic hikes in far-Southwest Virginia.

*If you are going to make this an overnighter instead of a day hike, you can either choose a backcountry campsite along the trail or take a side-trip to the forest service's **Lake Keokee Campground** (with pit toilets, but no drinking water).*

The (possibly unmarked) eastern trailhead is reached by driving north from Big Stone Gap on US Alternate 58/23 for a little more than a mile. Once you cross the bridge over **Roaring Branch**, look for a small parking spot on the right side of the road. Walk back along the road and cross it to begin the hike by ascending stone steps (constructed by the Youth Conservation Corps in the 1970s) along the rushing waters of Roaring Branch. Even before you get away from the sound of the highway, the beauty of this place begins to enfold you. The stream cascades over giant boulders as it tumbles through a narrow defile decorated by the lush greenness of towering hemlock and a thick understory of rhododendron. Even if you don't plan to hike this whole trail, you should at least walk to this point – few places this outstanding are so easily accessible.

Rising to the ridgeline, come to **High Butte** at about four miles with views to the north of the mountains in Kentucky and to the south of the Powell River Valley and the mountains of Southwest Virginia. Descend to the **Olinger Gap Trail** [FS327] at six miles. This side-route drops to the right for one mile to the 3½-mile **Lake Keokee Trail**, which loops around the lake, providing access to the **Lake Keokee Campground**.

Continuing on the Stone Mountain Trail, rise from Olinger Gap and follow the ups and downs of the ridgeline to the top of **Stone Mountain** at about 10½ miles into the hike. Bypass the little-used Payne Branch Trail [FS213] and begin the long, switchback descent to the end of the hike at **Cave Springs Campground**. (See the *Camping* section below for driving directions to the campground.)

CHIEF BENGE SCOUT & LITTLE STONY NR TRAILS: The Chief Benge Scout Trail [FS401] and the Little Stony National Recreation Trail [FS331] can be combined into an outstanding 19-mile one-way hike. Since there is road access at both ends and at two campgrounds and a picnic area, you can make the walk as short or as long as you wish.

The western terminus is reached by driving VA 619 south from Norton. Make a left onto FDR 238 and follow it to the intersection of the High Knob Tower Road, which leads you to the parking area. Begin the hike by climbing the observation tower, from which, on clear days, you can see the mountainscape of five different states.

Descending on the yellow blazes of the Chief Benge Trail, come to the **High Knob Recreation Area and Campground** (see *Camping* below, for driving directions) in a little over a mile. Going by a four-acre lake, the pathway parallels the waters of Mountain Fork in a heavy forest before crossing FDR 704 to rise to a wildlife clearing about seven miles into the hike. After crossing VA 706, you will begin to descend along Little Stony Creek, eventually arriving at the **Bark Camp Campground** (see *Camping* below, for driving directions), 10 miles into the hike.

Walking along the shore of 60-acre **Bark Camp Lake**, cross VA 822 and make use of an old railroad grade, continuing to descend. Expect to get your feet wet as you will cross the stream a number of times.

The Chief Benge Trail comes to an end at 16½ miles as you cross FDR 701 to begin following the Little Stony National Recreation Trail. As nice as the hike has been, it is even prettier from here on out. Within the first few hundred yards are several waterfalls, one with a drop of more than 20 feet. Continuing, you will be treated to numerous cascades and large pools as the stream gurgles down the narrow gorge, with large rock outcroppings and ledges towering hundreds of feet above. Mountain laurel and rhododendron grow in copious groves under the spreading branches of large hemlock trees. All of this comes to an end as you reach the hike's eastern terminus at 19.4 miles at the **Hanging Rock Picnic Area** on FDR 805. (This picnic area may be reached by driving south from Coeburn for eight miles on VA 72.)

THE APPALACHIA LOOP TRAIL: One other hike within the vicinity of Big Stone Gap is also worthy of your time. Drive south from Appalachia on US Alternate 58/23 for a half-mile to turn left onto Town Road (TR) 1321, following it to TR 319. Bear left for one block and make a right onto TR 1322, which is followed to its end. The four-mile Appalachia Loop Trail [FS214] begins by following an old maintenance road along a stream. Rising to the heights of Little Stone Mountain, you will be treated to a vista taking in the town of Appalachia and Black Mountain across the Kentucky border.

Outfitters

The Mountain Empire Outdoor Center (PO Box 1210, St. Paul, VA 24283, ☎ 540-762-7500) has hiking, biking, canoeing, horseback riding, and other outdoor activity tours, with or without lodging or guides. Equipment rental is available, as are lectures and easy nature walks.

Breaks Interstate Park Area

The park received its name from the break in Pine Mountain which was created by the grinding and cutting action of the Russell Fork River as it slowly carved a five-mile, thousand-foot gorge through sandstone. Fifteen pathways totaling about nine miles, wander through the park, providing views of the gorge and its lush vegetative ground cover.

- The .15-mile **Towers Trail** begins at the park office to descend to an overlook of the massive rock formations rising from the mountain ridge above the Russell Fork Gorge.

- The easy .4-mile **Loop Trail** follows an old road from Picnic Shelter #2 to a natural spring to join with the **Tower Tunnel Trail**. Blueberry bushes line the .2-mile pathway, which descends slightly to a view of the railroad tunnel cutting through the mountain.

- Running along the edge of the cliffs at the top of the gorge, the .75-mile **Overlook Trail** has almost continuous views of the canyon. Be prepared for frequent ups and downs.

- The park's longest route, the 1½-mile **Prospector's Trail** may also be its most enjoyable. Skirting the base of the cliffs below the major overlooks, it has views of the rock formations above and of the deep canyon below.

- The one-mile **River Trail** splits off from the Prospector's Trail to descend to the Russell River on a steep series of switchbacks. Paralleling the river for a distance, it meets up with the half-mile **Grassy Creek Trail**, which ascends along the creek.

 The River and Grassy Creek trails probably receive the least amount of traffic because of their steepness, so they are the ones to walk if you are looking for some solitude.

- Extending from the lower end of Laurel Lake to the Grassy Creek Trail is the 1.25-mile **Laurel Branch Trail**, which passes through rhododendron and The Notch, an interesting rock formation.

- Rising from the Laurel Branch Trail is the half-mile **Grassy Overlook Trail**, which leads to a vista of Grassy and Center creeks and VA 80 crossing into Kentucky.

- The half-mile **Cold Spring Trail** follows the bed of a small stream to meet up with the Laurel Branch Trail.

- The .35-mile **Geological Trail** and the half-mile **Ridge Trail** combine to make up a self-guiding nature trail whose numbered stops are keyed to a brochure available from the visitors center.

- Accessed from the visitors center, the dam, or Potter's Knoll, the half-mile **Lake Trail** wanders along the undeveloped side of Laurel Lake with its marshes and wildlife.

- The **Beaver Pond Trail** and the **Deer Trail** are short pathways dropping from the cottage area to Beaver Pond. Combined, they are no more than one mile.

The Cumberland Mountain Trail

One of the most rewarding hikes (also open to equestrians) in all of far-Southwest Virginia is along the Kentucky/Virginia border. Listed by the forest service as the Cumberland Mountain Trail [FS201], but locally known as the **Pine Mountain Trail**, the route has more than 20 miles of wonderful isolation, punctuated by numerous views from precipitous rock outcroppings.

The (possibly) unsigned western trailhead may be reached by driving US 23 north from the town of Pound to Pound Gap on the state line. Heading east, the trail starts out as a road, but soon becomes a blazed pathway through a hardwood forest mixed with pine and mountain laurel. In one mile, the **Austin Gap Trail** [FS201A] descends to the right to VA 630. Another side trail, the **Bobs Gap Trail** [FS201B] also descends right at about six miles into the journey.

The only dirt road of the entire hike, providing access for horseback riders, is encountered at the eight-mile point. Rising to the highest point on Pine Mountain, the trail skirts Birch Knob (named for the large birches that once grew on its Kentucky side) and drops to the Arminta Mullin's cabin site. A bit beyond, you will come to the site of the **Dutton Bottom Farm,** where Mrs. Mullin's husband was murdered while being accused of possessing moonshine.

Dropping to Blowing Rock Gap, through which muleteams and wagons carried supplies from Skeetrock, VA to Ashcamp, KY, you will rise to **Blowing Rock.** This small natural tunnel was formed by erosion and ends in the face of a cliff on the Kentucky side. Cool winds blowing through the hole are always welcomed on a hot summer day. Rock outcrops beyond this point provide spectacular views into Kentucky, marred only by the sight of large strip mine operations chewing up the mountaintops.

At 13 miles, the **Counts Cabin Trail** [FS201C] descends to the right and is a favorite horseback riders' access point from VA 611. There is one viewpoint after another as you continue along the crest of the mountain. About 19 miles into the hike, the route makes a long descent of several miles that leads to a woods road. At a second old road, the trail officially continues to Potters Flats along the Russell River to come to an end after crossing a railroad trestle. However, to avoid this unsafe crossing of the river, it is suggested you follow, as horseback riders do, the second old road downhill for a couple of miles to end the hike near Elkhorn City, KY.

Blacksburg

PANDAPAS POND TRAIL: Very popular with the locals and only three miles west of Blacksburg off US 460, Pandapas Pond Trail [FS74] is a moderately easy one-mile loop around the eight-acre man-made pond. Located on the edge of the Eastern Continental Divide, the pond has a marshy area along its northeast corner and beavers have established a wetland below it on the waters of Poverty Creek. The Pandapas Pond area also provides access to the Poverty Creek and Gap Mountain Horse trails.

Continuing to drive west on US 460 past Pandapas Pond gives you access to a number of other hiking areas:

JOHNS CREEK MOUNTAIN TRAIL: You can reach the trailhead for the Johns Creek Mountain Trail [FS57] by turning right onto VA 42 for 9½ miles to make a left onto VA 658. The road has already brought you up to the ridgeline, so you will only have minor ups and downs as you hike the crest of the mountain. Rock outcroppings in the mixed hardwood forest provide views of Sinking Creek Mountain and Valley. The Johns Creek Trail comes to an end as it intersects the **Appalachian Trail** [FS1] at three miles. You can either backtrack to your car or decide to continue walking along the AT. (One option is to turn left and hike for approximately one more mile past Big Pond – a bog in the making – to enjoy wintertime views from Kelly Knob.)

NATURE CONSERVANCY TRAIL: An outstanding (and extremely popular) day hike may be reached by driving west on US 460 from Blacksburg past Newport and making a right onto VA 613. Approximately three miles later, bear left onto VA 714. Continue 3½ miles to a fork, where you need to make a sharp left to reach the beginning of the Nature Conservancy Trail [FS7013] beside an old fire tower. The bald knob gives great views of the mountains to the north before the trail winds along the southern slope of the mountain through thick growths of rhododendron and across small water runs. The first side trail leads to **Barney's Wall** overlooking Little Stony Creek Gorge, while the second side path brings you to the upper falls of **The Cascades**.

About 3½ miles into the hike, the main route connects with **The Cascades Trail** [FS70]. This pathway will bring you to the 60-foot waterfall before you follow it downstream to a parking area on VA 623, ending the 7½-mile hike. (This parking area may be reached by driving US 460 west of Blacksburg to Pembroke, where a right turn onto VA 623 brings you to the trailhead.)

Outfitters

Providing all of the equipment you need (except clothing and personal items) and preparing tasty meals, David Trible of **The Virginia Wilderness Company** (10468 Fortune Ridge Road, Bent Mountain, VA 24059, ☎ 800-683-1831 ext. 3461) specializes in half- and full-day hikes, overnight backpacking trips, and full-day or overnight fly fishing excursions. Mr. Trible is a certified EMT, certified wilderness EMT, and has First Aid and CPR certification.

Backcountry Ski and Sports (3710 South Main St., Blacksburg, VA 24060, ☎ 540-552-6400) has canoes, kayaks, backpacking, camping, ski, and just about any other type of equipment you need for active outdoor pursuits.

■ On Wheels

Mountain Biking

Radford/Pulaski

 TRACT FORK TRAIL: Northwest of Pulaski it is possible to combine two forest service trails with a bit of roadway for a long afternoon's worth of riding. Drive north from Pulaski on VA 738 for four miles to make a right onto VA 641. Follow this road to its end at FDR 692 which, in turn, is driven to its end. Tract Fork Trail [FS6516] is a wide route bordered by rhododendron and hemlock. About one mile into the ride, bypass the Polecat Trail coming in from the left and continue to rise to the ridgeline. Skirting around the northern side of Piney Mountain, reach the end of the trail on VA 600 at four miles into the ride.

Make a left onto VA 600, following it for close to 1½ miles to make another left onto FDR 707. In 2.8 miles you will bear left onto the **Polecat Trail** [FS6517], which runs along a railroad grade to make a couple of crossings of Polecat Creek. Rising to cross a ridgeline, descend and turn right onto the Tract Fork Trail to return to your car and complete this 10.7-mile ride.

NEW RIVER TRAIL STATE PARK: This is one of the best success stories of rails-to-trails conversions in the country. When Norfolk Southern donated a right-of-way, the Commonwealth established it as a state park and developed the former railroad bed into a hiking, biking, and horseback riding trail.

For 57 miles (which includes a spur route to Fries), the trail runs from Pulaski to Galax, rising at an imperceptible grade as it heads south. Close to 40 miles of the route runs along the banks of the New River, providing scenery and ample spots to fish, canoe, or take a break. Six places along the way have restrooms. The state has also developed a few facilities and a concessionnaire rents canoes and bicycles at Foster Falls – about mid-point along the trail. Within a very short time, this has become one of the most popular outdoor recreation areas in Southwest Virginia. The state estimated that more than 40,000 people made use of some section of the trail in June, 1997!

In addition to its trailheads in Pulaski and Galax, other major road access points to the New River Trail with parking are Bryson's Store on VA 658 east of Draper; Foster Falls, drive US 52 to VA 608 and follow signs; Shot Tower Historical State Park, from I-77 Exit 24, drive east on VA 69 to US 52 and follow signs; Ivanhoe, east on VA 639 to VA 94; Byllesby Dam, east on VA 602 to VA 94 and park at the dam; Fries, park at town park; Chestnut Yard, drive VA 721 north through Cliffview to VA 607, which is followed to Chestnut Yard; Cliffview, drive US 58 to

New River Trail State Park.

Galax, then north on VA 887 to VA 721, park across from Cliffview Trading Post.

Outfitters

Cliffview Trading Post (Cliffview Road, Galax, VA 24333, ☎ 540-238-1530) rents horses and bicycles.

At Foster Falls is **New River Adventures** (office – 1007 North 4th St., Wytheville, VA 24382, ☎ 540-228-8311), which rents bicycles, canoes, kayaks, and inner tubes. In addition to providing shuttles, they put together guided overnight backpacking trips and have a full-service bike shop.

Less than a mile from the New River Trail in Draper, **New River Bicycles** (Route 1 Box 175, Draper, VA 24324, ☎ 540-980-1741) sells, services, and rents bicycles and provides shuttle service. They also claim to do a free safety check for any bike.

Near the northern end of the New River Trail is **Tangent Outfitters** (PO Box 1827, Dublin, VA 24084, ☎ 540-674-5202) in Dublin. Not only do they provide canoe and bike rentals and shuttles, but they will arrange for overnight pedal and paddle trips along the New River or customize a fishing trip for you.

Wytheville/Mount Rogers Area/Abingdon

THE CHANNEL ROCK TRAIL: A 10-mile ride, also open to hikers and horseback riders, is reached from Rural Retreat, I-81 Exit 19. Drive VA 680 north for 2½ miles, turn left onto VA 645 for four miles and then follow FDR 227 to its end. The Channel Rock Trail [FS6506] (not shown on the official Jefferson National Forest map) starts in beautifully isolated Crawfish Valley, crosses Bear Creek, and climbs to the top of Brushy Mountain. Following the ridgeline for four miles, descend into Channel Rock Hollow back to Crawfish Valley and the end of the ride. Expect rocky terrain along the creek bottoms and on the dry ridges.

GRAYSON HIGHLANDS STATE PARK: Grayson Highlands State Park opened a portion of its trail system for mountain biking in the mid-1990s. The park's rugged terrain and absolutely stunning scenery make it an ideal riding place. With four access points along the park's roadways, available trails include the **Horse Trail** from Massie's Gap to the campground; the **Seed Orchard Road**; the old **Upchurch Road**; and the **Service Road**. All of the routes have gravel and/or dirt, with rocky sections and stream crossings.

VIRGINIA CREEPER TRAIL: If you start the Virginia Creeper Trail at Whitetop Station, at an elevation of 3,576 feet, you will have an almost continuous downhill ride – at more than a 2% grade – for almost 17 miles into Damascus. The final 16 miles will rise to Abingdon at about a 1.5% grade. A couple of outfitters in Damascus provide shuttles allowing you to ride the entire trail in the downhill mode.

In addition to trailhead parking in Abingdon and Damascus, other major access points are Whitetop Station, drive US 58 east from Damascus for close to 16 miles to make a right onto VA 726; Green Cove, drive US 58 east from Damascus about 15 miles and turn right onto VA 600; Creek Junction, US 58 east from Damascus for 10 miles to a right turn onto VA 728; Alvarado, US 58 west from Damascus for approximately five miles to a left onto VA 711.

Outfitters

In Damascus, **Mount Rogers Outfitters** (110 Laurel Ave., Damascus, VA 24326, ☎ 540-475-5416) is located on the Appalachian Trail and is less than a block from the Virginia Creeper Trail. In addition to having a full range of hiking and camping equipment, they also rent bicycles and provide shuttles.

Also in Damascus, the **Blue Blaze** (PO Box 982, Damascus, VA 24326, ☎ 540-475-0595) rents bicycles and provides shuttles on a reserved, scheduled basis.

MOUNT ROGERS NATIONAL RECREATION AREA: Many of the trails in the Mount Rogers National Recreation

Area are open to mountain bikes and rides of varying lengths can be accomplished. Among the many available, some of the most popular riding pathways include to the 50-mile **Iron Mountain Trail** [FS301], the 60-mile **Virginia Highlands Horse Trail** [FS337], the **Feathercamp Ridge Trail** [FS 4550], the **Henley Hollow Trail** [FS 306], and the **Beartree Gap Trail** [FS4551].

ROWLAND'S CREEK FALLS CIRCUIT: The highlight of this challenging ride is the 150-foot **Rowlands Creek Falls**, but the entire journey has great scenery and flowing mountain streams. The beginning of the trip can be reached by driving VA 16 south from I-81 Exit 16 (in Marion) to Sugar Grove. Turn right onto VA 601 – which becomes VA 670 in Teas – to a left turn onto VA 656. Continue for 1.7 more miles to a left onto VA 668, which becomes FDR 643. Parking is at several pull-offs near the trailhead.

Begin by traveling along gated FDR 845. At 2.8 miles, the road ends and, crossing a stream, you will ascend steeply along **Jerry's Creek Trail** [FS165] to 4.1 miles and a left along Old 84. When this roadway comes to FDR 84, bear left and go through a gate to follow **Rowlands Creek Trail** [FS164] to return to the starting point and the end of this 12-mile ride.

The roads and trails of this ride are not identified on the official Jefferson Forest map.

Big Stone Gap

The forest service has identified four circuit rides in the High Knob area south of Norton. All the roadways, both paved and unpaved, are marked on the Jefferson National Forest Map of the Clinch Ranger District:

HIGH KNOB LOOP: The 13.2-mile High Knob Loop begins at the CCC parking lot on FDR 238 and proceeds past the High Knob Recreation Area, Coon Gap, and Osborne Rock to VA 706. Looping back to the west, the route follows FDR 704 past Mountain Fork to VA 619, where a right will return you to the starting point.

BACK VALLEY LOOP: At 26.7 miles, the Back Valley Loop is the longest ride in the area – and is all on unpaved roadway. Beginning at the intersection of FDR 704 and VA 619, ride south along VA 619 to turn to the left onto VA 653. Riding through quiet Back Valley, bear left onto FDR 776. Going by several junctions, come to VA 706, and then make a fairly quick turn onto FDR 822 to cross over Little Stony Creek and go by the Bark Camp Recreation Area. A left onto FDR 704 will bring you back to where you started.

BURNS CREEK LOOP: Also completely on unpaved roads, the Burns Creek Loop is an approximately 11-mile ride. Beginning at the intersection of FDR 238 and FDR 2020, the journey starts by heading south along FDR 238 to connect with and follow VA 706 to the left past Glades Cabin. At the junction with VA 699, keep to the left on VA 706 (shown on the forest service maps as both 151 and 706), descending into Shingle Hollow. Near the Guest River, make a left onto FDR 2020 and climb back to the starting point.

OSBORNE RIDGE LOOP: The Osborne Ridge Loop, another 11-mile route, begins at the junction of VA 706 and FDR 704 by heading south along VA 706. Riding through Edith Gap, make a left onto VA 822, passing by the Bark Camp Recreation Area and through Turkey Gap to the junction of VA 822, VA 699, and VA 706. Bearing left onto VA 706, return to the starting point.

GUEST RIVER GORGE TRAIL: Officially dedicated in 1994, after the Norfolk Southern Railroad donated the land to the forest service, this trail [FS216] is a wide, 5.3-mile route of dirt, gravel, and crushed cinders open to hikers and bikers. Always within sound of the river, the pathway has several trestles that cross the river. In just a very short time, this rail-trail has become very popular – and with good reason. The riding is easy and the scenery – with waterfalls, towering cliffs, deep forests, and churning whitewater – can't be beat.

The Guest River Gorge Trail may be reached by driving south from Coeburn for four miles to the signed access road on the left. There is no road access to the lower end of the trail, so all rides or hikes will involve backtracking.

Breaks Interstate Park Area

Breaks Interstate Park has a two-mile pathway dedicated to mountain bikes. The ride begins close to the cottage area beside the mountain bike rental shack (bikes by the hour or day) and loops through the forest on single track and a former railroad bed.

Blacksburg

Except for the Poverty Creek and Gap Mountain horse trails near Pandapas Pond, most of the forest service trails around Blacksburg are closed to mountain bikes. However, the backroads of the forest are lightly traveled and make for some good riding, especially in the Dismal Creek area.

In recent years, **Mountain Lake Resort** has opened a number of the pathways on its 11,000 acres. In fact, the trails have now become the site of several officially sanctioned races and rides.

 Be sure to ask permission before you go riding if you are not a guest at the resort.

Road Biking

The TransAmerica Bicycle Route

There are more than 225 miles of the TransAmerica Bicycle Route in Southwest Virginia – more miles than any other section of the state. Entering the Commonwealth at Breaks Interstate Park, the route follows VA 80 through the towns of Haysi, Davenport, and Honaker before crossing the Clinch River, the North Fork Holston River, and I-81. Arriving in Damascus, there is the option of continuing along roadways or of using the Virginia Creeper Trail to reach US 58. With many ups and downs through the Jefferson National Forest, the route goes by Konnarock, Sugar Grove, and Rural Retreat – where US 11 is followed to Wytheville. Crisscrossing I-81 into Draper, Newbern, and Radford, it swings to the west into Christiansburg and passes through the Ellet Valley. Continuing north, it leaves

Southwest Virginia in the Catawba Valley to enter the Shenandoah Valley Region.

Radford/Pulaski

A moderately easy nine-mile round-trip ride follows VA 710 west out of **Radford to the Gatewood Park and Reservoir**, where you can do some fishing, canoeing, or camping before heading back to town.

Wytheville/Mount Rogers Area/Abingdon

If you do not mind a bit of traffic and a lot of stiff ups and downs, a long day's ride begins by following US 58 east out of **Damascus**. About a mile out of town is a view of one the railroad trestles along the Virginia Creeper Trail; a parking area for the trail is another mile further along the highway. Passing by the forest service's **Beartree Campground**, stay on US 58 where VA 603 comes in from the left.

Making the long, slow climb to the ridgeline with Whitetop Mountain looming high to the east, the payoff comes as you descend quickly to make a sharp right onto VA 726. Having left the traffic of US 58, enjoy the peace along the creek as you drop into beautiful **Taylors Valley**, where VA 726 ends and you turn left onto VA 725. You will rise as you enter Tennessee for a few miles to make a right onto TN 91, which will return you to US 58 and Damascus.

Scott County

A moderately easy morning loop ride around Rye Cove begins in **Natural Bridge State Park** and heads along VA 646. Coming to the head of the cove, bear right onto VA 652 to make another right onto VA 649. One more right onto VA 650 takes you through the middle of the cove to the left turn onto VA 646 and the return to the state park.

Tazewell

A ride through beautiful scenery can start at the intersection of US Business 19/460 and VA 16 west of Tazewell. Riding south along VA 16, make a left onto VA 604 and enter bucolic **Thompson Valley**, where green fields dotted with sheep rise up to meet the forests crowning Knob Mountain. Swinging around the western edge of the mountain, make a right onto VA 91 and, riding in the shadow of the mountain's north facen, return to the start.

The postmaster in Burkes Garden told me to be sure to tell readers that there was absolutely nothing to do here, but I discovered she was wrong. This bowl of gently roaming farmland surrounded by **Garden Mountain** has one of the premier 20-mile loop rides in the state. Purchase a snack and ask permission to leave your car at the General Store, then ride your bike on VA 623 toward the mouth of the garden, soon making a right onto VA 666. Swinging around the eastern end of this huge cove, you pick up VA 625 along its northern edge. Make a left onto VA 623, and then a right in a short distance onto VA 667. Coming to VA 727, bear left onto the dirt road for just a few hundred yards to the **Shady Pine Country Store**. Ring the handbell attached to the fence and someone will come out to sell you some homemade Amish-baked goods. Retrace your route and follow VA 727 out to VA 623 (next to the Post Office) and make a left to return to your car. What a great ride!

Blacksburg

Close to 21 miles of bikeway, some on shared roads and some on separate paved bike paths, connect the Virginia Tech campus with other parts of Blacksburg. An approximately 12-mile, moderately easy loop with a bit of a climb at the end follows US Business 460 south through town to take VA 603 out of Blacksburg. Several miles later, make a left onto VA 723 and ride it four miles to another left onto VA 785. This roadway will return you to downtown Blacksburg.

A favorite local loop ride of close to 60 miles begins by leaving town on VA 624 (Mount Tabor Road, later known as Newport Road). Heading north, you will be riding through one of the prettiest valleys in the area, which provides a view of **Dragon's**

Tooth, a monolithic rock structure along the Appalachian Trail. About 20 miles into the ride, make a right onto VA 311 – watch for heavy traffic – for close to two miles and bear right onto the **TransAmerica Bicycle Route**, VA 785 (Blacksburg Road, known further on as Harding Ave.). If you want to make this an overnight ride, a pleasant place to spend the evening is the **Crosstrails B&B** (see *Where To Stay*). VA 785 is followed through pastoral Catawba Valley all of the way to Blacksburg.

> **! TAKE**
> **• CARE**
> *Be aware that VA 624 and VA 785 may not have much traffic, but they are narrow, twisting roads with no paved shoulders.*

■ On Horseback

Wytheville/Mount Rogers Area/Abingdon

 HUNGRY MOTHER STATE PARK: North of Marion, this park is the only one in the state park system to rent horses. Rides of a half-hour and one hour are along an easy loop trail next to the stables. During most years the rides are offered during the summer from 10 am to 5 pm. After Labor Day, they are available on the weekends only from 12 noon until 5 pm, weather permitting.

MOUNT ROGERS NATIONAL RECREATION AREA: Hundreds of miles of interconnecting pathways and designated horse camping sites and staging areas allow you to explore the many facets of this beautiful spot.

THE VIRGINIA HIGHLANDS HORSE TRAIL: Beginning on VA 94 south of Wytheville, the Virginia Highlands Horse Trail [FS337] heads west through almost the entire length of the recreation area before ending 67 miles later at Elk Garden on VA 600 (east of Damascus). Along the way are side trails to the Raven Cliff Horse Camp, the Hussy Mountain Horse Camp, and the Fox Creek Horse Camp.

Trails that connect with the Virginia Highlands Horse Trail include the 3½-mile **Big Branch Trail** [FS4500], 1.6-mile **Ewing Trail** [FS4614], 1.6-mile **Henley Hollow Trail** [FS306], 1.3-mile **Scales Trail**, and the 50-mile **Iron Mountain Trail** [FS301]. Adding even more miles of riding possibilities is the fact that there are many other paths connecting to the Iron Mountain Trail and in Grayson Highlands State Park (with a campground complete with horse stalls).

HORSE HEAVEN LOOP: An example of the circuit rides that can be accomplished is the nine-mile Horse Heaven Loop. Beginning at the **Hussy Mountain Horse Camp**, the ride heads west along the **East Fork Trail** [FS4617], crossing FDR 14 three times. Making a right, climb to the height of the mountain on the **Virginia Highlands Horse Trail** [FS337], following that pathway for six wonderful miles. Dropping back down, turn right onto FDR 14 and follow it back to the **East Fork Trail** and the campground.

Outfitters

With a campground and fully furnished log cabin for rent, **Hungry Horse Farm** (Route 1 Box 316, Ivanhoe, VA 24350, ☎ 540-744-3210) is the perfect base from which to take off and explore the wooded trails and scenic ridges. Stalls are available for your horse and the Trading Post offers meals.

If you do not own a horse, **Mount Rogers Country Outdoor Center** (PO Box 151, Troutdale, VA 24378, ☎ 540-677-3900) has guided day rides from its base camp into the high country. Overnight horse trips with pack mules are also offered. If you want to journey back in time, try one of their covered wagon trips (day or overnight). Catering to everyone, the center will arrange trips, dropoffs, pickups, and even move equipment for mountain bikers and hikers.

Cumberland Gap

Cumberland National Historical Park has over 45 miles open to horseback riders, including most of the park's main pathway, the **Ridge Trail**. (See *On Foot* for details on the trails.) Riding is restricted on a few of the routes because of heavy visitor use or because they are too steep and rough for safe horse travel. In addition, there are three backcountry camping areas for horse use. Each contains fireplaces, a pit toilet, and a hitch rack. Untreated water is available, but is not recommended for drinking. The required (free) permits are available from the visitors center.

Breaks Interstate Park Area

Horse and pony rides are available daily from Memorial Day to Labor Day at Breaks Interstate Park. (Weekends only after Labor Day.) The stables are open from 10 am to 6 pm weekdays and from 10 am to 8 pm on Saturdays and Sundays.

One of the best rides in all of far-Southwest Virginia is along the more than 20-mile **Cumberland Mountain Trail** [FS201]. The *On Foot* section above describes the trail in detail. The access points that are most popular with equestrians are the Mullins Road (FDR 616) and the Counts Ranger Cabin Site, both along VA 611.

The **Cumberland Pine Mountain Trail Riders Club** holds several rides each year along this trail with as many as 150 riders participating in each ride. For more information you can contact them at: Route 3, Clintwood, VA 24228, ☎ 540-926-4956.

In the same vicinity, a number of routes are open to horseback riders on the 8,274 acres surrounding the **John W. Flannagan Reservoir**. Since regulations may change from time to time, it is best to contact reservoir headquarters for the most current information.

Blacksburg

There are more than 15 miles of pathways included in the system of equestrian trails known as the **Poverty Creek** [FS1001] and **Gap Mountain** [FS1002] trails. One of the trailheads can be reached by driving west from Blacksburg on US 460 to make a left onto FDR 188.2. If you see the sign for Pandapas Pond you have gone too far. Turn around at Pandapas Pond and return east for almost a mile to make the turn onto FDR 188.2. A couple of trails descend from this road to connect you with the main Poverty Creek and Gap Mountain trails and their several side routes.

The **White Pines Horse Camp** is a small primitive camping area designed to accommodate equestrian needs. Nearby, and marked by orange blazes, are the **Hoof and Hill** [FS1061], **Pearis Thompsom** [FS1059], and **Standrock Branch** [FS1060] trails, which have close to six miles of pathways open to horses. By using the numerous dirt and woods roads which connect with these trails, you could easily spend a full day or more riding along mountain streams bordered by hemlock and rhododendron. The camp can be reached by driving west to Pearisburg to turn south onto VA 100. In 10 more miles, turn right onto VA 42 for 10 miles to another right onto VA 606. Just past a small grocery store, make a right onto FDR 201, which is followed to the camp.

Outfitters

Only three miles from Virginia Tech, **Walnut Springs Stables** (3587 Glade Road, Blacksburg, VA 24060, ☎ 540-552-7207) offers trail rides on their 555 acres of open and wooded country terrain. Riding lessons and boarding are also available.

■ On Water

Radford/Pulaski

 CLAYTOR LAKE: With more than 21 miles and over 4,000 acres of surface water, Claytor Lake is large enough that people with motorboats, water skis, pontoon boats, and even small sailboats are attracted to it. Boats with motors can be rented from a shed next to the marina in the state park, while a ramp is provided for those who have brought their own watercraft. Do not come here in the summer looking for a quiet place to paddle; you won't find it. However, in late

Claytor Lake.

spring and early summer when the kids are in school, you would be hard-pressed to find a lake this large with so few people using it.

Wytheville

HUNGRY MOTHER STATE PARK: The six miles of shoreline around the small lake at Hungry Mother State Park can be explored by rowboats and paddleboats that are available for rent by the hour, day, or week. A boat launch at a different location on the lake can be used by those who bring their own canoes or kayaks. Bordered by the campground, rental cabins, swimming area, and gravel road, this is not the most pristine of areas, but the flatwater and green hillside rising above the lake are worth it if you happen to be in this neck of the woods.

THE NEW RIVER: From where it enters the state at Mouth of Wilson (east of Mount Rogers) to where it leaves the Commonwealth at the West Virginia border, the New River has well over 150 miles of water that can be paddled throughout most of the year.

Despite its name, the New River is actually the oldest river in North America and many geologists believe it to be the second oldest in the world, only the Nile in Africa being older. It is also one of the few rivers in the country that flows in a south-north direction. The river's popularity is evidenced by its numerous trailerable launch sites. Among the major ones are Bridle Creek Landing on VA 601 southwest of Independence; US 21/221 south of Independence; US 58/221 west of Baywood; Fries Landing at Fries; Allisonia Landing on VA 693; Claytor Lake State Park Landing and Claytor Lake Dam south of Radford; Whitehorn Landing on VA 623 north of Radford; and Rich Creek and Glen Lyn landings west of Narrows.

See the *Mountain Biking* portion of the *On Wheels* section (above) as many of the same outfitters that rent bicycles in Southwest Virginia also provide canoes, kayaks, and shuttles for the New River.

The New River.

Scott County

THE CLINCH RIVER: Flowing from the northeast toward the Natural Tunnel State Park, the Clinch River has many, many miles of enjoyable paddling through some great mountain scenery. From a state Game Commission put-in at St. Paul, it is possible to paddle – pretty much year-round – all of the way into Tennessee and never encounter anything more than Class II obstacles. Additional put-in and take-out sites include VA 65 in Dungannon; VA 65 at Clinchport; and the boat ramp downstream from VA 625 on the Tennessee border.

Cumberland Gap Outfitters

Cumberland Gap Outfitters (124 Brooklyn Drive, Cumberland Gap, TN 37724, 423-869-2999) is a one-stop shop for outdoor adventures of all kinds. They provide canoe, inner tube, and bike rentals and shuttles in addition to custom-designing overnight bike, canoe, or hiking journeys. Guided day hikes in the Cumberland National Historical Park are available, and they can even teach you how to scuba dive.

Big Stone Gap

LAKE KEOKEE: Although it covers only 90 acres, Lake Keokee is a nice spot for a lazy afternoon paddle. Boats with gasoline motors are prohibited, so things will be quiet and there is a good chance that you may be the only one out on the lake. Lake Keokee can be reached by driving US Business 23 north of Big Stone Gap to make a left onto VA 68. About eight miles later, bear left onto VA 623 and you'll arrive at the lake.

THE NORTH FORK OF POUND LAKE: North of Norton, the North Fork of Pound Lake is large enough to accommodate motorboats and can get busy at its lower end on summer weekends. It does, however, have so many little fingers and coves that a kayaker or canoeist could spend a goodly amount of time exploring in solitude. If you want to extend your stay, head to the **Laurel Fork Primitive Camping Area**. It can be reached only by foot or boat, so it is usually quiet and uncrowded.

THE GUEST RIVER: Only for those with expert boat handling capabilities and experience, the Guest River has close to eight miles of nearly constant Class IV-V rapids and one Class VI that must be portaged.

Travel with someone who is familiar with the river your first time out as there are no easy access spots to scout from and visibility is quite bad as you go downstream. There is even one spot where the river drops at the rate of 200 feet per mile.

The wild trip begins at the VA 72 bridge just south of Coeburn and ends after you join up with the Clinch River and come to its bridge on VA 72. (About mid-way through the trip is another access point at the parking lot for the Guest River Gorge Trail.)

Breaks Interstate Park Area

Pedal boats are available for rent daily during the summer to ride around the small lake here. The dock is open from 10 am to 6 pm weekdays and 10 am to 8 pm on Saturdays and Sundays. (Rentals are available on weekends only after Memorial Day.)

THE RUSSELL FORK RIVER: On weekends in October when the US Army Corps of Engineers releases water from the reservoir, the Russell offers the most intense, technical, and challenging commercially rafted whitewater in the Eastern US. For some perspective on how extreme this is, consider that the Class V Upper Gauley River in West Virginia drops 50 feet per mile and the Class V Upper Youghiogheny River in Pennsylvania has a drop of 116 feet per mile. Passing through a 1,000-foot gorge along the border of Breaks Interstate Park, the Russell River has a Class V+ rating with a drop of 230 feet per mile. The Triple Drop is three major ledges where the river drops over 30 feet and El Horrendo has a total drop of over 25 feet.

Most commercial rafting companies require that you have prior Class V experience to go through the gorge, although some do offer trips above the gorge that are not quite as intense. Among the many companies flocking to the Russell Fork in October are:

Outfitters

Sheltowee Trace Outfitters, PO Box 1060, Whitley City, KY 42653, ☎ 800-541-RAFT.

Advanced Whitewater Adventures, PO Box 37, Shady Valley, TN 37688, ☎ 800-THE-FORK.

Wahoos Adventures, PO Box 1915, Boone, NC 28607, ☎ 800-444-RAFT.

Precision Rafting, PO Box 185, Friendsville, MD 2153, ☎ 800-477-3723.

Individual paddlers can also run Russell Fork, but remember that is only for those who have tested their mettle on other extreme rivers. It is always wise to go with someone familiar with the route on your first trip down; do not underestimate the river's difficulty as lives have been lost here.

For a Class III-IV run, you can put in below the Flannagan Dam on the Pound River and take out at the Bartlick Bridge on VA 611 or at the Garden Hole pool, where a park service road is open from May through October from dawn until 9 pm. After the Garden Hole you are committed to the wild rapids of the Russell Fork Gorge and can not take out until KY 80 or Elkorn City in Kentucky.

Tazewell

THE CLINCH RIVER: South of Tazewell from the VA 80 bridge at Blackford to the Tennessee state line, the Clinch River flows for close to 125 miles through some great mountain scenery and narrow gorges, giving access to a beautiful part of the state that, unfortunately, has no large tracts of public land on which to hike or bike.

The upper 18-mile stretch, usually runnable into the early part of summer, starts at the hand-carry put-in at the Blackford Bridge on VA 80 north of Rosedale. After a bit of fairly easy paddling, the stream enters an isolated gorge where you are going to encounter some Class III rapids and ledges. The take-out is a bit upstream from the VA 646 bridge at Nash's Ford.

Blacksburg Outfitters

Providing canoe rentals and shuttles between Claytor Lake State Park and Bluestone Dam on the New River is the **New River Canoe Company** (PO Box 100, Pembroke, VA 24136, ☎ 540-626-7189) in Pembroke, west of Blacksburg.

Where To Stay

Radford/Pulaski

 Set on a quiet knoll away from the highway, the **Dogwood Lodge** [$] (7073 Lee Highway, Radford, VA 24141, ☎ 540-639-9338) has rates that can't be beat.

Sharing the same address and the same swimming pool are the **Best Western Radford Inn** [$$] (1501 Tyler Ave., Radford, VA 24241, ☎ 540-639-3000) and the **Comfort Inn** [$$] (1501 Tyler Ave., Radford, VA 24241, ☎ 540-639-3000). Rates are almost identical.

Set in Radford's historic district, the **Alleghany Inn B&B** [$$$ to $$$$] was built near the beginning of the 20th century and is furnished with period antiques.

In Pulaski, the **Count Pulaski B&B** [$$ to $$$] (821 North Jefferson St., Pulaski, VA 24301, ☎ 800-980-1163) is so used to cyclists that an indoor bicycle storage area is provided. The host is well versed in the many outdoor activities available in the area.

Wytheville

At the crossroads of I-81 and I-77, Wytheville has hundreds of rooms from which to choose. Sadly, there are no real standouts here; most are national chains providing a clean, but somewhat bland environment.

Almost right at the junction of the two interstates, **Super 8** [$ to $$] (130 Nye Circle, Wytheville, VA 24382, ☎ 800-800-8000) will usually have some of the lowest rates in the area, along with the **Interstate Motor Lodge** [$ to $$] (705 Chapman Road, Wytheville, VA 24382, ☎ 800-654-9290).

Accessed from the same I-81 exit, the **Best Western** [$ to $$] (355 Nye Road, Wytheville, VA 24382, ☎ 540-228-7300) also has rates at the lower end of the scale. Pets are permitted for a fee. Swimming pool.

The **Comfort Inn** [$$] (315 Holston Road, Wytheville, VA 24382, ☎ 800-228-5150) offers a free continental breakfast and has a pool.

Pets are permitted for a small additional fee at the **Days Inn** [$$] (150 Malin Dr., Wytheville, VA 24382, ☎ 800-DAYS INN).

The **Hampton Inn** [$$] (1090 Pepper's Ferry Road, Wytheville, VA 24382, ☎ 540-228-6090) is one of newest to join the pack of motels in Wytheville. It has a swimming pool and data ports.

Many of the rooms at the **Holiday Inn** [$$ to $$$] (1800 East Main St., Wytheville, VA 24382, ☎ 800-842-7652) have views of the nearby mountains. Pets are permitted.

With more character than all of the above motels combined, the historic Georgian Colonial **Boxwood Inn B&B** [$$] (460 East Main St., Wytheville, VA 24382, ☎ 540-228-8911) is in a semi-residential district away from the interstate. Each of the eight rooms has a private bath and individual heating and air conditioning. If you call them several weeks in advance they will be able to put together a package that includes some hiking, biking, and/or canoeing.

Mount Rogers Area

The meeting place of the Appalachian Trail, the TransAmerica Bicycle Route, and Virginia Creeper Trail, Damascus has an abundance of bed and breakfasts.

Built in 1904, **The Maples B&B** [$$ to $$$] (203 Laurel Ave., Damascus, VA 24326, ☎ 540-475-3943) served as a home for local teachers before becoming a B&B. Breakfast includes homemade bread and jellies, local fruits, and gourmet coffee.

Situated on the river in the middle of Damascus, the **Lazy Fox Inn B&B** [$$ to $$$] (133 Imboden St., Damascus, VA 24326, ☎ 540-475-5838) has three bedrooms with a shared bath and one room with a private bath. Hosts Ben and Ginny Adams provide a full country breakfast.

Next to the Virginia Creeper and Appalachian trails, the **Appalachian Inn** [$$ to $$$$] (219 First St., Damascus, VA 24326, ☎ 540-475-3415) is not a B&B (there is no caretaker), but a place where you can rent just one room or the entire house. Everything is provided except food.

In nearby Troutdale, the **Fox Hill Inn** [$$ to $$$$] (Rural Route 2 Box 1A1, Troutdale, VA 24378, ☎ 800-874-3313) is less than a 10-minute drive from the Appalachian Trail and has a patio with a panoramic view of the surrounding mountains.

Abingdon/Bristol

The grande dame of accommodations in Abingdon is the **Martha Washington Inn** [$$$$ to $$$$$+] (150 West Main St., Abingdon, VA 24210, ☎ 540-628-3161). Built in 1832 and later used as the Martha Washington College for women, the antebellum mansion became a fashionable hotel in the 1930s. Winding staircases with gleaming hardwood rails, rooms appointed with antiques, and monogrammed bathrobes speak of the graciousness you will experience.

The **Alpine Motor Inn** [$ to $$] (882 East Main St., Abingdon, VA 24212, ☎ 540-628-3178) and the **Empire Motor Lodge** [$$] 887 Empire Drive, Abingdon, VA 24210, ☎ 540-628-7131) will suffice for those seeking a clean, comfortable place to spend the night.

The **Super 8 Motel** [$$] (298 Town Centre Drive, Abingdon, VA 24210, ☎ 540-676-3329) also has some of the lower rates in town.

Within Abingdon's historic district, all three rooms of the **White Birches B&B** [$$ to $$$] (268 Whites Mill Road, Abingdon, VA 24210, ☎ 800-BIRCHES) have private baths. Afternoon refreshments are served.

Also in the historic district, and within easy walking distance of the Virginia Creeper Trail, the post-Victorian **Summerfield Inn B&B** [$$ to $$$$] (101 West Valley St., Abingdon, VA 24210, ☎ 800-688-5905) has seven rooms with private baths, a large covered porch, and a pantry open to guests for the preparation of refreshments.

With each room having a private deck overlooking the North Fork of Holston River, the **River Garden B&B** [$$$] (19080 North Fork River Road, Abingdon, VA 24210, ☎ 800-952-4296) is only a 15-minute drive from downtown Abingdon. Fishing equipment, inner tubes, and a canoe are available for guest use.

The lowest rates you are likely to find in Bristol will be at the **Syland Motel** [$] (15545 Lee Highway, Bristol, VA 24202, ☎ 540-669-0166) and the **Siesta Motel** [$] (1972 Lee Highway, Bristol, VA 24201, ☎ 540-669-8166).

La Quinta Inn [$$] (1014 Old Airport Road, Bristol, VA 24202, ☎ 800-531-5900) has a swimming pool and permits you to bring your small pets into the rooms.

With a downtown location, the **Ramada Inn** [$$] (2221 Euclid Ave., Bristol, VA 24201, ☎ 540-669-7171) has an outdoor swimming pool and more than 120 rooms.

The four rooms of the **Glencarin Manor B&B** [$$ to $$$] (224 Old Abingdon Highway, Bristol, VA 24201, ☎ 800-466-GLENN) each have a private bath. With high ceilings and a number of fireplaces, the building dates from 1842.

Scott County

Just a short drive from Natural Tunnel State Park, the **Ramada Inn-Duffield** [$$] (PO Box 260, Duffield, VA 24244, ☎ 540-431-4300) has a large outdoor pool with mountain vistas and a staff that is attentive and friendly. The restaurant serves one of the best breakfasts around.

Cumberland Gap

Built in 1914, the **Monte Vista B&B** [$$$$ to $$$$$] (Route 2 Box 441, Ewing, VA 24248, ☎ 540-445-4141) is now the retreat of acclaimed artist Dale Benedict, whose landscape works add a warmth and personal touch to the mansion. Three huge porches and a second floor balcony overlook the Cumberland Mountains. Expect friendly and lively conversation in the evening with the Benedicts and a generous Southern-style breakfast in the morning. The antique-furnished great room, sitting room, and living room are all open to guests.

Just across the border in Tennessee, the **Holiday Inn-Cumberland Gap** [$$] (Box 37, Cumberland Gap, TN 37724,

☎ 800-HOLIDAY) has the closest accommodations to the National Historical Park. The outdoor pool has a view of the mountainsides. In conjunction with the Cumberland Gap Outfitters next door, the motel offers several canoe, raft, inner tube, bike, and scuba dive packages.

Big Stone Gap

With some of the lowest rates in all of Virginia, the **Trail Motel** [$] (509 Gilley Ave., Big Stone Gap, VA 24219, ☎ 540-523-1171) is close to the town's museums and the site of the Trail of the Lonesome Pine outdoor drama.

Showing some signs of age, the **Country Inn** [$] (627 Gilley Ave., Big Stone Gap, VA 24129, ☎ 540-523-0374) has 42 rooms. Small pets are permitted.

Small pets are also permitted in the **Super 8** [$$] (US 23/Alt 58, Norton, VA 24273, ☎ 540-678-0893) in nearby Norton.

Almost next door, the **Holiday Inn** [$$ to $$$] (551 Highway 58 East, Norton, VA 24273, ☎ 540-679-7000) has indoor and outdoor pools. The Norton Grill and Rotary Restaurant is located in the motel.

About 20 miles southwest of Big Stone Gap in Pennington Gap, the **Convenient Inn** [$] (131 Industrial Drive, Pennington Gap, VA 24277, ☎ 540-546-5350) has an outdoor pool and some of the lowest rates in the region.

Breaks Interstate Park Area

Only open from April to December, the 34 lodge rooms of the **Breaks Interstate Park** [$$] (PO Box 100, Breaks, VA 24607, ☎ 800-982-5122) were built on the edge of the Russell Fork Gorge. The rooms' picture windows and individual balconies provide almost-breathtaking views onto (and into) the steep canyon. Housekeeping cottages that are open year-round and can accommodate up to five people are available for rent by the week.

Located about one mile from the park is the **Gateway Motel** [$] (Route 80, Breaks, VA 24607, ☎ 540-531-8481), which has an outdoor pool and is also a short drive from the Russell Fork River. Small pets are permitted.

About a 20-minute drive from the park, **Our House Inn** [$ to $$] (Route 1 Box 593, Clincho, VA 24226, ☎ 540-835-9634) stands along the edge of Lick Creek and a scenic trail follows the roadbed of an old lumber railroad. Three bedrooms share two baths; a continental breakfast is served.

East of the park on US 460, the **Shortridge Motel** [$] (Route 460 Box 6A, Vansant, VA 24656, ☎ 540-935-2968) has basic motel rooms.

Tazewell

About a 10-mile drive from downtown Tazewell in Pounding Mill, **The Bedrock Inn B&B** [$$ to $$$] (PO Box 105, Pounding Mill, VA 24367, ☎ 540-963-9412) is nestled on a hilltop overlooking the Pounding Mill Quarry. Constructed in the early 1900s by Charles Hunter as the quarrymaster's home, the inn is now the home of the fourth generation of Hunters. The home is decorated in antiques, hundreds of photos of the Hunter family, quarry memorabilia, and animal trophies. The landscaped and manicured grounds include a uniquely designed outdoor hot tub. All three guest rooms have private baths.

Also in Pounding Mill is **Cuz's Cabins and Resort B&B** [$$$$ to $$$$$] (US 460, Pounding Mill, VA 24637, ☎ 540-964-9014). Sitting on a hillside far removed from the highway, the two newly constructed cedar cabins each have a hot tub, fireplace, TV, and stereo system. A delicious breakfast complete with fresh fruit and freshly squeezed juice is delivered to your front porch, which has pleasant views of the pastoral countryside. The extensive grounds include a clay tennis court, swimming pool, and stocked fishing pond; hiking on adjacent lands is permitted. See *Where To Eat* for information on Cuz's Uptown Barbecue.

Blacksburg

One of the lowest cost places to stay in this university town (and close to campus) is the **Comfort Inn** [$ to $$] (3333 South Main

St., Blacksburg, VA 24061, ☎ 540-951-1500), with a pool, exercise room, and some in-room whirlpools.

Also with some of the lowest rates is the **Best Western Red Lion Inn** [$$] (900 Plantation Road, Blacksburg, VA 24060, ☎ 540-552-7770), which sits on 13 acres on the outskirts of town along US 460. A swimming pool, tennis courts, fireplace in the lobby, and outside gazebo make this more than just a typical motel.

You will pay a bit more, but the **Blacksburg Marriott** [$$$] (900 Prices Fork Road, Blacksburg, VA 24060, ☎ 800-228-9290) is conveniently located close to campus and shopping centers. Amenities include two pools (one heated outdoor, one indoor), tennis court, whirlpool, and refrigerators and microwaves in some rooms.

The **Holiday Inn** [$$] (3503 Holiday Lane, Blacksburg, VA 24060, ☎ 800-645-4329) is also centrally located. Some rooms have coffeemakers and refrigerators.

One block from campus, **L'Arche B&B** [$$$] (301 Wall St., Blacksburg, VA 24060, ☎ 540-951-1801) is a Federal Revival home situated among terraced gardens. Breakfasts feature homemade breads, jams, jellies, and cakes.

About a 25-minute drive from downtown, the **Bed and Breakfast at Blackacre Estate** [$$$] (6694 Blacksburg Road, Catawba, VA 24070, ☎ 540-384-6941) is a huge 7,600-square-foot structure tucked into a mountain valley. Towering open beam ceilings, massive fireplace, and stained glass windows add to the feel of spaciousness. The outdoor swimming pool is surrounded by a 4,700-square-foot deck which looks out upon the nearby hillside.

A five-minute drive from Blackacre Estate, **Crosstrails Bed & Breakfast** [$$] (5880 Blacksburg Road, Catawba, VA 24070, ☎ 540-384-8078) is on the spot where the Appalachian Trail and the TransAmerica Bicycle Route meet. *Roanoke Times* outdoor writer Bill Cochran and his wife Katherine will provide shuttles to nearby locations to hike, bike, canoe, kayak, or pursue other outdoor activities. If you exhaust their extensive knowledge of local spots, their library contains a large collection of hiking and outdoor-oriented books. Road bikes and cross-country ski equipment are available for guests. Tranquil evenings may be spent relaxing in the outdoor hot tub overlooking the 15-acre property, which is joined on three sides by national park lands.

■ Camping

There may be more campsites in Southwest Virginia than there are motel rooms. Nearly two dozen forest service campgrounds are scattered throughout the region. With few exceptions, backcountry camping is allowed on all national forest lands, while there are literally hundreds of spots along forest service roads where you are permitted to pull off and set up camp. In addition, state, municipal, and commercial campgrounds abound, both close to the interstate and in more isolated sections of the region.

Radford/Pulaski

The campground at **Claytor Lake State Park** is usually open from mid-March to early December and has a dump station, showers, and flush toilets. Camping cabins are also available for rent. Reservations may be made by calling ☎ 800-933-7275.

The **J&K Camper Corral** (Route 1 Box 2038, Dublin, VA 24084, ☎ 540-674-5561) is less than one mile from I-81 Exit 101. A dump station, flush toilets, and phone and cable TV hookups are available.

You can do some camping under the pines in Pulaski at the **Gatewood Park and Reservoir** (PO Box 660, Pulaksi, VA 24301, ☎ 540-980-2561). The 480-acre park has hiking trails and the reservoir is available for canoeing.

The **Horseshoe Campground** (Route 1 Box 233, Draper, VA 24324, ☎ 540-980-0278) borders the New River Trail State Park and has canoe and boat rentals.

Wytheville

Just off I-81 Exit 77 is the **Wytheville KOA** (Route 2 Box 122, Wytheville, VA 24382, ☎ 540-228-2601). Within its 22 acres are a heated pool, playground, dump station, flush toilets, rec room, camp store, and cable TV hookups.

 Something to consider: By the time you pay to camp at the KOA, you could add just a few dollars and stay in one of the Kamping Kabins.

The **Rural Retreat Lake and Campground** (PO Box 429, Rural Retreat, VA 24368, ☎ 540-686-4331) is located west of Wytheville via US 11. This municipal facility has a 90-acre lake, boat rentals, picnic grounds, and 72 wooded sites with hookups.

A short drive north of Wytheville, via US 21/52 and VA 717, are the 52 sites of heavily wooded **Stony Fork Campground**. Quite deluxe by forest service standards, it has a dump station, flush toilets, and hot showers.

South of Wytheville and close to Speedwell on VA 619 is the forest service's primitive **Cripple Creek Campground**. There is a dump station, but only pit toilets.

The 43 sites of the campground at **Hungry Mother State Park** can fill up quickly on nice summer weekends. Flush toilets, dump station, showers, swimming in the lake, and horseback riding are all draws to the park. Reservations may be made by calling ☎ 800-933-7275.

Nearby, the **Hungry Mother Campground** (PO Box 106, Marion, VA 24354, ☎ 540-783-2046) has 100 sites on 25 acres of maintained grounds. Here you will find a dump station, flush toilets, camp store, laundromat, and a swimming and wading pool.

Mount Rogers Area

Be sure to pack some warm clothes if you're camping at **Grayson Highlands State Park**. Even in the dead of summer, temperatures can get downright cold at 5,090 feet above sea level. A dump station, flush toilets, and showers are available. Call ☎ 800-933-7275 to make reservations. The views on the trails radiating out from the campground are some of the best in all of Virginia.

There are numerous forest service campgrounds within or near the Mount Rogers National Recreation Area:

East of Damascus via US 58 and FDR 837 is the **Beartree Campground** with almost 80 sites. One of the most deluxe forest service campgrounds in the area, it has a dump station, flush toilets, and showers.

Further east along VA 603, **Grindstone Campground** has 100 sites and it, too, has a dump station, flush toilets, and showers.

Four miles west of Troutdale on VA 603, **Fox Creek Campground** has facilities for equestrians. Be aware that there is no drinking water available.

Hurricane Campground is northwest of Troutdale off VA 650. Even though it is one of the smaller campgrounds, it does have flush toilets and showers.

North of Troutdale on VA 16 is the small **Raccoon Branch Campground**. It has drinking water and flush toilets.

Also with drinking water and flush toilets is **Raven Cliff Campground**. It may be reached by driving US 21 south of Wytheville to make a left onto VA 619.

If you were to continue south from Wytheville on US 21 past the turn off to Raven Cliff, a left onto FDR 14 would take you to **Hussy Mountain Campground** (equestrian facilities) and a right onto FDR 57 would lead to **Comers Rock Campground**, which has only pit toilets and a hand pump for water. There is no fee to stay at the latter.

Abingdon/Bristol

Reached from I-81 Exit 14, the **Riverside Campground** (18496 North Fork River, Abingdon, VA 24210, ☎ 540-628-5333) offers a dump station, flush toilets, swimming pool, laundromat, and a few shaded sites overlooking the river.

Southeast of Abingdon on VA 75, the **Lakeshore Campground** (Highway 75, Abingdon, VA 24210, ☎ 540-628-5394) has 200 campsites, a boat ramp, and swimming in the lake.

Sugar Hollow Recreation Area (Robert E. Lee Highway Bristol, VA 24201, ☎ 540-645-7275) has a small network of trails coursing through its 450 acres. The campground, operated by the city of Bristol, has a dump station and flush toilets.

Scott County

There are only 29 campsites at **Natural Tunnel State Park**, so you should make your reservations as soon as possible by calling ☎ 800-933-7275. The campground has a dump station, flush toilets, and showers.

Cumberland Gap

For those wishing to do some backcountry camping, four designated sites are available in the **Cumberland Gap National Historical Park**. The required (free) permits can be obtained at the park's visitors center.

If you do not want to carry all of your camping equipment on your back, the historical park has a campground on the Virginia side of the park. Located on US 58, the **Wilderness Road Campground** has running water and flush toilets. There are no RV hookups.

Big Stone Gap

West of Big Stone Gap via US Alternate 58 and VA 621 is the forest service's **Cave Springs Campground**; sites are available on a first-come, first-served basis. Swimming, a beach, showers, dump station, and flush toilets are available.

North of Big Stone Gap, the forest service has developed a couple of campgrounds around the shore of the North Fork of Pound Lake. On VA 671 west of Pound, **Cane Patch Campground** has a dump station, flush toilets, and showers. There is no fee to stay at **Laurel Fork Campground**, which can be reached only by foot or boat and only has pit toilets.

Operated by the Norton Parks and Recreation, the **Flag Rock Recreation Area** (c/o 618 Virginia Ave., Norton, VA 24273, ☎ 540-679-0754) is four miles northwest of Norton on VA 619.

The campground has 231 sites, a dump station, flush toilets, hot showers, and electric hookups.

Beside a 60-acre lake southeast of Norton is the forest service's **Bark Camp Recreation Area**. The area is reached driving US Alternate 58 east from Norton. Make a right in Tacoma onto VA 706. Four miles later, bear left onto VA 699, only to soon make a right onto VA 822. Another 1.7 miles brings you to the recreation area. With 19 campsites, there is a dump station, central water supply, and flush toilets. There is no fee to stay here.

Also developed by the forest service, the **High Knob Recreation Area** is reached by driving VA 619 south of Norton for close to four miles and turning left onto FDR 238 for 1.6 miles. Centered around a four-acre lake with a swimming beach, the campground has flush toilets, showers, drinking water, and a dump station.

Breaks Interstate Park Area

No reservations are accepted for the campground at **Breaks Interstate Park**, which is usually open from the first of April into October. There are well over 100 sites fanning out from three separate designated campgrounds, so, except for a very rare occasion, you should be able to find an unoccupied site. Some of the sites in Campground B are specifically situated for tent campers. Water, flush toilets, and hot showers are provided.

Three campgrounds, **Cranesnest, Lower Twin**, and **Pound River**, are administered by the US Army Corps of Engineers and are found along the shore of John W. Flannagan Reservoir. All three have flush toilets, showers, horse shoe pits, playground, boat launch ramp, and a dump station (no dump station at Pound River).

Blacksburg

With primitive sites that are almost never crowded, the forest service's **White Rocks Campground** is a long drive from Blacksburg. Head west on US 460, and when you have gone through the small town of Pembroke, look for a sign directing you to make a right for many more miles of driving before reach-

ing the campground. Drinking water, flush toilets, and a dump
station are provided.

Where To Eat

Radford/Pulaski

In the college town of Radford you will find an abundance of fast food, hamburger, sub, taco, Chinese, and
pizza restaurants.

A favorite of the students – and not quite fast food – is **Maca-
doo's Restaurant and Delicatessen** [$ to $$] (510 Norwood
St., Radford, VA 24141, ☎ 540-731-4879). Sandwiches in an
endless variety are the specialty, with a few entrées and salads
also on the menu. The sinfully rich desserts are popular and the
wine list amazingly extensive.

Across the street from the university is **BT's Restaurant** [$ to
$$] (218 Tyler Ave., Radford, VA 24141, ☎ 540-639-1282), with
appetizers, deli sandwiches, burgers, prime rib, seafood, and se-
lections from the bar.

One block down the street, **Chancey's** [$] (118 Tyler Ave., Rad-
ford, VA 24141, ☎ 540-639-0930) probably has the best strom-
boli in town, in addition to pizza, calzones, subs, burgers, and
salads.

Of the several Chinese spots, the **Beijing Restaurant** [$ to $$]
(307 5th St. Northeast, Radford, VA 24141, ☎ 540-980-2888) is
one of the favorites with students.

The national chain, **Damon's Ribs** [$ to $$] (1501 Tyler Ave.,
Radford, VA 24141,☎ 540-731-3141) has a restaurant in Radford.

In Pulaski, **Main Street Café** [$] (227 East Main St., Pulaski,
VA 24301, ☎ 540-980-5616) packs them in for breakfast, lunch,
and dinner.

For a quick breakfast, head to **MimiAnne's Gourmet Coffee
and Pastries**, [$] (93 West Main St., Pulaski, VA 24301, ☎ 540-
980-6464).

In downtown Pulaski, **The Renaissance** [$ to $$] (55 West Main St., Pulaski, VA 24301, ☎ 540-980-0287) serves seafood, pasta, chicken, and beef in a casual, yet refined atmosphere.

Wytheville

The interstate exits are awash with the chain restaurants. Pick an exit and you are likely to find Arby's, Bob Evans, Burger King, Dairy Queen, Hardee's, Kentucky Fried Chicken, McDonald's, Pizza Hut, Waffle House, and more.

Also in abundance are a number of "southern-style home cooking" restaurants.

Many of the local folks head downtown to **Durham's** [$ to $$] (150 North 11 St., Wytheville, VA 24382, ☎ 540-228-5241), which has been serving hearty breakfasts and home-style lunches and dinners since 1949.

The **Wilderness Road Restaurant** [$ to $$] (1025 Pepper's Ferry Road, Wytheville, VA 24382, ☎ 540-228-9437) claims to serve "home cooking at its best" and **Mom's Country Store and Restaurant** [$] (200 Nye Road, Wytheville, VA 24382, ☎ 540-228-5068) says it has "the best of Southern Home Cooking."

For a change of taste, **El Puerto** [$] (713 Chapman Road, Wytheville, VA 24382, ☎ 540-228-3159) is a regional chain of Mexican restaurants.

In a complex of motels, the **Peking Restaurant** [$ to $$] (105 Malin Drive, Wytheville, VA 24382, ☎ 540-228-5515) is the place to head for Chinese cuisine.

The most unusual spot for lunch and dinner (and possibly the best food in town) is the **1776 Log House** [$ to $$] (520 East Main St., Wytheville, VA 24382, ☎ 540-228-4139). With an 18th-century atmosphere and Colonial motif, this is where people come for special occasions. Beef stew, stuffed chicken, tenderloin steak, and other Virginia dishes are featured on the menu.

Abingdon/Bristol

Open early in the morning, the **Bonfire Restaurant** [$ to $$] (897 Empire Dr., Abingdon, VA 24210, ☎ 540-628-6131) is the place to go for breakfast. It also serves lunch and dinner.

As the name implies, the **Starving Artist Café** [$$] (134 Wall St., Abingdon, VA 24210, ☎ 540-628-8445) is the gathering place of the town's aesthetes, with rotating exhibits on the wall. Gourmet sandwiches for lunch and crab cakes and prime rib for dinner. Vegetarian entrées available.

You will also find some vegetarian offerings and other sandwiches at **The Secret Garden Restaurant** [$ to $$] (130 Pecan St., Abingdon, VA 24210, ☎ 540-623-1111).

Around the corner, and run by the same folks, **The Tavern** [$$ to $$$] (222 East Main St., Abingdon, VA 24210, ☎ 540-628-1118) has more upscale menu offerings of London broil, quiche, veal marsala, wiener schnitzel, and shrimp scampi.

The Hardware Company Restaurant [$ to $$$] (260 West Main St., Abingdon, VA 24210, ☎ 540-628-1111) has outdoor dining with period decor inside the 1895 hardware store structure. Seafood and pasta are featured prominently.

Hunan, Szechuan, Mandarin, and Cantonese cuisines are all available at the **Hunan Restaurant** [$ to $$] (558 Cummings St., Abingdon, VA 24210, ☎ 540-676-2875).

There is no doubt that the fanciest spot in town is the historic **Martha Washington Inn** [$$$] (150 West Main St., Abingdon, VA 24210, ☎ 540-628-3161). Delicacies such as roast quail, veal Oscar, and mountain trout stuffed with crab are not found in many other restaurants in Southwest Virginia.

In Bristol, the **Athens Steak House** [$ to $$] (105 Goodson St., Bristol, VA 24201, ☎ 540-466-8271) features a Grecian menu along with lobster tails and steaks.

Your meal is prepared at your table at the **Tokyo Japanese Steak House** [$$ to $$$] (28 Commonwealth Ave., Bristol, VA 24201, ☎ 540-645-0399).

La Carretta [$ to $$] (530 Volunteer Parkway, Bristol, VA 24201, ☎ 540-989-3361) is a regional Mexican restaurant chain.

Vinyard [$ to $$$] (603 Gate City Highway, Bristol, VA 23210, ☎ 540-466-4244) serves breakfast, lunch, and dinner.

Scott County

In a departure from most motel restaurants, **Winfield's** [$ to $$] (PO Box 260, Duffield, VA 24244, ☎ 540-431-4300), in the Ramada Inn, has a varied menu of nicely prepared dishes.

The **Hob-Nob Drive-Inn** [$] (RFD 1, Gate City, VA 24242, ☎ 540-452-4538) will do for a quick bite.

Cumberland Gap

Just across the state line in Tennessee, the **Holiday Inn restaurant** [$ to $$] (PO Box 37, Cumberland Gap, TN 37724, ☎ 423-869-3631) serves breakfast, lunch, and dinner and has daily buffets.

Big Stone Gap Area

The chain restaurants, such as Hardee's, McDonald's, Dairy Queen, Burger King, Bonanza, and Western Steer rule in the towns of Big Stone Gap, Norton, and Wise. It takes a bit of looking around to find an alternative.

One such option is the locally owned **Stringer's Restaurant** [$ to $$] (412 East 5th St., Big Stone Gap, VA 24219, ☎ 540-523-5388). Steaks, homecooked meals, and a huge buffet are offered.

The option in Norton is **Mosby's Restaurant** [$ to $$] (Piggly Wiggly Shopping Center, Norton, VA 24273, ☎ 540-679-1046) for meals at reasonable prices.

The offerings at the **China Garden** [$ to $$] (Wise County Plaza, Wise, VA 24293, ☎ 540-679-5201) are always fresh.

Sadly, one of the most eclectic restaurants in the region, **Robert's House** [$ to $$$] (146 Robert's House St., Wise, VA 24293, ☎ 540-328-2277) was for sale as this book went to press. If it is still open, be sure to stop for some interesting lunch presentations, such as a cream cheese, cucumber, and rye sandwich or peanut butter and pineapple on homemade bread.

For plain old home-style food with an atmosphere to match, try **Appalachia Country Cooking** [$ to $$] (717 West Main St., Appalachia, VA, ☎ 540-565-5088), north of Big Stone Gap.

Tazewell

A chain restaurant, **Sonic Drive-In** [$] (611 Market St., Tazewell, VA 24651, ☎ 540-988-2343) serves the usual burgers, sandwiches, fries, and shakes.

South of Tazewell in Pounding Mill, **Cuz's Uptown Barbecue** [$ to $$$] (US 460 Pounding Mill, VA 24638, ☎ 540-964-9336) may be one of the most peculiar places you will ever dine. I'm not sure what to call the decor – unsophisticated chic maybe. This is not meant as a negative, but a positive description. You'll find Dayglo paint on the walls and Elvis memorabilia inside a converted dairy barn. But what a wonderfully unique menu this place has – and all of it prepared close to perfection. The menu changes and at any given time you may find crab rangoons with sweet and sour sauce, smoked emu, wild mushroom soup, trout mousse, ostrich steak, prime rib with Burgundy gravy, Thai curry, barbecued pork and beef, and French silk or butterscotch pie.

Blacksburg

Across the street from the Virginia Tech Campus, **Gillies** [$] (153 College Ave. Northwest, Blacksburg, VA 24060, ☎ 540-961-2703) serves breakfast, lunch, and dinner, with many vegetarian and healthful items available.

Bogen's [$ to $$] (622 North Main St., Blacksburg, VA 24060, ☎ 540-953-2233) is crowded for both lunch and dinner, serving steak, burgers, seafood, and some vegetarian choices. Cappuccino, desserts, a sports bar, and a cyberbar keep folks hanging around.

Serving what it calls "casual Brazilian cuisine" is the **Ipanema Restaurant** [$$] (107 Ellet Road, Blacksburg, VA 24060, ☎ 540-951-4501).

Anchy's [$ to $$] (1600 North Main St., Blacksburg, VA 24060, ☎ 540-951-2828) has a fine dining menu of live lobster, Norwegian salmon, crab legs, ribs, duck, veal, mussels, blackened dishes, and pasta in a relaxed casual atmosphere.

Those with a taste for sushi should try the **Bamboo House Restaurant** [$ to $$$] (713 North Main St., Blacksburg, VA 24060, ☎ 540-552-4876).

Mexican food is the specialty of **El Guadelupes** [$ to $$] (1410 South Main St., Blacksburg, VA 24060, ☎ 540-953-0706).

For special occasions, local people head to nearby Christiansburg and **The Huckleberry** [$$ to $$$] (2790 Roanoke St., Christiansburg, VA 24073, ☎ 540-381-2382). Fireplaces add romance to the decor and menu of prime rib, baby back ribs, steaks, broiled lobster tail, chicken Dijon, and pasta.

Index

Index

Index